Game of Thrones versus History

Praise for *Game of Thrones versus History: Written in Blood*

By unlocking the history behind the hugely popular books and TV series, this collection demonstrates how pop culture can be just as important as scholarship in defining what we mean by the "Middle Ages."

-**Matthew Gabriele**, Associate Professor of Medieval Studies, Department of Religion and Culture, Virginia Tech

Game of Thrones versus History takes Martin's novels back to their avowed roots in medieval history, revealing the supports underpinning one of the most remarkable cultural phenomena of the past decade. In doing so, the authors illuminate not only the novels themselves but also a wide variety of episodes from our own bloody and conflicted past.

-**Ross King**

Fantasy isn't born in a vacuum; it's actually a studied tweaking of the real, the recognizable, and the historical. This collection masterfully explores that artful blurring, unlocking Martin's world-making wizardry.

-**Benjamin Woodring**, Ph.D., English, Harvard University, J.D., Yale Law School

This thoughtful and thought-provoking work clearly demonstrates the power of popular culture to simultaneously educate and entertain.

-**Kristine Larsen**, Professor of Astronomy, Central Connecticut State University

Game of Thrones versus History

Written in Blood

Edited by Brian A. Pavlac

WILEY Blackwell

This edition first published 2017
© 2017 John Wiley & Sons, Inc.

Registered Office
John Wiley & Sons, Inc., 111 River Street, Hoboken, NJ 07030, USA

Editorial Offices
350 Main Street, Malden, MA 02148-5020, USA

For details of our global editorial offices, customer services, and more information about Wiley products visit us at www.wiley.com.

The right of Brian A. Pavlac to be identified as the author of the editorial material in this work has been asserted in accordance with law.

Wiley also publishes its books in a variety of electronic formats and by print-on-demand. Some content that appears in standard print versions of this book may not be available in other formats.

Library of Congress Cataloging-in-Publication data applied for

ISBN: 9781119249429 (paperback)

Cover image: Antique Paper © skodonnell/Getty Images; Sword © Kornelia Karkowska / EyeEm/Getty Images
Cover design: Wiley

Set in 10/12pt Warnock by SPi Global, Pondicherry, India
Printed and bound in Malaysia by Vivar Printing Sdn Bhd

10 9 8 7 6 5 4 3 2 1

Contents

17   By Whisper and Raven: Information and Communication in *Game of Thrones*   *227*
      Giacomo Giudici

18   What's in a Name? History and Fantasy in *Game of Thrones*   *241*
      Sara L. Uckelman, Sonia Murphy, and Joseph Percer

19   Setting up Westeros: The Medievalesque World of *Game of Thrones*   *251*
      Gillian Polack

      Appendix: List of Books and Episodes   *261*
      Index   *265*

Notes on Contributors

Danielle Alesi received her BA in history and political science at Hartwick College, New York, and her MA in Renaissance, Reformation, and Early Modern Studies from the University of Birmingham. She is currently a PhD student of history and Medieval and Renaissance Studies at the University of Nebraska-Lincoln, studying queenship and female power.

Maureen Attali is senior history teacher and PhD candidate in history and anthropology of ancient religions at Paris–Sorbonne University in France. She has published several articles about history and religion-related themes in fantasy fiction, most notably "Rome in Westeros" and "Religious Fundamentalism and Demonic Feminity: Remarks on the Character of Lilith in *True Blood*."

Shiloh Carroll teaches in the writing center at Tennessee State University. She is currently working on a book examining the medievalisms and neo-medievalisms of Martin's *A Song of Ice and Fire* and HBO's *Game of Thrones*. She has previously published work on *A Song of Ice and Fire* and the works of Joss Whedon.

Daniel J. Clasby is assistant professor of history and coordinator of the global studies general education curriculum at King's College in Wilkes-Barre, Pennsylvania, where he teaches European Mediterranean history and Jewish studies. His research focuses on Jewish diasporic questions of cultural identity and expressions of religiosity.

Brian de Ruiter earned his PhD with a dissertation on North American indigenous cinema and identity. He frequently attends popular culture conferences in Canada and the United States and is currently examining depictions of the North in popular culture.

Jacopo della Quercia is a scholar with the New York Council for the Humanities and the author of two books: *The Great Abraham Lincoln Pocket Watch*

Conspiracy (2014) and *License to Quill* (2015). His work has been featured in the *New York Times* bestseller *You Might Be a Zombie and Other Bad News (2011)*, BBC America, CNN Money, Cracked.com, *The Huffington Post*, *Reader's Digest*, Slate, and Princeton University's *Electronic Bulletin of the Dante Society of America*, among other places.

Kavita Mudan Finn earned her PhD in English Literature from the University of Oxford and has taught Medieval and Renaissance literature, Renaissance history, women's studies, and writing at several universities, including Georgetown University and the University of Maryland at College Park. In 2012 she published a book on fifteenth-century queens; she is now working on a second book, on representations of premodern women on television. She also edited *Fan Phenomena: Game of Thrones* (in press).

Giacomo Giudici recently completed a PhD in history at Birkbeck, University of London. His research on the relationship between textual practices, sociopolitical practices, and material culture has received awards from both the Royal Historical Society and the Society for Renaissance Studies in the United Kingdom. He has held visiting fellowships at the University of Illinois at Urbana–Champaign and at the Huntington Library of San Marino, California.

Mat Hardy is senior lecturer in Middle East studies at Deakin University, Australia. His research interests include the use of role-play in teaching political science and aspects of leadership in Libya. A youth misspent in pursuit of fantasy role-playing games and fiction has also encouraged him to marry fantasy with academic writing about the East.

Robert J. Haug is assistant professor of Islamic world history before 1500 in the Department of History at the University of Cincinnati, where he has taught a course titled "Playing the Game of Thrones: Kingship and Court Politics in the Premodern World." His research interests focus on the eastern frontiers of the Abbasid caliphate and its successors throughout eastern Iran, Afghanistan, and Central Asia; and on the continuity of local elites from the pre-Islamic period until the arrival of the Seljuqs.

Helle Strandgaard Jensen is assistant professor of contemporary cultural history at Aarhus University in Denmark. She is the author of *From Superman to Social Realism: Children's Media and Scandinavian Childhood* (2017). She has written on the history of children's media, media history in a digital age, and the epistemological failures of "moral panic" theory. Her current research project, funded by the European Commission, is entitled "Shaping Childhoods through Television: The Transfer and Demarcation of *Sesame Street* in 1970s' Europe."

Janice Liedl is professor of history at Laurentian University in Sudbury, Ontario, Canada. She co-edited and contributed to *The Hobbit and History* (2014) and *Star Wars and History* (2012). She also researches English women's struggles with both royal courts and law courts since the time of Henry VIII.

Nicole M. Mares is associate professor of history and director of women's studies at King's College in Wilkes-Barre, Pennsylvania. There she teaches the history of western civilization, women's and gender studies, and British and European history. Her research centers on the nineteenth-century British imperial history of southern Africa and on questions of race, gender, and identity.

Steven Muhlberger, before his recent retirement, was professor of history at Nipissing University in North Bay, Ontario. He has researched and published in a variety of areas, including chivalry and warfare in the later Middle Ages, democracy as a worldwide phenomenon, and the chronicles of late antiquity.

Sonia Murphy is an amateur medievalist and a long-time fan of *Game of Thrones.*

Brian A. Pavlac lives a dual life as professor of history at King's College in Wilkes-Barre, Pennsylvania, and priest-in-charge of St. Stephen's Episcopal Pro-Cathedral. Published books authored by him are *A Concise Survey of Western Civilization* (2010) and a general interest work on *Witch Hunts in the Western World* (2010); he also translated a medieval biography, *A Warrior Bishop of the 12th Century by Balderich* (2008). His research interests include witch hunting, medieval Germany, and prince bishops of the Holy Roman Empire (for example Nicholas of Cusa).

Joseph Percer is currently the chief heraldic and onomastic officer of a worldwide medieval non-profit organization devoted to the study of the Middle Ages.

Gillian Polack is currently based at the Australian National University. Her recent books include *The Middle Ages Unlocked: A Guide to Life in Medieval England* (2015); *The Time of the Ghosts* (2015; novel); and *The Art of Effective Dreaming* (2015; novel). Her monograph *History and Fiction: Writers, their Research, Worlds and Stories* was published in 2016.

Magnus Qvistgaard, an independent scholar, holds a PhD in history and civilization from the European University Institute in Florence. He works on processes of cultural exchange and on how public negotiations of aesthetic concepts shape cultural values. He has previously published on Scandinavian drama and on the interplay between theater and literature in the late nineteenth century.

Don Riggs studied myth at Dickinson College, where he focused on the mythical underpinnings of both ancient and modern literature. At UNC-Chapel Hill he earned degrees in comparative literature, which included the study of the French, Latin, and English Middle Ages. He has since published on Renaissance astrology, medieval and modern literature, and Tolkien. He has also translated, with Jerome Seaton, *Chinese Poetic Writing* by Francois Cheng (1984).

Kris Swank is library director at Pima Community College, Tucson, Arizona. She holds master's degrees in library science, international management, and language and literature with an emphasis on Tolkien studies. She has published in the field of fantasy literature, in the journals *Tolkien Studies* and *Mythlore* and in the edited collections *Fantasy and Science-Fiction Medievalisms: From Isaac Asimov to A Game of Thrones* (2015) and *Harry Potter for Nerds II* (2015).

Sara L. Uckelman is lecturer at Durham University in the United Kingdom and is affiliated to the Medieval and Early Modern Studies Institute. She is the editor-in-chief of the *Dictionary of Medieval Names from European Sources*.

Foreword

William Irwin

What a great idea! *Game of Thrones* versus history. Historians are storytellers, and the best historians, like the best storytellers, have ways of making their subject matter come to life. The challenge for the historian in the classroom is to find a hook or produce an example that will speak to a captive audience of students.

It's particularly effective when a teacher can start from something everyone thinks they know to be true, and then proceed to show that it wasn't exactly true. Something like "people think Columbus believed the earth was flat, but really he knew it was round." In this sense, a negative example can be just as effective as a positive example.

All too often, though, students do not know much about the past and so do not have incorrect ideas about it to be supplanted. Thus the historian's task becomes even more challenging. She needs to both explain and intrigue. This is where connections to popular culture can come in handy. When we can draw on what students are already interested in and knowledgeable about, we are halfway to the goal of engaging them with history.

I had a similar experience while teaching philosophy in the late 1990s. That's why they asked me to write this foreword, so please forgive the self-reference as I explain. Practically all my students were familiar with my favorite television show, *Seinfeld*. Many of them were even bigger fans than I was and could quote lines and cite episodes like scholars. It was only natural, then, to use the show to jump-start explanations and discussions of philosophy. Jerry Seinfeld's stand-up routine and observational humor could be compared to Socrates' questioning of his fellow citizens in the marketplace of Athens. It wasn't a perfect comparison, but that was part of the point. Seeing the initial similarity, students became interested in the differences as well.

I wasn't alone in doing this. Far from it.

Philosophers have always looked for vivid examples to illustrate complex ideas, and lots of professors were seizing on *Seinfeld*. When it was announced that the show was going off the air at the end of its ninth season in 1998, I was saddened as a fan and worried as a teacher. No longer would George, Jerry, Kramer, and Elaine deliver new philosophy resources. There was nothing left for me to do but build a memorial. There would be many tributes to mark the end of the show, but my idea was to capture in a book what had been happening in the classroom, not just in my classroom but in classrooms all over the country.

Seinfeld and Philosophy and the many books that followed have all been team efforts, in which many writers and editors brought diverse points of view together between the covers of a book. A recent success among the books is *Game of Thrones and Philosophy: Logic Cuts Deeper Than Swords*, edited by Henry Jacoby. As you might expect, the volume includes essays about understanding Westeros in terms of the political philosophies of Plato, Hobbes, Machiavelli, and Nietzsche. But the book also includes musings on the nature of happiness, magic and metaphysics, moral luck, and just-war theory. Like other books in its genre, *Game of Thrones and Philosophy* works because it speaks to fans. The writers are fans who can quote Tyrion Lannister and speak Dothraki. They relish the chance to discuss *Game of Thrones* as much as they appreciate the chance to spread philosophy. This same infectious enthusiasm pervades the pages of the book you hold in your hands.

Despite its subtitle, *Game of Thrones versus History* is not actually written in blood. It is, however, written instead with verve, insight, and enthusiasm, displaying love for both history and literature. Connections to the kings and castles of medieval England would be expected in a book of this nature, but other, less likely connections also lurk in what lies ahead. There were no real dragons in medieval Europe, of course, but examining the Seven Kingdoms reveals surprising insights into cultural history concerning the nature of childhood, the lives of powerful women, pagan religions, and forgotten celibate societies.

We can learn history by comparing it to *Game of Thrones*, and *Game of Thrones* can teach us something about history by making us reconsider it in terms of alternative possibilities. Historians face the difficult task of constructing a narrative from multiple sources that sometimes conflict with one another. The authors of this book face a similar problem concerning their sources: the differences between the accounts given by the books and the television show. What really happened in Westeros and the rest of the known world?

Game of Thrones versus History works brilliantly, not just because its authors are excellent historians, but also because their source material is wonderfully rich. The smart, compelling writing in the books and on the television show takes us on flights of imagination and keeps us at the sword's end of excitement. Appealing to a mass audience well beyond readers of fantasy literature, *Game of Thrones* is a pop culture force. Indeed, with its huge following of intelligent and devoted fans, *Game of Thrones* wins Emmy awards and takes the ratings crown. George R. R. Martin may be an American J. R. R. Tolkien, but he has created a global phenomenon. As evidence, consider the contributing authors in this book, who hail not just from the United States and our wintry neighbor to the north but from far-flung kingdoms in Australia—and from Europe as well. Take my advice and let them be your guide through worlds of fantasy and reality. If you read carefully, you may even get to keep your head.

Acknowledgments

In my tender years, my brother, Ross R. Pavlac, lit a fire in me for fantasy and science fiction. Despite several efforts, though, I could not follow him into that strange world of fandom, where he met George R. R. Martin long before *A Game of Thrones* was written. Tragically, my brother's life ended far too early: he died from cancer 20 years gone. I, meanwhile, pursued a path to academia, which by good fortune led me to my position as a history professor at King's College in Wilkes-Barre, Pennsylvania. There I watched my friend and colleague Bill Irwin launch a book series comparing popular culture and philosophy. The series "Philosophy and…" made me think about "History versus…"—and I am indebted to Bill for his help with this project. My daughter, Margaret Mackenzie Pavlac, got me watching the series. I am also grateful to Janice Liedl, whose books on Harry Potter and on the Hobbit and history caught my attention and led to my proposal for this volume. I offer thanks to Andrew Davidson, who welcomed my proposal with enthusiasm. My appreciation goes to Denisha Sahadevan, my editor at Wiley, and her assistant, Maddie Koufogazos for bringing this work to the world; to the commissioning editor, Haze Humbert; to the erudite editing of Manuela Tecusan; and also to the production editor, Nivetha Udayakumar. Much credit, of course, goes to the many authors of this book, who took the time and the risk to offer their hard work and scholarship to make it a reality. What virtues exist in the essays are theirs; what deficiencies appear are mine, as editor.

Lastly, this book's appearance owes a great debt to my spouse, Elizabeth S. Lott, PhD, without whom it, and much else in my life, could not have been accomplished. Her advice, her discipline, her editing, and her inspiration have been treasures beyond compare. *Yer Jalan Atthirari Anni*—You are the moon of my life.

Introduction

The Winter of Our Discontent

Brian A. Pavlac

People have surely been enjoying stories based on history since the first tales were told around fires in the night. Sometimes the stories are true, or at least as true as people can make them. Sometimes they are improved through creativity, adding elements that did not happen, or even could not happen. In our cultures, the oldest surviving stories were written down with huge doses of imagination. The first such story to survive was *The Epic of Gilgamesh*, which told of the founding king of Uruk in ancient Mesopotamia. King Gilgamesh not only interacted with gods and goddesses but, being partly divine, had superhuman strength himself. *The Iliad* and *The Odyssey*, the two ancient Greek epic poems traditionally attributed to Homer, centered around what was believed to have been a historical conflict in a very distant past: the Trojan War. The heroes of these epics, Achilles and Odysseus (or Ulysses, by his Latinized name), possessed respectively strength and intelligence within human capacity, although the narratives also included divine beings and dangerous monsters who wielded powers far greater than mere mortals.

Today we call such stories "myths," even if they refer to events that may have happened and the characters in them might once have been living people. But for the listeners entertained by these stories, the tales held truth.[1] First, they offered answers around the fundamental question of human existence: What is the meaning of life? Gilgamesh intentionally goes off in search of an answer to that question (and the one he finds is not reassuring). Achilles and Odysseus address the same question more obliquely, in the heat of battle and in the excitement of adventure. Of course, one big part of any awareness of life or of the human condition is the reality of death. "*Valar Morghulis*," say the Braavosi. "All men must die."[2]

Second, the tales also allowed readers and listeners to escape mundane burdens and the boredom of everyday life. As George R. R. Martin hesitantly explains:

> Conflict and ... and, uh, conflict and danger and, uh, all of these things are ... are the strong spices that we want. You know when they occur in our real life, we hate them. But they're part of what makes life "life," as opposed to just unending days of boredom. And, uh, I think we crave them in our ... our fiction.[3]

Third, the tales helped form values, perspectives on right and wrong beliefs and actions. Until modern times, people, as noted above, saw these stories as true, believing that they had actually happened. Learning the important stories was part of a person's education. Moral lessons came from interaction with characters and their choices, whether the tragically flawed hero or the comedically gifted fool.

Today we call these stories literature and classify them in our libraries as "fiction." Books in that part of the library are "made up," written from their authors' imaginations. Even in ancient times, though, historians began to write accounts that aimed to separate myth from fact. The earliest historians, such as Herodotus and Thucydides, tried to write about what people actually did, deleting any alleged involvement of supernatural beings and incredible occurrences. In libraries, history books are filed in sections called "non-fiction"—the opposite to fiction. This is a rather awkward name: it is like calling empirical reality "non-imaginary."

Among the most popular genres in recent writing are historical fiction and fantasy.[4] In historical fiction, authors start with what they know about the real past, then they fill in the blanks with imaginary speeches, conversations, meetings, and conflicts. In the Middle Ages conscious works of historical fiction were tales of knights and kings. *The Song of Roland, El Cid*, and even tales of the Knights of the Round Table included some historical rulers and historical events, although medieval audiences probably didn't know or care about historical accuracy. The great English playwright William Shakespeare certainly knew that his "historical plays" fleshed out history, adding dialogue and events to improve dramatic needs. The opening lines of his *Richard III*, "Now is the winter of our discontent/Made glorious summer by this son of York," make a clever transition from his play *Henry VI* but were surely never spoken by Richard III in real life—not even if you turn them into prose.[5]

The genre of fantasy writing reaches back again to those ancient epics—Gilgamesh, the Homeric poems—which placed human characters in environments of supernatural beings, magic, and monsters. Leading the way to modern fantasy were the works of two scholars who worked together at Oxford: J. R. R. Tolkien and C. S. Lewis. Tolkien's *The Lord of the Rings* (1954–1955) in particular brought fantasy writing to an adult audience.[6] Almost all other works in the fantasy genre are now measured against Tolkein's. *The Lord of the Rings* drew on Norse myth, classical epics, medieval history, and an overarching concept of Good at war with Evil, all set in an imaginary world where everyday life is similar to that of the European Middle Ages. Key heroes were regular folk —"hobbits"— who found in themselves strength they did not know they possessed.

In 1996 George R. R. Martin added his contribution to the genre with the publication of *A Game of Thrones*, originally planned, following Tolkien, as the first part of an epic trilogy called *A Song of Ice and Fire*.[7] The increasingly popular television series on HBO, which is based on these books and called simply *Game of Thrones*, has turned Martin's creation into a worldwide entertainment phenomenon. While Martin is not a professional scholar, as Tolkien was, his colorful and richly complex realms clearly derive from wide reading and reflect a deep knowledge of history.[8] Like Tolkien's Middle-Earth, Martin's Known World is set in a culture similar to our Middle Ages and touched by sorcery and dragons. His characters, like people throughout our history and literature, struggle with making the right choices in perilous times and places. As one way of appreciating Martin's work, this collection of essays connects *Game of Thrones'* fantasy fiction with historical fact.

You Know Nothing

For historians, the first step in answering any problem is to find the sources. Any record of past human activity is a source, but most useful for historians are written records: letters, diaries, memoirs, autobiographies, writs, laws, accounts, speeches, and literature. Without sources we know nothing of what happened in the past. And, even with sources, our knowledge is incomplete, tentative, and uncertain. The word "versus" in the title of this book underscores the tension of understanding facts and reality, whether in fiction or in history. The narrators in *Game of Thrones* are sources, and, like all people, they offer individual perspectives that contradict and confuse one another.[9] The Byzantine historian Procopius of Caesarea (c. AD 500–560) offers the most famous example of such a discrepancy. In *The Wars of Justinian*, Procopius openly and fulsomely praises his emperor and patron. Hundreds of years later, however, historians discovered his *Secret History*, in which he denounces Justinian. Some historians are not bothered by such ambivalence and the discrepancies it produces, while others strive to determine a single, definitive "truth" about the past. Fiction is, of course, another matter, since it is—well, fictional. Nevertheless, many fans prefer one flawless canon, even though the reality of producing the television series and adapting Martin's books has created two divergent versions of his story; and Martin is fine with that.[10]

To get a handle on the confusing sources, scholars have established what is known as the historical method.[11] In an imitation of the scientific method, historians propose a hypothesis supposed to answer a historical question, collect and study the sources, draw conclusions, then share their results with other historians at conferences and in academic publications. When the results are published in articles and books, key parts of the historical argument are contained in references, or in notes such as the ones the reader of this book will find at the end of each essay. References serve two functions. Explanatory or content notes add detail to an argument in the main text or give additional information on a related topic. Source notes show the origins of the historian's information. The second type is essential to scholarly argument; it allows other scholars to retrace and review the research, forming an independent evaluation of its conclusions.

By asking questions about the sources, historians try to resolve the conflicting points of view apparent within the sources themselves, decided upon by the writers of history, and brought to the material by the readers. Until the 1960s, historians mostly chose to write about political, diplomatic, and military subjects. This choice was partly due to people's fascination with violence in the past, such as reflected in the American Civil War or in World War II. Martin himself comments:

> I have to take issue with the notion that Westeros is a "dark and depraved place." It's not the Disneyland Middle Ages, no, and that was quite deliberate [...] but it is no darker nor more depraved than our own world. History is written in blood. The atrocities in "A Song of Ice and Fire," sexual and otherwise, pale in comparison to what can be found in any good history book.[12]

Historians chose to write about wars also because sources on political–military topics were readily available. The historical record is replete with what men of means have accomplished. It is women and children, the poor and the oppressed who died unrecorded.

Since the 1960s, though, historians have increasingly concentrated on social and cultural topics that typically include underrepresented people.[13] Feminists began gender studies by identifying and questioning patriarchy, or how social structures have been dominated by men for most of the past.[14] More recently masculinity studies have begun to look at how men decided that they were men. And as for the oppressed, they can still be found in sources only by reading between the lines and by using the concept of "the other" or "otherness."[15] People of privilege, who write history, define and capture themselves in their historical records by identifying others, the evil, and opposite versions of themselves as embodying faults and vices that the privileged claim not to have. But, as historians argue, even when marginalized, oppressed or "subaltern" people still possess "agency," the ability to make choices on their own behalf, if only to subvert or work against the powers that dominate them.

Definitions of what is good and bad throughout history have often been drawn from religion and faith. This is a delicate matter for historians. Today's scholars uphold a position of skepticism about things like divine intervention, miracles, the supernatural, or the paranormal. No good evidence exists that any of these things actually has changed history, except insofar as people have taken action on the basis of their personal or communal beliefs in them. Most notoriously, the witch hunts clearly happened because people believed that witches conspired with the Devil to overthrow Christian society, even though there was never any proof of a diabolic conspiracy, much less of the efficacy of curses and spells.[16] Many of Martin's characters are skeptical or dismissive of religion. But fantasy fiction such as Martin's usually assumes that the supernatural is real, especially as manifest in characters that defy biological science— whether creatures in their own right (White Walkers, wights, dragons), perfect disguises like the Faceless Men, or resurrected dead.[17] The historical profession does not, in the absence of proof, preclude the possibility of the supernatural and takes a neutral stance toward the relative truth of one religious belief or another. Importantly, historians recognize the significance of religion and how much it has shaped people's lives and decisions in the past.

Scholarly opinions can be as massive and enduring as the Wall in *Game of Thrones*. Yet the wildlings can go around, climb over, and even pass through its gates; this suggests that scholars, too, should be flexible enough to find alternative explanations. Scholarly ideas can be as grand as the castle Harrenhal, only to be burned down by dragonfire when new evidence destroys them. Scholarly theories can be blown up like the Great Sept of Baelor, leaving other scholars to rebuild a thesis from the rubble. Readers like to be reassured that history offers the definitive explanation of the past; but our understanding of history is constantly changing.

When Things Were Rotten

Popular images of the medieval period often begin and end with the label "dark ages" (which is used for other periods of history as well). The word "dark" raises expectations of ignorance, barbarism, and cruelty.[18] The phrase "Middle Ages" also evokes the image of medievalism, a time of lords and ladies that exists only in the popular imagination. But the historical period of the Middle Ages was much more rich and complex. One reason historians use the plural form "Ages" is that an enormous amount of change happened during medieval history.

The way historians define the Middle Ages, however, raises a fundamental problem. First, they love to argue about dates. Periodization means clumping various years into one category (a century, an age, an epoch, a period) that experiences common political, social, and ideological trends. In the grand sweep of chronology, historians of western civilization usually recognize four great categories or historical periods.[19] The first is prehistory, which started before 3500 BC, the date assigned to the invention of writing. "BC" refers, of course, to the time "before Christ," while AD abbreviates *anno Domini*, which means in Latin "in the year of the Lord" (namely Christ).[20] The second historical category is ancient history, which starts from the invention of writing and lasts until the beginning of the Middle Ages—the third period. Lastly, there is modern history, which begins at the end of the Middle Ages.

Where, then, does that third period of the Middle Ages begin and end? For historians, medieval history begins with the fall of the western half of the Roman Empire, which is traditionally placed in AD 476. (The eastern half of the Roman Empire continued for another thousand years, as the Byzantine Empire, until the Ottoman dynasty conquered it in 1453; and this date is sometimes conventionally given as the "end" of the Middle Ages.) But many events are significantly associated with the fall of the western half of the Roman Empire—from the Sack of Rome by the Visigoths in AD 410 to the removal of Emperor Romulus Augustulus in 476. Sometimes an arbitrarily rounded date like 450 or 500 is used. The label "dark ages" does fit the first few centuries after these events. Civilized Rome, with its wealthy cities, imperial bureaucracies, formal legal systems, paid armies, and schools had collapsed under the occupation of "barbarian" Germanic tribes with poor rural villages, kings who ruled through personal rule, oral legal traditions, armies held together by loyalty oaths, and widespread illiteracy. Only the Christian church managed to maintain a few centers of learning and knowledge. But the church placed limited value on needs of this world. Christianity urged believers to live an earthly life that would determine what their eternal life would be after death: either to suffer in hell or to rejoice with God in heaven. The influence of Christianity on medieval culture was so important that some historians call the Middle Ages the "age of faith."

After an initial "dark age" that followed the fall of Rome, stability and culture began to return during the reign of Charlemagne, crowned emperor of the Romans in AD 800 by the pope. But this return, called "Carolingian Renaissance" (after Charlemagne's Latin name, Carolus Magnus), collapsed soon after his death, through civil wars and through invasions by Magyars (Hungarians), Northmen (Vikings), and Saracens (Muslims). New military innovations of knights (armored warriors on horseback) and castles (fortified homes of the knights) enabled western Europeans to survive the political chaos. Knights banded together as lords and vassals, swearing oaths of fealty or loyalty to each other. They would then come to fight together in battle and celebrate together at their castle courts. Society became rigidly stratified, the clergy being the most respected members, nobles the most powerful, and peasants standing at the bottom and doing the farming that fed everyone. The priests prayed, the knights slayed and ruled, and the serfs toiled. With this restoration of some semblance of order, the early Middle Ages passed into the high Middle Ages.

The conventional dates for this transition range from AD 900 to the millennial year 1000 (a date that was not as frighteningly apocalyptic or notable as some modern myths suggest), and maybe even to 1050.

The high Middle Ages embody the "forsoothly" medieval way of life that is popularly imagined. An improving economy encouraged trade; some simple manufacturing began, especially of textiles; and towns started to flourish. Townspeople were something new; they did not fit into the previous threefold division of clergy, nobles, and peasants. Slowly the "bourgeois" increased their rights and privileges. Kings began to claim power over clearly delineated territories. Knights fought for the king and against each other. The clergy, headed by popes who claimed true sovereignty in Christendom, briefly offered a serious alternative to leadership. But by the end of the High Middle Ages kings had reduced the pope's authority over political affairs, although his dominance in the Latin church was vastly increased.

The event most closely linked with the beginning of the late Middle Ages is the Black Death, the spread of plague that began about 1348. Many thought that the world was ending, but the plague actually killed only about a third of the population. "Only." The ensuing period—the late Middle Ages—was a time of questioning and hesitation. Expansion into Eastern Europe collided with the advance of the Ottoman Empire. The increased wealth generated by bankers and the new banking system drove criticisms of materialism. Royal authority struggled to accommodate demands for representative bodies. The Hundred Years War (1337–1453) saw the decline of knights on the battlefield and the end of castles as strategic points, most importantly as a result of the use of gunpowder weapons. The authority of the papacy was much weakened, first through transfer from Rome to the city of Avignon, then through the Great Western Schism, when multiple rival popes were elected, all living in growing opulence.

The end of the Middle Ages is marked by the great changes in culture, religion, and geography that also mark the beginning of modern history. The Renaissance (which might have begun around 1400, 1450, or 1494) broke the intellectual monopoly of the Latin Christian church in Western Europe. The Reformation, traditionally taken to begin in 1517, with Martin Luther, shattered the unity of the church in the West. Various denominations—Lutherans, Calvinists, Anabaptists, and Anglicans—rejected the papacy to form their own Protestant versions of a Christian church. European ships sailing out into the Atlantic soon unleashed the power of Europe around the world. Some historians suggest that the Middle Ages lingered until the end of the Thirty Years' War in 1648, or even until the beginning of the French Revolution in 1789. To choose reasonably significant dates, though, we could say that the early Middle Ages lasted from about 450 to 1050, the high Middle Ages from about 1000 to 1350, the late Middle Ages from 1300 to 1500, the Renaissance from 1400 to 1600, and the early modern period from 1517 to 1648 or 1789.

'All this Divided, York and Lancaster, Divided in their dire Division'

Perhaps the greatest historical influence on George R. R. Martin has been that of the Wars of the Roses (1455–1485), a civil war in late medieval England.[21] Given this reality, it is worth offering a brief history of the conflict. William Shakespeare also tackled the subject in a tetralogy (i.e. a group of four linked history plays); the line that heads this section comes from one of them.[22] Shakespeare's previous tetralogy ended at the point where Henry V (r. 1413–1422) of the Plantagenet dynasty defeated the French royal army at Agincourt, married a royal princess, and won the French throne for England. Unfortunately Henry died young.

Shakespeare begins his account of the Wars of the Roses with three plays that cover the reign of Henry VI (r. 1422–1461, 1470–1471), Henry V's son, who inherited the French and English thrones when he was only nine months old. Various factions fight to control him even when he becomes an adult, since he keeps suffering bouts of mental illness perhaps inherited from his maternal grandfather, Charles VI "the Mad" (r. 1380–1422). One faction supports the Lancaster branch of the Plantagenet house and has a red rose for its emblem; the other faction supports the York branch and is symbolized by a white rose— hence the name of the conflict. In spite of Henry V's successes, England had lost the Hundred Years' War and people were looking for someone to blame. Richard, duke of York (1411–1460), used popular resentment to attack the factions around the king, but lost his life at the Battle of Wakefield. A few weeks later, though, at the Battle of Towton, his son won the throne as Edward IV (r. 1461–1470, 1471–1483). Edward's unpopular marriage to Elizabeth Woodville and enmity of his main supporter—Richard Neville, earl of Warwick, called "the Kingmaker"—cost him the throne and forced him into exile in 1470. The next year he returned with an army and won the throne back. He enjoyed being king and lived the high life until an early death.

His brother Richard, duke of Gloucester, was supposed to act as guardian to Edward's two young sons. But, as portrayed in Shakespeare's *Richard III*, a villainous Richard of Gloucester seized the throne for himself, becoming King Richard III (r. 1483–1485). Richard sent the two princes to the Tower of London and they never emerged again. He had other enemies and rivals executed, in the fashion of his time, but not enough of them, apparently. Henry Tudor had a weak claim to being a legitimate heir to the throne, but was supported by the Lancastrians. He invaded the realm and killed Richard in the closely fought Battle of Bosworth Field. The new king, Henry VII (r. 1485–1507), ended the Wars of the Roses and established the Tudor dynasty, which had its own ups and downs over the next century.

Martin drew on this historical conflict to create his novel: at its core lie the houses of Stark (York) and Lannister (Lancaster).[23] The doomed Richard of

York influences the character of Eddard Stark. Robert Baratheon resembles Edward IV both in his warrior prowess and in his neglect for rule. Robb Stark, also like a valiant Edward IV, makes a politically foolish marriage. Among the Lannisters, Tywin is a bold and sharp ruler, just like Edward I, "the Hammer of the Scots." Richard III's wit, insight, and alleged hunchback are exaggerated in the character of the dwarf Tyrion. His sister Cersei receives the same kind of abuse hurled at Margaret of Anjou (1430–1480), the wife of Henry VI. And young Danaerys combines the attributes of an inspirational Joan of Arc with those of the claimant to the throne, Henry Tudor. For more on these characters, see the brief summary below and many of the chapters in this volume.

The Story so Far

To go by the title that Martin has given the whole series, *A Song of Ice and Fire*, the overriding storyline involves fantasy elements. On an unnamed planet (sometimes called "the Known World"), humans live on the continents of Westeros and Essos, while the environment fluctuates between long and short spells of warm or cold weather. The "song's" first element is ice. "Winter is coming," says the original protagonist Ned Stark repeatedly. The Others or the White Walkers represent that winter. In the opening prologue they assault rangers of the Night's Watch, who normally defend the Wall. Then, progressively through the story, the Night King slowly, glacially builds up forces of White Walkers and wights (the old-fashioned term for zombie-like undead), eventually to attack the Seven Kingdoms to the South.[24]

The overwhelming bulk of the story so far is, however, about people trying to use power. At the highest level, the "game of thrones" involves struggles over the constituent Seven Kingdoms of Westeros. At the lowest level, Martin tells about outsiders trying to make a place for themselves in turbulent times. This human problem is, of course, universal, which is how the book can appeal to many folk who will never approach the power of a king who sits on the Iron Throne, a perilous seat made of swords.

The good guys are the Stark family: patriarch Ned, the Warden of the North, lord of the castle Winterfell; his wife Catelyn; and his legitimate children, Robb, Sansa, Arya, Bran, and Rickon, along with Ned's alleged illegitimate son, Jon Snow.[25] The wealthy and well-connected Lannisters are the opposing family. Patriarch Tywin is ruthlessly building his family's fortunes even as his gold mines run dry. His twin children, Jaime and Cersei, are in an incestuous relationship, although she has married the current king, Robert Baratheon. Their three royal offspring, Joffrey, Myrcella, and Tommen, are actually issue of the incest between Jaime and Cersei. Their younger brother, Tyrion Lannister, is trying to find his own place, which is complicated by his stature as a dwarf. A third family is the Targaryens, who had held the royal dynasty until Robert seized the throne. Two surviving Targaryen children, Viserys and his sister Daenerys, scheme to return to Westeros and reclaim the crown. Daenerys represents the second element in the novels' title, "fire": it is connected to her dragons, which help to bring magic back into the world.

These various characters' efforts to manipulate power for their own ends or for the benefit of others drive the various plots, all seen from first-person perspectives. The storyline begins after the suspicious death of the king's "Hand"— his chief advisor and the administrator of the realm. King Robert asks his old friend Ned Stark to take his place, drawing Ned and his family into the "game" of royal intrigue. This request leads to Bran's crippling, Ned's beheading, Robb's rebelling, Sansa's constraining, and Arya's wandering. Ned's exposure of Jaime and Cersei's incest provokes King Robert Baratheon's death and the War of the Five Kings. As king, vicious Joffrey spreads cruelty, Robert's brothers Stannis and Renly rebel against the illegitimate king, and Stannis commits magical fratricide on Renly through the Red Woman, Melisandre. Meanwhile old grudges encourage the rebellion of the ironmen from the Iron Islands, who attack both Stark and Lannister. Stannis' attack on the capital, King's Landing, fails, due to Tyrion's strategy and courage, along with Tywin's warfare and plotting ("swords and spears [...] quills and ravens").[26] Tywin also arranges the murder of Robb and his mother Catelyn Stark by the Frey and Bolton families, at the "Red Wedding." Stannis is briefly diverted northward to defeat the wildlings in their assault against the Night's Watch on the Wall. His attack against the Boltons who hold Winterfell fails and leads to his death.[27] Jon Snow, who had become Lord Commander, is murdered by mutinous members of the Night's Watch, but he comes back from the dead in a good way. Season 6, which is based on the novel *The Winds of Winter* (still unpublished at the time of this writing), ends with Jon and his half-sister Sansa reunited and back in Winterfell, having defeated the Boltons. Their sister Arya is beginning a career as an assassin, and their crippled brother Bran has become a seer, the three-eyed crow or raven.

Meanwhile the wealthy Tyrell family gains influence in the capital. As a result, Tywin's grandson, King Joffrey, is poisoned at his own wedding—the Purple Wedding—which leaves his vulnerable and weak brother Tommen, now king, to marry Joffrey's widow, Margaery Tyrell. Tyrion is about to be wrongly executed for the crime but escapes with the help of his brother Jaime although he stops on the way in order to kill his father, Tywin. Cersei tries to outflank her enemies by appointing a zealous preacher, the High Sparrow, as High Septon, leader of the main religion in Westeros. The High Sparrow arrests not only Tyrell's enemies, but also Cersei herself. Forced into a humiliating walk of atonement and threatened with still more punishment, Cersei wreaks vengeance on many of her enemies by blowing them up. As season 6 ends, Cersei takes the iron throne as the first regnant queen of the Seven Kingdoms.

Across the Narrow Sea in Essos, Daenrys Targaryen has been developing from a shy slip of a girl to a charismatic and dominating queen. Her marriage to Khal Drogo of the Dothraki horse-riding warriors was supposed to provide her brother with an army, but her sibling's foolishness got him gruesomely killed.[28] Drogo dies soon after, although out of his funeral pyre an unburnt Daererys appears with three dragons. She slowly builds allies and armed forces, conquering the slaver cities of Yunkai, Astapor, and Meereen. She gets stalled for a while in Meereen, where she tries to rule a rebellious population while gathering resources for an invasion of Westeros. At the end of season 6, with a vast fleet combining forces from Dorne, the ironmen, and the Dothraki and advised by Tyrion Lannister, she has set sail to reclaim the Iron Throne. But, as Ser Davos Seaworth warns: "The real war isn't between a few squabbling houses. It's between the living and the dead, and make no mistake, my lady, the dead are coming."[29]

Scholarly Studies

This volume proposes to help readers understand and appreciate the vast tapestry of George R. R. Martin's fiction by hanging it alongside the great vista of history. From various perspectives, the authors take a look at Martin's plots, characterizations, and settings and discuss, from the vantage point of history, whether Martin's creations are possible or fantasy. Each author has his or her own voice, own perspective, and own methodology in applying sources. Such a collection of chapters is perforce not comprehensive; it cannot cover every relevant facet of *Game of Thrones*. There is also some repetition and redundancy among the authors, as well as some disagreement of interpretation. But, because of that, the collection offers insights into the real practice of historians. Point by point, a scholar takes a thesis and argues it out, until a stately edifice is built to encompass our understanding of the past.

The chapters are grouped into five parts. Part I covers largely political issues. The opening chapter of Kavita Mudan Finn appraises women rulers, who have become increasingly important over the course of the *Game of Thrones* and in our own view of the past. Jacopo della Quercia quizzes Machiavelli for advice that he might offer to historical or fantasy rulers, either male or female. Steven Muhlberger analyzes the role of knights and their behavior in medieval and Westerosi society. Then Brian A. Pavlac probes the moves by which kings win and play with power.

Part II digs into the cultural history of those on the fringes of Western Europe or Westeros. Shiloh Carroll surveys how invaders and conquerors transform societies. Brian de Ruiter then constructs a more narrow argument around Hadrian's Wall. Turning eastward, Mat Hardy illustrates how foreign both Essos and Asia might seem—or not. Robert Haug then sharpens the argument on the use of slave-soldiers in both places.

Part III raises issues of women and children, to whom Martin's stories give pride of place, even if history often has not. Janice Liedl starts from the top of the family unit, the parents, and what choices they typically made in medieval or made-up society. Helle Strandgaard Jensen and Magnus Qvistgaard continue from the bottom up, presenting the limited perspectives of children. Nicole Mares examines the overall possibilities for women to direct their own lives, while Danielle Alesi concentrates on Sansa Stark.

Part IV covers religious issues. Don Riggs compares religions in Europe with those in Westeros. Maureen Attali exposes the more violent sides of people of faith. Daniel Clasby blends together the tension between tendencies for violence among religious believers and their attempts to live in harmony. Finally, Kris Swank takes a peek at the world from under the covers of those believers who practice sexual abstinence.

Part V does, admittedly, collect essays without any thematic cohesion. Giacomo Giudici's piece on communication speaks to some accurate and inaccurate methods of writing and talking. The article by Sara Uckelman, Sonia Murphy, and Joseph Percer identifies qualities of medieval and fantasy names. Concluding the volume, Gillian Pollack highlights various means by which Martin evokes the Middle Ages.

We hope these scholarly efforts will feed an interest in history while deepening an appreciation for George R. R. Martin's *Game of Thrones.*[30]

Notes

1 C. S. Lewis, "The Dethronement of Power," in *Tolkien and the Critics: Essays on J. R. R. Tolkien's* The Lord of the Rings," edited by Neil D. Isaacs and Rose A. Zimbardo (Notre Dame, IN: University of Notre Dame Press, 1968), 16, notes that myth helps us rediscover reality.

2 George R. R. Martin, *A Song of Ice and Fire, Book Three: A Storm of Swords* (New York: Bantam, 2011 [2000]), 910. J. R. R. Tolkien, "On Fairy-Stories," in *The Tolkien Reader* (New York: Ballantine Books, 1966), 67–68, notes how stories can address the desire to escape from death, partly through the concept of the "happy ending," which he calls a *eucastastrophe* (from the ancient Greek compound adjective *eukatastrophos*, "turned well, turned to a good conclusion," and by analogy with the Aristotelian concept of *catastrophē*, "reversal").

3 "Game of Thrones: A Dance of Dragons and the Winds of Winter Original Trilogy, George R. R. Martin and Robin Hobb—Exclusive Event!" 2014, August 26 (accessed October 25, 2016 at https://www.youtube.com/watch?v=tXLYSnMIrXM &feature=youtu.be).

4 Martin thought to combine "epic fantasy that had the imagination and the sense of wonder that you get in the best fantasy, [with] the gritty realism of the best historical fiction. If I could combine those two threads, I might have something fairly unique

and well worth reading" (John Hodgman and George R. R. Martin, "George R. R. Martin, Author of 'A Song of Ice and Fire,' Series: Interview on The Sound of Young America," 2011, September 19. Accessed August 3, 2016 at http://www.maximumfun.org/sound-young-america/george-r-r-martin-author-song-ice-and-fire-series-interview-sound-young-america).

5 William Shakespeare, *The Tragedy of King Richard III*, Act 1, Scene 1, lines 1–2.

6 For more on the origins of modern fantasy, see the chapter by Uckelman, Murphy, and Percer in this volume.

7 George R. R. Martin, "The Long Game … of Thrones," in Not a Blog (on his website), 2016, August 1 (1: 13 a.m.) (accessed August 2, 2016 at http://grrm.livejournal.com/496185.html). Tolkien's "trilogy" was actually in six books, each with its own title; his first words were: "This tale grew in the telling" (J. R. R. Tolkien, *The Fellowship of the Ring, Being the First Part of the Lord of the Rings*, 2nd edn., Boston: Houghton Mifflin Company, 1965), 1. Martin's work has reluctantly grown to seven planned books; see Dave Itzkoff, "His Beautiful Dark Twisted Fantasy: George R. R. Martin Talks 'Game of Thrones,'" *New York Times ArtBeat*, 2011, April 1 (accessed August 8, 2016 at http://artsbeat.blogs.nytimes.com/2011/04/01/his-beautiful-dark-twisted-fantasy-george-r-r-martin-talks-game-of-thrones).

8 For some of his book recommendations, see George R. R. Martin, "FAQ," in For Fans (on his own website), 2016 (accessed August 4, 2016 at http://www.georgerrmartin.com/for-fans/faq).

9 Laura Miller, "George R. R. Martin Reveals Which Inconsistencies in 'Game of Thrones' Are Actually Deliberate," 2015, June 1 (accessed October 12, 2016 at http://uk.businessinsider.com/george-rr-martin-game-of-thrones-inconsistencies-2015-6).

10 George R. R. Martin, "The Show, the Books," in Not a Blog, 2015, May 18 (12: 55 p.m.) (accessed January 20, 2016 at http://grrm.livejournal.com/427713.html).

11 An updated classic is Jacques Barzun and Henry F. Graff, *The Modern Researcher* (6th edn., Belmont, CA: Wadsworth/Thomson Learning, 2004 [1957]).

12 David Itzkoff, "George R. R. Martin on 'Game of Thrones' and Sexual Violence," *New York Times ArtBeat*, 2014, May 2 (accessed August 8, 2016 at http://artsbeat.blogs.nytimes.com/2014/05/02/george-r-r-martin-on-game-of-thrones-and-sexual-violence/?).

13 For a good survey of new trends, see John Tosh with Seán Lang, *The Pursuit of History: Aims, Methods and New Directions in the Study of Modern History* (4th edn., Harlow: Pearson Longman, 2006).

14 Martin draws on medieval patriarchy for his novel. See the unsigned "Patriarchy in Westeros," in *The Citadel: So Spake Martin*, 1999, January 7 (accessed August 6, 2016 at http://www.westeros.org/Citadel/SSM/Entry/962). Nevertheless, many of his female characters fight against the restrictions of patriarchy. On this topic, see the chapters by Mares and Alesi in this volume.

15 Aside from the wildlings covered in this chapter, other "others" who are truly "other" are the "White Walkers," the blue-frozen undead humanoids whom Martin calls "Others" in the books. The producers of the television series changed their name, worried that viewers might be confused in oral references to "others" (see "Episode One: 'Winter Is Coming' with Commentary," in the DVD *Game of Thrones: The Complete First Season*, USA: Home Box Office, Inc., 2014).

16 See Brian A. Pavlac, *Witch Hunts in the Western World: Persecution and Punishment from the Inquisition through the Salem Trials* (Westport, CT: Greenwood Press, 2009).

17 Beric Dendarrion and John Snow, who have returned from the dead, are clearly different from wights. Wights become killers of former friends, such as those who attack Lord Commander Mormont. Beric Dendarrion and John Snow retain most of their memories and personality and do not continue to physically rot (although they continue to suffer some damage from wounds).

18 A readable counterpoint is Régine Pernoud, *Those Terrible Middle Ages! Debunking the Myths*, translated by Anne Englund Nash (San Francisco: Ignatius Press, 2000 [1977]).

19 For more on western civilization, see Brian A. Pavlac, *A Concise Survey of Western Civilization: Supremacies and Diversities throughout History* (2nd edn., Lanham, MD: Rowman & Littlefield, 2015).

20 Some historians nowadays prefer to use instead the abbreviations BCE (before the common era) and CE (common era), but such usage often comes from political correctness or simply from the desire to conform to fashion. At any rate it does not reflect a true classification, that is, any historical trend or event meaningful enough to function as a criterion by which our history could be split into two parts—as the birth of Christ is traditionally supposed to have done.

21 "More Wars of the Roses" (unsigned), in *The Citadel: So Spake Martin*, 1998, November 27 (accessed August 6, 2016 at http://www.westeros.org/Citadel/SSM/Entry/950). For a general treatment, see Charles Ross, *The Wars of the Roses: A Concise History* (London: Thames & Hudson, 1976).

22 Shakespeare, *Richard III*, Act 5, Scene 5, lines 27–28.

23 See "The Real History Behind the Game of Thrones," in the DVD *Game of Thrones: The Complete Fifth Season* (USA: Home Box Office, Inc., 2016).

24 Each of the old kingdoms is dominated by a powerful dynasty: Stark in the North, Tully in the Riverlands, Lannister in the Westerlands, Baratheon in the Stormlands, Arryns in the Vale, Tyrell in the Reach, and Martell in Dorne. Dorne itself is a mixture of Spain, Palestine, and, oddly, Wales (see the unsigned "Historical Influences for Dorne," in *The Citadel: So Spake Martin*, February 29, 2000, accessed August 7, 2016 at http://www.westeros.org/Citadel/SSM/Entry/999).

25 Stark's hostage and ward, Theon Greyjoy of the Iron Islands, switches back and forth between being a "good guy" and being a "bad guy."

26 Martin, *A Storm of Swords*, 260.

27 The former Kingsguard of Renly, Brienne of Tarth, a woman warrior, finds and executes the wounded Stannis for the murder of her lord.

28 He is given a "crown" of molten gold; see Rachel Nuwer, "Here's What Actually Happens During an Execution by Molten Gold," 2014, June 10 (accessed August 3, 2016 at http://www.smithsonianmag.com/smart-news/heres-what-happened-people-who-were-executed-having-molten-gold-poured-down-their-throat-180951695).

29 "The Broken Man," directed by Mark Mylod, written by Bryan Cogman, in *Game of Thrones*, season 6, HBO, first aired on June 5, 2016.

30 For further browsing, consider the following websites and articles: A Wiki of Ice and Fire, at http://awoiaf.westeros.org/index.php/Main_Page; *Game of Thrones Wiki*, at http://gameofthrones.wikia.com/wiki/Game_of_Thrones_Wiki; Winter Is Coming: The Game of Thrones News Source, at http://winteriscoming.net; History Behind the Game of Thrones, at http://history-behind-game-of-thrones.com; and the site dedicated to this volume: *Game of Thrones versus History*, at http://gameofthronesversushistory.com.

Part I

Kings, Queens, Knights, and Strategy

1

High and Mighty Queens of Westeros

Kavita Mudan Finn

"Courtesy is a lady's armor," advises Septa Mordane, governess to Lady Sansa Stark, who, early in *Game of Thrones*, is engaged to the crown prince of Westeros, Joffrey Baratheon. Sansa is the perfect aristocratic girl, versed in courtesies, songs, and good behavior, unlike her tomboyish younger sister Arya. But Sansa and the viewer quickly learn that being a perfect lady is far from being a perfect queen. Queens in Westeros, like their real-world historical counterparts, have a dirtier and more complicated job than is generally acknowledged, and they are under attack in subtler ways than by the sword.

The cultural standards in *A Song of Ice and Fire* and *Game of Thrones* hew closely to traditional fantasy tropes, themselves a product of J. R. R. Tolkien's training as a medieval literature scholar. While Tolkien focuses on plotlines that largely exclude women, George R. R. Martin includes six women among his fourteen major point-of-view (PoV) characters.[1] Instead of telling stories of kings, as is traditional in medieval romance and modern fantasy, Martin focuses on the people surrounding the king: his advisors, his family, his servants—and sometimes his queen.

The first queen whom viewers encounter is Cersei Lannister, the consort of King Robert Baratheon. Even before she appears, she is defined first and foremost as a *Lannister*, more loyal to her blood relations than she will ever be to her husband. Royal marriages in medieval and early modern Europe were founded on military and diplomatic ties, so a married queen was expected to maintain a relationship with her family—within certain limits. King Edward IV of England (r. 1461–1470, 1471–1483) faced this problem when he secretly married the beautiful Elizabeth Woodville (c. 1437–1492). The introduction of Elizabeth's large and ambitious family at Edward's Yorkist court upset the balance among the established families and led to a resurgence of civil war.[2] Within several years, Edward lost his throne to the rival house of Lancaster and had to invade his own country to get it back. Controversy over the marriage also contributed to the chaos after Edward's death in 1483, the disappearance

Game of Thrones versus History: Written in Blood, First Edition. Edited by Brian A. Pavlac.
© 2017 John Wiley & Sons, Inc. Published 2017 by John Wiley & Sons, Inc.

(and probable murder) of his two sons, and his younger brother's usurpation of the throne as King Richard III (r. 1483–1485).[3]

If all this sounds familiar, so it should. *Game of Thrones* makes no secret of its medieval roots—it's a short step, after all, from York to Stark and from Lancaster to Lannister. Even though the series includes direwolves, fire-breathing dragons, and the walking dead, its complicated plot hinges on a quintessentially medieval problem: a disputed succession that leads to civil war. Historically, the fifteenth century saw civil wars erupt in England, France, Burgundy, Spain, and the Italian Peninsula—wars that only got worse after the sixteenth-century Reformation. During this turbulent period, a queen's role was especially important and often controversial. Studying the queens in *Game of Thrones* and their historical sources of inspiration can tell us a great deal about how women were perceived then—and are now.

The Making of a Queen

Prior to Robert's rebellion 15 years before *Game of Thrones* begins, almost all the queens of the Seven Kingdoms came from the Targaryen family.

> The line must be kept pure [...] theirs was the kingsblood, the golden blood of old Valyria, the blood of the dragon. Dragons did not mate with the beasts of the field, and Targaryens did not mingle their blood with that of lesser men.[4]

The practice of incestuous brother–sister marriage sets the Targaryens apart from the rest of Westeros, while also giving each child born to the family a fair chance of turning out insane, thanks to generations of inbreeding.[5] *The World of Ice and Fire* (2014), which provides a detailed history of Westeros, includes instances of Targaryens marrying outside the family, usually to shore up alliances or to gain additional territory, but the overall tendency was to preserve the royal bloodline. In short, Targaryens make their own rules, and those rules do not apply to any other family, whether in Westeros or in medieval Europe.

Medieval nobility commonly negotiated multiple marriage agreements for daughters who might potentially become queens. When Robert Baratheon takes the Iron Throne from the Targaryens, he chooses for his queen Cersei, the only daughter of Lord Tywin Lannister, the richest man in the Seven Kingdoms. Although Tywin had delayed supporting Robert until the last moment, his seizure of King's Landing secured Robert's victory. Viewers learn later that Cersei had already been offered to the last Targaryen prince, but the "mad" king, fearful of Tywin's growing power, had refused. When Cersei marries Robert, she is therefore fulfilling the promise that she would become a queen—a promise she had made in her youth.[6] Following a similar succession of marriage arrangements, Margaery Tyrell, a wealthy daughter of Highgarden, states her ambition unambiguously: "I don't want to be *a* queen. I want to be *the* queen."[7] She marries first Renly Baratheon, then King Joffrey (if only for a few hours), and finally King Tommen.

Decades of war in medieval Europe created a multitude of widows and many found themselves remarried, with or without their consent. Elizabeth Woodville, for instance, was the widow of a Lancastrian knight before becoming the wife of the Yorkist king, Edward IV. Roughly a decade later, Edward's brother Richard married Lady Anne Neville (1456–1485), who was previously married to the son of the Lancastrian king, Henry VI (r. 1422–1461; 1471). Unlike Elizabeth, Anne was from a prominent noble family, with a massive dowry and substantial landholdings in the north of England. Some chroniclers even hinted that Anne's money and family influence made it possible for Richard to claim the throne later.[8]

She is not the most extreme case, however. Lady Margaret Beaufort (1443–1509), whose bloodline gave her a complicated claim to the English throne, was constantly being married off in order to either advance or control that claim. She was briefly married to the Lancastrian Edmund Tudor, who died in prison of plague and by whom Margaret had her only child. When the Yorkists came to power in 1461, she was married to one of Edward IV's supporters. After he died in battle, Margaret married for the last time, and her third husband's talent for double-dealing and raising large armies made it possible for her son to become King Henry VII in 1485. As queen mother she set her stamp on the English court and took charge of her royal grandchildren, including the future King Henry VIII. As far as we know, Margaery Tyrell's ferocious grandmother Lady Olenna had only one husband, but her influence on her children and grandchildren certainly evokes Margaret Beaufort, who would never be queen in her own right but was nonetheless a force to be reckoned with.

In *A Storm of Swords* and during the second season of *Game of Thrones*, Sansa Stark's elder brother Robb, declared "King in the North" after his father's execution, contracts a secret marriage not unlike that of King Edward IV, and with similarly bloody results. In the book, Robb sleeps with and impulsively marries a young woman named Jeyne Westerling, despite being betrothed to a daughter of the irascible Lord of the Crossing, Walder Frey. Although this marriage is the "honorable" thing to do in one sense (because they had had sexual relations), the breaking of his word to his betrothed leads to Robb's murder at the hands of Lord Frey and his allies. We later learn that even Robb's initial encounter with Jeyne was a deep-rooted conspiracy begun by Tywin Lannister, liege lord to Jeyne's parents, and designed to destroy the northern alliances from within.[9] The television series replaces Jeyne with a lady physician from Volantis named Talisa, who, while similarly unsuitable, has no connection to the rest of the characters. Unlike Jeyne, she is murdered at the Red Wedding alongside her husband.

Some queens in *Game of Thrones* claim thrones in their own right rather than through marriage. The most significant is Daenerys Targaryen, who possesses the only three living dragons in the world and intends to use them to take back her inheritance. Unfortunately, Daenerys is forced to rely on men for her armies and her councils, and it remains to be seen whether or not she will succeed. Another woman, Asha (or Yara) Greyjoy, claims the Seastone Chair of the Iron Islands through force of arms as well as through lineal succession, but fails when faced with her more powerful uncle Euron. Conscious of the danger Euron represents, Yara flees the Iron Islands and makes an alliance with Daenerys, who promises to support her claim. Lastly, Arianne Martell, daughter of Prince Doran Martell of Dorne, is recognized throughout the region as his heir—although this detail was changed between the books and the television series, where Doran is murdered by his brother's paramour Ellaria Sand, who takes control of Dorne. These, however, are exceptional cases in *Game of Thrones*, just as there were only a few queens regnant in medieval Europe. Princess Isabella of Castile, for example, played a major role in the unification of Spain. Several marriage contracts came and went before she wed Prince Ferdinand of Aragon in 1469. When she inherited Castile (r. 1474–1504) and he inherited Aragon (r. 1479–1516), they together created a united Spain they passed on to their children and grandchildren. She herself actively ruled, at times leading her own armies. Fortunately queens did not need to rule in their own right to be a dominant force. Queen consorts, although dependent on men (whether husbands, sons, or other family members), could still wield considerable power within those limits.

Responsibilities of Queenship

The Targaryen queens held a great deal of power since, as blood relatives to the king, their bloodlines were equal to his. More importantly, they had dragons. Dragons are a gender equalizer, as queens and kings, princes, princesses, and royal bastards alike ride their fiery mounts to battle—more often than not to their deaths. This unusual balance of power led to several uprisings during the Targaryens' 300-year rule over Westeros. The most infamous of these, the so-called Dance of the Dragons, raged between Queen Alicent, second wife of Viserys I, who fought on behalf of her young son Aegon, and Princess Rhaenyra, Viserys' eldest daughter by his first wife.[10]

Historically, a similar civil war began in England in 1135 when King Henry I declared his daughter Matilda his heir. The aristocracy refused to follow a woman and crowned her cousin Stephen of Blois instead. Eighteen years of brutal civil war followed, during which chroniclers claimed that "Christ and his saints slept." Finally the realm was united under Matilda's son, King Henry II

(r. 1154–1189). The Dance of the Dragons lasted only two years, but "the Targaryen power [was] much diminished, and the world's last dragons vastly reduced in number."[11] Echoing the resolution of the English Civil War, the war only ended when Rhaenyra's son Aegon became King Aegon III and married Aegon II's daughter. The seeds of the Targaryens' downfall can be found in this conflict, as most of their dragons—arguably their main source of power—were killed during the war.

With the dying out of the dragons, the military function of Targaryen queenship diminished and the role of queens became more ceremonial. "Good" Queen Alysanne, for instance, is revered for her charity and her kindness, particularly to the Night's Watch, while Queen Naerys, wife to Aegon the Unworthy, survives in song for her beauty and her sadness. The Water Gardens in Dorne were constructed for the Targaryen queen Daenerys. She filled these gardens first with her own children, then with children of the Dornish nobility, and, finally, with the children of all those who served in her household, a tradition that endures into the period in which the series is set.[12] By the time of the War of the Five Kings, the queen's job is, first and foremost, to provide heirs to the throne and, second, to promote harmony at court. When queens step outside those prescribed areas of influence, as Cersei Lannister repeatedly does, they meet with strong opposition from the surrounding men.

Although Cersei appears to fulfill all the expectations one had from a queen (by providing heirs, being gracious and charming in public, and acting as an intermediary between the Lannisters and the Baratheons), this is only a façade, soon demolished. Viewers quickly discover that all three of her children came from an incestuous affair with her twin brother Jaime and that she would stop at nothing to preserve her royal power. Her dismissive attitude and short-sighted policies—as well as her inability to control her sadistic and bloody-minded son Joffrey—result in her being almost universally despised, both within the story and among critics and fans. Martin, however, gives us Cersei's point of view in the fourth and fifth books, where it becomes clear that her worst decisions are driven by desperation, paranoia, and frustration with her lack of real power. As she complains early in Season 2: "This is what ruling is: lying on a bed of weeds, ripping them out by the root, one by one, before they strangle you in your sleep!"[13]

Cersei's flaws are highlighted by her rivalry with her prospective daughter-in-law, Margaery Tyrell. Not only is Margaery the perfect candidate on the surface, she also cultivates the queenly attributes that Cersei abandons:

> When she was feeling pious she would leave the castle to pray at Baelor's Sept. She gave her custom to a dozen different seamstresses, was well-known among the city's goldsmiths, and had even been known to visit the

> fish market by the Mud Gate for a look at the day's catch. Wherever she went, the smallfolk fawned on her, and Lady Margaery did all she could to fan their ardor. She was forever giving alms to beggars, buying hot pies off bakers' carts, and reining up to speak to common tradesmen.[14]

Margaery, in short, is gaining public support independently of the king. Queens in medieval Europe were able to sway public opinion through ceremonial interactions with the general population. For instance, when the city of London unsuccessfully rebelled against Richard II in 1392, his queen, Anne of Bohemia, interceded on behalf of the citizens, to spare them from the king's wrath—an incident immortalized in Richard Maidstone's poem *Concordia*. Like Margaery, medieval queens could also wield influence through smaller acts of patronage: buying goods from local merchants and craftsmen or encouraging the cultural life of the court. Eleanor of Provence (1223–1291), wife of Henry III of England (r. 1216–1272), presided over one of the most splendid courts of the thirteenth century. The same held true for Queen Isabeau of France (c. 1370–1435), who patronized many artists and writers, including Christine de Pizan, considered the first professional woman writer in Europe.

This patronage extended to religion. Queens in medieval Europe would give generously to monasteries and abbeys, fund a variety of church projects, and sometimes even retire to convents late in life. Whatever their personal beliefs, they had to conform to what the church deemed to be appropriate behavior. Queen Isabella of Castile, for instance, encouraged the Spanish Inquisition and expelled both Jews and Muslims from the Iberian Peninsula on the pope's orders. In season 6, Margaery Tyrell ingratiates herself with the powerful and deeply pious High Septon (who had been the High Sparrow) in order to protect her family and her status as Tommen's queen. This again contrasts her with Cersei, who pays for her antagonism against the High Septon with the public humiliation of a walk of shame (although her fiery revenge by burning down the Great Sept has no historical basis).

Royal women sometimes exercised power by serving as regents for their young sons, as Cersei does to a limited extent. When those sons reached the age of majority, married, and had children of their own, queen mothers were expected to retire gracefully and allow their successors to rule unhindered. Most of them did. Some kings, however, saw fit to keep their mothers close, even at the expense of their wives. The redoubtable Eleanor of Aquitaine (1124–1204) ruled as regent in England while her son Richard I joined the Third Crusade (1189–1192). It is she who is forever associated with "the Lionheart," rather than his wife Berengaria of Navarre. King Louis IX (r. 1226–1270), canonized as Saint Louis, brought his mother, Blanche of Castile (1188–1252), out of a convent to rule France when he led the Seventh Crusade (1248–1254). Louis' wife, Marguerite of Provence (1221–1295), accompanied her husband

and, when he was imprisoned in Egypt, took charge of the French army, briefly becoming the only woman ever to lead a crusade.

A crusading queen earned herself a reputation for piety and courage. A queen during a civil war was lucky if her reputation survived the conflict. Isabeau of Bavaria had been married for seven years to Charles VI of France (r. 1380–1422) and had borne him four children before he manifested signs of insanity. When Isabeau took over the kingdom as regent, she was repeatedly accused of adultery and mismanagement, though she was likely innocent of both.[15] Similarly, Margaret of Anjou (1430–1482) had been married for eight years when her husband, Henry VI of England (r. 1421–1461, 1470–1471), fell into catatonia in 1453, one month before their only son was born. Margaret was slandered in diplomatic letters, in attempts to discredit her son's claim to the throne.[16] These accusations first appear in sources hostile to the queen's party and were almost certainly untrue. Although the accusations of adultery brought against Cersei Lannister happen to be true, several other women are falsely accused during the series; this is meant either to punish them or to discredit their sons and husbands. Witchcraft accusations were another popular weapon used against queens. Joan of Navarre, wife to Henry IV of England (r. 1399–1413) was convicted of witchcraft in 1419 and forced to hand over most of her jointure to her stepson Henry V (r. 1413–1421) in order to fund his wars against France. There is no indication that anyone believed she was guilty and her relationship with the king remained cordial—perhaps an indication of how dependent she was on his goodwill.

Although Daenerys Targaryen rules in her own name as the Mother of Dragons, she is no less bound by social and cultural strictures—indeed, she refers to her court manners in Meereen as "floppy ears" that she must wear to preserve her position. After a traumatic miscarriage at the end of the first book and season 1, it is prophesied that Daenerys can no longer bear children. This poses an obvious problem for the inheritance of the Iron Throne. Historically, Isabella of Castile successfully used her marriage to Ferdinand of Aragon to shore up support against her uncle Enrique, who threatened to divert the succession of Castile elsewhere. But her marriage to her ambitious and frustrated husband brought her other problems, particularly when she tried to ensure that Castile would pass on to her daughter Juana after her own death. Ferdinand conspired with Juana's husband to have her declared mad and imprisoned, so they could split the kingdom between themselves, thus countermanding Isabella's dying wishes. Similarly, Mary I of England (r. 1553–1558), a queen in her own right, found little comfort and many problems in her marriage to Philip II of Spain a century later. Philip constantly nagged her for more power in England, while the English parliament stood firmly against allowing a Spaniard (and a Roman Catholic) to rule over it. It is therefore not too surprising that Mary's half-sister Elizabeth I (r. 1558–1603) refused to marry and reigned for 44 years as the Virgin Queen.

The Unmaking of Queens and Other Cautionary Tales

A queen's position, while potentially powerful, was by no means invulnerable. Many kings found excuses to rid themselves of unwanted wives. Most infamous is Henry VIII of England (r. 1509–1547) with his six wives; but he was far from being the first. In 1483, just before he inherited the throne, Charles VIII of France (r. 1483–1498) was betrothed to Margaret of Austria (1480–1530), who was only three years old at the time. She came to the French court as a child and grew up there. In the autumn of 1491, however, Charles repudiated the betrothal and married instead Duchess Anne of Brittany (1477–1514), for blatantly political reasons. Brittany was an important strategic barrier between France and England and Charles' marriage to Anne gave France control over its territories. When he died without an heir, his cousin, Louis XII (r. 1498–1515), inherited the throne. Although Louis was already married to his cousin Jeanne of France (1464–1505) he had the marriage annulled and wed Anne, the previous king's queen. Like his cousin Charles, Louis also died without a male heir, but France ultimately kept Brittany.[17] Meanwhile Margaret of Austria, the jilted fiancée of Charles VIII, went on to marry and be widowed twice and then vowed never to marry again. Her father, Emperor Maximilian I (r. 1486–1519), who had also been betrothed to Anne of Brittany, appointed Margaret regent of the Netherlands, thus giving her a significant political role for the rest of her life. Meanwhile Jeanne of France, the abandoned wife of Louis XII, retired to a convent and was eventually canonized. These women were given no choice in their repudiation and were forced to make the best of embarrassing and potentially damaging situations.

Though Sansa Stark begins the series as the daughter of a powerful lord betrothed to the king's son, she loses much of her value as a potential queen after her father is executed and she becomes a hostage to the Lannisters. The alliance with the Tyrells gives King Joffrey an excuse to repudiate Sansa and take Margaery as his queen instead (while threatening to keep Sansa as an unwilling mistress).[18] As discussed above, Robb Stark's decision to break his betrothal to Lord Frey's daughter proves equally fatal to him and to his wife in *Game of Thrones*. But not all changes in marriage plans were scandalous. What is not reflected in Westerosi politics is the many routine cases of betrothals cancelled or altered for a variety of normal reasons, not least because the parties involved were children. While it is a common belief that child marriage was normal in the medieval period, this is simply not true: royal and aristocratic children were often promised in marriage with the caveat that the marriage itself should not take place before they reached the age of majority.

As mentioned above, queens were sometimes accused of adultery. When these accusations were made for obviously political reasons, they were usually taken with a grain of salt. If, however, they were proven true, the results could be catastrophic. In 1314, the three daughters-in-law of King Philip IV "the Fair" of France (r. 1285–1314) were tried for infidelity and treason, a turn of events that destroyed the French succession and ushered in the Hundred Years' War (1337–1453). As for the former princesses, one was exonerated—probably owing to her substantial dowry—and the other two were publicly shamed before being sentenced to lifetime imprisonment. A year later, when Philip IV's successor, Louis X (r. 1314–1316), was unable to obtain a divorce, his unfortunate wife, Marguerite of Burgundy (1290–1315), was found mysteriously strangled in her cell. Henry VIII of England was more vicious. Anne Boleyn (1501–1536) and Katherine Howard (c. 1522–1542) were both beheaded after being convicted of adultery, though it is likely that neither was guilty. Anne Boleyn was even accused of sleeping with her brother George—one possible inspiration for the incestuous relationship between Cersei and Jaime in *Game of Thrones*. In *A Feast for Crows* and in season 5 of *Game of Thrones*, Cersei accuses Margaery Tyrell of adultery and incest, only to find herself implicated in the same crimes—crimes of which she is undoubtedly guilty.

Cersei's public penance in King's Landing, which occupies one of her two chapters in *A Dance with Dragons* and a substantial portion of the season 5 finale in *Game of Thrones*, is a conflation and exaggeration of actual medieval punishments inflicted upon women. Convicted for witchcraft in November 1441, Eleanor Cobham, duchess of Gloucester, was forced to walk through the streets of London, wearing only a simple shift and carrying a candle. Nearly 20 years earlier, Eleanor had married the duke of Gloucester after an adulterous affair. His subsequent divorce from his first wife, Jacqueline of Hainault, no doubt contributed to Eleanor's notoriety long before her trial. Although witnesses did not hurl garbage, her penance was scandalous enough to appear in most English chronicles thereafter.[19] In 1483 Richard III forced Edward IV's favorite mistress, Jane Shore, to do a similar penance for her involvement in a treasonous plot against him. The punishment backfired, however. Instead of shaming the victim, it confirmed instead that Mistress Shore was more popular in London than Richard III.

In *Game of Thrones* Cersei has no such support during her public penance, as she has antagonized the citizens of King's Landing at every opportunity. Furthermore, not only is she forced to walk all the way across the city barefoot— as both Eleanor and Mistress Shore did—she does so "clad only in gooseprickles and pride," having been shaved and stripped beforehand.[20] During her walk, she regrets her penance:

> *I should not have done this. I was their queen, but now they've seen, they've seen. I should never have let them see.* Gowned and crowned, she was a queen. Naked, bloody, limping, she was only a woman, not so very different from their wives, more like their mothers than their pretty little maiden daughters. *What have I done?*[21]

Since Cersei, rightly or wrongly, identifies her beauty as the source of her power, she sees the ridicule and disgust of the crowd as the fulfillment of the curse of the *maegi* of Lannisport whom she had encountered as a child.[22]

In addition to the penance, the Faith Militant initially intended for Cersei to have a trial by combat. While trials by combat appear in medieval romance, they rarely if ever happened in actuality.[23] In contrast, such trials in Westeros are imbued with religious significance, and their verdicts cannot be countermanded. Although Cersei appears to have set herself up for success by naming, as her champion, a monster knight raised from the dead, her son Tommen's decision to ban trials by combat late in season 6 forces her to take more drastic measures. Through her master of whisperers Qyburn, Cersei engineers a catastrophic explosion of wildfire beneath the Sept of Baelor, killing most of the Tyrell family, her uncle Kevan, and the High Septon and prompting her own son to throw himself from a window of the Red Keep. When she is named "Queen on the Iron Throne" at the end of the season's finale, clad as she is in a black, high-necked gown in sharp contrast to the flowing dresses she wore earlier in the series, her hair shorn, she bears a closer resemblance—both in expression and in costume—to her late father, Lord Tywin, which suggests that her rule is likely to be as merciless as his.

Cersei's reign may come to an end at the hand of her unknown rival, Daenerys Targaryen rather than Margaery Tyrell, whom she had suspected and tried to undermine. By the end of season 6, Daenerys has taken control of a Dothraki horde, recaptured Meereen, and set sail for Westeros at the head of an enormous fleet, ready to take the Iron Throne for herself. Margaery, unlike Cersei and Daenerys, had the support of the population in King's Landing and the southern regions as well as a network of allies, both men and women. This is unusual. Most of the main female characters in *Game of Thrones* find themselves either the only woman or one of few women surrounded by men in male-centric situations. Cersei, who views other women as competitors, prefers it this way. The women of Highgarden and Dorne represent a different kind of collaborative female power. Margaery has been well taught by her grandmother Olenna, whose nickname "Queen of Thorns" reflects both her cleverness and her ruthlessness. Similarly, the princesses and even the illegitimate royal daughters of Dorne (known as the "Sand Snakes") take an active role in both governance and espionage, and they are given considerably more sexual freedom than their northern counterparts. In contrast, both Cersei and Daenerys suffer as a result of their isolation, as do all three women of the Stark family.

Historically, European queens were able to form networks and alliances, most frequently ones based on blood ties. Marguerite of Provence, wife of King Louis IX, had three sisters who married other European monarchs. Although their relationships were often fractious, they maintained contact with one another and held firm in their allegiance to their native Provence while their husbands squabbled.[24] By the fifteenth century, however, when civil wars overtook wars of conquest, even family alliances came under tremendous strain. Within *Game of Thrones*, the Queen of Thorns, to avenge her lost family and destroy the Lannisters, joins forces with the Sand Snakes and their mother in Dorne, in support of Daenerys. With Yara Greyjoy and the Iron Fleet along with the levies of Dorne and Highgarden at her side, Daenerys has created a powerful alliance of women to take down Cersei Lannister, thus making it almost completely certain that she is the younger and more beautiful queen in Cersei's prophecy.

The queens of *Game of Thrones* are formidable women in their own right, as were their medieval and early modern counterparts in Europe. Queenship was an unpredictable and dangerous undertaking, since the actions of a queen reflected not only upon the king, but also upon the country she adopted through marriage. It is not surprising, therefore, that one of the most popular works of Christine de Pizan's during her lifetime and in the century following her death was an advice book addressed to queens and aristocratic ladies, instructing them on how to keep their positions. *The Treasury of the City of Ladies* (c. 1405) was written in the tradition of "mirrors for princes," books intended to teach rulers how to rule. "There is no doubt," Christine observes, "that a lady is more feared and respected and held in greater reverence when she is seen to be wise and chaste and of firm behaviour."[25] Calling on the examples of Blanche of Castile and other queens of France and addressing herself not just to queens but to women of all classes, Christine advises patience, prudence, and, above all things, discretion—advice that one might argue Margaery Tyrell follows and Cersei Lannister flouts. Where the institution of queenship is going in Westeros remains to be seen, as the Mother of Dragons can make her own rules. Queens may follow the philosophy of Septa Mordane, that "courtesy is a lady's armor," but it seems more likely that they will take the advice of Shakespeare's Lady Macbeth: "Look like the innocent flower,/But be the serpent under't."[26]

Notes

1 Éowyn of Rohan and Galadriel of Lothlórien are the only significant female characters in *The Lord of the Rings*. Major female PoV characters in *A Song of Ice and Fire* are Catelyn, Sansa, and Arya Stark, Daenerys Targaryen, Cersei Lannister, and Brienne of Tarth. Minor female PoVs are (so far) Asha Greyjoy, Arianne Martell, and Melisandre of Asshai.

2 Elizabeth's mother, Jacquetta, was from the royal family of Luxembourg and had been married before to King Henry VI's uncle. After his death, she remarried a young knight named Richard Woodville, against the king's command.

3 Richard died at the hand of rebels two years after his coronation, in the Battle of Bosworth Field, and has the dubious distinction of being the only king of England whose body wound up buried beneath a car park.

4   George R. R. Martin, *A Song of Ice and Fire, Book One: A Game of Thrones* (New York: Bantam, 1996), 26.

5   In order to preserve bloodlines and territories, royal families throughout Europe intermarried during the medieval and early modern periods. Although marriages between close relations (often within four degrees) required papal dispensation, such sanctions were usually easy to obtain. The consequences are on display in the last generations of the Hapsburgs, who suffered from a variety of illnesses as a result of being too closely related or the Wittelsbachs; it may be disputed that "Mad" King Ludwig II (r. 1864–1886) of castle-building fame was actually insane, but his brother Otto certainly was.

6   George R. R. Martin, *A Song of Ice and Fire, Book Four: A Feast for Crows* (New York: Bantam, 2005), 360–362.

7   "The Ghost of Harrenhal," directed by David Petrarca, written by David Benioff and D. B. Weiss, in *Game of Thrones*, season 2, HBO, first aired on April 29, 2012.

8   Nicholas Pronay and John Cox, *The Crowland Chronicle Continuations: 1459–1486* (London: Alan Sutton, 1986), 175.

9   Martin, *A Feast for Crows*, 660–663.

10 George R. R. Martin, "The Princess and the Queen," in *Dangerous Women*, edited by George R. R. Martin and Gardner Dozois (New York: Tor, 2013), 703–786.

11 Martin, "Princess and Queen," 703.

12 George R. R. Martin, *A Song of Ice and Fire, Book Five: A Dance with Dragons* (New York: Bantam, 2011), 505–506.

13 "The Night Lands," directed by Alan Taylor, written by David Benioff and D. B. Weiss, in *Game of Thrones*, season 2, HBO, first aired on April 8 2012.

14 Martin, *A Feast for Crows*, 424.

15 See Tracy Adams, *The Life and Afterlife of Isabeau of Bavaria* (Baltimore, MD: Johns Hopkins University Press, 2010).

16 For Margaret of Anjou, see Helen Maurer, *Margaret of Anjou: Queenship and Power in Late Medieval England* (Woodbridge: Boydell, 2003). On her reputation and on slanders against her, see Kavita Mudan Finn, *The Last Plantagenet Consorts: Gender, Genre, and Historiography, 1440–1627* (New York: Palgrave, 2012), 22–24.

17 Owing to the lack of direct heirs, the French crown passed to François of Angoulême (1515–1589), Louis' cousin. See Sharon L. Jansen, *The Monstrous Regiment of Women* (New York: Palgrave, 2002), 56–62, 83–96.

18 George R. R. Martin, *A Song of Ice and Fire, Book Three: A Storm of Swords* (New York: Bantam, 2002 [2000]), 662.

19 Eleanor Cobham's afterlife is both fascinating and complicated. See Kavita Mudan Finn, "Tragedy, Transgression, and Women's Voices: The Cases of Eleanor Cobham and Margaret of Anjou," *Viator* 47.2 (2016), 277–303.

20 Martin, *A Dance with Dragons*, 855.

21 Martin, *A Dance with Dragons*, 858.

22 "Queen you shall be […] until there comes another, younger and more beautiful, to cast you down and take all that you hold dear" (Martin, *A Feast for Crows*, 179; see "The Wars to Come," directed by Michael Slovis, written by David Benioff and D. B. Weiss, in *Game of Thrones*, season 5, HBO, first aired on April 12, 2015).

23 For trials by combat, see Carolyne Larrington, *Winter Is Coming: The Medieval World of Game of Thrones* (London: I. B. Tauris, 2016), 39–42.

24 Marguerite's sisters were Eleanor, married to Henry III of England; Beatrix, married to William of Sicily; and Sancia, married to Richard, king of the Romans. See Nancy Goldstone, *Four Queens: The Provençal Sisters Who Ruled Europe* (New York: Penguin, 2007).

25 Christine de Pizan, *The Treasury of the City of Ladies*, translated by Sarah Lawson (London: Penguin, 1985), 76.

26 William Shakespeare, *Macbeth*, Act 1, Scene 5, lines 65–66.

2

A Machiavellian Discourse on *Game of Thrones*

Jacopo della Quercia

Are the political theories proposed five centuries ago by Niccolò Machiavelli (1469–1527), the Renaissance Florentine statesman, playwright, philosopher, and historian, relevant to the kingdoms and characters in George R. R. Martin's *A Song of Ice and Fire* and in HBO's *Game of Thrones*? Machiavelli's *Il Principe* (*The Prince*) has been described by scholars and political strategists as "the most famous book on politics ever written."[1] The treatise first appeared in 1513 as an analysis on how a prince's power over a newly acquired territory could be developed and maintained—or lost. Machiavelli was writing in response to a series of invasions that had torn apart the Italian Peninsula. Florence had just experienced a golden age under Lorenzo de' Medici, "the Magnificent," who had died in 1492. Then in 1494 the king of France claimed the throne of the kingdom of Naples. A massive French army tore the Italian Peninsula apart, beginning a series of wars that lasted more than 50 years, as petty Italian states fought against one another and against other foreigners such as Germans, Swiss, and Spanish. Machiavelli's political treatise not only provided practical realistic advice but also called on a prince to unite Italy and bring peace once more.

Machiavelli supported his theories with examples from the lives and times of numerous historical figures, among them Alexander the Great (356–323 BC), Julius Caesar (100–44 BC), and Pope Alexander VI (r. 1492–1503), as well as biblical, literary, and mythological figures such as Moses, Achilles, and Chiron the Centaur. Machiavelli made few distinctions between the fictional and historical figures featured in *The Prince*, because his theories focused on fundamental human behaviors consistent throughout history and evident in humanity's most enduring heroes of lore. Since Machiavelli referenced figures like Moses and Achilles when proposing theories about the fundamental use of political power, who's to say that he—or we—can't do the same using some of the most popular characters from *Game of Thrones*?

Game of Thrones versus History: Written in Blood, First Edition. Edited by Brian A. Pavlac.
© 2017 John Wiley & Sons, Inc. Published 2017 by John Wiley & Sons, Inc.

The Flames of Time

Like *The Prince*, George R. R. Martin's *A Song of Ice and Fire* borrows heavily from the lives and deeds of numerous historical figures, some of whom were Machiavelli's contemporaries and even mentioned in his writings. One such figure was Girolamo Savonarola (1452–1498), a Dominican friar whom Machiavelli himself heard preach in Florence.[2] Savonarola offers an excellent example of how Martin and Machiavelli not only tapped into the same reservoirs of history but wrote about them in comparable ways. Although Machiavelli was skeptical of Savonarola's abilities as a prophet, he recognized that the friar did not need supernatural abilities to attract his enormous following.[3] Savonarola came to power by encouraging a revolution in Florence that overthrew the de' Medici family and replaced it with an elected republican form of government. He stirred up passions through fiery sermons and actual "bonfires of the vanities," where Florentines could repent of their sins by tossing their material possessions into the flames. At the height of the cultural flowering of the Renaissance, his believers paradoxically burned the books of ancient and recent authors, lutes and flutes, caps and gowns, and, of course, mirrors. Savonarola created meaning by blaming the corrupt church and warring rulers for the misfortunes of the people.

The same applies to the High Sparrow in *Game of Thrones* because his behavior, as noted by one Machiavelli scholar, caters to "human" nature.[4] It's only natural for a suffering people to embrace a social revolutionary, be that Savonarola against the Medici in Florence and the Borgia in Rome or the High Sparrow against the Tyrells and the Lannisters in King's Landing. Just as Savonarola cultivated devoted *piagnoni* ("wailers" or "weepers") from among the youth of Florence so that his followers came to be known by this name, the High Sparrow recruited fanatic "Sparrows" in King's Landing.[5] The High Sparrow also condemned excess, sodomy, and heresy at all levels of society.

Both men thought they spoke for the divine, but both suffered fiery deaths.[6] The Sparrow appeared for a moment to be at the height of his power and influence, but instead was consumed in wildfire at the hand of a former patron and then enemy, Cersei. Savonarola also died at the hand of his former supporters, who had ceased to believe. Some challenged him to prove his prophetic role by literally walking through fire. When he failed to go through with the test, a mob attacked his convent. Savonarola wound up arrested and confessed, under torture, that he had lied about his visions. A crowd hanged him and then burned his body at the stake. Misplaced faith, it seems, proved as human as hubris—for both figures.

The High Sparrow and Savonarola suffered fiery ends after accusing their respective adversaries, Cersei and Pope Alexander VI Borgia, of sacrilege, illegitimacy, and fornication.[7] Does this mean that George R. R. Martin based the character of Cersei on Alexander VI, who, like her, allegedly engaged in incest? According to HBO's experts, no.[8] The High Sparrow's rise and fall does, however, demonstrate how closely the world of *Game of Thrones* resembles Machiavelli's, from its urban youth to its religious radicals and its cruelest monarchs. One scholar summarized Machiavelli's opinion of Savonarola's political posturing as "a sick power-play," and the same could easily be said of the High Sparrow.[9] Similarly, if Machiavelli could remark on Moses, Cyrus, and other figures of fact and fiction in the same sentence in which he mentions Savonarola in *The Prince*,[10] there's no reason why we cannot do the same with the High Sparrow, Cersei, or any characters from *Game of Thrones* whenever appropriate to Machiavelli's arguments.

Here is a thought that Machiavelli offers in *Discourses on Livy*: [11]

> Whoever wants to foresee the future needs to consult the past; for all human events, in every era, are a reflection of ancient times. This arises because they are the work of men who have always been animated by the same passions, which, by necessity, produces the same results.

Since the characters in *Game of Thrones* are animated by the same passions that have lured men and women toward good and evil throughout history, it should not be too surprising how well Machiavelli's theories mesh with the histories and politics of Westeros. There's a good chance Machiavelli watched one of Florence's most prominent residents burn five centuries before we watched something analogous on HBO.

A Clash of Kingdoms

You know how every episode of *Game of Thrones* opens with that nifty mechanical pop-up map of the known world? Imagine that sequence—along with its stirring music—as we take a similar tour of Machiavelli's Italy beginning in the backyard of that other famous Florentine, whose cogs and wheels inspired *Game of Thrones'* epic opening: Leonardo da Vinci (1452–1519), the famous Renaissance artist, inventor, and contemporary of Machiavelli.[12]

In this reimagined opening, our floating eye zooms in on Machiavelli's Florence with a few words from George R. R. Martin:[13]

> Florence was a city state occupying and controlling only a very small portion of a very chaotic Italy, surrounded by other city states that were allies on Tuesday, enemies on Wednesday, and then allies again on Thursday. The situation was constantly changing. It was very treacherous. You didn't know who your friends were, and you couldn't trust anyone. So they had to be clever.

If the papal seat in Rome was the Renaissance equivalent of King's Landing, then Florence was very much Machiavelli's Winterfell. It was his heart, his home, and the place where nearly every episode of his life took place. As our sweeping view in the opening shifts west to Genoa and north to the duchy of Milan's mountainous boarders, viewers might think that the icy Alps protected Italy from *barbari* just as the Wall safeguarded Westeros. This may have been the case in prior centuries, but in 1494 an army of French soldiers and Swiss mercenaries (a sort of unstoppable Unsullied of their time) invaded the Italian Peninsula. That invasion ignited a series of Italian Wars (1494–1559) between Italy's divided city-states and their larger, more powerful French, Spanish, and Germanic neighbors.

After a few blinks from our astrolabe, our soaring eye swoops down on the east, to Venice and its many holdings along the Adriatic and across the narrow sea. We might see shades of Braavos in Venice, from its canals to its reputation, worthy of a "Free City," and to the many masques its inhabitants wear during Carnival. Further east, the Ottoman Empire looms as a large and growing adversary: a Daenerys with a massive army and mighty navy. As our gaze shifts back to Italy, we cross the narrow sea again to the southern kingdoms of Naples and Sicily, controlled by the same Spanish kingdoms that inspired Dorne.[14] Such was Renaissance Italy: a dangerous, disrupted, hopelessly divided tangle of city-states surrounded by deadly enemies.

The first few chapters of *The Prince* define and describe the many different kinds of governments that typify nearly every dominion in both Machiavelli's Europe and Martin's Westeros and Essos. They are either "republics" (like Venice or Braavos) or monarchial "principalities" (akin to England, the conquered states of the Ottoman Empire, or any of the Seven Kingdoms). Principalities come in two forms: "hereditary" (like France or Dorne), or some "new" kind (such as Spanish-held Naples or Daenerys' budding queendom in Slaver's Bay).[15] Such principalities have been established in *Game of Thrones* through conquest (Aegon I, Daenerys), rebellion (Robert Baratheon, Balon Greyjoy), support from the elite (Robb Stark) or from the masses (the wildlings the Dothraki), treachery (Roose Bolton, the Lannisters), or chance (Stannis Baratheon, who was aided by Cersei's incest and Melisandre's magic). Although this may seem a superficial relationship between *The Prince* and *Game of Thrones*, the commentary Machiavelli might offer each corresponding principality is uncanny for a political theorist who has never seen the HBO series. Watch how his political advice for the princes of the Renaissance is reflected in the rulers of Westeros and Essos.

In Praise of King Robert

There's a reason why Robert Baratheon not only seized the Iron Throne but successfully held onto it for so long: he was one of the most formidable military *and* political figures that Westeros has seen since Aegon's conquest. Robert won his rule through strength in arms and through bloodlust. His bold action during rebellion resembles that of a young man Machiavelli idealized in *The Prince*, a ferocious one (*aggressivo*). Robert seemed as determined to seize lady fortune when his own betrothed, Lyanna Stark, was stolen from him. Robert's heedless aggression is comparable with that of the bellicose Pope Julius II (r. 1503–1513). Machiavelli praised this pope for invading Perugia and Bologna in 1506 impulsively and without "everything in order" and thus forcing his French, Spanish, and Venetian adversaries to either act accordingly or avoid him.[16] Robert's similar urgency to rescue Lyanna earned him many victories in quick succession. In one day, Robert won three battles when his rebellion seemed at its weakest.[17] Had Julius II launched his attacks cautiously, Machiavelli determined, "his ruin would have followed."[18] Had Robert also hesitated, it's unlikely that his rebellion would have lasted long enough for him to swing his war hammer into the chest of Rhaegar Targaryen, Lyanna's abductor, and usurp the Iron Throne.

As king, however, Robert did not hide his annoyance with the mechanics of rule. He left such matters to Jon Arryn, a capable man, while asserting that "fear and blood" preserved the Seven Kingdoms better than "honor."[19] Ned Stark considered him "no better than the Mad King" on account of having such sentiments. But Machiavelli distinguished between being *feared* and being *hated*, as had happened to the "mad" king, Aerys II. Robert illustrated awareness of this difference when he told Cersei that a "cowardly" defense of King's Landing during a hypothetical Dothraki invasion—namely sitting behind castle walls while commoners were slaughtered—would cost him popular support.[20] In contrast, Robert's son Joffrey learned a different lesson from his mother Cersei: "fear is better than love."[21] More personally, Rhaegar's abduction of Lyanna Stark made House Targaryen "hated above all" to Robert, while Machiavelli noted that a prince's preying on his subjects' women or property leads to hatred.[22] Notably Robert engaged in violence in order to put down rebellion against his authority, despite his self-described "fear and blood" doctrine. His usual passions were for whoring, hunting, tourneys, and telling drunken war stories. While such vices were costly burdens that impaired Robert's relationship with his Small Council, they more likely made him more lovable to the people rather than hated.

King Robert was a warrior. His reputation and his ability successfully preserved the Seven Kingdoms using the same methods Machiavelli prescribed for the city-states of Italy. Robert's understanding of the need for a single army "united behind one leader with one purpose" echoes what Machiavelli stressed numerous times throughout *The Prince*.[23] A national army comprised entirely of fellow countrymen, like "Rome and Sparta," Machiavelli thought, would always be superior to an army formed of allied soldiers.[24] Aerys Targaryen proved to have missed this lesson when he invited a Lannister army into King's Landing, expecting that it would help defend the city. Instead the army sacked it. A national army is also superior to an army bolstered with auxiliary or mercenary soldiers, as Stannis Baratheon learned when so many troops deserted him during his long march to Winterfell. Most importantly of all, a national army is superior to an army comprised entirely of mercenaries—like the Second Sons who betrayed the Qohorik and Yunkai, although not yet Daenerys herself.

King Robert acquired the Seven Kingdoms through his own "arms and virtue," and Machiavelli would have admired that aspect of Baratheon authority. He wrote that a prince "should have no other object, nor thought [...] than the art of war."[25] On this standard alone, Machiavelli might have compared Robert Baratheon favorably with the Greek mythological hero Achilles for his ferocity, with the Carthaginian commander Hannibal (247–183/182 BC) for his military prowess (with or without the elephants), and with Cesare Borgia (1475–1507) for his conquests in the Italian Peninsula.

Ned Stark: The Hand without a Head

Alas, if King Robert had a singular crowning failure, it was appointing a "Hand" as ineffectual as Eddard "Ned" Stark to replace Jon Arryn. Machiavelli issued the following warning to all the Ned Starks of the world:[26]

> How one lives is so distant from how one ought to live, that he who abandons what is done for what ought to be done sooner learns his ruin than his preservation. For a man who wishes to demonstrate his goodness in every deed will come to his ruin among so many who are not good.

Martin, who by his own admission read *The Prince* and "obviously absorbed quite a few of its lessons," embodied the dangers of excessive goodness in Ned Stark.[27] At first glance it seems that Stark's greatest failing was his unbending moral rectitude. The fault that ultimately cost him his head, however, was not his refusal to do something he deemed immoral: it was how *bad* Ned was at doing wrong when circumstances required it.

According to Machiavelli, it is necessary for a prince "wanting to preserve his power" to know when and how "to do wrong."[28] Martin shared this sentiment, adding:[29]

> It's tough to be a ruler, whether in Machiavelli's time or today [...] A lot of the fantasy that went on before me has this unspoken assumption that if you are a good man you will be a good king, or a good prince. But if you look at the real world, if you look at real history, or if you look at contemporary times, it's not enough just to be a good guy.

This was true for King Robert, who, as mentioned above, understood when to be cruel and when not to. The out-of-control cruelty of the Mad King and of King

Joffrey led to the rebellion, betrayals, and conspiracies that ended their lives. The Starks' cruelty was tied to beheadings, beginning with Ned's execution of a Night's Watch deserter in the first episode. That killing had few consequences, unlike the decapitation by his son Robb. The "King of the North" beheaded one of his lords, Richard Karstark, for insubordination. As a result, the Karstark forces hated him and withdrew from Robb's army, which led directly to his failure. In contrast, the Lord Commander of the Night's Watch, Jon Snow, publicly beheaded Janos Slynt for disobedience, yet this action solidified his authority as Lord Commander of the Night's Watch, gained the grudging approval of King Stannis, and temporarily muzzled critics like Ser Alliser Thorne. But, just as there are two sides to every sword, Jon's excessive mercy in letting wildlings pass through Castle Black lost him credibility among key members of the Watch, who then assassinated him.[30]

Whether or not Ned could have preserved his rule—and neck—through more cruelty, the fact is that several of his actions as Hand were both immoral and (sadly) ineffective. First was his lie in claiming responsibility for his wife Catelyn's capture of Tyrion Lannister. This resulted in the deaths of three members of his household guard and nearly cost Ned his life. Evidently Ned could choose to lie. It's just a shame he was so bad at lying (except about Jon Snow's true parentage).

A second act of dishonesty occurred during Ned's last moments with King Robert. While recording Robert's will, Ned deliberately wrote "my rightful heir" instead of the king's words of "my son Joffrey." This falsehood denied the Iron Throne to the boy whom Ned knew to be illegitimate, although he had refused to tell the king.[31] Nevertheless, Ned gained no advantage over Cersei through this deception, because, out of mercy, he told the queen about his plan. Even worse, he failed to secure sufficiently many allies and troops, betting on the City Watch as if it were a *mercenary* army—the kind that Machiavelli describes as "unfaithful [...] cowardly," and "useless."[32] Ned's attempt to usurp the Iron Throne for Robert's brother Stannis without even telling him was doomed to fail. The crime of forgery, which depended on a scribble on a piece of paper that Cersei could and did rip up, simply did not work.

Nevertheless, by falsifying Robert's will, Ned aligned himself with those whom Machiavelli considered to have "attained a principality through crimes."[33] Machiavelli uses two rulers as examples of successful seizure of rule through crime. Agathocles of Syracuse (361–289 BC) rose from being a mere potter to tyrant of the powerful ancient city-state. He began his rise by taking advantage of a powerful man in Syracuse who fell in love with him, gave him wealth, then got him into the military. As a soldier and commander, Agathocles showed his prowess and won the support of common people. He then exploited class conflict in the city. He called together the Six Hundred, a body of elite Syracusans, for a conference and, once they had come, he stood in front of the masses and accused the gathered elites of plotting against him. Agathocles had his troops arrest and kill many of the Six Hundred, while the people turned into a mob who plundered, murdered, and raped their way through the neighborhoods of the wealthy. More than 4,000 people were killed before Agathocles allowed himself to be proclaimed tyrant and restore order.[34]

In a second example, Machiavelli cites his contemporary, Oliverotto Euffreducci (1475–1502), who seized power in Fermo. After years of fighting and gaining military leadership, Oliverotto returned to the city in 1501 and held a banquet for his uncle and other leading citizens at his uncle's palace. After dinner, as conversation turned to serious political issues, Oliverotto invited his guests into another room for further discussion in private. Once the guests were thus gathered inside, his troops killed them. He then bullied the fearful government still extant into handing over the city-state to him.

This is remarkably similar to the most famous criminal act in the *Game of Thrones*, the "Red Wedding." The Starks expected hospitality from the Freys but were butchered instead. It is well known that George R. R. Martin based this event on two incidents from Scottish history: the "Black Dinner" and the "Glencoe Massacre."[35] In 1440, the regents for the 10-year-old King James II (r. 1437–1460) suspected that the sons of the late regent, the Douglas brothers, were conspiring against the crown. They invited the brothers to a dinner with the king on the pretext of a renewal of friendship ties but, upon the brothers' appearance in Edinburgh castle, had them arrested and executed. The Glencoe Massacre followed from the reluctance of some Highland Scots to recognize the rule of King William III "of Orange" (r. 1689–1702). His government decided to make an example of the MacDonald clan at Glencoe. Royal troops under the command of a Campbell arrived in the village at the beginning of February 1692. The local people fed and housed the troops for 12 days as respected guests. Then, early on on the morning of February 13, according to plan, the troops began to kill as many of the villagers as they could—nearly 40. Roughly the same number of people managed to escape when a sudden snowstorm gave them cover, although the same storm also caused some to die from exposure.

At the end of season 6, Cersei removes many of her enemies in one stroke through the destruction of the Sept of Baelor. This is similar to Guy Fawkes' failed Gunpowder Plot designed to overthrow the religious domination of the Protestants in England. Fawkes and his Roman Catholic conspirators had planned to blow up Parliament on November 5, 1605 with 36 barrels of gunpowder in the cellar. Only the chance discovery of Fawkes the night before by a justice of the peace foiled the plan, just in time.

Machiavelli believed that anyone who seizes a state through treachery must kill his or her enemies "all at a stroke," to mitigate the act. Renly Baratheon urged Ned to do just than, even though Lord Renly had a reputation as a courtly and considerate prince. But even he, like Machiavelli, appreciated "how to do wrong [...] according to necessity."[36] Ned only possessed the ability to do wrong the *wrong* way, and for his errors Stark lost his life, and the kingdom plunged into civil war.

Before we leave Westeros, let's take a moment to examine what Machiavelli would have thought about the cruelty of Roose Bolton by comparison to that of Cesare Borgia, whom Machiavelli knew well and praised as an ideal prince who very nearly dominated Italy. Cesare, sometimes known by the title duke of Valentinois, which earned him the nickname Valentino (*il Valentino*), was the illegitimate son of Pope Alexander VI, who made him a cardinal. When Cesare's elder brother mysteriously died, however, Alexander put Cesare in charge of the papal military forces that were to regain the pope's authority over the various cities and towns recognized as the Papal States. When Cesare invaded the Romagna region, he appointed Remirro de Orco its governor. He knew that Remirro, "a cruel man," would quickly subjugate the region with extreme brutality. Once the unruly realm was quelled, however, Cesare made quite a spectacle of his stooge. He had Remirro "cut into two" and displayed in a public square, "with a piece of wood and a bloody knife" beside him. Machiavelli claimed that the sight left Romagna's conquered people "satisfied and terrified"—a result he approved of and felt was worthy of "being imitated by others."[37]

For a while it looked as if Roose was using his bastard son Ramsey in a similar fashion. His weak warning "You can't rule the North through terror alone," however, had no effect on his son, who used Reek/Theon to trick the ironmen at Moat Cailin into surrendering (after which they were flayed).[38] Bolton again warned Ramsay that things were going too far: "If you acquire a reputation as a mad dog, you will be treated as a mad dog, taken out back and slaughtered for pig feed."[39] Roose knew that Ramsay's "rapacious" cruelty was making him "hateful and contemptible" throughout the North, just as Machiavelli warned.[40] But, as Machiavelli noted, fortune favors the young and the forceful; and the son murdered the father.[41] Despite his crimes, Ramsey found many still willing to fight for him.

Why Daenerys Nearly Lost Meereen

Across the Narrow Sea, Daenerys Targaryen was trying to rule her newly conquered cities around Slaver's Bay. She possessed a unique advantage with her three fire-breathing dragons. Sadly, there are no dragons in Machiavelli's *The Art of War*, but he does mention war elephants a few times. When discussing Pyrrhus' use of elephants against Roman cavalry at the Battle of Heraclea (280 BC), Machiavelli noted that the beasts caused "great confusion and disturbance" among Romans, an effect not entirely dissimilar to what happens whenever Daenerys says "dracarys."[42] Although intimidating, war elephants had a weakness that the Roman general Scipio Africanus exploited when facing Hannibal at Zama (202 BC)—another battle that Machiavelli discussed.[43] Scipio had deduced that Hannibal's elephants could only move in straight lines; thus, when they charged at Zama, Scipio ordered his soldiers to reposition into columns, allowing Hannibal's elephants to pass harmlessly through his army. In short, the secret to defeating the most formidable creatures ever ridden into battle was to avoid providing a target for them. Such a tactic also saved the Dornish kingdom from being conquered by the Targaryens Dornishmen did not come together in armies, ready to be burned, but scattered throughout the desert. At Meereen, though, Daenerys could hardly use her dragons to burn her own city.

The situation in Meereen was constantly tense because of hostility between freed slaves and former masters, a situation not covered by Machiavelli. Daenerys' attempt to enforce justice by executing the murderer of one of her prisoners went nearly as badly as it did for Robb Stark. Her public beheading of a freed slave accused of killing an alleged Son of the Harpy while in her custody caused a riot against her.[44] Such a conflict only gave support to her foes, as in the case of the Roman Emperor Maximinus Thrax (r. 235 to 238), whose cruelty, according to Machiavelli, created "so many enemies" that his own troops murdered him.[45]

That riot then prompted Daenerys to question her own leadership, which highlights her problem with advisors. Of her male counselors, she had banished Jorah Mormont; Grey Worm lay wounded; and Barristan Selmy had been slain. This left Daenerys only with her lover Daario Naharis, whose best talents were making love and killing. According to Machiavelli, however, lack of counselors is not a problem: a prince should only consult advisors when he wants to, not the other way around.[46] Daenerys' translator, Missandei, also counseled Daenerys that she herself often saw a solution that her advisors could not see; the queen therefore should rely on her own instinct.[47] Machiavelli also reasoned that "good counsel, from wherever it comes, must arise from the prudence of the prince, and not the prudence of the prince from good counsel."[48]

It's an enormous credit to George R. R. Martin that his characters can serve as profiles in leadership comparable to great literary and historical figures. Few writers create even one such figure, an Atticus Finch or a Captain Ahab, and even fewer fill our literature with families as captivating as the Corleones or the house of Montague. *Game of Thrones* contains an entire world of characters with histories so closely modeled after our own that it's impossible to examine them without seeing ourselves reflected in them. The same applies to Machiavelli's *The Prince*, which after five hundred years still holds a mirror to some of the darkest sides of human nature.

Notes

1 Harvey Mansfield, "Introduction," in Niccolò Machiavelli, *The Prince* (Chicago, IL: University of Chicago Press, 1985), vii.

2 Niccolò Machiavelli, *The Letters of Machiavelli*, translated by Allan Gilbert (Chicago, IL: University of Chicago Press, 1988), 57.

3 Niccolò Machiavelli, *Discourses on Livy*, translated by Harvey C. Mansfield and Nathan Tarcov (Chicago, IL: University of Chicago Press, 1998): Book I, chapter xi.

4 Mark Jurdjevic, *A Great and Wretched City* (Cambridge, MA: Harvard University Press, 2014), 28.

5 For more on the Faith Militant, see the chapter by Attali in this volume.

6 "The Winds of Winter," directed by Miguel Sapochnik, written by David Benioff and D. B. Weiss, in *Game of Thrones*, season 6, HBO, first aired on June 26, 2016.

7 Tamar Herzig, *Savonarola's Women: Visions and Reform in Renaissance Italy* (Chicago, IL: University of Chicago Press, 2008), 495.

8 "The Real History Behind *Game of Thrones*," DVD, in *Game of Thrones: The Complete Fifth Season* (USA: Home Box Office, Inc., 2016).

9 Nevio Cristante, *Machiavellis Revivus: Slashing a Sword on the Western Classical Tradition* (Newcastle upon Tyne: Cambridge Scholars Publishing, 2011), 88.

10 Niccolò Machiavelli, *Il Principe*, edited by Luigi Firpo (Turin: Einaudi, 1961): chapter vi. All translations in the present chapter are by Jacopo della Quercia and Marino D'Orazio. Many other English versions are readily available.

11 Niccolò Machiavelli, *Discorsi sopra la prima Deca di Tito Livio* (Florence: Sansosi, 1971): Book III, chapter 43. In this work Machiavelli discusses the politics of republics with elected democratic governments rather than that of monarchies and principalities such as we find in *The Prince*. He himself was a member of such a government in Florence, until the regime arrested, tortured, then exiled him.

12 Tim Appelo, "Secrets Behind 'Game of Thrones' Opening Credits," *Hollywood Reporter*, April 19, 2011 (accessed July 15, 2016 at http://www.hollywoodreporter.com/race/secrets-game-thrones-opening-credits-179656).

13 George R. R. Martin, interviewed in "Who's Afraid of Machiavelli?" directed by Clare Beavan, in *Imagine*, season 22, BBC, first aired on December 3, 2013.

14 George R. R. Martin, "Trying to Please Everyone Is a Horrible Mistake," in *Adria's News*, October 7, 2012 (8: 58 p.m.) (accessed July 15, 2016 at http://www.adrias news.com/2012/10/george-r-r-martin-interview.html).

15 Machiavelli, *Il Principe*, chapters i–xi.

16 Machiavelli, *Il Principe*, chapter xxv.

17 "Complete Guide to Westeros: Robert's Rebellion," Blu-ray, in *Game of Thrones: The Complete First Season* (USA: Home Box Office, Inc., 2011).

18 Machiavelli, *Il Principe*, chapter xxv.

19 "The Wolf and the Lion," directed by Brian Kirk, written by David Benioff and D. B. Weiss, in *Game of Thrones*, season 1, HBO, first aired on May 15, 2011.

20 "The Wolf and the Lion," HBO.

21 George R. R. Martin, *A Song of Ice and Fire, Book Two: A Clash of Kings* (New York: Bantam, 2011 [1999]), 489.

22 Machiavelli, *Il Principe*, chapter xix.

23 "The Wolf and the Lion," HBO; Machiavelli, *Il Principe*, chapters xii, xiii, xxvi.

24 Machiavelli, *Il Principe*, chapter xii.

25 Machiavelli, *Il Principe*, chapter xiv.

26 Machiavelli, *Il Principe*, chapter xv.

27 "Who's Afraid of Machiavelli?" BBC.

28 Machiavelli, *Il Principe*, chapter XV.

29 *Imagine*, "Who's Afraid of Machiavelli?"

30 The justification for assassination is stronger in the book, since Snow breaks his vows to try and take Winterfell back from the Boltons; see George R. R. Martin, *A Song of Ice and Fire, Book Five: A Dance of Dragons* (New York: Bantam, 2013 [2011]), 995–1000.

31 "You Win or You Die," directed by Daniel Minahan, written by David Benioff and D. B. Weiss, in *Game of Thrones*, season 1, HBO, first aired on May 29, 2011.

32 Machiavelli, *Il Principe*, chapter xii.

33 Machiavelli, *Il Principe*, chapter viii.

34 The ancient source is the beginning of Book XIX in Didodorus Siculus, *The Library of History* (accessed July 20, 2016 at http://penelope.uchicago.edu/Thayer/E/Roman/Texts/Diodorus_Siculus/19A*.html).

35 James Hibberd, "Game of Thrones' author George R. R. Martin: Why He Wrote The Red Wedding – Exclusive," *Entertainment Weekly*, June 2, 2013 (accessed April 15, 2016 at http://www.ew.com/article/2013/06/02/game-of-thrones-author-george-r-r-martin-why-he-wrote-the-red-wedding/2); "The Real History Behind *Game of Thrones*," DVD, in *Game of Thrones: The Complete Fifth Season* (USA: Home Box Office, Inc., 2016).

36 Machiavelli, *Il Principe*, chapter xv.

37 Machiavelli, *Il Principe*, chapter vii. Just after this he tricked Oliverotto Euffreducci into his hands and executed him. Machiavelli judges that Cesare Borgia only failed because his papal father died unexpectedly while Cesare was ill, and his nemesis became Pope Julius II.

38 "High Sparrow," directed by Mark Mylod, written by David Benioff & D. B. Weiss, in *Game of Thrones*, season 3, HBO, first aired on April 26, 2015.

39 "Home," directed by Jeremy Podeswa, written by Dave Hill, in *Game of Thrones*, season 6, HBO, first aired on May 1, 2016.

40 Machiavelli, *Il Principe*, chapter xix.

41 Machiavelli, *Il Principe*, chapter xxv.

42 Niccolò Machiavelli, *The Art of War*, translated by Ellis Farnesworth (Cambridge, MA: Da Capo Press, 2001): chapter iv.

43 Machiavelli, *Art of War*, chapter iv.

44 "The House of Black and White," directed by Daniel Minahan, written by David Benioff and D. B. Weiss, *Game of Thrones*, season 5, HBO, first aired on April 19, 2015.

45 Machiavelli, *Il Principe*, chapter xix. For the ancient source, see "The Two Maximini," chapters 1–23, in *Historia Augusta* (the Loeb edition, as reproduced at Lacus Curtius: accessed July 22, 2016 at http://penelope.uchicago.edu/Thayer/E/Roman/Texts/Historia_Augusta/Maximini_duo*.html).

46 Machiavelli, *Il Principe*, chapter xxiii.

47 "Kill the Boy," directed by Jeremy Podeswa, written by Bryan Cogman, *Game of Thrones*, season 5, HBO, first aired on May 10, 2015.

48 Harvey Mansfield, ed., *The Prince*, chapter xxiii.

3

Chivalry in Westeros

Steven Muhlberger

Chivalry is easier to discuss as an ideal than as a historical phenomenon. Students and fans of chivalry often try to identify and live up to some impossible standard of "true chivalry." This idolatrization often leaves chivalry unexplained, however. In *Game of Thrones* chivalry is key to understanding the culture of Westeros as well as that of the later Middle Ages in Western Europe (roughly the fourteenth and fifteenth centuries). In both places, chivalry is both a noble ideal to be lived up to and a set of practices central to aristocratic life and the culture as a whole. This double nature can create problems when discussing chivalry.[1]

In both the Middle Ages and Westeros, chivalry grew out of "the life of arms." The warrior's life was a difficult, yet respected way of life. In a world often torn by war, foreign and domestic, this life was dangerous and uncertain. Nevertheless, it was seen by many as the ultimate expression of masculinity. It also held out the possibility of social advancement and wealth. In the Westeros of King Robert's time, as in the later Middle Ages, a knight was the best kind of warrior. Not all warriors in Westeros are knights, just as they were not in fifteenth-century Europe. But all kinds of warriors manifested chivalry to some degree or another. If they failed to live up to the cultural expectations of knighthood, they were blamed for not being chivalrous. Such cultural expectations were complicated and sometimes contradictory.

Types of Knights

What was a knight? In the Middle Ages, knights were highly trained warriors in armor, mounted on large, powerful war horses, who fought alongside other knights in battle. Knights were typically used as heavy cavalry, shock troops that fought with swords, lances, maces, and battle-axes. In every European

Game of Thrones versus History: Written in Blood, First Edition. Edited by Brian A. Pavlac.
© 2017 John Wiley & Sons, Inc. Published 2017 by John Wiley & Sons, Inc.

language, the word meaning "knight" is derived from the word meaning "rider" (e.g., *chevalier, caballero, Reiter*). Only in English does the noun *knight* have its origins in a word meaning "servant" (*cniht*, like the modern German *Knecht*), indicating how knighthood was also bound up with service. For this discussion of chivalry, historical and fictional, let's start by describing three different kinds of medieval knights, their most important characteristics, and their similarities to the knights of Westeros.

First, vassal knights performed military and political service as a subordinate to their lord. When the centralized rule of kings broke down after the collapse of the Carolingian Empire in the ninth century, powerful men bound armed followers to themselves and made them their vassals by endowing them with arms, horses, training, and, preferably, a fief (i.e., piece of land). These bonds have become known to historians as feudal relationships, from the Latin word meaning "fief" (*feudum*). Many early medieval knights might have started with a low status, being dependent on a particular lord to whom they owed everything. Ideally a vassal was expected to have two virtues: prowess (a combination of courage and skill at arms) and loyalty to his lord. An eleventh-century bishop, Fulbert of Chartres, when asked to define what made a good vassal, said that the vassal "should not be injurious to [his lord] in his body [or] in his secrets or in the defences through which he is able to be secure."[2] Although this ideal of the loyal military vassal was not originally or exclusively attached to knights, it became and remained a key part of chivalry.

Second, knights and chivalry became identified with nobility. Vassals themselves could be powerful enough to be feudal lords with their own vassals. Thus a complicated "feudal network" of sworn loyalties connected knightly lords and vassals to one another. To exclude the "unsuitable" kind of people, knighthood became restricted to members of the nobility. Knights had to demonstrate noble lineage—membership of important families going back generations. The privilege of belonging to the class of nobles elevated knights to a high social status. From the twelfth century on, only the wealthier nobles could afford the costs of heavy cavalry: obtaining and maintaining weapons, armor, travelling baggage, and supplies, not to mention horses with their feed, stabling, and care. It required much time and wealth to train from early youth to ride and fight from horseback. Hence many knights needed to be rich—and nobles were by definition rich. Rare were the instances of a commoner being knighted on account of his valiant deeds. More commonly, poor knights could become powerful, most famously William Marshall (c. 1146–1219). Starting with nothing but the most basic of arms, William rose in status through victory in tournaments, success in battle, and wisdom in advising kings, until he became the greatest lord in England.[3] Class consciousness also played a part in chivalric attitudes in battle. For example, knights were reluctant to kill enemy knights of noble stock, especially since capturing and ransoming rich knights was more profitable.

As nobles, knights became associated with authority. One story told by medieval writers about the origin of kings emphasized that the first kings were those men who had the best physical qualities and the highest standard of moral conduct.[4] The same characteristics, said those writers, were the ones that made a good knight. Like emperors, kings, and princes and unlike the earlier vassal knights, noble knights were political leaders, participating in the governance of the kingdom. Even more, knights were meant to be a force for justice, for instance by defending non-combatants, especially clergy, women, and children.

A third kind of knight is the courteous knight. He is the knight of song and story, of whom ladies (like Sansa Stark) are so fond. Tales about such knights began to appear in France in the late twelfth century—stories that were the first "romances." Epic stories up to this point, like the *Song of Roland* (c. 1000), were almost exclusively about men. While romances told of chivalric adventures such as single combat between knights, they also focused on ladies, damsels to be rescued and loved. Like the noble knight, the courteous knight was a man of good breeding. He had manners appropriate to behavior at court and an appreciation of the rarefied cultural atmosphere that surrounded princes. Further, the courteous knight was a man of finer feeling, who could inspire and be motivated by romantic love. Some medieval knights even wrote love poetry, which not only celebrated a lady as the object of desire, but also reflected well on the knight as her suitor. Courtesy (refined manners) became so important to chivalry that life at court came to be to a great extent a celebration of chivalry and of the knight as a perfect man.

Starting in the fourteenth century, kings and other high lords created chivalric orders, such as the English Order of the Garter and the Burgundian Order of the Golden Fleece.[5] Princes selected and inducted members only if they truly embodied knightly virtues. Knights in orders wore distinctive dress and badges and participated in rituals that marked them as worthy continuers of traditions identified with the legendary Round Table of King Arthur. Such traditions inspired tournaments and jousts that were the high points in the courtly calendar.

These three groups of knights—vassal, noble, courteous—overlap and share characteristics. First, all knights were expected to have prowess—practical military skill, physical toughness, and courage. Thus what makes the courteous knight so desirable is not just his good manners, but his military ability. The prominent French knight Geoffroi de Charny wrote in the 1350s that "noble ladies should [...] love and honor these worthy men-at-arms who [...] expose themselves to so much physical danger as the vocation of arms requires."[6] He also asked his readers to imagine how a lady who loves a miserable wretch—a man who is unwilling to bear arms—will feel when he comes into a hall and no one shows him any honor.[7] Second, all knights were expected to show loyalty to their lords. Third, even the lowest level of knight, the dependent military retainer, could claim authority in order to enforce order.

Knights in the Seven Kingdoms

Turning to Westeros, we see that the characteristics present in the knights of late medieval Europe are also found in the knights of the Seven Kingdoms. Westeros has its hedge knights, who scramble to maintain respectability through unglamorous but effective service. There are also knights of noble lineage and lordly position, who are pillars of the realm. And some knights aspire to a reputation for great courtesy. Westeros' different kinds of chivalry sometimes come into conflict with each other, too.

In Westeros almost no one thinks that knights are obsolete. People naturally look to knights for both individual military performance and leadership. All knights are expected to manifest prowess. To be a knight is to be a warrior: the status is not granted to rich grocers, or bankers, or other non-combatants. Whether or not all Westeros knights are actually effective on the battlefield or on campaign, failure to live up to the standard of prowess is a cause for deep scorn. Ser Dontos, having publicly shown himself to be a fool, is demoted by King Joffrey to being a court fool (and only Sansa's attempt at mercy saves him from execution). Even knights of high lineage meet (or try to meet) the cultural expectations that leaders must be physically powerful and dangerous men. Jaime Lannister's reputation as a combat champion and warrior helps make him the fearsome figure that he is (although his notorious act as "the Kingslayer" and his ruthless leadership in war cut the other way as well, as seen below).

Two characters reinforce the identification of chivalry with consummate manhood and male privilege. Jaime's brother Tyrion is a figure of contempt, not just because of his peculiar appearance, but because he cannot fulfill the fighting role that comes so easily to his brother. Wealth, rank, and family connection in Tyrion's case are practically cancelled by his physical inability to be a warrior, or even a man. By many people's reckoning, not only is a knight the best kind of man, but any man who cannot fight is hardly a man at all. Tyrion knows that he cannot act as his own champion in a trial by combat because he would be soundly defeated and executed, and also because he would suffer utter ridicule.[8] Even his leadership, heroism, and combat ability at the Battle of Blackwater are taken from him, and credit is granted to his father and Loras Tyrell. People's willingness to believe the worst of Tyrion shows how badly he is positioned in his culture.

Tyrion has had a lifetime to learn that physical skill and power are necessary for someone to be accepted as that privileged figure, a man. Yet physical skill and power do not always bring respect. Brienne of Tarth fights better than most men, yet men treat her as a freak, despite (or because of) her amazing skill at arms. Most men view her skill as not legitimate in a woman, and they scorn her for trying to be a man. Only a few knights, such as Renly Baratheon and Jaime Lannister, recognize her devotion to chivalry.

What about men who were good fighters but who were not of noble birth? They were excluded from chivalric social roles, but prowess by itself could give its possessor a certain amount of grudging respect. Richard Kaeuper, a leading scholar of medieval chivalry, has said that prowess was practically a demigod for medieval knights.[9] Similarly, men whose lineage is unremarkable can find advancement on the basis of strength, ruthlessness, or generalship in the Seven Kingdoms, torn as these are by civil wars and by the distrust of noble households toward one another. Davos, the Onion Knight, for instance, found advancement through his blunt honesty, prudent counsel, and simple courage, just like Robert Knowles. Originally a mere archer, Knowles rose to a position of command over English armies during the Hundred Years' War (1337–1452) and died very wealthy. Likewise, military talent has enabled Davos to attain first knighthood and later the rank of lord. (Knowles never advanced that far.) Davos regrets his rise, fearing that his success would attract the deadly hostility of members of established families. Yet his lord, King Stannis, can neither do without his talents nor use them without giving Davos the formal rank of knight, which an admiral or a King's Hand requires if he is to command respect.

In contrast, Ser Gregor Clegane, called "the Mountain that Rides," and his brother Sandor, known as "the Hound," are striking examples of how raw fighting ability, or prowess, can have devastating effects. At first, neither the Mountain nor the Hound has any other laudable characteristics whatsoever; even their loyalty cannot be taken for granted. In an era when human strength and skill rule the battlefield and even intimidate the court, the Mountain is a terrifying weapon that is not just tolerated: he is used. The lords of Westeros are willing to play with fire in his case. His ability to overawe their political rivals is too valuable a tool to ignore.

Nevertheless, the very presence of the Mountain at court tends to erode decent aristocratic standards. The most notable example is the ungoverned rage he exhibits when losing a joust to Loras Tyrell, called "the Knight of Flowers." Unused to losing at anything, the Mountain kills his stallion in front of the king and the whole court. Much greater crimes can be ascribed to Ser Gregor, but this was an immensely shocking act in a horse-obsessed culture. That no one did anything about it, that King Robert let the Mountain go unpunished and unrebuked, indicates either that chivalric sensibilities were numb or, more probably, that everyone was afraid of the Mountain.

Chivalry in Westeros is not always prized or praised. Members of the mainstream nobility more than once express a certain contempt for the very word "chivalry." They think that the word has come to designate only one narrow aspect of the total picture of chivalry: the courtly aspect. People who have no manners or play cruel tricks on others may be labeled unchivalrous, but being called chivalrous is not always a compliment. In this view, chivalry may be admirable in a way but is actually impractical, especially if it sacrifices an advantage in wartime for the sake of fair play or "decent behavior." For example,

Catelyn, on finding that King Renly's army is staging a tournament in his war camp, sees this traditional recreation as foolish play while serious business is being ignored.

> This is madness, Catelyn thought. Real enemies on every side and half the realm in flames, and Renly sits here playing at war like a boy with his first wooden sword.[10]

Perhaps she has a point, at least about Renly: later on Renly rejects the idea of a nighttime attack on Stannis, equating it with treachery and lack of chivalry since his brother and rival has—for his own devious reasons—previously specified dawn as the hour to engage each other in formal battle.

Contempt for chivalry's perceived lack of ruthlessness leads to disrespect for chivalry's courteous behavior. In fact chivalry is losing its hold on many of the inhabitants of Westeros, commoners and nobles alike. One gets the impression that too many people have seen too much bad behavior from knights. At the beginning of the tale, the starry-eyed child Sansa Stark believes most strongly in chivalry. She expects the actual inhabitants at the royal court to have the virtues and romantic allure of the characters she has heard of in the songs that still are the meat and drink of all working minstrels in Westeros. The true believer Sansa is savagely punished for her loyalty to the old high standards, and on one memorable occasion suffers brutality and humiliation at the hands of the worst members of King Joffrey's court, all knights.[11] Afterwards, the Hound gives to Sansa his disillusioned judgment on chivalry:

> "What do you think a knight's *for*, girl? You think it's all taking favors from ladies and looking good in gold plate? Knights are for *killing*." [...]
> "True knights protect the weak."
> He snorted, "There are no true knights, no more than there are gods."[12]

Sandor Clegane's contempt for chivalry is partly based on his personal experience of the knight closest to him, his brutal brother. The Hound certainly doesn't want to be a knight. Yet his moral view seems to be moderating to be less murderous, which is as first shown by his almost fatherly conduct toward Arya Stark. By season 6 he takes up with the Brotherhood without Banners, a loose order of fighters led by knights who try to fight for justice—for something higher than themselves.[13]

Twilight of Knights

In addition to the widespread disrespect for chivalric standards, the Seven Kingdoms have also experienced an erosion of the institutions that helped define chivalry in the past. One remnant of chivalric tradition is the Night's

Watch. It is analogous to the historical monastic crusading orders of the Middle Ages, the most famous being the Templars, the Hospitallers, and the Teutonic Knights. During the Christian crusades against Muslim-held territories, some crusading warriors decided to dedicate their entire life to the cause. They became monk-knights, organized into religious–military orders that combined monastic discipline in daily life with a fierce dedication to fighting the infidel in the Holy Land or the Iberian Peninsula and to converting the pagans in the Baltic Sea region.

The Night's Watch ideal is similarly one of lifelong self-sacrifice in the service of the civilized world as a whole—a special kind of chivalry. But, just as the crusading orders of our fourteenth and fifteenth centuries were past their period of greatest prestige and effectiveness, the Night's Watch of King Robert's era is also in decline. Those who "wear the black" are no longer respected for their service. The danger posed by the forces of winter now seems too remote to inspire either a practical or an idealistic response, and those who enter the brotherhood are no longer men dedicated to a cause. They are simply people with nowhere else to go. Many are condemned criminals who serve for life at the Wall rather than die at the headsman's axe on the block.

Kingsguard knights in Westeros are similar to the royally sponsored orders of chivalry of the late Middle Ages mentioned above, such as the Garter or the Golden Fleece. In contrast to these orders, however, the Kingsguard knights have a more active mandate: to guard and serve the monarch. Even though this "brotherhood" is in better shape than the Night's Watch, the Kingsguard is also declining. It has a long and glorious history of heroes whose names and accomplishments can still be rhymed off by people who love chivalric lore, just as people in the Middle Ages could name the Nine Worthies or the Twelve Peers of Charlemagne. Stories about these figures, who were both historical and legendary, provided role models of the best kind of chivalry. To "wear the cloak" of the Kingsguard is still a source of pride for those who are chosen to serve the king. But, increasingly, the politics of membership do not inspire respect. The limited number of positions is filled not by the best, the strongest, or even the most inspiring candidates. Instead, positions are allocated on the strength of purely political considerations, by using this great gift to tie some family more closely to the throne.

Jaime Lannister, the Kingslayer, is an example of how political complications can cripple a paragon of chivalry. On the one hand, he is the best example of what a knight could be: of noble background, extraordinary male beauty, and extraordinary prowess. King Aerys chose him as guard at a very early age. But that appointment was a poisoned gift. It struck at the house of Lannister because the position required celibacy. Through this appointment Jaime, the only acceptable male heir to his mighty father, was removed from the succession to Casterly Rock, and doubt was cast on the future of the dynasty. Jaime in his early youth may well have been a tremendous symbol of what knighthood should be, the acceptable face of ancient chivalry, but the political machinations that put him in Westeros' premier chivalric order blighted his full potential.

Furthermore, Jaime accepted the appointment partly in order to be near his lover, his own sister Cersei. The incest between Jaime and Cersei completely betrays the ideal of chivalry (just as the fictional adultery between Lancelot and Guinevere did for King Arthur). Eventually their actions undermined the Lannisters and tore apart the Seven Kingdoms. Almost as subversive was Jaime's most heroic act, which shook the belief in chivalry to its very core. No one forgets that Jaime killed his liege lord, "Mad" King Aerys. The King had gone mad, killing and burning. A knight who was a noble lord would not hesitate to kill such a monster. In a way, this could be seen as an act worthy of the greatest heroes of chivalric legend (although there is no comparable example of the murder of a murderous monarch in the European age of chivalry).

Yet defending the innocent against the king's injustice required Jaime Lannister to violate his oath as a vassal knight, as loyal retainer and sworn defender of his lord. Loyalty, especially loyalty pledged to such a symbol of traditional authority as a king, is so central to the structure of aristocratic life that many cannot forgive Jaime, even if he saved them from the monster. Even the normal knightly practices of warfare—killing foes, holding prisoners, and ravaging the land of one's enemies—turn into grounds for condemning Jamie's character in the eyes of his captive Edmure Tully, who wonders how Jaime could imagine himself a decent person and manage to sleep at night.[14]

Once knights had become the greatest perpetrators of violence in medieval Europe, only the power of oaths reined in their deadly power. Yet even that constraint was only a temporary way to organize society. In late Medieval Europe, the personal loyalty and vassalage of noble knights to one another was being replaced by the sovereign power of kings and queens, who required obedience of all subjects. Any reader of *A Song of Ice and Fire* or viewer of *Game of Thrones* can see that, if chivalry depends on a deep-felt need to uphold sworn commitments of honor, then chivalry in Westeros has failed as well.

Notes

1 The best treatment of medieval chivalry is still Maurice Keen, *Chivalry* (New Haven, CT: Yale University Press, 1984).
2 Paul Halsall, ed., "Fulbert of Chartres: On Feudal Obligations, 1020," in *Internet Medieval Sourcebook*, 1996 (accessed October 29, 2015 at thttp://legacy.fordham.edu/halsall/source/fulbert1.asp).
3 A classic study on him is Georges Duby, *William Marshal: The Flower of Chivalry*, translated by Richard Howard (New York: Random House, 1985); for a recent one, see David Crouch, *William Marshal* (3rd edn., New York: Routledge, 2016).
4 Ramon Llull, *The Book of the Order of Chivalry*, translated by Noel Fallows (Woodbridge and Rochester: Boydell Press, 2013), 40.
5 On these and similar orders, see Keen, *Chivalry*, 179–199.

6 Geoffroi de Charny, *A Knight's Own Book of Chivalry*, translated by Elspeth Kennedy with an introduction by Richard W. Kaeuper (Philadelphia: University of Pennsylvania Press, 2005), 67.

7 Geoffroi de Charny, *Knight's Own Book of Chivalry*, 66.

8 George R. R. Martin, *A Song of Ice and Fire: A Storm of Swords* (New York: Bantam, 2011 [2000]), 899.

9 Richard W. Kaeuper, *Chivalry and Violence in Medieval Europe* (Oxford: Clarendon, 1999).

10 George R. R. Martin, *A Song of Ice and Fire: Book Two: A Clash of Kings* (New York: Bantam, 1999), 340.

11 "Garden of Bones," directed by David Petrarca, written by Vanessa Taylor, in *Game of Thrones*, season 2, HBO, first aired on April 22, 2012.

12 Martin, *A Storm of Swords*, 756–757.

13 "No One," directed by Mark Mylod, written by David Benioff and D. B. Weiss, *Game of Thrones*, season 6, HBO, first aired on June 12, 2016.

14 "No One," HBO.

4

Of Kings, Their Battles, and Castles

Brian A. Pavlac

Kings rule in our imaginations. On the one hand, the attraction of kingship is clear. Mel Brooks as Louis XVI, the French king, tells us: "It's good to be the king."[1] Or a medieval peasant can identify Arthur as king of the Britons because he "hasn't got shit all over him."[2] On the other hand, being king has its burdens. "Uneasy lies the head that wears a crown," sighs Shakespeare's King Henry IV.[3] And Robb Stark, King of the North, laments: "Why would any man ever want to be king?"[4] The title of the television series *Game of Thrones* literally makes kingship a central theme. Familiarity with similar historical kings therefore enriches our understanding of Martin's turbulent Westeros.

Although the history of kingship begins with the history of civilization, our images of kings in western culture are strongly shaped by the Middle Ages. A king wears long robes, often trimmed with gold and fur. On his head rests a crown.[5] He sits on a special chair, a throne, holding in one hand an orb or a scepter, in the other a sword, all symbols of his authority to rule, to punish, to kill. These attributes make a king appear different from all other people, and above all from the subjects over whom he wields royal authority.

This chapter reviews the three main elements of kingly rule and power in medieval Europe and in Westeros. First, both in the past and today, a king was and is an inspirational figure, binding together the people of a realm. Second, a king must administer that realm, provide peace and justice for his people. Third, a king is a war leader. In this last function, medieval warrior-kings maintained royal power through feudal relations and a strategy of castles.

The King Is Dead, Long Live the King

The origins of kings are lost in myth. Thousands of years ago, men who claimed kingship usually proclaimed that they represented the gods and therefore held sway over the subjects in their kingdoms. They often asserted their claims to

Game of Thrones versus History: Written in Blood, First Edition. Edited by Brian A. Pavlac.
© 2017 John Wiley & Sons, Inc. Published 2017 by John Wiley & Sons, Inc.

some sacred or divine inheritance in their ancestry. This concept carried over into Christianity when the Germanic barbarian kings who conquered the Western Roman Empire converted to Christian belief and saw themselves as God's representatives on earth.

These kings possessed a very natural human drive to pass on their royal power to their descendants. They tried to create dynasties in which kingship was inherited through lines of succession based on family connections, preferably from father to son. Meanwhile, the subjects of kings, especially the more powerful ones, wanted to have a choice in who would be their ruler; such a choice would be expressed preferably through election or at least through acclamation—a ritual in which those present shouted their approval.

Elections came into play most frequently when a dynasty died out in the male line. The other option was civil war between claimants, often cousins and heirs through female lines of descent. In Anglo-Saxon England, the Witan chose among *aethelings*, descendants of previous kings, legitimate or not. They held a meeting (*moot*) to choose a king, a method that Martin borrows for his Iron Islands.[6] Catelyn Stark also suggests (though in vain) an election designed to end the War of Five Kings.[7]

Because of the tension between inheritance and election, royal dynasties in Western Europe started out very fragile. Since death came for kings as well as for paupers, a king often tried to get his son elected as successor king while he was still alive. If he did not, others might try and seize the throne once he was cold in the tomb. Sometimes a crowned son tried to toss out his father while still warm. For example, sons led rebellions against the Carolingian Louis the Pious (r. 813–840), Henry II of England (r. 1154–1189), and Henry IV of Germany (r. 1056–1105). A rare outright parricide was Chlodoric, who had his father Sigebert assassinated (d. 505).[8] Chlodoric assumed that his neighboring king, Clovis, would approve. Instead Clovis executed Chlodoric and confiscated his realm. Occasionally an illegitimate son would try to claim the crown. During the Hundred Years' War (1337–1453), the bastard Henry/Enrique of Trastámara fought to depose his half-brother King Peter/Pedro I of Castile (r. 1350–1369), called "the Cruel" or "the Just" depending on one's point of view. Both Enrique and Pedro bribed the French knight DuGuesclin to arrange a meeting between them. In DuGuesclin's tent, Enrique stabbed Pedro to death. King Enrique II (r. 1369–1379) then founded the new Trastámara dynasty.[9]

By the Grace of God

Once a king is designated, he must be anointed, crowned, enthroned, and acclaimed in a litany of ceremonies involving the church. These rituals granted kings charism,[10] that is, a certain kind of power, endowed with miraculous properties (such as to heal the sick) and sanctified by a divine representative:

the power to rule as the vicar of Jesus Christ. A large part of royal duties, as still demonstrated by the queen of England, was to symbolically unite the people under God.

To fulfill this role, kings should display certain qualities of character. Renly Baratheon lists virtues suitable for being a king (he extrapolates them from himself, of course): "strong, yet generous, clever, just, diligent, loyal to my friends and terrible to my enemies, yet capable of forgiveness, patient."[11] It is "unkingly" for a king like Robert, as a paragon of morality, to strike his wife Cersei in private; and it is even worse that her son Joffrey has a household knight beat his betrothed publicly.[12] These were not good kings.[13] People believed that a good king cared; a good king fought the evil.[14] It was his duty to promote "peace and prosperity where powerful [do] not prey on the powerless."[15]

Kings were supposed to inspire passionate loyalty. In the stirring words of little Lady Mormount, "we know no king but the king in the North whose name is Stark. He is my king from this day until my last day."[16] Such loyalty and obedience made people willing to lay down their life for the ruler, to obey his commands, and even to kill others.

In the Christian Middle Ages kings were allied with the church, whose official task was to get people to heaven. Baptized and anointed kings felt that they, too, played a key part in establishing a moral community. Many medieval believers would have agreed with the Westerosi sentiment that "faith and crown are the two pillars that hold up the world."[17] Early medieval kings used bishops from their kingdoms as advisors, educators, and even administrators. In Germany, kings especially favored prince-bishops, clerical nobles who held a kind of political power equivalent to that of secular princes and dukes.[18] The growing papacy, however, didn't always like to share power. Popes quarreled with kings over whose authority was superior: the spiritual sword's or the secular sword's. These fights caused excommunications, condemnations, and invasions.[19] By 1300, though, a rough equilibrium of cooperation allowed kings to retain their divinely sanctioned aura.

For the Good of the Realm

Administration was vital to royal rule, even if all that stuff about "coin and crops and justice" bored Robert Baratheon to tears.[20] For a long time in the Middle Ages kings were peripatetic: they wandered about the kingdom. This nomadic lifestyle served two purposes. First, by bringing the sovereign to different provinces and towns, it showed the realm who was king. Second, it allowed the kings and their large courts to live off the wealth of their scattered estates or the hospitality of local barons. Since there was little money in the economy, actual foodstuffs had to be acquired near the place where they were produced.

As kingship came into its own in the high Middle Ages, administration had evolved from a style of government that was personal to one that was official. Early medieval kings often had to be present in person to make their influence felt. To be more effective, on the other hand, kings needed to delegate duties related to some facets of governance. Kings therefore began to employ bureaucrats and other administrators who helped royal authority go beyond the person of the king. High medieval kings created a whole staff of officials such as chancellors, seneschals, marshals, constables, bailiffs, treasurers, secretaries, and even butlers. They collected various revenues from taxes, tolls, custom duties, mints, manors, forests, fishing rights, fines, and fees of all sorts. Centers where people could find these royal officials helped designate capital cities like London or Paris by the late twelfth century.

Royal administration requires financing. In *Game of Thrones*, banks, especially the Iron Bank of Braavos, stand at the ready to take on enormous debts. But there seems to be no real mechanism to enforce repayment. The government of the Seven Kingdoms stops payments on its debt until after the war, despite the warning that "the Iron Bank will have its due."[21] Medieval kings did not fear their banks' wrath, being much more willing to declare bankruptcy. In 1343, when King Edward III (r. 1327–1377) completely defaulted on Italian banks for loans used to pay for the Hundred Years' War, no bank could recoup the losses and many collapsed into insolvency.[22]

In *Game of Thrones* finding money is often a simple matter for kings, and it is achieved by raising taxes. This was not possible in the real Middle Ages. Sometimes kings exploited royal wards, young heirs to great fiefs. A king could draw on revenues from the ward's lands and arrange marriages of his choosing. In *Game of Thrones*, vassals with their own financial resources, such as the Lannisters with their gold mine, could lend money to the king. Gold mines were hardly existent in the Middle Ages. Even silver mines, from which most money was coined, were few and far between. Wealth was not so easily dug out from the ground. It was created by farm labor and commerce.

Just as Robert Baratheon has no interest in ruling, Martin does not cover the nitty-gritty of royal administration. Instead he conveniently conflates all the functions of royal governance into the office of a single viceroy called "the King's Hand":

> the second-most powerful man in the Seven Kingdoms. He spoke with the king's voice, commanded the king's armies, drafted the king's laws. At times he even sat upon the Iron Throne to dispense justice, when the king was absent, or sick, or otherwise indisposed. [...] a responsibility as large as the realm itself. [23]

Historical kings, however, needed many bureaucrats. The English writer Geoffrey Chaucer (c. 1343–1400), for example, served in various administrative positions while writing books such as *The Canterbury Tales.*[24] Chaucer's son was even a member of parliament, an institution that had become a key tool for royal government.

Most people at most times want peace and the chance for prosperity. Maintaining the well-being of the realm was an explicit requirement for kings in Westeros and throughout the Middle Ages.[25] Henry II's son and successor, King Richard I "the Lionheart" (r. 1189–1199), swore at his coronation

> that he would all the days of his life observe peace, honor, and reverence towards God, the Holy Church, and its ordinances. He also swore that he would exercise true justice and equity towards the people committed to his charge. He also swore that he would abrogate bad laws and unjust customs, if any such had been introduced into his kingdom, and would enact good laws, and observe the same without fraud or evil intent.[26]

While the "king's justice" is exercised throughout Westeros, medieval kings had to assert their judicial role over the rights of feudal lords and vassals, who also administered justice in their own spheres.[27] At first the kings themselves heard the complaints; then they started to rely on bishops and select magnates to render justice. In England, by the twelfth century, university-trained royal judges traveled on court circuits to hear cases and suits. The system functioned through writs—specific legal forms for plaintiffs to fill out and file in court. The crown kept the records.

The growing royal judicial power sparked a counter-reaction, especially if the people saw the king as a tyrant. Rebellions against the crown, such as the barons' against King John (r. 1199–1217) for royal abuses, led to restrictions on royal authority. The first step—the Magna Carta, issued at the beginning of the thirteenth century—led to the establishment of parliament by the century's end. This gathering of the clergy, barons, and townspeople actually increased the power of the king by letting representatives talk over and agree to laws and taxes before they were passed. Thus centralized power became much easier to enforce, since the people could not complain of being treated tyrannically.

The Warlord

As a commander of armies, a king was to crush internal rebellions; he was to defend his realm against foreign invaders; and he might chose to expand his power by conquering neighbors. Like many government systems, monarchy sought a monopoly on violence. Within their kingdoms, medieval kings needed to restrict feuds and private wars between their feudal vassals. By 1100 knights had created an alternative governmental process, feudal politics, in which they swore fealty to one another as vassals to lords, promising *auxilium et consilium* ("help and counsel," Latin).[28] The "help" usually came in the form of a vassal's military service to his lord, often for 30 days, at the vassal's own expense. Knights naturally developed loyalty to and affection for their local districts and lords rather than the far-off king. But a king did reign as suzerain, the highest feudal lord in a network of knights,[29] and he did try to demand liege homage for himself.[30] To do so, the "king became the chief patron of chivalry," setting up chivalric orders of knights and holding tournaments.[31]

In *Game of Thrones*, the military power of the king of the Seven Kingdoms seems to come from descendants of former kings who have been demoted to "Wardens." As heads of great houses, Wardens have many troops of their own. They can also call on "bannermen," leaders of various less noble houses who, in the manner of feudal hosts, provide still more men-at-arms. Through the course of the high Middle Ages, however, kings increasingly turned away from the military service required of feudal vassals, looking to other ways of raising armed forces. The king arranged for the upkeep and maintenance of knights at court. The personal household guards provided a core fighting force. As time went on, kings paid money directly to knights, perhaps in contracts called "fief rents," trying to combine the old system with the new.[32]

Although mercenaries had a reputation for being unreliable, kings depended on them as often and as much as they could afford them.[33] To help pay for mercenaries, the English kings established a policy of *scutage* (shield tax), a fee that all vassals paid to the crown in proportion to the size and number of their fiefs and vassals. Soon vassals, too, could pay, as a way to avoid military service entirely.

By the time of the Hundred Years' War, very few troops served out of a sense of feudal obligation. The crown negotiated with nobles and magnates to supply troops, paying them with tax money and plunder. Contracts of money for service replaced bonds of personal loyalty. In any case, actual knights were becoming fewer in number because of the high cost of armor and horse, not to mention the risk.

A king's power ultimately rested on his ability to survive any and all military assaults. And that survival depended on warriors' loyally risking their lives to fight for him in battle. Three strategic factors figured into royal victory: the ability of commanders; the numbers and quality of fighters; and the places chosen to defend. In the Middle Ages and in Westeros, that meant battles with knights and castles.

The Face of Battle

To win a war usually means defeating the enemy's armies and compelling him to surrender. Contrary to popular imagination, set-piece battles with two sides of medieval knights on horseback charging at each other were uncommon. One reason was that medieval warfare often took the form of a series of sieges of castles and towns (see below). Additionally, supplying combatants of more than a few thousand was too difficult logistically. Strategy likewise advised medieval commanders not to rush to fight: as in Tywin Lannister's metaphor, "the lion and the fawn," each side preferred to lie in wait for the other to make a false move, then pounce.[34]

Such hesitation by no means indicated a lack of courage; knights were notoriously bellicose. Their extensive training and state-of-the-art weapons made then eager to fight. Encased in armor and high on their horses, high medieval knights usually faced more risks of disease than of getting wounded in combat. Their social standing also sheltered them: knights were worth more alive with ransom than dead. The ransom of a king could be more disastrous for a kingdom. The most famous ransom, that of King Richard "the Lionheart," inspired much later stories in the Robin Hood legend about tensions in England to pay huge sums.[35] During the Hundred Years' War, when King Edward III of England held for ransom both King John II "the Good" of France (r. 1350–1364) and King David II of Scotland (r. 1331–1371), the hundreds of thousands of pounds of silver for their release impoverished their kingdoms and sparked peasant revolts.[36] Instead of looking for a decisive battle, many a medieval (or Westerosi) commander preferred instead to ravage the lands of his enemy.[37] The English often relied on the tactic of *chevauchée* in the Hundred Years' War, pillaging and plundering French farms and towns and killing peasants and townspeople in order to damage the economy.

If battle was unavoidable, one side usually chose the field, preferably in a defensive position on a hill, flanked by obstacles such as forests or streams, to limit attacks from the sides. When two armies faced each other, the idea was sometimes floated of deciding the battle through a duel of champions.[38] King Philip II "Augustus" (r. 1179–1223) offered five champions from each side in order to decide a battle, but changed his mind when King Richard "the Lionheart" insisted that the kings be among the champions. The advantage would have gone to Richard, one of the greatest knights of his time, over Philip, who was not really a fighter. At the siege of Tournai at the beginning of the Hundred Years' War, King Edward III challenged King Philip VI to settle their differences either between the two of them alone or with 99 other knights. A similar offer came at the siege of Calais (1346–1347). "The Last Knight," Emperor Maximilian, suggested a duel to King Francis I of France. Just as in *Game of Thrones*, though, no one ever took up such offers; they remained fantasy.

This meant that battles would be fought by feudal forces. The heavy cavalry of armored knights on horseback was rarely alone on the field. The infantry— foot soldiers—was often set on the flanks to protect against attacks. The cavalry was also supported by artillery or by archers with either bows shooting arrows or crossbows shooting bolts or quarrels. When the time came to fight, the classic form of medieval combat had three units of cavalry. They were called "battles" and were arranged in a long front line, followed (or flanked) by infantry and archers, and ending with a reserve unit in the rear. Depending on personal choice, the commander either fought in the front lines or stayed with the reserve. While attacked by enemy archers, the two opposing lines charged at each other, clashing in the center of the field. If neither side was able to overwhelm, push back, or outflank the other side into a retreat, combat degenerated into a mêlée. "The battle is over the instant one army breaks and flees."[39] Usually the last side to commit its reserve unit to battle was the victorious side. The Battle of the Bastards in Westeros best reflects this sort of battle in the portion that depicts the cavalry charge and the resulting mêlée.[40]

In some battles, for instance those at Stirling Bridge (1297), Courtrai (1302), and Bannockburn (1314), infantry actually managed to defeat heavy horse cavalry. The English then developed a technique in their wars against the Scots that won them many a battle during the Hundred Years' War. Their knights dismounted and stood on a fortified hill, and backed up their archers with longbows. As the enemy cavalry recklessly charged, sometimes trampling their own infantry, the English archers rained death from the sky. Any French knights who made it to the English line were unchivalrously hacked down from their horses by the armored knights. In three crucial battles, at Crécy (1346), Poitiers (1356), and Agincourt (1415), this tactic defeated armies of French knights that greatly outnumbered the English. At Agincourt, the tactic succeeded even though the English army was suffering from dysentery. In a detail that Shakespeare left out but Martin enjoys, the "runs" made the longbowmen "take off their pants whilst awaiting the French charge. Come the battle, they shot and shat, shot and shat, shot and shat."[41]

Still, as Robb Stark discovered, one could win all the battles and still lose the war. Despite these great victories, the French eventually won the Hundred Years' War, while the English went on to tear themselves apart in the Wars of the Roses. By that time—that is, the mid-fifteenth century—the battlefield was dominated by infantry carrying pikes to defend soldiers armed with guns. And, with these new early modern armies, kings gained more power than ever.

Once More unto the Breach

Back in the Middle Ages, royal lordship required control over castles. Castles were fortified places for warriors to defend strategic points; but they were also people's homes. The saying "a man's home is his castle" reflects the situation where medieval lords lived with their families and servants, all being together in a walled fort: women, children, the elderly, peasants, workers, clergy. As the seat of a lord, castles were also centers of government authority, whence the lord dispensed justice and collected revenues.

Castles rose as defenses against the invaders and warriors rampaging through Western Europe after the collapse of the Carolingian Empire in the ninth century. Kings were not able to defend everyone, so they defended themselves. Men of power convinced others to acknowledge them as overlords, an authority enforced by castles. At first castles were simple wooden towers on hills. Over the centuries, engineers built massive complexes of stone with layers of defensive works. Lords went on the offensive as knights, while they used castles for defense. These combined strategies brought relative peace and order to Western Europe by the eleventh century.

Kings, however, did not like so many layers of lords impinging on their traditional authority. Before 1050 or so, there was not much that they could do about it. But, as royal resources and authority improved, they began to bring the knights to heel. As a first step, kings built their own castles. William the Conqueror is famous for planting castles all over his new English realm, most famously the White Tower, just outside medieval London. Kings enfeoffed some royal castles to lords; others they staffed with paid garrisons. A king sometimes claimed the right to enter all his castles, or required licenses for new ones to be built. A generation after William the Conqueror, during the Civil War in England between Queen Mathilda and Stephen of Blois (1135–1154), unapproved castles arose everywhere. It was said that

> every powerful man made his castles [...] and filled the land full of castles. They oppressed the wretched men of the land hard with work on the castles, and when the castles were made they filled them with devils and evil men. Then they took people they believed had any goods, both by night and by day, men and women, and put them in prison; they were after gold and silver and tortured them with unspeakable tortures.[42]

Those who defied royal authority over castles, of course, ultimately had to be dealt with by force. After Mathilda's son Henry II came to power and ended the Civil War, he vigorously went after illicit castles. He slighted (damaged) or razed (tore down) many of them, keeping the best, however, for himself.[43]

While Henry seemed to seize castles easily, that was not normally the case. Unlike the quick charges of horses into the heat of battle, sieges forced opponents to sit in a cold contest of endurance. Castles got bigger and stronger, in parallel with the refinement of siege weapons, catapults, and trebuchets, which became ever more accurate and destructive. A commander might try frontal assault on a castle, escalading or taking it "by storm," the preferred method of the iron men of the Iron Islands.[44] Yet any prudent commander, even a fictional Jaime Lannister at Riverrun, recognized this tactic as disadvantageous to the attacker: it was sure to attract high casualties.[45] In a storming, the attackers might use a battering ram to break gates, or just planks to cross ditches and ladders to scale walls, all the while being hit with missiles (arrows, quarrels, and even rocks) and perhaps having boiling water thrown over them (but rarely boiling oil). A slower approach was to breech the walls by undermining and sapping or battering with catapults and trebuchets. Another means to get a castle was by ruse or trickery. Besiegers were known to use disguises to gain entry, to find a secret entrance, or even to get the garrison drunk on a gift of strong wine. Treachery or betrayal was a common occurrence, especially as the defenders began to starve. The besiegers could just threaten to slaughter everyone who did not surrender within a reasonable time limit. Meanwhile, the job of those under siege was to outwait the besiegers until circumstances changed. No castle could endure forever, but a garrison could outlast besiegers long enough for them to freeze, starve, or mutiny, as Roose Bolton in *Game of Thrones* suggests.[46]

One of the most famous castles, comparable to Harrenhal, was Chateau Gaillard in northern France. It was built by King Richard I "Lionheart" of England in 1198 to defend his province of Normandy against King Philip II "Augustus" of France. Richard boasted that he could hold Chateau Gaillard even if its walls were made of butter.[47] Richard's successor, King John, however, failed in his defense. Beginning in August 1203, Philip set a siege, having his men dig trenches and fortifications. To save supplies for his soldiers, the English commander expelled hundreds of townspeople, who were allowed to pass safely through French lines. A few months later, however, when winter made John expel a few hundred more, the French refused them passage. Since the English in turn refused to let them back in, many stayed in no-man's-land, suffering and starving for three months, until the French let them go. In the spring, siege towers breached the outer wall, but the inner wall still held firm. Finally a few French soldiers dared to climb up a latrine shaft and got into the chapel. The noise they made frightened the garrison into abandoning that middle wall and retreating to the keep. John's attempt to relieve the siege by attacking Philip failed miserably. Philip then had a corner of the keep undermined; it collapsed, forcing the remaining English garrison to surrender on March 8, 1204. After that, Philip quickly conquered the rest of Normandy: so strategically important was that one castle.

King John used what he had learned during his own siege of rebels in Rochester castle in October and November of 1215. His miners collapsed the first wall of defenses, but the garrison, of course, withdrew to the keep. John then had his men dig a shaft under the keep, stuffed it with the fat of 40 pigs, and set it on fire.[48] Unfortunately, the resulting breach only opened part of the keep. The garrison fought on, although they also expelled unnecessary people, who were then allegedly mutilated by John's men. When reinforcements for the castle failed to arrive, the garrison surrendered, just like Chateau Gaillard. John's ability to take the castle caused some to question its military value.[49] Nonetheless, castles remained central to strategy for a few more centuries.

A walled town, which could be considered a castle writ large—a fortification in which families lived—was also besieged. During the Hundred Years' War, the year-long siege of Calais in 1346–1347 ended in a notable English victory. The French army, recently defeated at Crécy, took too long to attack the English besiegers and the city surrendered. King Edward declined to execute the town's leading burghers when his visibly pregnant queen pleaded for their lives (a scene famously commemorated in a sculpture by Rodin).[50]

The invention of gunpowder, used in cannons against castles and in hand-guns against knights, ended the era of feudal warfare. Similarly, if the Targaryen dragons overwhelmed castles and kings in Westeros' fictional past, in the current (unfinished) story Daenerys will likely do so with her new dragons. In our own time, kings remain predominantly figures of a fanciful past, made irrelevant by modern forms of government. Looking at the failed achievements of kings, Davos and Tormund lament: "Maybe that was our mistake, believing in kings."[51] Ultimately kings had power because people believed that royal power upheld the correct order of the world. Kings had authority at all, though, because people chose to surrender their own power to them. Cersei reinforces this idea in her confrontation with Littlefinger, pointing out: "Power is power." By "power" she means the ability to get people to kill upon command.[52] Yet, as Varys tells Tyrion in his riddle:

> "Power is a curious thing [...] Three great men, a king, a priest, and a rich man. Between them stands a common sellsword. Each great man bids the sellsword kill the other two. Who lives, who dies? [...] Power resides where men believe it resides; it's a trick, a shadow on the wall."[53]

Whether kings can maintain power or not, in Westeros, the Middle Ages, or today, requires that leap of imagination.

Notes

1 *History of the World: Part 1*, directed by Mel Brooks, 20th Century Fox, 1981.
2 *Monty Python and the Holy Grail*, directed by Terry Gilliam and Terry Jones, EMI films, 1975.
3 William Shakespeare, *The History of Henry the Fourth, Part 2*, Act 2, Scene 1, line 31.
4 George R. R. Martin, *A Song of Ice and Fire, Book Three: A Storm of Swords* (New York: Bantam, 2011 [2000]), 280.
5 This chapter will use the male gender pronoun for the kings covered in this article, since during the high Middle Ages there were almost no queens with any power. For more on queenship, see the chapter by Finn in this volume.
6 "Home," directed by Jeremy Podeswa, written by David Hill, in *Game of Thrones*, season 6, HBO, first aired on May 1, 2016.

7 George R. R. Martin, *A Song of Ice and Fire, Book Two: A Clash of Kings* (New York: Bantam Books Mass Market Edition, 2011 [1999]), 501.

8 Gregory of Tours, *The History of the Franks*, translated with an introduction by Lewis Thorpe (Harmondsworth: Penguin Books, 1974): Book II, chapter 40, 155.

9 John Froissart, *The Chronicles of England, France and Spain* (New York: E. P. Dutton, 1961); see Book I, chapter iv, 110–112, in H. P. Dunster's condensation of Thomas Johnes' translation.

10 Not to be confounded with the better known charisma; both words have the same etymon in the ancient Greek *charis*, "grace."

11 Martin, *A Clash of Kings*, 481.

12 George R. R. Martin, *A Song of Ice and Fire, Book One: A Game of Thrones* (New York: Bantam, 2011 [1996]), 430; Martin, *A Clash of Kings*, 488–489.

13 Tywin begins to teach the new king, his grandson Tommen, that a good king's most important quality should be wisdom rather than holiness, justice, or strength and he cites Joffrey and Robert as bad examples: see "Breaker of Chains," directed by Alex Graves, written by David Benioff and D. B. Weiss, *Game of Thrones*, season 4, HBO, first aired on April 20, 2014.

14 Martin, *A Clash of Kings*, 561.

15 "The Wars to Come," directed by Michael Slovis, written by David Benioff and D. B. Weiss, in *Game of Thrones*, season 5, HBO, first aired on April 12, 2015. Many of these characteristics are emphasized in the twelfth century by John of Salisbury, *Policraticus: Of the Frivolities of Courtiers and the Footprints of Philosophers*, edited and translated by Cary J. Nederman (Cambridge: Cambridge University Press, 1990); see especially Book IV, 27–64.

16 "The Winds of Winter," directed by Miguel Sapochik, written by David Benioff and D. B. Weiss, in *Game of Thrones*, season 6, HBO, first aired on June 26, 2016.

17 "High Sparrow," directed by Mark Mylod, written by David Benioff and D. B. Weiss, in *Game of Thrones*, season 5, HBO, first aired on April 26, 2015.

18 See for example, *A Warrior Bishop of the 12th Century: The Deeds of Albero of Trier, by Balderich* (Medieval Sources in Translation 44), translated with an introduction and notes by Brian A. Pavlac (Toronto: Pontifical Institute of Medieval Studies, 2008).

19 But not explosions: Cersei's blowing up her enemies in "The Winds of Winter," HBO has a parallel in Guy Fawkes' Gunpowder Plot to destroy parliament in 1605; Fawkes' religious motive was to destroy Protestantism in England by killing the king and the members of parliament in one stroke.

20 Martin, *A Game of Thrones*, 193.

21 Martin, *A Feast for Crows*, 348–349.

22 Jack Weatherford, *The History of Money* (New York: Random House, 1999), 76.

23 Martin, *A Game of Thrones*, 47.

24 Carolyne Larrington, *Winter is Coming: The Medieval World of Game of Thrones* (London: I. B. Tauris, 2016), 130–131.

25 Martin, *A Game of Thrones*, 233.

26 Roger of Hoveden, *The Annals, comprising the History of England and of Other Countries of Europe from* AD *732 to* AD *1201*, translated by Henry T. Riley (London: H. G. Bohn, 1853; reprinted New York: AMS, 1968). The passage quoted here comes from the chapter "The Order of Coronation of Richard I, 1189" (vol. 2, pp. 117–119), which can be found at http://sourcebooks.fordham.edu/source/hoveden1189a.asp (accessed October 16, 2016).

27 E.g., Martin, *A Game of Thrones*, 13, 202, 292, 421, 469–471.

28 Following Elizabeth A. R. Brown, "Tyranny of a Construct: Feudalism and Historians of Medieval Europe," *The American Historical Review* 79.4 (1974), 1063–1088, most medieval historians avoid the word "feudalism." Nevertheless the adjective "feudal," used throughout this book, does help define social and political relationships that have connections to receiving and giving fiefs.

29 Often these mutual bonds are called "feudal pyramid," but such a term implies more order than this collection of connections warrants.

30 Even in Westeros, kings want homage; Martin, *A Clash of Kings*, 121.

31 Richard Barber, *The Knight and Chivalry* (New York: Harper Colophon 1982 [1970]), 293.

32 Norman Housley, "European Warfare c. 1200–1300," in *Medieval Warfare: A History*, edited by Maurice Keen (Oxford: Oxford University Press, 1999), 124.

33 See William Urban, *Medieval Mercenaries: The Business of War* (St. Paul, MN: MBI Publishing, 2006).

34 Martin, *A Clash of Kings*, 320–321.

35 On the origins of the stories, see J. C. Holt, *Robin Hood* (London: Thames & Hudson, 1982).

36 Froissart, *Chronicles*, Book I, chapter iii, 49–50, 69, 79. John even returned to honorable captivity after being released on parole, since his son had broken his word; David was captured by an army with the English queen at its head.

37 Martin, *A Clash of Kings*, 119.

38 For Westeros, see "Fire and Blood," directed by Alan Taylor, written by David Benioff and D. B Weiss, in *Game of Thrones*, season 1, HBO, first aired on June 19, 2011; and "Battle of the Bastards," directed by Miguel Sapochnik, written by David Benioff and D. B Weiss, in *Game of Thrones*, season 6, HBO, first aired on June 19, 2016.

39 Martin, *A Clash of Kings*, 780.

40 "Battle of the Bastards," HBO; See Nate Jones, "How Accurate Was *Game of Thrones'* Battle of the Bastards?" *Vulture*, 2016, June 22 (accessed August 11, 2016, http://www.vulture.com/2016/06/battle-of-the-bastards-game-of-thrones-historical-accuracy.html).

41 George R. R. Martin, "Odds and Ends and Mystery Men: History Mrs. Grundy Never Taught You," in For Fans (on his own website), 2016 (accessed August 3, 2016, http://www.georgerrmartin.com/for-fans/knights/odds-and-ends-and-mystery-men).

42 *The Anglo-Saxon Chronicles*, translated and collated by Anne Savage (New York: St. Martin's/Marek, 1983), 265 (year 1137).

43 W. L. Warren, *Henry II* (Berkeley: University of California Press, 1973), 58–62, 141–142.

44 Martin, *A Clash of Kings*, 545.

45 "No One," directed by Mark Mylod, written by David Benioff and D. B. Weiss, in *Game of Thrones*, season 6, HBO, first aired on June 12, 2016. Jaime's idea for a quick resolution is to threaten to kill a hostage, Edmure Tully's son. This echoes what happened with King Stephen and William Marshall; for more on this subject, see the chapter by Liedl in this volume.

46 "Hardhome," directed by Miguel Sapochik, written by David Benioff and D. B. Weiss, in *Game of Thrones*, season 5, HBO, first aired on May 31, 2016.

47 John Gillingham, *Richard I* (New Haven, CT: Yale University Press, 2002), 303.

48 W. L. Warren, *King John* (New York: Norton, 1961), 246–247.

49 Julian Humphreys, *Enemies at the Gate: English Castles under Siege from the 12th Century to the Civil War* (Swindon: English Heritage, 2007), 46–47.

50 Froissart, *Chronicles*, selected, translated, and edited by Geoffrey Brereton (Harmondsworth: Penguin Books, 1973): Book I, pp. 97–110 ("The Siege of Calais"), at 104–109.

51 "Battle of the Bastards," HBO.

52 "The North Remembers," directed by Alan Taylor, written by David Benioff and D. B Weis, in *Game of Thrones*, season 2, HBO, first aired on April 1, 2012.

53 "What Is Dead May Never Die," directed by Alik Sakharov, written by Bryan Cogman, in *Game of Thrones*, season 2, HBO, first aired on April 15, 2012.

Part II

Slaves, Barbarians, and Other Others

5

Barbarian Colonizers and Postcolonialism in Westeros and Britain

Shiloh Carroll

George R. R. Martin has been quite vocal about basing *A Song of Ice and Fire*'s culture and history on the real Middle Ages. Distinct parallels to historical events and people can be found throughout the novels, especially between waves of colonization in Westeros and in Britain. Of course, Martin does not aim for allegory or other types of one-to-one mirroring of history. Rather he says, "I take it, and I file off the serial numbers, and I turn it up to eleven, and I change the color from red to purple, and I have a great incident for the books."[1] Thus his indigenous people and the waves of colonizers—the Children of the Forest, the First Men, the Andals, and the Valyrian Targaryens—share historical characteristics with the peoples who colonized and settled Britain—the Romans, the Anglo-Saxons, and the Normans—but blend those characteristics in new and interesting ways, which create a unique approach to colonialism and postcolonialism.

The Children of the Forest

In the earliest history of Westeros, roughly 15,000 years before the events of *A Song of Ice and Fire*, the only inhabitants of the Isles were Children of the Forest and giants.[2] The Children had a close affinity to nature. They worshipped their gods as faces carved on trees, through which their greenseers could observe people and places at a distance, and even through time (as we see in Bran Stark's later chapters). In the first few novels, all information about the Children comes from scholars called maesters, who only rely on hearsay and rumors about the early days of the First Men. Samwell Tarly laments this paucity of information in *A Feast for Crows*:

> The oldest histories were written after the Andals came to Westeros. The First Men left us only runes on rocks, so everything we think we know about the Age of Heroes and the Dawn Age and the Long Night comes from accounts set down by septons thousands of years later.[3]

Game of Thrones versus History: Written in Blood, First Edition. Edited by Brian A. Pavlac.
© 2017 John Wiley & Sons, Inc. Published 2017 by John Wiley & Sons, Inc.

The maesters mythologize the Children of the Forest in much the same way that the Romans and the Anglo-Saxons mythologized the original tribes that occupied the British Isles. According to Barry Cunliffe, the Romans saw the British Isles as mysterious and otherworldly, "places where anything could happen."[4] Most of our own information about the early British Celts comes from Roman sources. One historian was the Roman general Julius Caesar (100–44 BC), who invaded Great Britain in 55 BC. He famously wrote that Britons "dye their bodies with woad, which produces a blue color."[5]

Medieval writers such as Nennius (AD c. 769–820), Geoffrey of Monmouth (c. 1100–1155), and the compiler(s) of the oral history *The Mabinogion* (c. 1350–1410) had a tendency to mythologize the British tribes and create stories or histories that served the authors' contemporary political needs and purposes. These writers were instrumental in creating a myth of the origins of the British in which Brutus, a (fictional) descendant of the hero Aeneas, survivor of the Trojan War, settles in Britain. Claiming Trojan noble ancestry for the Britons served a political purpose: it provided a pedigree just as impressive as that of the Romans, who were also descendants of the mythical Aeneas. Additionally, with no indigenous people to be displaced, Britain seemed a land destined for habitation by the authors' noble patrons.

Some beings did precede Brutus and his settlers, however, and those creatures were giants. Geoffrey of Monmouth's *History of the Kings of Britain* (c. 1138) tells that Albion, as Britain was known at that time, was unoccupied except by giants, who were nothing but monsters.[6] Brutus and his army of Trojans pushed the giants into the mountains, leaving them to live in caves. Eventually the Trojans eliminated the giants altogether.[7] Similarly, when Bran discovers the remaining Children of the Forest, they are dwelling in caves to the far north of Westeros, beyond the Wall. Giants reside in that region as well. Yet in Martin's version, the giants had a claim on the land, being almost human, with a language and a culture of their own.

The persistent legends about the Children that still permeate Westeros have much in common with ideas—both Roman and modern—about the ancient British Celts and their religion: Druidism. Both are thought to be living close to nature, worshiping trees, and respecting the spirits of the forest. The wars between the Children and the First Men began because the First Men were destroying forests to build their forts and towns. Story and history also have in common human sacrifice. Caesar wrote that the Druids practiced it, and Maester Yandel, credited with writing the history of Westeros, mentions blood sacrifices to the Old Gods.[8] Further, the contemporary Romantic mysticism that surrounds the Druids is mirrored in the "greenseers" of the Children of the Forest—the ability to inhabit the bodies of animals or trees, talk to animals, and otherwise directly commune with nature. Of particular interest in Westeros is the Order of the Green Men, a group charged with protecting the

Isle of Faces, where the pact ending hostilities between the Children and the First Men was signed. The Maester claims that people who glimpse the Green Men report having seen beings who are literally green and horned. This invokes both the British Green Man carvings and the Celtic Horned God.[9]

Much of the history of early Britain written in antiquity and in the Middle Ages is little more than mythology. Archaeology indicates that Britain has been continuously occupied by humans for about 11,000 years, not settled by Trojan colonists at some unspecified time before the founding of Rome.[10] Martin, meanwhile, draws on the more fantastic medieval pseudo-histories, which allows for a grander, more epic fantasy. In Westeros, mythology is true history.

The First Men

While the Children of the Forest have been driven to near extinction, only a few survivors hiding in the far north, the wildlings are the counterpart to the British tribes confronted by the Romans. Although descended from the First Men, they have adopted the Children's religion. They live outside the political system of Westeros, choosing instead to remain "free" on the "wrong" side of the Wall, along with the giants. They are the "barbarians" of Westeros, comparable to the ancient tribes of Picts who constantly raided to the south of Hadrian's Wall, built by the Romans. As described by Caesar, they resemble hunter-gatherers; they are dressed in skins and have no agriculture to speak of.[11] The wildlings are tribal and fight among themselves, failing to pull together well enough to pose a true threat to the southern kingdoms, just as the British tribes were unable to unify against the Romans. HBO's *Game of Thrones* pushes the characterization of the wildlings even further on the "barbarian" side by depicting the Thenns, one of the wildling tribes, as bloodthirsty cannibals who carve up their own skin in ritual scarification.[12]

Prior to becoming northern barbarians, however, the First Men had much in common with the civilized Romans. They came from Essos to Westeros, just as the Romans crossed from Gaul to Britain. Both groups entered from the south—the First Men in Dorne, the Romans around Kent. Both the Romans and the First Men took many years to completely conquer their respective islands. Indeed, the Romans required several generations to acculturate the south of Britain, and they never really occupied the north beyond Hadrian's Wall. Maester Yandel reports that, according to tradition, the First Men completely settled Westeros within only a few years, but he rejects that assertion as absurd.[13] Viewers would agree, since Westeros is much larger than Britain and the First Men were not nearly the organized force that the Romans were. The Maester believes instead that the war between the Children and the First Men lasted 100 years before both sides grew tired and drew a pact.

Perhaps the clearest parallel to the Romans comes in the form of the Wall, a massive structure of ice built in the north to divide the territory of men from the territory of the White Walkers—the mysterious beings who bring winter and prey on mankind. The Wall represents an uneasy peace between the First Men and the White Walkers. This peace was facilitated by the Children of the Forest, who helped Bran the Builder construct the Wall. Martin has made no secret that the Wall was inspired by Hadrian's Wall, though he obviously scaled it up.[14] The historical wall was commissioned by Emperor Hadrian in AD 122. It marked the farthest reach of the Roman occupation of Britain at that time. Both the Night's Watch and the Roman troops were stationed at forts along the Wall and, respectively, Hadrian's Wall and patrolled to defend it against "barbarian" invaders. Sometimes they sent expeditions north but were unable to conquer and hold more land there.

Some differences exist, of course. Roman soldiers occupied Britain for only about 450 years. After that, the troops withdrew back to Rome, abandoning many Roman colonists and Romanized Britons to new invasions by the Anglo-Saxons. Without troops, Hadrian's Wall fell apart into a ruined jumble. In contrast, the First Men colonized Westeros and stayed, while their Wall endured for eight thousand years. Another difference concerns religion. While Christianity replaced Celtic paganism in the British Isles, the First Men adopted the Children's Old Gods rather than introducing their own religion to the indigenous people. In this way, the First Men show similarities to the Anglo-Saxons, who settled permanently in Britain after the Romans left. They converted to Christianity rather than spreading their native Germanic paganism to the Christian Britons.

Other striking cultural similarities between Anglo-Saxons and First Men also exist. Samwell Tarly's remark about "runes on rocks" (quoted above) calls to mind Germanic runic writing. The early Anglo-Saxons used a system called *futhorc*, descended from Old Norse runic. Only after Irish missionaries introduced the Latin alphabet (and Christianity) to the Anglo-Saxons did the latter shift to the writing modern people are more familiar with from *Beowulf* and other Anglo-Saxon texts.[15] Speech also shows similarities. In Westeros, the language of the First Men, the Old Tongue, is nearly extinct south of the Wall, where only the wildlings claim to speak it. Old English has also become extinct (as discussed below). It is now indecipherable to English speakers who have not studied it.

Beowulf and other Anglo-Saxon poems in Old English give us an idea of the ethos of the Anglo-Saxons—at least as an ideal. Whether or not the Anglo-Saxons actually lived up to the heroic moral principles shown in their literature is a question that many scholars have tackled.[16] The "fourfold Germanic ethic" upholds loyalty to one's lord, loyalty to one's kin, the duty to avenge the death of one's lord or kin, and the belief in *wyrd* (fate). These moral principles are echoed in the culture of the First Men, at least as practiced by the Starks. They have a deeply entrenched sense of duty and loyalty. Ned Stark articulates part of his code of conduct when he explains his decision to behead a Night's Watch deserter early on in *A Game of Thrones*:

> If you would take a man's life, you owe it to him to look into his eyes and hear his final words. And if you cannot do that, then perhaps the man does not deserve to die.[17]

Not all crimes, however, necessitated a death sentence. The Anglo-Saxons used the ancient law of *wergild*, which specified an amount of money that had to be paid by the person who had committed an offense to the injured party (whether a family, a lord, or the king). The First Men, too, had a "blood price" by which a person could make restitution for an offense against another, including injury to or the death of a family member. Payment of the blood price could prevent further bloodshed, feud, or outright war. In a Hedge Knight story, Ser Eustace tells Ser Duncan the Tall that he is willing to abide by the rules of "the green kings" and pay a blood price for one of his knights who injured a peasant from a neighboring duchy.[18] Neither *wergild* nor a blood price could ensure peace, but they did provide a way to avoid the vengeful violence of blood feuds, and even war.

The Andals

As their name implies, the First Men did not remain in control of Westeros for long. The next invaders were the Andals, who also bear notable similarities to the Anglo-Saxons. Fleeing the advance of the Valyrian Empire, the Andals landed on the Fingers in eastern Westeros, then began pushing inland. Their weapons were iron instead of bronze, and these gave them an advantage over the First Men. After about 1,000 years of war and colonization, the Andals had essentially conquered Westeros and the land was divided into the Seven Kingdoms.[19]

Like the Andals, the Anglo-Saxons divided their conquered territory, most of the island of Great Britain, into seven kingdoms known as the "heptarchy": East Anglia, Mercia, Northumbria, Wessex, Essex, Sussex, and Kent. Like in the kingdoms of the Andals, the size, power, and number of these kingdoms vacillated depending on wars, alliances, rebellions, and other political maneuverings. The Anglo-Saxon kingdoms were based on location of territory, family groups, alliances, and victories against rivals. Historians Nicholas J. Higham and Martin J. Ryan claim that, in the Anglo-Saxon kingdoms, "a successful war-leader may well have established his influence from the beginning over several peoples, through family connections, patronage, negotiation, marriage, the widespread recruitment of followers and/or intimidation."[20] Eventually the various quarreling kingdoms needed to unite and fight against new invaders, the Vikings. They became one kingdom of England under a single king, Alfred the Great (r. 871–889).

One notable difference between the Andals and the Anglo-Saxons concerns religion. The Andals brought with them to Westeros the Faith of the Seven, while the Anglo-Saxons converted to Christianity, Britain's religion under the Romans. Not only did the Anglo-Saxons convert to Christianity, they used Christianity as a method of forging peace with the Vikings, insisting that the latter convert as part of peace treaties. In any case, both the Andals and the Anglo-Saxons were ultimately unified by a single codified religion.

Through much of the Middle Ages, church and state were symbiotic, kings appointing church leaders and church leaders strengthening royal positions. Higham and Ryan believe that Anglo-Saxon leadership likely embraced Christianity because it offered unity and a link to the Roman past: "The Old Testament presented a style of kingship which was divinely ordained and quasi-sacral, while the imperial government of the New Testament had law-making and tax-raising powers."[21] A similar symbiosis between sept (house of worship) and throne is evident in *A Song of Ice and Fire*. Frequently the condition of the kingdom is reflected in the type of person who holds the title of High Septon. For example, the High Septon under Robert is "a great glutton, and biddable," mirroring Robert's indolence and proneness to being manipulated by those around him.[22]

Although the Andals' invasion of Westeros is similar to that of the Anglo-Saxons, their southern culture more closely mirrors that of high medieval England after the Norman conquest of 1066. In contrast, northern Westeros remains in a kind of pre-conquest "dark age." While the north is still tribal, southern Westeros is feudal. The north continues to follow an ancient (pagan) religion, while the south's religion, the Faith of the Seven, has much in common with medieval Christianity. *Game of Thrones* costumers and set designers underscore this difference. While the north is dark, with heavy fabrics and fur and simpler braids, the south is portrayed with bright colors, flowing fabrics, and elaborate hairstyles. If the north reflects *Beowulf* and other Germanic tales, the south reflects the world of Chaucer. This dichotomy might be partially explained by the Targaryen invasion of Westeros, which resembles the Norman conquest of England. Both led to a radical shift in language, literature, and culture.

The Targaryens

The Targaryen invasion, the final occupation of Westeros so far, took place roughly 300 years before the events in *Game of Thrones*. The Targaryens were one of the few surviving families of the Valyrian Empire after "the Doom"—a catastrophic volcanic eruption in the mountainous peninsula that destroyed nearly everyone and everything.[23] The Targaryen invasion of Westeros parallels the Norman invasion of England. Unlike previous invasions, neither the Norman conquest nor the Targaryen invasion involved an entire race, tribe, or other group of people settling the conquered territory. Rather a relatively small force led by a determined commander took the power, in Westeros as in England.

In AD 1066, at the time of the Norman conquest, England had been mostly united for about 200 years. Two centuries before, in 865, the "Great Heathen Army" of the Vikings had successfully attacked the squabbling Anglo-Saxon kingdoms in Great Britain. The Scandinavians took about half the realm and threatened the last remaining kingdom of Wessex. But its king, Alfred "the Great" (r. 871–899), fought the Vikings to a standstill. Although the Vikings retained a large portion of the territory called "the Danelaw," Alfred united the realm under the name "England." Soon enough, the Vikings were Christianized and became English.[24] At the turn of the eleventh century, Danish kings had held the throne of England and interventions from Denmark and Norway remained dangerous. The last Anglo-Saxon king, Edward "the Confessor" (r. 1042–1066), had reinstalled an Anglo-Saxon dynasty to rule over England, but his lack of children foreshadowed trouble (as did a comet in the heavens). Westeros was even less stable just before Aegon Targaryen's invasion, being still divided into seven parts—the Seven Kingdoms—without a high king or central government. Archmaester Gerold's account of the invasion describes the Seven Kingdoms as "quarrelsome," claiming that "there was hardly a time when two or three of these kingdoms were not at war with one another."[25]

Both invasions were instigated by perceived insults. Upon Edward the Confessor's death, Harold Godwinson, Edward's brother-in-law and son of an important earl, claimed that Edward had committed the kingdom to his protection. The leaders of England endorsed his election and crowned him the next day. But Edward's cousin, Duke William "the Bastard" of Normandy, claimed that both Edward and Harold had recognized William's right of succession. Edward supposedly made this promise after Harold's father had briefly driven Harold into exile in Normandy in 1051. Apparently Harold's recognition had also taken place while he was in Normandy, either as guest in 1051 or as prisoner in 1064. When Harold refused William's demands to honor his pledge and give up the throne, William planned an invasion. Harold waited for weeks for the Normans to cross the English Channel, then suddenly had to march his army northward to fight an invading army led by his brother Tostig, supported by Harald "Hardrada" ("Hard Ruler"), king of Norway. Shortly after defeating and killing them at the Battle of Stamford Bridge, Harold's army had to turn and march back south again, at the news that William had landed in England.

In Westeros, an insult by King Argilac of the Stormlands instigated Aegon's invasion. Argilac wanted a strong husband for his only direct heir, a daughter, because he was worried about his neighbor, Harren Hoare or "Black Harren," who had built the massive castle Harrenhal. He offered his daughter's hand to Aegon, who at that time was living with his sister-wives on Dragonstone, not yet part of Westeros. Aegon refused the suit but offered a counter-proposal: the daughter's marriage to his bastard half-brother, Orys Baratheon. This suggestion so offended Argilac that he cut off the messenger's hands and sent them back to Aegon. In reaction, Aegon decided to invade and conquer Westeros. He began his campaign with a grand gesture, calling for the immediate surrender and fealty of all seven kings.

Both groups of invaders were relatively small. Aegon brought perhaps only a few hundred troops, not more than 300. Aegon landed at the mouth of the Blackwater, the place of the future King's Landing, and immediately fortified the hill that would be known as Aegon's High Hill. William was able to land several thousand troops at Pevensey Bay and moved to Hastings, which he fortified. Despite their small sizes, both armies had definite advantages over the inhabitants who opposed them. Aegon's special forces were his dragons. He and his sisters had three, while no one else had any. William's special forces were his well-trained armored cavalry. Knights fighting on horseback had been common in continental Europe since the stirrup was introduced there in the eighth century. Such combat was, however, uncommon in Britain, where warriors generally fought on foot with axes.

Both invasions consisted of a single, decisive battle that set the stage for the invaders to conquer the remainder of the country. In Westeros, Aegon faced Lord Darklyn of Duskendale and Lord Mooton of Maidenpool and their combined armies. Both lords were slain in the battle and their sons immediately swore fealty to Aegon. William and Harold faced each other at the Battle of Hastings on October 14, 1066, fighting for most of the day. William's cavalry had hard work, as it had to charge uphill against Harold's infantry several times. Then Harold was wounded in the eye with an arrow and finished off by William's knights. Once the Anglo-Saxon line broke, they were routed. The entire story of the Norman invasion, along with the Battle of Hastings, is shown on the Bayeux Tapestry, almost like a graphic novel. One of the most important examples of Romanesque art, this 230-foot embroidery was commissioned by William's half-brother in the decade after the invasion.

Of course, in neither case did a decisive battle put an end to the conflict. There was no immediate acknowledgment of the kingship of either Aegon or William. Nevertheless, the outcomes of the battles were crucial in that they allowed the two men to fully conquer Westeros and England. Aegon's sister Visenya crowned him shortly after the battle at the Blackwater, and the dragons enabled Aegon to fully conquer the Seven Kingdoms (except for Dorne) in two years. Often all he had to do was show up on the back of Balerion the Black Dread, and surrender quickly followed. And, while William was crowned in December of 1066, two months after the Battle of Hastings, he struggled with English rebellions and uprisings until 1075.

Since the Targaryen and Norman invading forces were relatively small, power over the conquered people was concentrated in the hands of Aegon's and

William's loyalists. Aegon granted lands and titles to his own men, creating the Small Council and the Hand of the King. He also bequeathed the Stormlands to Oryn Baratheon. Yet, in Westeros, many of the Andal lords were allowed to keep their lands and titles after they swore fealty to Aegon and turned over their swords, which were forged into the Iron Throne. In England, however, repeated uprisings enabled William to replace most of the local English lords with his own men. Cunliffe claims that the Normans concentrated 4,000–5,000 individual English estates into the hands of only 144 Norman lords, nearly all of England's political and religious governance being placed in the hands of William's Norman, Breton, and Flemish vassals.[26]

These final invasions had an enormous political and social impact on both England and Westeros. In England, Anglo-Saxon English was no longer the language of power; French took its place. All official state and church business was conducted in French and Latin. Without a central official role, English language splintered into dialects, spoken primarily by the common folk. Old English turned into Middle English as it borrowed vocabulary and grammar from French. Not until Edward I Plantagenet (r. 1272–1307) did England again have a king whose primary language was English. In fictional Westeros, Targaryen rulers formed a new central government, and the kings of the Seven Kingdoms became vassal lords.

Yet in both England and Westeros the conquered land may have changed the invaders just as much as they changed it. Kenneth Henshall says that,

> as is often the case with an occupying people, especially when relatively few in number, despite their power-holding it can be argued that the Normans became "indigenised," and ended up being Anglicised as much as, if not more than, they Normanised the Anglo-Saxons.[27]

This syncretism can also be seen in Westeros. It is not clear what religion, if any, the Targaryens practiced before their invasion but, once they began ruling, it became necessary for them to conform to (most of) the tenets of the Seven.

In both Westeros and Britain, the effect of waves of invasion and colonization was profound. Entire peoples, cultures, and religions were wiped out, or at least pushed out of their dominant place and into a subordinate one. Native peoples were forced out of their homes and resettled on the fringes of Westeros (in the far north, beyond the Wall) and of Britain (in the outlying areas of Scotland, Ireland, and Wales). Those who remained on their lands were absorbed into the new dominant society, lost much of their ethnic identity, and were subsequently mythologized or ignored by the new owners of the land. As Catherine Hills puts it,

> if the prehistorical peoples of Britain were successively replaced [by the Romans and Anglo-Saxons], we are not descended from them, they do not form part of our roots, and they can safely be put aside as curiosities who left strange stone monuments we can visit on days out.[28]

Martin does not gloss over the destruction of culture that occurs when one civilization takes over another. The effects of this destruction are shown and discussed frequently in the novels, from Maester Luwin lamenting the loss of the Children of the Forest to the wildlings and people of the North clinging to the culture of the First Men. Yet very little emotional connection to the Children exists even among the descendants of the First Men, and even less connection to the First Men exists among the Andals. They are seen as curiosities of the past rather than as the roots of the country; all that is left of them is "runes on rocks," trees with eyes, crumbling towers, and burial mounds. While Martin's fascination with history does not create exact correlations between historical peoples and peoples in the novels, the themes and broad strokes still clearly show the profound influence of British history on the history of Westeros.

Notes

1 "The Real History Behind *Game of Thrones*," Blu-ray, in *Game of Thrones: The Complete Fifth Season* (USA: Home Box Office, Inc., 2016).

2 George R. R. Martin, Elio M. García, and Linda Antonsson, *The World of Ice and Fire: The Untold History of Westeros and the Game of Thrones* (New York: Bantam, 2014), 5–6; the book is presented as if it were history by a writer called "Maester Yandel."

3 George R. R. Martin, *A Song of Ice and Fire, Book Four: A Feast for Crows* (New York: Bantam, 2006 [2005]), 114.

4 Barry Cunliffe, *Britain Begins* (Oxford: Oxford University Press, 2013), 1.

5 Julius Caesar, *The Gallic War*, translated by H. J. Edwards (Cambridge, MA: Harvard University Press, 1963), 253.

6 Geoffrey of Monmouth, *The History of the Kings of Britain*, translated by Lewis Thorpe (New York: Penguin Books, 1966). The image of woad was reused in the movie *Braveheart*, although it had long been out of fashion by the turn of the fourteenth century.

7 Geoffrey of Monmouth, *The History of the Kings of Britain*, 72–73.

8 Martin, García, and Antonsson, *The World of Ice and Fire*, 6. See "The Door," directed by Jack Bender, written by David Benioff and D. B. Weiss, in *Game of Thrones*, season 5, HBO, first aired on May 22, 2016: this episode shows the Children ritually murdering a human in order to create a White Walker as a weapon against human invaders. It backfired.

9 The Green Man is a widespread image in the British Isles, and many theories have arisen regarding its meaning and origin. For a short but thorough overview of the Green Man, see Kathleen Basford, *The Green Man* (Cambridge: D. S. Brewer, 1978). The Horned God is more complicated; while horned deities appear in many carvings worldwide, little historical or literary evidence exists to explain the significance of this figure. Modern Wiccans have adopted the Celtic version and worship

him as the male half of the divine. For more on the Horned God, see Phyllis Fray Bober, "Cernunnos: Origin and Transformation of a Celtic Divinity," *American Journal of Archaeology* 55.1 (1951), 13–51.

10 Cunliffe, *Britain Begins*, 128.

11 Caesar, *The Gallic War*, 253.

12 "Two Swords," directed by David Benioff and D. B. Weiss, written by David Benioff and D. B. Weiss, in *Game of Thrones*, season 4, HBO, first aired on April 6, 2014.

13 Martin, García, and Antonsson, *The World of Ice and Fire*, 8.

14 "The Real History behind *Game of Thrones*." Hadrian's Wall was 84 miles long and about 20 feet high; the Wall in Westeros is 300 miles long and 700 feet high. For more on the latter, see the chapter by de Ruiter in this volume.

15 See *Beowulf*, translated by R. M. Liuzza (Buffalo, NY: Broadview Press, 2012 [1999]). For other popular Anglo-Saxon poems, riddles, maxims, saints' lives, and charms, see Greg Delanty and Michael Matto, eds., *The Word Exchange: Anglo-Saxon Poems in Translation* (New York: Norton, 2011).

16 See, for example, Milton McC. Gatch, *Loyalties and Traditions: Man and His World in Old English Literature* (New York: Pegasus, 1971) and John Lindlow, *Comitatus, Individual and Honor: Studies in North Germanic Institutional Vocabulary* (Berkeley: University of California Press, 1975). For a contemporary example of how Anglo-Saxons were *not* living up to their ideals, see Wulfstan II's *Sermo Lupi ad Anglos*, translated as *The Sermon of the Wolf to the English* and posted on February 17, 2014 at https://thewildpeak.wordpress.com/2014/02/17/the-sermon-of-the-wolf-to-the-english (accessed October 28, 2016).

17 George R. R. Martin, *A Song of Ice and Fire: Book One: A Game of Thrones* (New York: Bantam, 2005 [1996]), 16.

18 George R. R. Martin, *A Knight of the Seven Kingdoms* (New York: Bantam, 2015), 123.

19 A more detailed history of these kingdoms can be found in Martin, García, and Antonsson, *The World of Ice and Fire* and in the "Histories & Lore" bonus features on the DVDs issued by HBO.

20 Nicholas J. Higham and Martin J. Ryan, *The Anglo-Saxon World* (New Haven, CT: Yale University Press, 2013), 141.

21 Higham and Ryan, *The Anglo-Saxon World*, 157.

22 Martin, *A Feast for Crows*, 142. After he is torn apart by a mob during a riot, Tyrion reflects that "starving men take a hard view of priests too fat to walk," which suggests that the populace rejected the extreme inequality between nobility and smallfolk as manifested in the High Septon's girth; see also George R. R. Martin, *A Song of Ice and Fire: Book Two: A Clash of Kings* (New York: Bantam, 2005 [1999]), 599–600.

23 The Doom of Valyria could easily be compared with the eruption of Mount Vesuvius and the subsequent destruction of Pompeii, though such an analysis would be beyond the scope of this essay.

24 Anders Winroth, *The Age of Vikings* (Princeton, NJ: Princeton University Press, 2014), 52–60.
25 Martin, García, and Antonsson, *The World of Ice and Fire*, 33.
26 Cunliffe, *Britain Begins*, 487.
27 Kenneth Henshall, *Folly and Fortune in Early British History* (New York: Palgrave, 2008), 212.
28 Catherine Hills, *Origins of the English* (London: Duckworth, 2003), 18.

6

A Defense against the "Other"

Constructing Sites on the Edge of Civilization and Savagery

Brian de Ruiter

The television series *Game of Thrones* opens with three men of the Night's Watch passing through the Wall, then heading north on a mission to find a band of wildlings. One of the men makes a grizzly discovery: the chopped-up corpses of the wildlings, strewn on the ground in a pattern. When he reports his findings to the commanding ranger, the ranger replies: "What do you expect, they're savages. One lot steals a goat from another lot, before you know it, they're ripping each other to pieces."[1] This scene sets up two important elements for the series. First it introduces the White Walkers, who attack and kill most of the rangers. Their grave threat to the Seven Kingdoms hangs over the entire story. But—and this is more pertinent to the present discussion—the scene provides the first visuals of the "harsh" lands north of the Wall and reveals how members of the Night's Watch view the wildlings, the humans who live there. The rangers instinctively blame those wildlings for atrocities that the truly monstrous White Walkers have actually done. These negative views represent not only those of the majority of the Night's Watch, but also the dominant attitude of the people in the Seven Kingdoms toward the people north of the Wall.

Hadrian's Wall and Points North

The concept of "the North" has featured prominently in many cultures over the course of centuries, with various descriptors, characteristics, and meanings. Britain held a large place in the Romans' definition of "the North." P. C. N. Stewart wrote that, for the Romans, "Britain was not a place, but an idea, and one which was inconstant and adaptable."[2] When examining *Game of Thrones*, our question is: how much do the Wall and what lies beyond it reflect Roman and medieval views of Hadrian's Wall and of the people in northern Britain?

Game of Thrones versus History: Written in Blood, First Edition. Edited by Brian A. Pavlac.
© 2017 John Wiley & Sons, Inc. Published 2017 by John Wiley & Sons, Inc.

The Roman Emperor Hadrian (r. 117–138) built the stone wall that was named for him. It stretched from one coast to the other, 84 miles long and about 20 feet high, and had forts occupied by troops. The wall marked the northernmost point of the Roman Empire. Roman and medieval literature demonstrate that writers viewed the tribes to the north of Hadrian's Wall in terms of "the other." Sociologists use this term to describe how societies (and individuals) represent their own self-identity as normal and correct, but that of other social groups (and persons) as abnormal and deviant. This distinction often leads to discriminations and hostility. Descriptions of people and the lands they inhabit tend to be interconnected. Roman writers saw the lands of the Britons and, even more, the lands to the north of Hadrian's Wall as cold, wet, and wild. Writers such as Cassius Dio (c. 155–235), Herodian (c. 170–c. 240), Ammianus Marcellinus (c. 330–395), Gildas (c. 500–570) and the Venerable Bede (c. 673–735) described the Caledonians, the Maeatae (a confederation of tribes beyond Hadrian's Wall), and the Picts as savage and warlike in their appearance, values, and activities. Similarly, the people of the Seven Kingdoms hold a corresponding image of the wildlings. In both cases, a wall defends against otherness.

At the opening of his book on Hadrian's Wall, Alistair Moffat stated: "Hadrian's Wall is the largest, most spectacular and one of the most enigmatic historical monuments in Britain."[3] It was probably its grandeur that attracted George R. R. Martin one day in 1981. Like other people who visited the site before him, Martin stood on top of the wall to get a better view of the countryside to the north, so he could imagine what lay beyond:

> I stood up there and I tried to imagine what it was like to be a Roman legionary, standing on this wall, looking at these distant hills. It was a very profound feeling. For the Romans at that time, this was the end of civilization; it was the end of the world. We know that there were Scots beyond the hills, but they didn't know that.[4]

Martin was mistaken, for the Romans were somewhat familiar with what existed beyond the wall. Roman invaders had penetrated into Scotland during the campaigns of Agricola (AD 69–73, 77–85), Severus (208–211) and Constantius (296). After the Romans finished building Hadrian's Wall (c. 128), they maintained a number of advance posts to its north (they even held the smaller, shorter Antonine Wall further north for a brief period) and used scouts for the purpose of reconnaissance. But Martin's experience on the wall echoes that of other people who have stood upon the stone structure and allowed their imaginations to conjure what lay in the lands of the Caledonians, Maeatae, and Picts. Historically and in the Seven Kingdoms, the Wall is the "end of the world."

Beside the peoples to the north of Hadrian's Wall, Roman writers described barbarians who lived beyond other frontiers of the Roman Empire. These writers applied the term "barbarian" to any foreign population that spoke a language unrelated to Greek and Latin and possessed cultural norms that the Romans judged to be inferior. In short, the term "barbarian" is connected to the concept of foreignness and was partially predicated on being different. This different-ness might derive from the barbarians' nature and physical appearance or from their social and political structures, with the result that their society seemed less complex than that of Rome. Also, historians have noted that these differences appeared more exaggerated to Roman writers the farther away the barbarians lived from the imperial center.[5] This is reflected in Strabo's (64/63 BC–c. AD 24) description of the Britons: "They live much like the Gauls but some of their customs are more primitive and barbarous."[6] Strabo's description of the indigenous population of Ierne [Ireland] follows a similar pattern: "About this island I have nothing certain to tell, except that its inhabitants are more savage than the Britons."[7]

Savage Garden in a Distant Land

Barbarians could be depicted as primitive savages or they could be romanti-cized and attributed idealistic qualities, depending on the perspective and agenda of the writer.[8] In his examination of Roman literature on Britain, Stewart argues that "difference serves to establish a foil to Roman civilization and culture."[9] Furthermore, the presentation of Britons as formidable adversaries could serve the empire's interest "to reinforce the concept of national cohe-sion" and reaffirm the military superiority of the Romans.[10] J. Mann reminds us that there is a storytelling element to these histories: "Content was often distorted by writers resorting to the 'stock' characters and 'stock' descriptions of literary conventions, in preference to the real facts. Telling a good story within the conventions was a primary aim."[11] In this respect, Roman authors and George R. R. Martin had the same goal. In Roman literature on Britain one recognizes a "dominant discourse of the conqueror."[12]

Stewart identified numerous writers who highlighted the "remoteness" of Britain.[13] He cited Horace (65–8 BC), who mentioned "the Britons at the end of the world," and Vergil (70–19 BC), who described "the Britons [as] totally cut off from the whole world."[14] In the third century AD, Cassius Dio remarked that Roman soldiers who participated in Claudius' invasion of Britain in AD 43 were reluctantly "campaigning outside the limits of the world they knew."[15] The unknown author of the *Panegyric of Constantine* (the sixth in Mynor's edition of the twelve panegyrics to Roman emperors),[16] conventionally dated to 310 (and probably written some time around 307 and 311), stated that northern Britain was "the farthest limit of the earth."[17] Ammianus Marcellinus described it as the "remotest parts of the earth."[18]

This Roman description of northern Britain is echoed in *Game of Thrones* in the way Tyrion Lannister refers to the remoteness of the Wall: he declares that he travelled to this structure so that he may "stand on top of the Wall and piss off the edge of the world."[19] Pypar also refers to the Wall as the "end of the world" when telling Jon Snow and Samwell Tarly how he came to join the Night's Watch.[20] Both Jon and Maester Aemon view the Wall in similar terms.[21] Furthermore, the notion that the Wall marks the end of the world is reflected in the kind of toponyms we find in the north: "Last River" and "Last Hearth."

In addition to remoteness, another common element in Roman texts is their reference to the harsh nature of the land, which to some extent mirrors the wild nature of the inhabitants. Peter Wells has identified a tendency in Roman writers to portray lands occupied by barbarians, such as Britain, as "wilder and less transformed by cultivation than those of the Romans and Greeks."[22] Cassius Dio wrote that "both tribes [Caledonians and Maeatae] inhabit wild and waterless mountains and desolate and swampy plains."[23] This notion of wild lands is echoed in Theon Greyjoy's views of the lands north of the Wall. He tells Osha: "you're not living in the wilderness anymore. In civilized lands, you refer to your betters by their proper titles."[24] The Byzantine historian Procopius of Caesarea (c. 500–c. 554 or later) was a bit more caustic in his account of what lay to the north of Hadrian's Wall:

> Now in this island of Brittia the men of ancient times built a long wall, cutting off a large part of it; and the climate and the soil and everything else is not alike on the two sides of it. For to the east [south] of the wall there is a salubrious air, changing with the seasons, being moderately warm in summer and cool in winter. And many people dwell there, living in the same fashion as other men [...] But on the west [north] side everything is the reverse of this, so that it is actually impossible for a man to survive there even a half-hour, but countless snakes and serpents and every other kind of wild creature occupy this area as their own. And, strangest of all, the inhabitants say that if any man crosses this wall and goes to the other side, he dies straightway, being quite unable to support the pestilential air of that region, and wild animals, likewise, which go there are instantly met and taken by death.[25]

Procopius considered Hadrian's Wall as a sort of dividing line that marked abrupt changes in the environment. The lands to the south were endowed with the characteristics of a pleasant locale, whereas those to the north were viewed as harsh and extremely hazardous.

Procopius' contrast between two environments is taken up in the visuals of the landscape in *Game of Thrones*. Although lands to the north of the Wall do not have a poisonous air, they are depicted as icy harsh, in stark contrast to the green and mild lands of the south. George R. R. Martin imagines that the land beyond the Wall is approximately the size of the Canadian landmass and that harsh conditions shaped the wildlings in terms of their worldview, their sense of community, their material culture, and their cultural diversity.[26] Toponyms like "Frozen Shore" and "the Land of Always Winter" emphasize the harsh, forbidding nature of the landscape north of the Wall. The difference in landscape between the territories on the two sides is best reflected visually when Ygritte and Jon Snow climb to the top of the Wall, in preparation for a wildling attack on Castle Black. During this scene, viewers share Jon and Ygritte's view: to the north is a barren, snow-covered land, while to the south is a green landscape with few traces of winter.[27]

In *Game of Thrones* the Wall was erected during the reign of Bran the Builder, 8,000 years before the start of the events presented in the series. Magical beings such as the Children of the Forest and giants helped Bran build a massive barrier that reached 300 miles in length and 700 feet in height. This barrier was intended to defend the people of the Seven Kingdoms "from the ancient evils that dwell beyond."[28] Clearly the primary purpose of the Wall was protection, even if many people in the Seven Kingdoms no longer believed in the magical entities that existed north of it.

In contrast, the primary function of Hadrian's Wall has long been disputed. It evidently served as a frontier marker, although opinions differ as to whether the wall was designed to observe and regulate movement or to defend Roman Britain against the tribes beyond.[29] David Breeze wrote that Hadrian's Wall offered "security," intending "to control access to 'our space.'"[30] Regardless of the wall's original function, a clear threat lay beyond the Roman frontier. The *Historia Augusta*, a late Roman compilation of biographies that covers the period from 117 to 284, confirms the warlike nature of the Britons and their military prowess: "the Britons could not be kept under Roman control."[31] Significantly, its authors (known collectively as Scriptores *Historiae Augustae*) specifically name the reason for constructing Hadrian's Wall: "to separate the Romans from the barbarians."[32] Inscriptions discovered in St. Paul's Church during the late eighteenth century confirm this view.[33] Hudson agrees, noting that Roman imperial policy meant the wall to be a marker that separated the "civilized" Roman Empire from the "uncivilized" people outside it, thereby reinforcing the division between "us" and "them."[34]

This notion of "our" space and "their" space reveals itself not only in the minds of the Romans, but also in the divergent development of the two regions. Romans in Britain had built a substantial network of roads and large towns, particularly in the south.[35] In contrast, writers like Cassius Dio wrote that these people north of the wall had "neither walls, cities, nor tilled fields."[36] Guy de la Bédoyère notes the significance of towns in Roman social life and in defining identity: "Town life was [...] synonymous with Roman culture [...] the town was an arena in which everything that made the Roman world work came together."[37] The lack of urbanization north of Hadrian's Wall is similar to the absence of cities and stone buildings in the lands of the wildlings. Even Ygritte assumes that the people south of the Wall "think we're savages because we don't live in stone castles."[38]

Take Your Picts

When commenting on the physical appearance of the tribes beyond Hadrian's Wall, Roman writers paid particular attention to tattoos. Herodian, for example, wrote: "Strangers to clothing [...] they tattoo their bodies with colored designs and drawings of all kinds of animals; for this reason they do not wear clothes, which would conceal the decorations on their bodies."[39] Benjamin Hudson believes that Herodian's comment on tattoos created "a visible difference between the Britons living within and outside Roman control."[40] This differentiation was adopted by later Roman writers. The very term "Pict"—from the Latin *picti*, which means "painted people"—(singular *pictus*; participle of the verb *pingere*, "to paint")—was used from the end of the third century AD on to describe a group of people who lived north of Hadrian's Wall. Hudson believes that "painted people" was much more than a descriptive term, as it "was clearly meant to differentiate between civilized Britons (those within the bounds of the empire) and the barbarians who lurked beyond Hadrian's Wall."[41] This Roman discussion of tattoos reiterated ideas of difference and primitiveness.[42]

Interestingly, in *Game of Thrones*, visible body disfigurement was rare among the tribes residing north of the Wall; they did not have such explicit marks of primitiveness. One instance of disfigurement, however, was the Thenns, who used scarification. Nevertheless, the Night's Watch does not seem to judge the scars of the Thenns as evidence of primitiveness. Scarification is probably an attempt to demonstrate the cultural diversity that Martin acknowledged exists north of the Wall.[43] On the other hand, the Thenns are also portrayed as menacing on account of their cannibalism, not to mention the kind of music that is played when they first appear.

But the question remains: other than being wild and savage, of what sort were the people who inhabited the lands to the north of Hadrian's Wall? Roman writers distinguished between themselves and the barbarian peoples by comparing values, governance, and clothing (or lack thereof). About the Maeatae and the Caledonians, Cassius Dio wrote: "They [...] possess their women in common, and in common rear all the offspring. Their form of rule is democratic for the most part, and they are very fond of plundering; consequently they choose their boldest men as rulers."[44]

In *Game of Thrones*, viewers witness cultural traits north of the Wall that are not normal for the people of the Seven Kingdoms, such as cannibalism among the Thenns (as discussed above). Furthermore, just as Cassius Dio wrote, wildlings select and follow a leader on the basis of factors other than hereditary rights. For instance, wildlings choose to follow Mance Rayder because he has a plan to flee from the White Walkers. Both Martin and D. B. Weiss wanted wildling society to be vastly different from that of the Seven Kingdoms, where birth and family were key to one's status. In fact the social hierarchy in the Seven Kingdoms is mocked by the wildlings: they label people south of the Wall "Kneelers."[45] This sentiment is held so strongly that, when Rayder's army is captured by Stannis Baratheon, the wildling leader ultimately chooses death over kneeling before Stannis.

Plundering on the frontier of Roman Britain also contributed to the Roman view that the tribes beyond Hadrian's Wall were wild and savage. Herodian, for instance, recorded:

> barbarians there were in revolt and overrunning the country, looting and destroying virtually everything on the island. [...] Extremely savage and warlike, they are armed only with a spear and a narrow shield, plus a sword that hangs suspended by a belt from their otherwise naked bodies.[46]

Raiding was a serious problem in the north of Roman Britain. Ammianus Marcellinus reported that "the savage tribes of the Scots and Picts were carrying out raids in Britain, having disrupted the agreed peace, and laying waste places near the frontiers."[47] He further wrote that "the most savage nations rose and poured across the nearest frontiers. Simultaneously [...] the Picts, Saxons, Scots and Attacotti harassed Britain in a never-ending series of disasters."[48] Benjamin Hudson summed up the situation when he wrote that the lands to the north of Hadrian's Wall "were rarely viewed [by the Romans] in benign terms."[49]

Walk on the Wildling Side

Although Roman writers only incidentally mentioned Hadrian's Wall, it is a subject that medieval writers dwelled on.[50] Both Gildas and Bede saw Hadrian's Wall as a barrier that protected southern societies from the savage populations beyond the old Roman frontier. Gildas spoke of the

> cruelty of two foreign nations – the Scots from the north-west, and the Picts from the north [...] differing one from another in manners, but inspired with the same avidity for blood, and all more eager to shroud their villainous faces in bushy hair than cover with decent clothing those parts of their body which required it.[51]

In the *Ecclesiastical History of the English People*, Bede recounted how the Britons did not want to see their nation "destroyed [...] by the barbarity of foreigners [Picts]" and called for the Romans to protect them against this northern threat. The Romans constructed "a strong wall of stone" and left the Britons to defend it unsuccessfully. After the Romans left Britain, the Picts continued their assault on the "sluggish people," and "the wretched Britons were torn in pieces by their enemies like lambs by wild beasts."[52] This notion of the north as representing a danger to the south continued even past the medieval period. Richard Hingley has argued that the importance attached to Hadrian's Wall continued to appear in English societal discourses whenever concern arose about Scottish aggression.[53]

If Roman and medieval writers saw barbarians as primitive, savage, and aggressive, in *Game of Thrones* the people of the Seven Kingdoms view the wildlings exactly the same way. And just as raiding occurred across Hadrian's Wall, the wildlings conduct raids in the north, plundering, abducting females, and acquiring the metal necessary for their weapons. Even the term "wildling" indicates a savage. When Theon asks Osha: "Why on earth would I trust the word of a lying little savage like you?"—Osha replies that she is "no liar." Theon counters that "all wildlings are liars and savages with no loyalty to anything or anyone." Even though Osha rejects the term "wildling," she nevertheless utilizes the image to engage in Theon's fantasies, replying "we know things [...] savage things."[54] David Benioff noted that children in the north would have grown up with tales of wildling raids that cemented the notion that the wildlings were savages and adversaries.[55] Jon Snow, for instance, recounts how he has heard since childhood that "six times you've [the wildlings] invaded and six times you've failed."[56] It is not just wildling raids and invasions that the north remembers, but tales of wildling savagery. Rickon recounts how he was told that wildlings "turn your skull into a cup and make you drink your own blood from it."[57] Jon was told similar stories.[58]

One of the primary objectives of the Night's Watch is to protect the Seven Kingdoms against wildling attacks and raids. These raids contribute to the animosity and fear that the north holds toward the wildlings, which is demonstrated in a number of scenes throughout the series. For example, the reception Lord Glover gave to Jon Snow when he came seeking aid to oust Ramsay Bolton from Winterfell shows Glover's hatred of the wildlings.[59] But viewers really become aware of the hatred between the Night's Watch and the wildlings in season 5. Olyvar resents Jon Snow for making an alliance with the wildlings, who massacred his community. Olyvar is afraid the wildlings may attack the Night's Watch after they have entered Castle Black.[60] Indeed, captains of the Night's Watch assassinate Jon Snow because of his alliance with the wildlings. Even more than the cultural differences that exist between the wildlings and the people of the Seven Kingdoms, it is undoubtedly the former's raiding and killing that contribute to the hatred that the Night's Watch and the north hold toward them. And this hatred of the wildlings is not restricted just to northern families. One of the reasons why Lord Randyll Tarly sent his son Samwell to the Wall was to "make a man" of him, which he would become "by killing some bloody wildlings"; and Randyll's hatred toward Gilly when he learns that she is a wildling is obvious to viewers.[61]

Although the belief in the wildlings' primitiveness and savagery is by far the dominant one among the people of the Seven Kingdoms, some characters see beyond the savage image and recognize the similarities that exist between the wildlings and the people of the Seven Kingdoms. Both Benjen Stark and Tyrion Lannister comment about this at Castle Black.[62] Martin and Weiss themselves have noted commonalities and shared histories between the people on both sides of the Wall.[63] For example, the people in the north and the wildlings believe in the Old Gods.[64] And Jon Snow's interaction and relationship with Ygritte demonstrates that two very different people can connect at a deep emotional level. When Jon Snow says "my ancestors lived here same as yours," Ygritte asks: "So why you fighting us?"[65] Jon actually then recognizes that the wildlings "were no different than the men of the Night's Watch."[66] Samwell comes to a similar conclusion as he tries to explain to Olyvar Jon's decision to help the wildlings at Hardhome.[67]

Of course, the Roman frontier along Hadrian's Wall was much more complex than suggested by Roman writings that reduce circumstances to a simple dichotomy. In fact, archaeological evidence indicates that Romans had amicable relations with some of the people there.[68] Similarly, friendly social interactions do take place between the Night's Watch and the wildlings.[69] In any case, many similarities clearly exist between how Roman writers and the people of the Seven Kingdoms viewed the populations beyond their respective Walls. Each "civilized" side saw the lands beyond their wall as remote, harsh, and wild and the people there as aggressive "barbarians." Beyond all doubt, Hadrian's Wall and historical views of the populations north of this wall influenced Martin's characterizations in *Game of Thrones*.

Notes

1 "Winter Is Coming," directed by Tim Van Patten, written by David Benioff and D. B. Weiss, in *Game of Thrones*, season 1, HBO, first aired on April 17, 2011.

2 P. C. N. Stewart, "Inventing Britain: The Roman Creation and Adaption of an Image," *Britannia* 26 (1995), 1.

3 Alistair Moffat, *The Wall: Rome's Greatest Frontier* (Edinburgh: Birlinn, 2008), 1.

4 Mikal Gilmore, "George R. R. Martin: The Rolling Stone Interview," *Rolling Stone*, 2014, May 8 (accessed July 9, 2016 at http://www.rollingstone.com/tv/news/george-r-r-martin-the-rolling-stone-interview-20140423).

5 Peter Wells, *The Barbarians Speak: How the Conquered Peoples Shaped Roman Europe* (Princeton, NJ: Princeton University Press, 1999), 100–101.

6 Strabo, *Geography*, in *Literary Sources for Roman Britain*, edited by J. C. Mann and R. G. Penman (London: London Association of Classical Teachers, 1977), 13. The reader should note that this and the next reference are not to Strabo's own text (which in this case would be 4.5.11), but to page numbers in Mann and Penman'a anthology. This holds for all the authors cited from Mann and Penman in this chapter.

7 Strabo, *Geography* (from Man and Penman's *Literary Sources*), 14 (translation amended).

8 Wells, *Barbarians Speak*, 100.

9 Stewart, "Inventing Britain," 6.

10 Stewart, "Inventing Britain," 7.

11 J. C. Mann and R. G. Penman, "Introduction," in *Literary Sources for Roman Britain*, edited by J. C. Mann and R. G. Penman (London: London Association of Classical Teachers, 1977), 4.

12 Wells, *Barbarians Speak*, 99.

13 Stewart, "Inventing Britain," 4.

14 Stewart, "Inventing Britain," 4.

15 Cassius Dio, *Roman History*, in *Literary Sources for Roman Britain*, edited by J. C. Mann and R. G. Penman (London: London Association of Classical Teachers, 1977), 22.

16 R. A. B. Mynors, *XII Panegyrici Latini* (Oxford, Clarendon, 1964).

17 *Panegyric of Constantine* (Pan. Lat. Vet. VI (VII)) by an anonymous orator, in *Literary Sources for Roman Britain*, edited by J. C. Mann and R. G. Penman (London: London Association of Classical Teachers, 1977), 38. For dating and other useful details, see also the introduction to the translation of this panegyric in *In Praise of Later Roman Emperors: The Panegyrici Latini*, edited and translated with introduction and historical commentary by C. E. V. Nixon and Barbara Rodgers and with the Latin text by R. A. B. Mynors (Berkeley, CA: University of California Press 1994), 211–217.

18 Ammianus Marcellinus, *The Roman History of Ammianus Marcellinus*, in *Literary Sources for Roman Britain*, edited by J. C. Mann and R. G. Penman (London: London Association of Classical Teachers, 1977), 44.

19 "The Kingsroad," directed by Tim Van Patten, written by David Benioff and D. B. Weiss, in *Game of Thrones*, season 1, HBO, first aired on April 24, 2011.

20 "You Win or You Die," directed by Daniel Minahan, written by David Benioff and D. B. Weiss, in *Game of Thrones*, season 1, HBO, first aired on May 29, 2011.

21 George R. R. Martin, *A Song of Ice and Fire: Book One: A Game of Thrones* (New York: Bantam, 2011 [1996]), 178, 205.

22 Wells, *Barbarians Speak*, 101.

23 Cassius Dio, *Roman History: Books 71–80*, translated by Earnest Cary (Cambridge, MA: Harvard University Press, 1927), 263.

24 "You Win or You Die," HBO.

25 Procopius, *History of the Wars*, Books VII and VIII, translated by H. B. Dewing (London: William Heinemann, 1962), 265–267.

26 See "Special Feature: Inside the Wildlings," in the DVD *Game of Thrones: The Third Complete Season* (USA: Home Box Office, Inc., 2014).

27 The onset of winter in season 5 minimized this difference, as a snowstorm descended on the North.

28 See "Special Feature: Complete Guide to Westeros," in the DVD *Game of Thrones: The Complete First Season* (USA: Home Box Office, Inc., 2012).

29 David Breeze, "John Collingwood Bruce and the Study of Hadrian's Wall," *Britannia* 34 (2003), 7.

30 David Breeze, *The Frontiers of Imperial Rome* (Barnsley: Pen & Sword Books, 2011, Kindle edn.).

31 *Historia Augusta*, in *Literary Sources for Roman Britain*, edited by J. C. Mann and R. G. Penman (London: London Association of Classical Teachers, 1977), 32.

32 David Breeze and Brian Dobson, *Hadrian's Wall* (London: Penguin Books, 1976), 5.

33 Moffat, *Wall*, 178.

34 Benjamin Hudson, *The Picts* (Oxford: Wiley Blackwell, 2014), 18.

35 Hudson, *Picts*, 19.

36 Cassius Dio, *Roman History: Books 71–80*, 263.

37 Guy de la Bédoyère, *Roman Britain: A New History* (New York: Thames & Hudson, 2013), 130–131.

38 "A Man without Honor," directed by David Nutter, written by David Benioff and D. B. Weiss, in *Game of Thrones*, season 2, HBO, first aired on May 13, 2012.

39 Herodian, *History of the Roman Empire since the Death of Marcus Aurelius*, 3.14.7. This and the subsequent passages from Herodian in this chapter reproduce Edward C. Echols' 1961 translation of Herodian and can all be found at http://www.livius.org/sources/content/herodian-s-roman-history/herodian-3.14 (accessed October 26, 2016).

40 Hudson, *Picts*, 23.

41 Hudson, *Picts*, 23.

42 Hudson, *Picts*, 23.

43 "Special Feature: Inside the Wildlings," DVD.

44 Cassius Dio, *Roman History: Books 71–80*, 263.

45 "Special Feature: Inside the Wildlings," DVD.

46 Herodian, *History of the Roman Empire*, 3.14.1, 3.14.8.

47 Ammianus Marcellinus, *Roman History* (from Man and Penman's *Literary Sources*), 43.

48 Ammianus Marcellinus, *Roman History* (from Man and Penman's *Literary Sources*), 43.

49 Hudson, *Picts*, 39.

50 Breeze, *Frontiers of Imperial Rome*.

51 Gildas, *On the Ruin of Britain*, chs. 14 and 18. This is the 1842 translation by J. A. Giles and T. Habington (pp. 12–13 and 14), which can be found at http://www. heroofcamelot.com/docs/Gildas-On-the-Ruin-of-Britain.pdf (accessed October 22, 2016).

52 Bede, *The Ecclesiastical History of the English People* (Oxford: Oxford University Press, 2008), 23–24.

53 Richard Hingley, Robert Witcher and Claire Nesbitt, "Life of an Ancient Monument: Hadrian's Wall in History," *Antiquity* 86 (2012), 764.

54 "The Old Gods and the New," directed by David Nutter, written by Vanessa Taylor, in *Game of Thrones*, season 2, HBO, first aired on May 6, 2012.

55 "Special Feature: Inside the Wildlings," DVD.

56 "The Bear and the Fair Maiden," directed by Michelle MacLaren, written by George R. R. Martin, in *Game of Thrones*, season 3, HBO, first aired on May 12, 2013.

57 "The Rains of Castamere," directed by David Nutter, written by David Benioff and D. B. Weiss, in *Game of Thrones*, season 3, HBO, first aired on June 2, 2013.

58 George R. R. Martin, *A Song of Ice and Fire, Book Two: A Clash of Kings* (New York: Bantam, 2011 [1999]), 271.

59 "The Broken Man," directed by Mark Mylod, written by Bryan Cogman, in *Game of Thrones*, season 6, HBO, first aired on June 5, 2016.

60 "Hardhome," directed by Miguel Sapochnik, written by David Benioff and D. B. Weiss, in *Game of Thrones*, season 5, HBO, first aired on May 31, 2015.

61 "Blood of My Blood," directed by Jack Bender, written by Bryan Cogman, in *Game of Thrones*, season 6, HBO, first aired on May 29, 2016.

62 "Lord Snow," directed by Brian Kirk, written by David Benioff and D. B. Weiss, in *Game of Thrones*, season 1, HBO, first aired on May 1, 2011.

63 "Special Feature: Inside the Wildlings," DVD.

64 George R. R. Martin, *A Song of Ice and Fire, Book Five: A Dance with Dragons* (New York: Bantam, 2013 [2011]), 296.

65 "A Man without Honor," HBO.

66 Martin, *A Dance with Dragons*, 782. That Olyvar takes the opposite meaning to what Sam intends shows, however, the power of prejudice.

67 "Hardhome," HBO.

68 W. S. Hanson, "Scotland and the Northern Frontier: Second to Fourth Centuries AD," in *A Companion to Roman Britain*, edited by Malcolm Todd (London: Historical Society, 2004), 148.

69 George R. R. Martin, *A Song of Ice and Fire: Book Three: A Storm of Swords* (New York: Bantam, 2011 [2000]), 101.

7

The Eastern Question
Mat Hardy

For the western world, the East has long represented a hostile and exotic realm: a source of threat, difference, and barbarism. Starting with the schism between the Greek and Latin churches in the early centuries of Christianity and then the rise and spread of Islam, the East and its inhabitants were feared and distrusted during the Middle Ages. Muslim victories, finalized by the eviction of the crusaders from the Holy Land in 1291, the ensuing hostile relations with the Byzantines, and then the fall of Constantinople in 1453 did nothing to improve relations. Throughout these centuries, and arguably until today, western relations with the East have been marred by religious differences that have led to conflict with "the other" (the name sociologists give to the idea that people often define their own unifying characteristics and sense of belonging as wholesome or good, while constructing for the opponent an identity that is indecent or evil).

Western Europe's interaction with the "orient" remained limited until around the sixteenth century. This was especially true for those nations that did not border the Mediterranean or Balkans. Nevertheless, as the expanding Ottoman Empire began to make incursions into Europe in the early 1500s, a greater awareness of the orient arose. The burgeoning trade and colonial networks of the European maritime nations also brought increased contact. From this point on, the East was more tangible for the West: not just as an unknown, un-Christian edge of the map, but as a real space.

Western popular imagining of the East developed a series of representations and characteristics influenced mostly by contact with the Ottomans, but they became universally attributed to various peoples, whether validly or not. These images became cemented over the centuries and served to depict all the lands and peoples anywhere between Morocco and India. Even more, many of these same images are still used in fantasy fiction to represent eastern cultures in other worlds: "deserts, oases, bazaars and slums, jewelled caravans and minaret topped edifices [...] beggars, houris, eunuchs, caliphs, viziers, adventurers."[1]

Game of Thrones versus History: Written in Blood, First Edition. Edited by Brian A. Pavlac.
© 2017 John Wiley & Sons, Inc. Published 2017 by John Wiley & Sons, Inc.

A certain talent for treachery and sexual licentiousness among easterners is also part of the standard depiction of the East in the western imagination, as is the ever present threat of sudden death or barbaric cruelty.[2]

Game of Thrones inherits some of our real-world baggage in its imagining of the orient. The eastern continent, Essos, is painted as a realm of alien menace: it is filled with swarthy, threatening and duplicitous inhabitants. The landscapes are harsh, arid, and empty, while the cities present exotic architecture or bustling bazaars. The natives are prone to treachery, dark mysticism, fanatic religious cults, slavery, and arbitrary slaughter. As in medieval Europe, in Westeros the threat of invasion from Essos, be it military or religious, is a major theme. Indeed, to some extent the depiction of this difference is a product of our own history. Nevertheless, the anachronisms and geographical conflations displayed in the fantasy world also offer intriguing differences.

Geography

Like so many fantasy authors, George R. R. Martin uses for his novels a standardized geography that is roughly based on Europe and the Middle East. Westeros has an amalgam of European-like geographies and cultures, from the Norse Celtic northern climes, through the Anglo-French center, down to the spicy Iberian Moorish civilization of Dorne. The north–south continental map bears something of a resemblance to the British Isles, and its terrain, climate, architecture and clothing are recognisably European. By contrast, Essos is strikingly similar to Turkey in outline and is more akin to Asia in every other way. Its lateral orientation includes sprawling steppes and deserts with a host of peoples that correspond to Levantines, Arabs, Turks, and Mongols. Another similarity is the free cities, such as Braavos and Myr, which act as halfway houses between the occident and orient, in the same way in which maritime powers like Venice and Genoa or islands such as Rhodes performed this role for Europe.

Martin is certainly not alone in using these standard geographies and cultures in his fictional universe. Fantasy authors such as J. R. R. Tolkien, Raymond E. Feist, Robert Jordan, and Robert E. Howard have all used such east–west dichotomies.[3] The eastern world in those sagas is invariably separated by mountains, deserts, or steppes and is often the location of some evil, or at least home to smaller, slyer, and more alien peoples. Generally this eastern setting is nothing more than a backdrop for culturally western characters to progress across. This is also the case with Essos, which is exposed only through the adventures of Daenerys, Tyrion, and others.[4]

This standard geography allows for many parallels to be drawn between history and the fantasy world of *Game of Thrones*. For example, the close proximity, yet lack of interaction between Westeros and Essos is similar to that of the European vis-à-vis the Ottoman world. People on both continents are aware of the other, yet there appears to be no significant exchange beyond certain luxury goods. Aside from traders and sailors, few people, even among the wealthy, will ever travel to the other continent or garner any personal experience of its people. Oberyn Martell is the exception that tests the rule. He claims to have spent five years in Essos precisely because he did not want to be like "most of us."[5] For the most part, however, the Westerosi rely upon hearsay, stereotypes, and xenophobic assumptions to form their impression of foreigners. In this respect, the characters of Martin's work are much like the people of Europe.

Looking East through Baroque Glasses

From the citadels of Westeros, the discussion of the East and its political and commercial facets is similar to the thoughts expressed by Europeans as they considered their Arab and Ottoman neighbors. Still, there is an important difference. On the whole, significant worry about eastern threats occurred later in European history than in the medieval setting of *Game of Thrones*. The crusades to the Holy Land (1096–1291) were, of course, a major interaction with the Middle East, but they were limited both in time and in space. Not until the fifteenth and sixteenth centuries did European leaders start paying more attention to the East, not least because Ottoman territorial expansion made it unavoidable. When Sultan Suleiman the Magnificent (r. 1520–1566) attacked the gates of Vienna in 1529 and when Ottoman armies again besieged the same city in 1683, the bulk of Christian Europe finally became more concerned with its Muslim neighbors.

Some awareness was occasioned by the atrocities committed in border wars between Christians and Muslims in the Balkans. Wallachia (now part of Romania) still resonates in our myth of vampires and Transylvanian castles. The reputation for bloodthirstiness acquired by Prince Vlad Dracula "the Impaler" (1431–1477) on account of slaughtering Ottoman invaders inspired the fictional character of Count Dracula the vampire. Vlad was reported to have butchered tens of thousands of men, women, children, both his own subjects and his enemies. His most infamous method was to run a long stake vertically through each human body (dead or alive), plant the stakes in the ground, and create a grisly forest of impaled corpses. Less well-known is that Vlad spent six years as a hostage of the Ottoman court, being schooled in Koranic law, the Turkish language, and military tactics.

Military issues point to a peculiar discrepancy between *Game of Thrones* and the history of western contact with the Islamic world. The combat technology of chainmail, swords, and castles in *Game of Thrones* is easy to identify as medieval. These items are relatively standard tropes in fantasy settings, where warfare never seems to progress beyond the thirteenth century. In its eastern relations, however, the world of *Game of Thrones* is much more akin to our early modern period, the sixteenth and seventeenth centuries. Even though the battlefield equipment and tactics are medieval, the globalized scale of informational, cultural, and economic development and exchange is clearly post-medieval. This is

> a world where merchants trade exotic drugs and spices between conti-
> nents, where professional standing armies can number in the tens or
> hundreds of thousands, where scholars study the stars via telescopes,
> and proto-corporations like the Iron Bank of Braavos and the Spicers of
> Qarth control global trade. It's also a world of slavery on a gigantic scale,
> and huge wars that disrupt daily life to an unprecedented degree.[6]

Thus, on the one hand, exchange between the two continents, at least in population and travel, was limited in *Game of Thrones*, as it was in the Middle Ages.
Yet, on the other hand, the world in *Game of Thrones* has a form of globaliza-
tion that did not exist in Europe until the early modern mercantile and colonial
era. Transport networks also appear to be superior to those of medieval Europe.
Uninterrupted travel in Westeros and Essos is not as difficult as it was in the
medieval period. Land and open sea journeys of thousands of miles are under-
taken by many characters without apparent need for much preparation or
transhipping. In contrast, when Thomas Dallam sailed from Britain to Istanbul
in 1599 to deliver a pipe organ to "the Grand Turk," Sultan Mehmet III, this was
considered an incredibly exotic journey for the time. Nevertheless, it was only
the same distance as King's Landing is from Winterfell. Even the prostitute Ros
makes that journey for the sake of a vague ambition.[7]

Assassinations in the East

While the most notorious political assassinations in *Game of Thrones* occur in
Westeros at the Red and Purple Weddings, the eastern realms actually have a
greater number of professional killings. Indeed, the close fight at the Twins and
the poisoning of Joffrey are crude affairs compared to the subtleties of the
Faceless Men, the Sorrowful Men, and the elaborate wine merchant plot to
poison Daenerys.

Historically, fear of assassination has long been associated with eastern
lands. For example, the Roman (western) occupation of Judea was challenged
by Jewish (eastern) zealots. One faction within this resistance was known as
Sicarii ("dagger men," from the Latin *sicarius*). They engaged in what would
be called today asymmetrical warfare: a small force against a dominant military power. The Sicarii carried out daring raids and a campaign of terror,

both against the Roman invaders and those among the native population whom they saw as collaborators or rivals. In *Game of Thrones*, the Sons of the Harpy in Meereen, opponents of Daenerys, are a reflection of this group. Their tactics parallel almost exactly those of the Sicarii, who, according to the contemporary historian Josephus,

> slew men in the day time, and in the midst of the city; this they did chiefly at the festivals, when they mingled themselves among the multitude, and concealed daggers under their garments, with which they stabbed those that were their enemies; and when any fell down dead, the murderers became a part of those that had indignation against them; by which means they appeared persons of such reputation, that they could by no means be discovered.[8]

Josephus records that such was the terror inspired by this campaign that citizens "expected death every hour" and became increasingly paranoid and mistrusting even of their friends.

Perhaps fortunately for the citizens of Meereen, Daenerys' response to the Sons of the Harpy is far milder than the Roman tactics. The juggernaut of Rome systematically crushed the Jewish revolt. It ended in AD 70 with a brutal siege of Jerusalem that saw most of the city destroyed and its population variously slain, crucified, enslaved, and dispersed. The Temple precinct was demolished, and some of the building blocks thrown down by the Roman engineers still lie at the foot of the walls today. It was to be another 1900 years before the Jews were again in control of their historic capital, after Israel's triumph in the Six-Day War (1967).

Political resistance through terror tactics is still often associated with the Middle East today. In addition, westerners also stereotype another kind of oriental violence: assassination. In *Game of Thrones*, the Faceless Men are professional assassins endowed with supernatural abilities of infiltration and with lethal expertise. The Faceless Men have historical parallels, starting with the very term that we use for the act of targeted killing. "The Assassins" is the name given to a medieval Islamic sect that inhabited the mountainous regions of Iran and Syria during the eleventh century and down to the thirteenth.[9] More properly known as the Nizaris, they were a splinter group of the Ismaili faith, itself a subgroup of Shia Islam. The Nizaris were just one of many factions at that time, but their reputation for attempting daring murders of political leaders has made their fame endure for a thousand years. Although their main targets were Muslim leaders, their clashes with the crusaders cemented the link in the European mind between eastern religions and cunning murder.

The tales of Nizaris being led by an "Old Man of the Mountain" and using mind-altering drugs in mystic ceremonies were largely manufactured by their opponents. They prompted the derogatory nickname Hashishin ("hash addicts"), which was reported back to the West by Marco Polo.[10] The word evolved into "assassin," which describes one who kills political leaders. In reality, only a small inner circle of highly trained Nizari devotees went on killing missions. They were never killers for hire; their assassinations were solely directed at enemies and opponents of their sect.

The Assassins made two attempts on the life of Saladin, who, before he become the bane of the crusaders, was also a political rival of the Nizari leader. The second attempt involved men who posed as soldiers in Saladin's army and attacked him during a ceremony. These Assassins were cut down before achieving their objective. In 1192 two Assassins killed Conrad of Monferrat, the king elect of Jerusalem, after spending months pretending to be Christians. Special operatives such as these had to be masters of disguise, able to blend in linguistically and culturally, and willing to strike against a wary target without hope of personal survival.[11] Within the Nizari community they were known as "the "Fidaiyin"—"the ones willing to sacrifice themselves." Today the name of these highly trained killers is often rendered as "Fedayeen," the same name adopted by an army of Saddam Hussein's loyalists in the final years of his power in Iraq.[12]

Assassination services in *Game of Thrones* are quite different from the reality of eastern history. Even when, historically, there was a link between religion and targeted killing, such as in the case of Nizari or Sicarii, assassination was always committed on behalf of a group, to further its overall political aspirations. The idea of a Middle Easterner travelling halfway around the world on a contract to kill someone else's business rival is ridiculous. Of course, just as in *Game of Thrones*, westerners themselves were no strangers to employing the tactics of assassination, as the toxic history of the Renaissance Italian states bears witness. The murder of Giuliano de' Medici by a rival Florentine family in front of 10,000 people attending mass in 1478, or the alleged poisoning fetish of the Borgias, would not be out of place in Westeros.[13] This infamous period in Italian history has even found its way into the *Assassin's Creed* series of video games—another fantasy series that spans the East–West divide.

Swords for Sale

Duplicity and betrayal are commonplace in Essos; but they are especially prevalent in warfare. The dependence on "sellswords" or bands of mercenaries is a standard feature in the campaigns of competing city-states, where the noble citizenry regards risking one's life in battle as supremely foolish.[14] The fickleness and treachery of these mercenaries is noted repeatedly in the novels. Deserting, switching sides for a better offer, and even intracompany betrayal all occur. This makes warfare a small-scale and chaotic enterprise in Essos, as well as emphasizing the overriding stereotype that easterners are a treacherous and cowardly bunch. The loyal (and thus expensive) Golden Company is the exception that tests the rule.

In our own history, the mercenary profession is more rooted in the West than in the East. Models for Martin's mercenary leaders were the *condottieri* of the Italian Peninsula in the fourteenth and fifteenth centuries. One such *condottiero* was the Englishman Sir John Hawkwood (1320–1394), who made great profits by exploiting the chaotic rivalry among the Italian city-states. After service with the English in the Hundred Years' War, Hawkwood joined one of the many "free companies" of mercenaries that sold their services to various factions throughout France and the Italian states. He contracted his allegiance to popes, doges, and kings for over three decades, eventually rising to command the well-regarded White Company. His battlefield success was mixed, but he was extremely good at enriching himself during the shifting struggles between papacy and the city-states of the Italian Peninsula. It was not unknown for Hawkwood to accept a lucrative contract to attack one city and then take a massive bribe from the target in order not to do so. On occasion, one rival might hire his company to do nothing, merely so that an opponent would not be able to co-opt his services. Some conflicts ended not in blood-shed, but with financial negotiation. By 1381 the White Company was turning over nearly as much coin as some of the smaller Italian cities.[15] Hawkwood's loyalty could definitely be bought, but only for an exorbitant price and for a limited time. A century later, Niccolò Machiavelli (1469–1527) referred to Hawkwood by the nickname "Giovanni Acuto"—"John the Sharp."[16]

Even when we look in the East for mercenaries, it is again Europeans, not easterners, who make the best examples. The Varangian Guard protected the Byzantine emperors. Formed of Norsemen and later of Anglo-Saxons and Normans, these bodyguards were famous for their loyalty and professional-ism.[17] They were showered with wealth and battlefield spoils for their efforts, but that was not all. The Varangian Guard also had the curious privilege of being able to "loot" the palace treasury upon the death of an emperor, each man being allowed one trip into the vault to take as much as he could carry with two hands. Like the sellswords of Essos, the members of the Guard were not always common freebooters. The noble exile Harald "Hardrada" ("Hard Ruler") amassed such wealth serving as the commander of the Varangians that it bankrolled his successful claim to the Norwegian throne and his unsuccessful attempt at the English crown in 1066. With their heavy armor and long axes, the Varangians may have inspired Martin's Areo Hotah, the captain of the Dornish prince's bodyguard.

The Unsullied

The martial prowess of the dehumanized Unsullied is the basis of the Astapori economy and then becomes the cornerstone of Daenerys' power. The Unsullied are slaves raised in a barracks and trained to absolute loyalty, which makes them highly prized as soldiers yet disconnects them from wider society. There are obvious parallels between the Unsullied and the Janissaries of the Ottoman Empire. The Janissaries formed the elite personal guards of the sultans and were a pillar of their authority. Originally they were slaves, Christian boys taken mainly from the conquered lands of the Balkans. The boys were converted to Islam and raised as a military brotherhood, trained in special schools. The Janissaries' origin as captured slaves was important: it guaranteed that they had no family ties or vested interest in the political machinations around the throne. They were loyal only to their sultan and to one another. In an echo of the Unsullied's demeaning names, the Janissaries used kitchen terminology for their rank system, their officers bearing titles such as "cook," "head scullion," and "soup man."[18]

Unlike the fictional Unsullied, the Janissaries were not castrated. They were, however, expected to be celibate and were not permitted to marry. Their masters believed that allowing Janissaries to reproduce would result in divided loyalty. Even without children, the institutional loyalty of the Janissary corps declined over the centuries as they realized their own power. They began to marry and engage in commercial enterprises. By the seventeenth century being a Janissary had devolved into a profitable sinecure, supported by corruption. The corps' ranks became bloated with thousands of ineffectual freeloaders. Eventually they so endangered the empire's stability that in 1826 Sultan Mahmud II mounted a military operation against them, killing or exiling all Janissaries and disbanding the institution for good. Still, the Janissary corps had lasted for nearly 500 years. That Daenerys might sustain the ranks of her Unsullied without their brutal training remains doubtful.

Slavery

The link between slavery and eastern lands is quite strong in *Game of Thrones*, given that slaving is prevalent in Essos, yet a capital offence in the Seven Kingdoms.[19] Slavery is a purely eastern institution, and the cities of Slaver's Bay show the apogee of that business. Sexual servitude is also apparent: cities such as Lys specialize in the training of "bed slaves."

Oriental slavery is depicted quite graphically both in the novels and in the television series. The excesses align with the stereotype that Europeans had of the Ottoman Empire. In the eighteenth and nineteenth centuries, orientalist painters such as Jean-Léon Gérôme titillated the European public with depictions of harem scenes and slave markets. Salacious reports of white Christian women kidnapped and sold to wealthy satraps were grist for the tabloid mill. The term "white slavery" was coined, and the plotline of abduction to a harem has been used ever since in everything from pulp romance novels to Hollywood film and pornography. The marriage of Daenerys to Khal Drogo is really a version of the story of a fair maiden sold into sexual servitude.

Campaigning against the Ottoman slave trade was a key policy of the British and Russians during the nineteenth century; the case of Daenerys and the retribution she exacted on the Masters of Slaver's Bay illustrates something similar. Initially the focus was on liberating "white" slaves, particularly Circassian women, who fetched high prices at auction. Although it is hard to fault ending slavery, this goal also expanded the idea that "the civilized West" needed to teach "the barbaric East." Moral and religious superiority went hand in hand with the Great Powers' territorial ambition. The Ottoman trade in humans was gradually outlawed in the second half of the nineteenth century, although the principle did not necessarily extend to the liberation of existing slaves. Illegal trading and ownership continued until the demise of the Ottoman Empire after World War I.

In Essos slavery is carried out on a sensational scale, not just in number but in terms of its luridness. Decrepit and obese merchant princes are borne on giant palanquins carried by cohorts of straining slaves. Young males and females serve as sexual playthings, the best being especially trained in erotic skills in order to provide maximum pleasure. In addition to the mutilations performed on the Unsullied, gladiators fight to the death in arenas. Even more cruel spectacles encourage animals to eat children: "A bear and three small boys. One boy will be rolled in honey, one in blood and one in rotting fish, and she [Daenerys] may wager on which the bear will eat first."[20] Yet more gruesomely, disemboweled slave children are nailed up on every one of the 163 mileposts along the road from Yunkai, to warn Daenerys away from Meereen.[21] Gratuitous as this may seem, the number of executions is small in comparison to the 6,000 rebellious slaves who were crucified along the Appian Way following their rise under Spartacus in Rome's Third Servile War (73–71 BC).[22]

The slave trade in Essos, however, differs from that practised by the Ottomans. Istanbul was at the intersection of Europe, Asia, and Africa, and this position made the trade logistically more practical there than in the remote cities of Slaver's Bay. In Essos, the end market for so many slaves is unclear. Only Volantis is mentioned as a significant consumer, and it is said that there are five slaves for every free citizen in that city. Such a proportion would be demographically perilous: slaves could rise up against their owners or outbreed them. In contrast, the proportion of slaves in the Ottoman Empire was the opposite: in 1609 roughly one fifth of the population was made up of slaves.[23] Furthermore, slaves in the Ottoman Empire were not all in chains. The civil and military services were filled with men bought as slaves but educated and raised freely. They themselves could own slaves; and they rose to high status in their professions. The stability of the empire rested to a large degree upon the skills of these servile specialists.

In the end, the real role of Slaver's Bay is to showcase oriental barbarism, especially in contrast with the western ideals of Daenerys. Furthermore, her missionary zeal in defeating these sinkholes of human bondage and the slaves' subsequent inability to make good use of their newfound freedom are yet other examples of the implicit assumption of western (or rather Westerosi) cultural superiority. The conundrums and frustrations of Daenerys' rule in the East are a fantasy version of Rudyard Kipling's "White Man's Burden." In this poem Kipling explains that imperial ambitions to improve the lot of less civilized peoples may be a noble undertaking, but is unlikely to result in success or gratitude:

> Take up the White Man's burden,
> The savage wars of peace—
> Fill full the mouth of Famine
> And bid the sickness cease;
> And when your goal is nearest
> The end for others sought,
> Watch sloth and heathen Folly
> Bring all your hopes to nought.[24]

Religious Threat

In centuries past, and even today, the relationship between East and West has often been couched in religious terms. Whether by way of Latin versus Greek or Christianity versus Islam, there has been an abiding framework of two cultures experiencing a "polemical confrontation" through religious difference.[25] The use of religious faith to define an eastern "other" is a basic tenet of orientalist cultural discourse.

The idea of an aggressive religion creeping in from the East is also present in *Game of Thrones*. The worship of R'hollr has seeped into the political fault lines between the two continents. Demanding almost fanatic adherence from its followers, it has an apparent intolerance to other faiths. Additionally, it has abhorrent practices, such as human sacrifice, dark magic, and iconoclasm. Compared with the more gentle Faith of the Seven (itself originally an invader from the East), the worship of R'hollr apparently has a degenerative effect upon its practitioners, corrupting them either through perverse paths to power (King Stannis) or through debilitating necromancy (such as in the cases of Melisandre in the TV series and Thoros of Myr in the books). Even when a more zealous interpretation of the Faith of the Seven occurs later in the story, its concern for the downtrodden still offers a positive contrast to the more shadowy cult of the Lord of Light. There is, for example, no indication that even the militant arm of the Seven is empowered by supernatural forces.

The binary notion of light and darkness in the religion of R'hollr may have roots in Manichaeism, which developed in antiquity in the Persian Empire and its descendants. This religion depicted an eternal cosmic struggle, waged both in the real world and in the soul of mankind, between light–good–spirituality and the opposing forces of darkness–evil–materialism. Warfare between the Sasanian practitioners of these faiths and the Byzantine Empire from the fifth to the seventh centuries is an early example of religious conflict between Christian society and an eastern creed. In the centuries since then, doing battle with perceived religious enemies has been a crucial factor in east–west relations. "Defender of the Faith," "Savior of Christendom," and similar titles have been bestowed upon rulers and heroes precisely to emphasize the centrality of such a worldview.

In *Game of Thrones* the mantle of Azor Ahai and "the Lord's chosen" is similarly conferred upon Stannis by his Red Priestess adviser, Melisandre.[26] Her belief in Stannis' messianic potential, along with her demands for the burning of false idols and their worshippers, proves that, for her at least, the conflict in Westeros is a holy war. Stannis thus becomes not just another claimant to the throne, but one tainted with spiritual inflexibility and unwholesome religious fervor. That Melisandre later transfers her belief to Jon Snow while one of her colleagues subsequently anoints Daenerys demonstrates a certain expedience among the prophets of R'hollr, or at least conveys the impression that the religion is somewhat spurious. In any case, the conflict between faiths reinforces the stereotype of a religious threat stemming from the East, both in the real world and in fiction.

East Meets West

The depiction of the eastern continent in Martin's books and in the television series follows patterns and images that are well entrenched in western literature and in the historical record. The landscape and the people of Essos are derivative of real-world geography and cultures. But, although parallels can be drawn, the links are seldom solid. Just as readers in centuries past were thrilled by the *Tales from the Thousand and One Nights*, modern audiences are now absorbed in the elaborate fantasy that is *Game of Thrones*. We should remember, however, that truth is vastly more complex than fiction and that, when we look east, even in a fantasy world, we do so through orientalist lenses that, like Valyrian steel, are nearly impossible to break.

Notes

1 John Clute and John Grant, *The Encyclopaedia of Fantasy* (New York: St. Martin's Press, 1997), 51.

2 Edward Said, *Orientalism* (New York: Vintage, 1979), 38–39, 190.

3 Lorenzo DiTommaso, "The Persistence of the Familiar: The Hyborian World and the Geographies of Fantastic Literature," in *Two-Gun Bob: A Centennial Study of Robert E. Howard*, edited by Benjamin Szumskyj (New York: Hippocampus, 2006), 107–119.

4 Mat Hardy, "Game of Tropes: The Orientalist Tradition in the Works of G. R. R. Martin," *International Journal of Arts & Sciences* 8.1 (2015), 409–420 (accessed May 27, 2016 at www.universitypublications.net/ijas/0801/pdf/U4K318.pdf).

5 "The Laws of Gods and Men," directed by Alik Sakharov, written by Bryan Cogman, in *Game of Thrones*, season 4, HBO, first aired on May 11, 2014.

6 Benjamin Breen, "Why 'Game of Thrones' Isn't Medieval—and Why That Matters," 2014, June 12, *Pacific Standard* (accessed April, 1, 2016 at http://www.psmag.com/books-and-culture/game-thrones-isnt-medieval-matters-83288).

7 "A Golden Crown," directed by Daniel Minahan, written by David Benioff and D. B. Weiss, in *Game of Thrones*, season 1, HBO, first aired on May 22, 2011.

8 Flavius Josephus, *The Great Roman–Jewish War* (Mineola, NY: Dover Publications, 2012, eBook version), 248.

9 See Bernard Lewis, *The Assassins: A Radical Sect in Islam* (London: Weidenfeld & Nicolson, 2011, Kindle edn.).

10 Marco Polo, *The Travels of Marco Polo* (Adelaide: Yule-Cordier, 2009): online edition from University of Adelaide Library, available at ebooks.adelaide.edu.au/p/polo/marco/travels (accessed May 26, 2016).

11 C. E. Nowell, "The Old Man of the Mountain," *Speculum* 22 (1947), 497–519, doi: 10.2307/2853134.

12 Sharon Otterman, *IRAQ: What Is the Fedayeen Saddam?* Council of Foreign Relations, 2003 (accessed May 27, 2016 at http://www.cfr.org/iraq/iraq-fedayeen-saddam/p7698).

13 The most famous poisoning is the alleged murder of Lucretia Borgia's second husband Alfonso of Aragon in 1500. Sarah Bradford, the author of a recent biography titled *Lucretia Borgia: Life, Love and Death in Renaissance Italy* (New York: Viking, 2004), also worked on the television series *The Borgias* (Showtime, 2011).

14 George R. R. Martin, Elio M. García Jr., and Linda Antonsson, *The World of Ice and Fire: The Untold History of Westeros and the Game of Thrones* (London: Harper Voyager, 2014), 264.

15 William Caferro, *John Hawkwood: An English Mercenary in Fourteenth-Century Italy* (Baltimore, MD: Johns Hopkins University Press, 2006), 339.

16 Niccolò Machiavelli, *The Prince* (New York: Open Road Media, 2014, eBook version), 73.

17 See Sigfús Blöndal, *The Varangians of Byzantium*, translated by Benedikt Bendikz (1st rev. edn., Cambridge: Cambridge University Press, 2008).

18 Jason Goodwin, *Lords of the Horizons: A History of the Ottoman Empire* (New York: Random House, 2011), 64.

19 A partial exception is the bondage of salt wives and thralls on the Iron Islands. But these individuals are captives taken in battle and never bought or sold for a "gold price."

20 George R. R. Martin, *A Song of Ice and Fire, Book Three: A Storm of Swords* (New York: Bantam, 2005 [2000]), 321.

21 Martin, *A Storm of Swords*, 775.

22 Appian, *The Civil Wars*, Book I, chapter xiv, 120. This online edition in the Perseus Digital Library, Tufts University, available at www.perseus.tufts.edu/hopper/text?doc=Perseus%3atext%3a1999.01.0232 (accessed on 27 May, 2016) reproduces the Macmillan edition of London 1899.

23 Karl Kaser, *The Balkans and the Near East: Introduction to a Shared History* (Vienna: Lit Verlag, 2011), 108.

24 Rudyard Kipling, *The White Man's Burden*, 2014, University of Adelaide Library, online version (accessed May 27, 2016 at ebooks.adelaide.edu.au/k/kipling/rudyard/five/complete.html#section22).

25 Said, *Orientalism*, 258.

26 Martin, *A Storm of Swords*, 349.

8

Slaves with Swords

Slave-Soldiers in Essos and in the Islamic World

Robert J. Haug

When Daenerys Targaryan is looking to raise an army to help her invade and take the throne of the Seven Kingdoms of Westeros, she arrives at the city of Astapor to look over the Unsullied, eunuch slave-soldiers.[1] Her advisor warns her against buying them:

> "My queen," said Arstan, "there have been no slaves in the Seven Kingdoms for thousands of years. The old gods and the new alike hold slavery to be an abomination. Evil. If you should land in Westeros at the head of a slave army, many good men will oppose you for no other reason than that. You will do great harm to your cause, and to the honor of your House."[2]

Ignoring his advice, Daenerys buys the slaves. But she sets them free, and they become a core element of her army. One of its leaders, Grey Worm, even becomes one of Daenerys' closest advisors. Outside a fantasy context, the idea of a slave army may seem odd to modern readers. Thoughts of armed slaves may turn to slave revolts such as those that occurred under the leadership of Spartacus (c. 111–71 BC), Toussaint L'Ouverture (1743–1803), and Nat Turner (1800–1831). In fact slave-soldiers have a basis in Islamic history, even though the fictional Unsullied are an extreme version.[3] Slave-soldiers were designated by the Arabic term *mamlūk* (pl. *mamālīk*), which literally means "property." They were an important and almost entirely unique aspect of armies in the Islamic world from the ninth to the nineteenth centuries.[4] Both the slave-soldiers used by Daenerys and the Unsullied in her army share a number of similarities with the slave armies used by Muslim rulers. This chapter explores such similarities. It considers the questions that slave-soldiers raise regarding the relationship between rulers, their armies, and their subjects, and it does so from the point of view of both Daenerys and a series of Muslim rulers who played their own "game of thrones."

Game of Thrones versus History: Written in Blood, First Edition. Edited by Brian A. Pavlac.
© 2017 John Wiley & Sons, Inc. Published 2017 by John Wiley & Sons, Inc.

The Origins of Slave-soldiers in the Islamic World

Institutionalized slave armies in the Islamic world began under the Abbasid caliphate (750–1258). They are most closely connected with Caliph Abu Ishaq al-Muʿtasim (r. 833–842), who, during the reign of his brother al-Maʾmun (r. 813–833), acquired a personal retinue of Turkish slaves who were later integrated into the imperial army. Like Daenerys' Unsullied, al-Muʿtasim's Turks emerged out of existing practices of slavery. Slaves performed many different roles across the caliphate, including domestic service, physical labor, entertainment, and concubinage.[5] They arrived in the Abbasid Empire, which at its height stretched from Tunisia to Afghanistan, from almost every neighboring land. Some slaves were victims of war, the spoils of either conquest or smaller raids across the frontiers (including piracy). Slaves also arrived in the Islamic world as commodities of slave traders or as tribute from neighboring states. Evidence for slave markets in most major cities proves the large demand for slaves in the Abbasid Empire. While we can paint a general picture of the slave trade in the early Islamic world, the details are often difficult to see. As Matthew Gordon wrote about the trade in Turkish slaves from Inner Asia:

> the sources fail to provide information even on such basic matters as identity of its participants (who were the traders? who were the captives—prisoners of war, tribute, orphans cast off to those willing to feed them?), the mechanics of the trade (how were the slaves transported, fed, housed?), and the levels of profit.[6]

Unlike the fictional cities of Slaver's Bay, this was not a society whose existence was based on or defined by the slave trade, although it was heavily reliant upon slavery.

Slave militaries grew in particular out of existing traditions of slave bodyguards and private retinues.[7] Illustrative of this connection, the Arabic term most often used to describe al-Muʿtasim's Turkish soldiers was *ghilmān* (pl. *ghulām*), which, besides "slave", can mean "young man," "servant," or "bodyguard." The origins of these bodyguards and private retinues in the early Islamic period are not clear. One of the earliest military forces in Islamic history that may have consisted of slaves belonged to ʿUbaydallah ibn Ziyad (d. 686), a late seventh-century military commander and governor in the Umayyad Empire (661–750). Following a campaign in Transoxania, Ibn Ziyad brought a private retinue of archers back from the city of Bukhara (in modern Uzbekistan) to Iraq. Some scholars argue that the Bukhariyya, as the group was known, consisted of enslaved prisoners of war. Others point to a pre-Islamic Iranian practice called *čākir*, in which a group of warriors, often foreigners, would enter the service of a lord as a unit, complete with their own leadership. According to this view, the people of Bukhara entered into a subservient relationship with

Ibn Ziyad willingly (or at least as willingly as one can make it when dealing with the commander of an army that has attacked your city).[8] By 833, when the reign of al-Muʿtasim started, units of *čākir* with the Arabicized name Shakiriyya were being employed in the imperial army alongside, but separately from, units of slave-soldiers.

From the second half of the eighth century on, we have better evidence for rulers employing their own private slave retinues in increasingly public roles. The Umayyads of Spain (711–1031) employed forces of European slaves called Saqaliba (derived from a word meaning "Slav")[9] in their military.[10] In the early ninth century, the Aghlabid (800–909) emir of Ifiqiyya, Ibrahim I (r. 800–812), had settled a retinue of *ʿabīd*, sub-Saharan African slaves, in his new capital of Abbasiyya.[11] Not long after this, the practice reached the center of the Abbasid Caliphate.

Why Would a Ruler Employ Slave-soldiers?

Scholars have debated why the Muslim caliphate and its successors came to place military and political power in the hands of imported slaves. A large part of this discussion has examined lack of participation in the public sphere on the part of subjects of the caliphate and the seeming absence of a strong, military-minded aristocracy in the early and medieval Islamic world.[12] Jürgen Paul has written that the choice to turn to slave-soldiers was really one of "efficiency, loyalty and expense."[13] For both Daenerys Targaryen and al-Muʿtasim, resorting to slave-soldiers effectively met these three requirements.

In Daenerys' case, she was a deposed Westerosi noble in Essos, a foreigner with very limited access to more traditional sources of military support: she had little more than a pair of wayward knights, a few loyal Dothraki, and very young dragons. Once she lost her horde, her two remaining options were hiring mercenaries or purchasing Unsullied. In convincing Daenerys to choose an Unsullied force, Ser Jorah Mormont argued that they were more loyal, better disciplined, and more effective than mercenaries—especially the Dothraki, whose raping and pillaging, along with their practice of enslaving the conquered, had been so distasteful to her.[14]

Al-Muʿtasim was similarly faced with problems of maintaining an army that should be effective, affordable, and ultimately loyal to him. In the early ninth century, the Abbasid caliphate was embroiled in a civil war between two sons of Caliph Harun al-Rashid of *One Thousand and One Nights* fame (r. 786–809): al-Amin (r. 809–813) and al-Maʾmun. This war was incredibly damaging to the empire, culminating in a year-long siege of the imperial capital of Baghdad, long remembered in the Arabic chronicles for the house-to-house fighting that was needed to overcome the city's defenders. Besides the rivalry between the two princes, this war represented competition between two factions within the empire. On one side were the Baghdad-based *abnā' al-dawla* ("sons of the dynasty"), an old guard of soldiers who had served the Abbasids six decades earlier, during the revolution that brought them to power.[15] On the other side were the people of Khurasan (or Khorasan, the grand province in the east that covered roughly today's northeastern Iran, Turkmenistan, and large parts of Afghanistan), mainly consisting of Persians and other Iranian peoples, in contrast to the Arabs who had dominated political life in the early caliphate. In the end, the Khurasanis and their preferred caliph, al-Ma'mun, were victorious. It was during al-Ma'mun's reign that his younger brother Abu Ishaq, the future al-Mu'tasim, began purchasing large numbers of Turkish slaves to fill the ranks of a personal bodyguard. This decision reflected not just a prince concerned for his own security; it was part of a larger attempt to reorganize the military after the civil war. Al-Mu'tasim understood the challenges of courting and maintaining the loyalty of existing imperial elites while controlling the growing rifts between various elite factions. He used his Turkish slaves to build a guard that was first and foremost loyal to him and substantively disconnected from the surrounding empire. Upon his ascension to the throne in 833, al-Mu'tasim engaged in his own large-scale reorganization of the imperial military. He promoted and expanded a regiment of Turkish slaves, making them a central piece of his imperial army.

In point of efficiency, affordability, and availability, Turkish slaves were an ideal choice. Above all, they were loyal, because they were outsiders without connections to local communities. As foreigners who spoke a language not too familiar in Arabic-, Persian-, and Syriac-speaking Iraq, they had few opportunities to build bonds outside their own communities. The Turks were also well known in the early Islamic world for their military prowess, especially in horsemanship and archery.[16] Their reputation as fearsome warriors is recorded even in two prophetic traditions. One encourages the Muslims to "leave the Turks alone as long as they leave you alone."[17] The other associates fighting the Turks with the end times, stating that "the Hour will not come until the Muslims fight with the Turks, a people whose faces are like hammered shields, wearing clothes of hair and walking (with shoes) of hair."[18] The Turks had been a thorn in the side of the caliphate while it expanded across its eastern and northern frontiers. Regular conflict increased the availability and affordability of slaves, as fighting brought new prisoners of war to markets.

What Are Slave-soldiers?

When the Unsullied are introduced in *A Song of Ice and Fire*, they are unquestionably slaves. They are commodities, objects to be bought and sold. As detailed by the slave trader Kraznys, the Unsullied's training is designed to create a kind of social dislocation—a combination of isolation and alienation, sometimes called "social death," that is a hallmark of slavery.[19] These slaves were taken from their families at a young age and castrated. They had their individual identities removed to such an extent that no Unsullied had his own name; each slave drew a new name from a bucket every day. Slaves were conditioned to be absolutely obedient. Kraznys claims that, if ordered, the Unsullied would stand at attention in the Plaza of Pride until the last one died of exhaustion. To demonstrate their stoic immunity to pain, Kraznys whips one across the face and cuts the nipple off of another.[20] Such slaves have lost all individual identity. They are incapable of connecting with broader society, except through masters upon whom they are completely dependent.

We lack evidence that the slave armies of the Islamic world went through this extreme conditioning. Nevertheless, the purchase and training of slaves under Islam created a sense of isolation and alienation from the rest of society, while reinforcing a collective group identity. The armies of al-Muʿtasim's Turkish *ghilmān*, the Umayyads of Spain's Saqaliba, or Ibrahim I's *ʿabīd* can be called slave armies mainly because the individual members of these forces were commodities purchased from beyond the frontiers of the Islamic world. In the case of al-Muʿtasim's Turkish *ghilmān*, most of its members came from the steppes of Inner Asia, through the slave markets of Khurasan. Stories of specific slaves tell us that many had been purchased from former owners, having previously lived as slaves in Baghdad and other cities of the Abbasid Empire.[21]

Their foreignness kept slaves apart, dislocated from the society in which they had come to live. Masters reinforced this otherness by physically separating the Turks from Abbasid society. For example, upon ascending to the caliphate, al-Muʿtasim founded a new capital, Samarra, approximately 125 kilometers north of Baghdad. He did this partly to keep uncouth Turks away from the busy, cosmopolitan streets of Baghdad. Contemporary sources tell many stories of wild Turks riding their horses at full gallop down the streets of the city, as if they were still on the steppes, with little regard for pedestrians. Al-Muʿtasim may also have meant to separate the Turks from the former soldiers whose jobs they had taken.[22]

In any case, Samarra was designed as a home for al-Muʿtasim's court and his army, away from the people of Baghdad. He granted land there to his commanders, so they could settle and provide for their soldiers. The resulting neighborhoods followed the divisions in the army itself, which ran largely along ethnic lines. Besides the Turkish *ghilmān*, grants were given both to the Maghariba ("westerners," most likely Arabs recruited in Egypt), and to the Shakiriyya from the East (who were discussed above).[23] The unique identities of each of these units increased competition across different groups within the military. Maintaining separation helped reduce the violence that occasionally broke out between different groups of slave-soldiers, as well as between them and the other factions within the military.[24] Al-Muʿtasim even provided his Turkish slaves with wives, so that they could settle into their communities, establish families, and produce a second generation of *ghilmān*. Unlike the Unsullied, Abbasid slave-soldiers were not eunuchs.[25] For the *ghilmān*, training also included indoctrination into certain aspects of Islamic civilization. Yet, while the Turks were instructed in Islam and converted, their education was limited, so that they could not function as full and active members of Muslim society. They remained instead dependent on the person of the caliph.[26] While the Turkish *ghilmān* may not have experienced the total breakdown of identity and personality that the Unsullied suffered, their otherness and their dependence on their masters kept them disconnected from the rest of society.

But Were They Really Slaves?

Can slaves who have been armed, trained to fight, and in some cases given positions of authority both within and outside the military still be considered slaves? Daenerys and her army raise this question. Daenerys is an antislavery abolitionist. Upon taking ownership of her Unsullied army, she immediately freed them and ordered them to free the slaves in Astapor by attacking the Good Masters.[27] The sack of Astapor and Daenerys' further abolitionist campaigns against other cities of Slaver's Bay, Yunkai and Meereen, earn her the title "Breaker of Shackles." Slavery had ended under Daenerys' rule—but, as the emissaries of Astapor, Volantis, and Yunkai rightly ask, is she not just a master by a different name?[28] Her own Unsullied patrolled the streets of Meereen, yet maintained their identity as a unit, separate and distinct from the rest of society. Even in freedom, they retain a certain social dislocation and aloofness that is a mark of enslavement.

We can see the Abbasid *ghilmān* existing in a similar intermediary space. At Samarra, the Turkish *ghilmān* quickly became a dominant force in the political life of the caliphate. From the beginning, these slave-soldiers had been led by commanders who were themselves slaves. These commanders achieved even higher positions of authority throughout the empire when al-Muʿtasim and his son and successor, al-Wathiq (r. 842–847), centralized power under a small group of officers and administrators. Three commanders of al-Muʿtasim's initial force were especially powerful: Ashinas (d. 844), who served as governor of Egypt from 834 until his death; Itakh (d. 849), who took over the governorship of Egypt after Ashinās' death and served as chamberlain until he was assassinated; and Wasif (d. 867), who served as chamberlain to both al-Muʿtasim and al-Mutawakkil. When al-Wathiq died at the young age of 36 without a designated successor, the Turkish commanders Itakh and Wasif were in the party of five prominent men who chose the new caliph, al-Wathiq's brother al-Mutawakkil.

Despite the political mobility and substantial power that these Turkish commanders wielded, they never integrated into larger society. Their relationship with the slave corps always defined their identity. They found themselves in rivalries with the secretarial class of imperial bureaucrats and with the Tahirids (a powerful Persian family from Khurasan whose members ruled the East as autonomous governors from 821 to 873 and Baghdad until 891).[29] Also competing with them were other military factions, including other units of slave-soldiers. Within these rivalries, the *ghilmān* essentially seized power over the caliphate. When Caliph al-Mutawakkil attempted to limit their power, first by ordering the assassination of Itakh and later by seizing the properties of Wasif, a group of *ghilmān* assassinated him in his own chambers, on the night of December 11, 861. Al-Mutawakkil's death kicked off a period known as the "anarchy" at Samarra, a decade that saw the violent succession of four caliphs who were little more than puppets in the hands of different military factions. During this period, the rivalry between the Samarran Turks and the Tahirids in Baghdad broke into full-out war. The Turkish *ghilmān* continued to dominate politics until Caliph al-Mu'tamid (r. 870–892) returned the capital to Baghdad in 892.

The accumulation and aggressive use of power by these commanders might give the impression that they were free men. Instead, as Patricia Crone has argued, such behavior actually resulted from their being slaves:

> It is in the nature of slave armies that they can easily get out of hand: because they are private in character, their discipline turns to a greater extent than is usually the case on the personal forcefulness of the ruler [...] Both the isolation and the homogeneity of the Samarran slaves probably exceeded the safety limit.[30]

The Turkish *ghilmān*'s distinct and separate identity, fostered by continued residence in Samarra, kept him (and the caliph) isolated from rival factions in Baghdad and other parts of the empire. Hence the *ghulām*'s interests did not ultimately lie in the betterment of the caliphate, or even in loyalty to the caliph, but in the improvement of their own position. When a strong caliph attempted to limit their power, authority, and wealth, they killed him and found a more pliable candidate. We can perceive here a similarity with Grey Worm, when he and the Unsullied initially refused to obey the commands of a weak ruler, Hizdahr zo Loraq, but responded positively to a stronger and better respected ruler, Ser Barristan Selmy.[31]

Slave Militaries beyond the Caliphate

Once the institution of slave-soldiers was introduced to the Islamic world, it not only continued but also expanded. These slave armies often proved difficult to control. In Transoxania and Khurasan, the Turkish slave-soldiers of the

Samanids (819–1005) seized power for themselves. They formed their own dynasty, the Ghaznavids (977–1186), famous for expanding the frontiers of the Islamic world into India.[32] In India, slave-soldiers known as the Mamlūk Dynasty (1206–1290) founded the Delhi sultanate (r. 1206–1526).[33] In the aftermath of Louis IX's (r. 1226–1270) failed invasion of Egypt during the Seventh Crusade (1248–1254), Turkish and Circassian slave-soldiers wrested control of Egypt and Syria from the Ayyubid Dynasty (1171–1260), which had been founded by the famous Kurd Saladin (r. 1171–1193). The new Mamlūk sultanate (1250–1517) endured for over two and a half centuries.[34]

Other states were more successful in managing their slave-soldiers. Beginning in the late fourteenth century, the Ottoman Empire (1299–1923) built a "new army" of Janissaries. This corps was formed by enslaving young Christian boys who had been forcibly "collected" from their Balkan homes through the *devşirme*, an annual tax.[35] While the *devşirme* came to an end in the early eighteenth century, the Janissaries continued to be at the center of the Ottoman military until 1826, when Sultan Mahmud II (r. 1808–1839) abolished them. In Morocco, the Alawite Dynasty (1631–) under Sultan Mulay Ismaʿil (r. 1672–1727) formed the ʿAbid al-Bukhari, a force made up of sub-Saharan slaves. This slave army survived until the late nineteenth century.[36]

One of the long-term effects of slave militaries in the Islamic world was a growing separation between rulers and their soldiers on the one hand, and the people they ruled over on the other. Increasingly the military became a world of its own, peopled by foreigners. In contrast, native locals usually ran the bureaucracy. Under this system society could become divided into camps, sometimes referred to in shorthand as "men of the sword" and "men of the pen." Such divisions could be rated positively, as when the great North African historian Ibn Khaldun (d. 1406) praised the arrival of the Mamlūks in Egypt:

> "God's benevolence [...] that He rescued the faith by reviving its dying breath and restoring the unity of the Muslim in Egypt [...] by sending to the Muslims, from this Turkish nation and from among its great and numerous tribes, rulers to defend them and utterly loyal helpers, who were brought from the House of War to the House of Islam under the rule of slavery."[37]

Although arming and training slaves as soldiers, let alone handing military and political power to them, may seem odd to us today, slave-soldiers were a historical reality in the Islamic world. They grew out of the need for an efficient, loyal, and affordable army. The story of Daenerys Targaryen and her Unsullied is not an exact replication of the story of slave-soldiers as it developed in the Islamic world. It does, however, depict familiar concerns and solutions, similar to the historical concerns and solutions of those who attempted to play their own "game of thrones" in real life.

Acknowledgment

This chapter is adapted from a presentation given February 8, 2014 at the Center for Medieval and Renaissance Studies at the Ohio State University as part of its annual Popular Culture and Deep History conference. The original paper was entitled "Between the Steppe and the Throne: The Rise of Daenerys Targaryen and Turko-Persian Empire Building." I wish to thank Alison Vacca, Nathan Gehoski, and Marc Reichardt for their comments on an earlier draft.

Notes

1 George R. R. Martin, *A Song of Ice and Fire, Book One: A Game of Thrones* (New York: Bantam, 2011 [1996]), 35.
2 The Unsullied had earlier appeared as guards at the manse of the Dothraki warlord Khal Drogo; see George R. R. Martin, *A Song of Ice and Fire, Book Three: A Storm of Swords* (New York: Bantam, 2011 [2000]), 320.
3 For a fuller discussion of orientalism in *A Song of Ice and Fire*, see Mat Hardy's "Game of Tropes: The Orientalist Tradition in the Works of G. R. R. Martin," *International Journal of Arts & Sciences* 8 (2015), 409–420, as well as his chapter in this volume.
4 For other examples of military slavery, see Christopher Brown and Philip Morgan, eds., *Arming Slaves: From Classical Times to the Modern Age* (New Haven, CT: Yale University Press, 2006).
5 On slavery in the Islamic world, see Robert Brunschvig, "'Abd," in *Enclopaedia of Islam* (2nd edn.), edited by P. Bearman, T. Bianquis, C. E. Bosworth, E. van Donzel, and W. P. Heinrichs (Leiden: Brill, 1960), 1: 24–40.
6 Matthew Gordon, *The Breaking of a Thousand Swords: A History of the Turkish Military of Samarra (*AH *200–275/815–899* CE*)* (Albany, NY: SUNY Press, 2001), 35.
7 "Appendix A: Retainer Forces in Early Islamic History," in Gordon, *The Breaking of a Thousand Swords*. For a fuller discussion of private retinues in early Islamic history, see Khalil 'Athamina, "Non-Arab Regiments and Private Militias during the Umayyad Period," *Arabica* 45 (1998), 347–378.
8 David Ayalon, "Preliminary Remarks on the Mamluk Military Institution in Islam," in *War, Technology, and Society in the Middle East*, edited by V. J. Perry and M. E. Yapp (London: Oxford University Press, 1975), 47 and Daniel Pipes, *Slave Soldiers and Islam: The Genesis of a Military System* (New Haven, CT: Yale University Press, 1981), 115, n. 42.
9 Words for "slave" in English, French (*esclave*), German (*Sklave*), and Italian (*schiavo*) also derive from Slav. Perhaps this reflects a seventh-century shift to the Balkans and to Slavic peoples as the main source of slavery in Europe. See Michael McCormick, *Origins of the European Economy: Communications and Commerce, ad 300–900* (Cambridge: Cambridge University Press, 2001), 739–740.

10 P. Guichard and Mohamed Meouak, "al-Ṣakāliba, 3. In the Muslim West," in *Encyclopaedia of Islam* (2nd edn.), edited by P. Bearman, T. Bianquis, C. E. Bosworth, E. van Donzel, and W. P. Heinrichs (Leiden: Brill, 1960), 8: 879–81. On the trade of European slaves to the Islamic world, see McCormick, *Origins of the European Economy*, 759–777. See also Matthew Gordon, "Preliminary Remarks on Slaves and Slave Labor in the Third/Ninth Century Abbasid Empire," in *Slaves and Households in the Near East*, edited by Laura Culbertson (Chicago, IL: Oriental Institute at the University of Chicago, 2011), 77.

11 Mohamed Talbi, *L'Émirat aghlabide* (Paris: A. Maisonneuve, 1966), 131–159.

12 See Patricia Crone, *Slaves on Horses: Evolution of the Islamic Polity* (Cambridge: Cambridge University Press, 1980) and Pipes, *Slave Soldiers and Islam*. For the role of religiously motivated warfare along the Arab–Byzantine frontier, see Michael Bonner, *Aristocratic Violence and Holy War* (New Haven, CT: American Oriental Society, 1996), esp. 4–5.

13 Jürgen Paul, *The State and the Military: The Samanid Case* (Bloomington,, IN: Research Institute for Inner Asian Studies, 1994), 4–5.

14 Martin, *A Storm of Swords*, 328–329.

15 John P. Turner, "The *abnāʾ al-dawla*: The Definition and Legitimation of Identity in Response to the Fourth *Fitna*," *Journal of the American Oriental Society* 124 (2004): 1–22.

16 Reuven Amitai, "The Mamlūk Institution, or One Thousand Years of Military Slavery in the Islamic World," in *Arming Slaves: From Classical Times to the Modern Age*, edited by Christopher Brown and Philip Morgan (New Haven, CT: Yale University Press, 2006), 45–46.

17 Abu Daʾud, *Sunan*, Book 37, Number 4288.

18 Muslim, *Sahih Muslim*, Book 41, Number 6959.

19 Orlando Patterson, *Slavery and Social Death: A Comparative Study* (Cambridge, MA: Harvard University Press, 1982).

20 Martin, *A Storm of Swords*, 313–319.

21 Gordon, *The Breaking of a Thousand Swords*, 21–23.

22 Gordon, *The Breaking of a Thousand Swords*, 50–55.

23 Osman S. A. Ismail, "Muʿtaṣim and the Turks," *Bulletin of the School of Oriental and African Studies* 29 (1966), 14–15.

24 Jere Bacharach, "African Military Slaves in the Medieval Middle East: The Case of Iraq (865–955) and Egypt (868–1171)," *International Journal of Middle East Studies* 13 (1981), 471–495.

25 For a brief look into the lives of these non-elite women enslaved to people who were themselves slaves, see Gordon, *The Breaking of a Thousand Swords*, 62–63. Slaves were free to marry under Islamic law and an enslaved man could marry up to two enslaved women: Fuad Matthew Caswell, *The Slave Girls of Baghdad: The Qiyān in the Early Abbasid Era* (London: I. B. Tauris, 2011), 11. The plan to have

these slave armies reproduce failed and future generations of *ghilmān* were purchased from abroad.

26 Crone, *Slaves on Horses*, 78–79.

27 Martin, *A Storm of Swords*, 380–381.

28 "Book of the Stranger," directed by Daniel Sackheim, written by David Venioff and D. B. Weiss, in *Game of Thrones*, season 6, HBO, first aired on May 15, 2016.

29 For the Tahirids, see C. E. Bosworth, "The Ṭāhirids and Ṣaffārids," in *The Cambridge History of Iran, vol. 4: The Period from the Arab Invasion to the Seljuqs*, edited by R. N. Frye, 90–135 (Cambridge, UK: Cambridge University Press, 1975).

30 Crone, *Slaves on Horses*, 82.

31 George R. R. Martin, *A Song of Ice and Fire, Book Five: A Dance with Dragons* (New York: Bantam, 2011).

32 For the early Ghaznavids, see C. E. Bosworth, *The Ghaznavids: Their Empire in Afghanistan and Eastern Iran 994–1040* (Edinburgh: University of Edinburgh Press, 1963).

33 Peter Jackson, "The 'Mamlūk' Institution in Early Muslim India," *Journal of the Royal Asiatic Society of Great Britain and Ireland* 2 (1990): 340–358.

34 See Robert Irwin, *The Middle East in the Middle Ages: The Early Mamluk Sultanate, 1250–1328* (Carbondale: Southern Illinois University Press, 1986).

35 See Baki Tezcan, *The Second Ottoman Empire: Political and Social Transformation in the Early Modern World* (Cambridge: Cambridge University Press, 2010), 191–223.

36 Allen R. Myers, "Slave Soldiers and State Politics in Early ʿAlawi Morocco, 1668–1727," *International Journal of African Historical Studies* 16 (1983): 39–48.

37 Quoted in Amitai, "The Mamlūk Institution," 67.

Part III

Women and Children

9

Rocking Cradles and Hatching Dragons

Parents in *Game of Thrones*

Janice Liedl

Robert Baratheon is gripped with dread on learning of the marriage between Daenerys Targaryen and Khal Drogo. Pausing between Winterfell to King's Landing, the king paints a grim picture for his friend, Ned Stark, of what this news represents. "A Targaryen boy crosses with a Dothraki horde at his back. The scum will join him," Robert predicts.[1] He thinks that Daenerys herself poses little direct threat to his dynasty, but her potential as a mother raises his concern. Beyond the last Targaryen's maternal prospects, Westeros teems with parents ready to fight to the death for their children and for the legacies they represent.

Medieval and Renaissance parents operated on similar principles: fathers and mothers built family legacies along with breeding new generations of sons and daughters. Women were not only expected to bear children: once mothers, they needed to raise and support their sons and daughters. A father's job was to protect his children as well as to see to their education and advancement. Some historical parents, such as Margaret Paston (1421–1484), an English noblewoman living during the Wars of the Roses (1455–1485), or France's Queen Blanche of Castile (1188–1252), withstood sieges and rallied armies to protect their children against rivals or rebels. Such were the stakes for noble parents in tough historical times.

It was just as easy for fathers or mothers to fumble these dangerous duties. Both John Marshal (d. 1165) and Diarmait, king of Leinster (c. 1110–1171), offered their sons as hostages for their own good behavior and then promptly broke those promises. John handed over his younger son as hostage to King Stephen (r. 1135–1154) during a civil war over the English throne in 1152. He then laughed off the royal threat to kill the boy, cheekily observing that he could produce more children if William died.[2] Fortunately for the little boy (who grew up to be the epitome of medieval knighthood), the hostage keeper backed down. Diarmait of Leinster was less fortunate in his gamble over his youngest son, whom he had yielded as hostage. The boy, not yet out of his teens when his

Game of Thrones versus History: Written in Blood, First Edition. Edited by Brian A. Pavlac.

father surrendered him to secure a peace, paid the ultimate price when Ireland's High King had him beheaded as the price of Diarmait's rebellion.[3] In *Game of Thrones*, Edmure Tully believed that Jaime Lannister would have his infant son hurled at the walls of Riverrun, and so surrendered the castle.[4]

What Robert Baratheon misses as he frets about the threat posed to Westeros by a child of Targaryen and Dothraki background is the power of parents. Both mothers and fathers shift the fates of the Seven Kingdoms, whether operating out of love or calculation, sacrifice, or vengeance, just as they did throughout centuries of history. Mothers such as Catelyn Stark, Cersei Lannister, and Olenna Tyrell fight fiercely for their children and grandchildren. Fathers of the Seven Kingdoms such as Ned Stark, Walder Frey, and Tywin Lannister run the gamut from caring parent to power-hungry patriarch. Even the childless sometimes operate as parents: consider the impact of Daenerys and Melisandre through their inhuman children, draconic and demonic. All attest to the power of parents in *Game of Thrones*. Not every child was grateful for such parental attention; nevertheless, even broken families show us the importance of parenting—in both history and George R. R. Martin's world.

Nature versus Nurture

What is it that makes a parent? From one perspective, the role begins with conception. Historical cultures did not have a modern scientific understanding of human genetics, but they knew that children reflected their parents. Ancient philosophers debated whether children were formed solely from the man's seed nurtured in a woman's body or shaped by both. This first branch of thought believed that children naturally resembled the father, unless the mother's womb was a defective environment. Such a view aligns with Westeros beliefs, as shown in Ned Stark's realization that the very fair royal Baratheon children cannot be Robert's get because for many generations the royal family has produced only children with black hair.

A second branch of medieval philosophers emphasized the role of the environment in shaping babies. Their idea of what constituted the environment differed, however, from modern definitions. They looked less at the air that pregnant women breathed or the food they ate and more at what they saw or heard. The medieval physician Maimonides (1135–1204) shared an old story about how one man ensured a handsome son. The hopeful father commissioned a portrait of a beautiful child and commanded his wife to look at it unblinkingly during marital relations. When she gave birth, Maimonides explained, the boy resembled the portrait and looked nothing like his (presumably less handsome) father.[5] Perception through any of the five senses could affect development in this way, they believed. For instance, if women listened to music a great deal, they supposedly bore children who were musical.

Sometimes, when the children's appearance or characteristics differed from those of their parents, the cause was not the environment, but rather conception out of wedlock. Such progeny did not have an easy time. Illegitimate children might get no support from their fathers, just as Gendry and Barra live as the unacknowledged bastards of Robert Baratheon. Historically, medieval law punished illegitimate families with restrictions on social recognition and job opportunities.

But even legitimate children could face a difficult life. Unless limited by the law of primogeniture (whereby the eldest son inherited all of the family property), fathers of legitimate children decided both how their children would live and what, if anything, they would inherit. Ancient Roman patriarchs, before the rise of Christianity, could abandon children to die, whether because they doubted their legitimate birth, worried about their viability, or thought that the family lacked the resources to feed another mouth. This practice is generally called exposure, because the infants were left exposed to the elements. Some of these infants might be taken by families who needed a slave, but more likely they faced a horrific death in a hostile world—unless they were summarily dispatched by the parent personally.[6] Tywin Lannister might have despised and disregarded Tyrion, but at least he did not abandon the child in infancy, as an ancient Roman might have done.

Some historians have argued that parents before the Renaissance had little emotional attachment to children, even their own, and that these societies did not see childhood as differing much from adulthood.[7] Child mortality in the medieval world was as high as one in three, due to disease, injury, and malnutrition. When medieval parents christened newborns with the name that a deceased older sibling had borne, this was considered proof of parental detachment.[8] Walder Frey's disconnected approach to his many daughters and granddaughters, all lined up as prospective brides for Edmure Tully before the Red Wedding in "The Rains of Castamere" (season 3), endorses the historical hypothesis of uncaring parents. The brutal Frey, however, is not much admired in the Seven Kingdoms for his harsh fatherly attitude: he is the model of a bad father. A more disturbing parental betrayal comes when Stannis and Selyse Baratheon sacrifice Shireen, seeking the favor of the Lord of Light in an upcoming battle ("The Dance of Dragons," season 5). These political ploys recall John Marshal's calculated surrender of his hostage son, William, showing that political advantage sometimes trumped the parent–child bond. Some medieval parents endangered their children for much less, such as when the Frankish Queen Fredegund (d. 597) tried to kill her daughter by slamming a chest lid down upon the young woman's neck, all in a fit of temper.[9]

Rather than seeing children as expendable pawns, historical fathers and mothers were normally expected to treasure them. Consider a fifteenth-century story about a young girl badly injured by a fallen tree. Her father rushed to her rescue, "his heart wrung with an agony of grief: yet, lifting the log with some difficulty, he raised her in his hands. Then the fountains of his eyes were loosed." The tale concludes with the desperate parents restoring their daughter to life and health through the miraculous intervention of the deceased King Henry VI (r. 1421–1471), to whom they prayed in their distress.[10] These medieval parents' devastation recalls the grief and worry weighing down Ned and Catelyn Stark after Bran's horrific fall in the first episode. While some historical parents may have felt little or no emotional bond with their offspring, the Starks' heartfelt love for their injured son would have been widely lauded in the Middle Ages.

Father Knows Best

The Starks' concern for Bran is complicated both by Ned's royal summons and by their responsibility for their other children. When Ned travels to the court, he brings his daughters with him, just as many historical parents did. Families advanced at court, making marriages and connections. Sansa is to marry Joffrey, a royal heir, while Catelyn hopes that the court will refine Arya. Similarly, Princess Myrcella is sent to Dorne as a promised bride to the heir, Trystane Martell, hopefully securing peace between the Lannisters and the Martells. These strategies were identical to those pursued by medieval and Renaissance noble parents placing their children with other families in hopes of cementing an alliance. This was known as fostering, a practice whereby children lived, usually for years at a time, with another family of equal or higher social rank. The foster parents would educate and supervise their young charge as if the child were their own son or daughter.

Many foster experiences ended in marriage, or at least in an enduring family friendship. Arthur Plantagenet, Lord Lisle (d. 1542), and his second wife, Honor Grenville (1492–1566), advanced their children's interests through fostering and courtly appointments. Arthur Plantagenet, an illegitimate son of Edward IV and companion to his nephew Henry VIII, was appointed the king's deputy of Calais in 1533. His stepdaughter, Anne, became a lady-in-waiting at the court of Henry VIII (r. 1509–1547) thanks to Lord Lisle's connections and her mother's lavish gifts to the royal household. Other Lisle children and stepchildren were fostered in elite households across both England and France. Like Ned Stark and Catelyn Stark, these parents used appointments and relations to secure their children's futures. Sadly, as Ned Stark also discovered, close connections with the royal family were no safeguard for the Lisle patriarch when crisis struck. Arthur Plantagenet was arrested for treason in 1540 and then died of a heart attack upon his vindication two years later. The heartbroken Honor Grenville retired to the country after Arthur's death, leaving their children to struggle at the treacherous royal court.[11]

Not every father or mother sent their children away of their own free will. Balon Greyjoy sends his only surviving son, Theon, to Winterfell less as an honored foster child than as a hostage, just as Diarmait of Leinster and John Marshal did with their boys in the twelfth century. Sons were the pawns most frequently taken as hostages for good behavior in the Middle Ages, probably because they were presumed the most valued family members. That Theon, as ward, is treated as well as a Stark child corresponds with medieval ideas about hostages. Nevertheless, hostages' lives were never without worry. Young William Marshal could have died for his father's resistance to King Stephen. Instead, and not unusually in the long history of hostage exchanges, he survived thanks to Stephen's code of conduct. Eventually William followed his father as England's Lord Marshal, the king's chief officer of horses, serving Stephen's rival, nephew, and successor, Henry II (r. 1154–1189). But it wasn't enough just to survive by being a hostage. Hostages also had to remain on good terms with their far distant family. One Welsh prince held as a hostage by Henry II was treated so well that, upon his eventual release, he was scorned by his fellow countrymen as "Sais," their word for Englishman.[12] So, too, is Theon scorned by the ironborn, even by his sister, for not having been raised in "the Old Way."

Clearly it was difficult for parents to both protect their children and launch them successfully into a dangerous world. Too many were judged to err on the side of caution and carefulness, raising children unable to cope with the harsh realities of life. Consider the observations of Konrad Sam (1483–1533), pastor of Ulm, a city on the Danube River in the Holy Roman Empire. His complaint has a timeless ring:

> Do not do as is now done in the world, where children are taught to rule, but not to serve; to curse and insult, but not to pray; to ride, but not to speak properly. Children today are badly raised; not only do parents permit them their every selfish wish, but they even show them the way to do it.[13]

Such condemnation might be equally made of Cersei's indulgence of Joffrey's every whim, first as heir to the throne and then as king, until she is shocked by his ingratitude. Both Tywin and Tyrion consider Cersei's permissive parenting to have a big part in why Joffrey is such a monster.

Cersei is not the only problematic mother in Westeros and not even the worst. Lysa Arryn, mother to Robin, the heir to the Vale, might be the worst in terms of preparing her child for adult life. Lysa indulges and coddles her son to a degree that appalls every visitor. Sweetrobin has never lifted a sword or seen much of the world until his mother is pushed through the Moon Door by her new consort, Petyr Baelish ("Mockingbird," season 4). Littlefinger, as stepfather to the bereaved young lord, belatedly introduces his charge to fighting and other physical activities. Petyr appears a better parent than Lysa has been.

Contrast Robin's stunted upbringing with the opportunities afforded Baldwin IV of Jerusalem (r. 1174–1185) at his father's court. Given an excellent physical and political education by his father, the teenage heir was ready to rule when the old king suddenly died. Courtiers exclaimed how Baldwin looked, talked, and walked like his father. The young king was acknowledged as skilled in horsemanship and scholarship. But these good qualities were sadly tempered by the horrible leprosy that eventually killed Baldwin IV at only 24 years of age.[14] Not all the preparation in the world could counter diseases or other dangers that lurked among the great houses.

Baldwin IV's story shows how many skills medieval parents expected their children to master. Not every child received such opportunities or appreciated his or her parents' attentions. Tywin Lannister works hard raising Jaime, his eldest son and heir, to be the epitome of Westeros nobility. When Jaime struggles to master reading, Tywin forces him to spend hours every day with books ("The Old Gods and the New," season 2). He also trains Jaime in the art of war. Tywin's parenting of his other children is less personalized. Tywin uses Cersei to cement alliances, first through an unhappy marriage to Robert Baratheon and then through an unwanted betrothal to Loras Tyrell. He treats Tyrion even worse. Tywin blames his youngest son for his wife's death in childbirth. Further deemed an embarrassment on account of his dwarfism, Tywin's most intelligent child suffers his father's cruelty and callousness. Tywin's parenting achieved results at the cost of strained family relations.

The Families That Fight Together

Even when he treats them harshly, Tywin believes that he protects the Lannister children and grandchildren. This determination began when Tywin betrayed the mad Targaryen king and continues up to the marriage he arranges between the new king and his only daughter. Tywin's behind-the-scenes approach to politics and family power mirrors that of one of medieval England's most infamous noblemen: "the Kingmaker," Richard Neville, earl of Warwick (1428–1471). Neville helped his cousin, the Yorkist King Edward IV (r. 1461–1470, 1471–1483), to seize England's crown from Henry VI in 1461. Warwick's estates were not as rich as Casterly Rock, but he became the most powerful individual in Yorkist England, perhaps even more than the king. Warwick had only daughters to provide for and, like Tywin, married the eldest off to the king's younger brother for political advantage. That marriage, however, did not cement a peace. Edward IV and the earl of Warwick fell out not just over the marriage of the latter's daughter, but also over the king's own love match, which stymied Warwick's planned French alliance. In 1470 Warwick changed sides and put Henry VI back on the throne. Edward returned the next year and the Kingmaker died in the Battle of Barnet.[15]

At least Warwick's death was not at his child's hand, as Tywin Lannister and Roose Bolton both experience. Parricide, parent killing, carried a high price throughout history. Roman law had this kind of offender sewn into a sack and tossed into the sea or a river, while in the Middle Ages father killers were usually beheaded or hanged.[16] Few parricides are documented among the medieval elite, probably because convicted murderers had to forfeit property. More than loss of life, the loss of property risked the entire family's land, wealth, and title. Bereaved relatives had good reason to stay silent if they suspected parricide among their kin.

Short of such killings, historical parents did experience wrenching disloyalty from their children and grandchildren. Edward II of England (r. 1307–1327) famously favored his male companions over his wife and son, the future Edward III (r. 1327–1377). When Queen Isabella (1295–1358) and Prince Edward fled into exile, Edward II seized their estates, threatening dire punishments, so that "all other sons shall take example thereby of disobeying their lords and fathers."[17] Edward and his mother countered the unpopular king by invading England with the support of many English nobles. Edward II panicked and fled the Tower of London, but was soon captured. The disgraced king was forced to abdicate his throne and soon died in mysterious circumstances, being rumored to have been murdered at the orders of his wife and her lover.[18] Edward III soon forced Isabella out of his inner circle, not unlike what Dowager Queen Cersei experiences in Tommen's zealously reformed court.

Such family disputes could be dangerous not just for individuals but for the future of the realm. Consider Sancho's Rebellion of 1282 against the aging Alfonso X of Castile (r. 1252–1284). Alfonso was famous as a poet and scientist but made bad financial and political decisions. His eldest son, Sancho (r. 1284–1295), revolted, proclaiming that Alfonso was a tyrant, possibly even a mad leper. The rebels dethroned Alfonso, who soon died, broken, in disgrace. Still, Sancho's younger brothers repeatedly caused trouble for the young king.[19] Sancho's rebellion has parallels with the crisis in Dorne that eliminates Doran Martell. Ellaria Sand decries Doran's failure to avenge the death of his brother and her lover, Oberyn, by going to war with the Lannisters. Once her attempt at assassinating Myrcella at the Dornish court is foiled, Ellaria feigns submission to Doran, only to poison the departing princess ("Mother's Mercy," season 5). Disobedience turns into a coup in which the Sand Snakes assassinate Doran and his son ("The Red Woman," season 6).

Every family has its conflicts, in Westeros and in history alike. Sometimes the stakes are far smaller. Arya Stark feels alienated from her mother, Catelyn, who emphasizes needlework and other conventionally feminine skills. Arya bonds with her father, who hires Syrio Forel from Braavos to tutor her in sword fighting. After Ned's execution, Catelyn is forced to fill both fatherly and motherly roles, for example when she negotiates for and advises her son, Robb, the successor to his father. Robb does not always appreciate this interference.

Historically, one interfering dowager was Catherine de' Medici (1519–1589), queen mother during much of the French Wars of Religion (1562–1598) between Roman Catholics and Protestants (known in France as Huguenots). According to popular lore, Catherine masterminded one of the wars' chief atrocities: the St. Bartholomew's Day massacre of 1572, an event that bears comparison with the Red Wedding (which costs Catelyn and Robb their lives). A marriage between Catherine's royal daughter Margot and the royal family's chief Protestant rival, Henry of Bourbon, was supposed to bring peace and compromise. But one political faction used the gathering to kill as many Protestants as they could find. The bloodbath began in the streets of Paris and spread across France. Henry only escaped death under the protection of his bride and by swearing to convert to Roman Catholicism. Many accounts described the queen mother in the most unmotherly terms and blamed her for the tragedy. One can compare Catherine's implication in the massacre with Cersei's masterminding of the wildfire attack on the High Sparrow and on all of those in the Sept of Baelor ("The Winds of Winter," season 6). In some stories, guilt over the massacre drove Catherine's son, Charles IX of France (r. 1560–1574), to penitential madness just before his untimely death.[20] Thanks to such tales, Catherine de' Medici is commonly described as a mother so ambitious that she destroyed her child in order to defend his throne—a chilling historical parallel to Tommen's suicidal leap.

Short of mass murder, mothers fought for their children and their children's benefit, both in history and in *Game of Thrones*. Cersei struggles to assert her power as Queen Regent for Joffrey and Tommen, but this proves to be a thankless task. In 1469 Margaret Paston had similar problems as she defended Caister Castle against the duke of Norfolk's forces until the family's small force surrendered. Her absent son had ignored his mother's many dire warnings until the castle was forfeit and the family nearly ruined.[21] Eleanor of Aquitaine (1122–1204), one of the most formidable medieval matriarchs, also fought tirelessly for her children's and grandchildren's interests. Married first to King Louis VII of France (r. 1137–1180) and then, after an annulment, to King Henry II of England, Eleanor held the rich duchy of Aquitaine in her own right. A mother many times over (she gave Louis only daughters but had both sons and daughters with Henry), Eleanor unwisely supported her sons' failed rebellions against their father and spent 15 years as Henry II's honored captive more than as his dear spouse.[22] Widowed, Eleanor continued her political machinations until her death, advising her royal sons and arranging marriages for her many grandchildren. After the horrific deaths of Mace Tyrell and his children Margaery and Loras in Cersei's bombing, his mother, Olenna Tyrell, makes alliances with Targaryen and Martell to seek vengeance for her losses ("The Winds of Winter," season 6).

Olenna's actions regarding Margaery's betrothal to Joffrey and her reminiscences about her own youthful road to marriage recall other aspects of Eleanor of Aquitaine's colorful life. As heiress of Aquitaine, Eleanor never had to compete for a suitor's interest, as Olenna revealed she did. Nevertheless, the two women share a similar style. There were scandalous stories that described Eleanor accompanying her pious first husband on his crusade while shamelessly garbed as an Amazon and riding a horse astride.[23] Olenna Tyrell, known as the "Queen of Thorns," also shows no shame for having seduced her sister's betrothed into marriage and for poisoning Joffrey ("Oathkeeper," season 4).

Both women were heavily invested in their grandchildren's lives. In 1200 Eleanor, now dowager queen, made the long journey to Castile, where one of her daughters was raising a royal family. Bypassing the elder granddaughter, Urraca, Eleanor picked 12-year-old Blanche as a more likely consort to secure a peace alliance between France and England. Blanche (1188–1252) married the young French prince Louis, a grandson of Eleanor's first husband, and her son eventually flourished on the French throne as "Saint" Louis IX (r. 1226–1270). Blanche's rivals sneeringly dubbed her "Dame Hersent" ("Lady Wolf"), but the widowed Blanche successfully quelled rebels while her son grew to manhood.

At 60 years of age Blanche of Castile still remained a formidable woman. She governed France as regent again when her son Louis IX led the Seventh Crusade (1248–1254). While King Louis suffered military defeat and debilitating disease on that ill-fated crusade, Blanche worried for her children. A younger son died crusading, while the king nearly succumbed to illness, languishing as a prisoner of war. Blanche herself died during the long wait for his return. She was mourned as a prudent, wise, and valiant queen who had been like a mother to her people: "she who never while she lived did know the people's spite nor blame."[24]

Some Fairly Odd Parents

In her dying days, Blanche joined a community of nuns. Among the cloistered women she found comfort and possibly even another kind of parental role. Medieval Christianity honored priests as fathers, while nuns who led cloistered communities were addressed as "mother." These terms reflected the power that churchmen and churchwomen wielded in politics and within communities due to their parental roles in religious orders.[25] In *Game of Thrones*, the High Septon in the Faith of the Seven held a similar paternalistic power, although the High Sparrow overextends his reach when he tries to control the crown. Meanwhile, the Hand of self-proclaimed King Stannis Baratheon, Davos Seaworth, lost his only son in the Battle of Blackwater, yet he comes to cherish young princess Shireen Baratheon. Upon discovering Melisandre's role in the sacrificial burning to death of the princess, Davos convinces Jon Snow to punish the Red Woman ("The Winds of Winter," season 6).[26] These examples show that fathering or bearing children was not the only way to parenthood, either in the Middle Ages or in *Game of Thrones*.

As for childlessness, sometimes it was less from choice than the result of tragedy. Daenerys Targaryen discovers this when she bears a stillborn, monstrous son because of the vengeful godswife Mirri Maz Duur ("Fire and Blood," season 1). Her parental care, however, soon has a new focus: the three firebreathers hatched on Khal Drogo's funeral pyre. Now known as "Mother of Dragons," Daenerys inspires awe and terror early on in her campaigns thanks to her devoted dragon children. The liberated slaves of Yunkai call Daenerys "mother," *mhysa*, after her army conquers their city ("Mhysa," season 3). In this respect, Daenerys echoes the great unmarried and childless English monarch, Elizabeth I (r. 1558–1603), who described herself as "a good mother of my country."[27]

Yet, even though Daenerys may be a mother to her many followers and to her three dragons, she can never escape her traumatic maternal loss, as her visions of Drogo and of her son prove in "Valar Morghulis" (season 2). Daenerys' pain might have something to do with how dark magic was implicated in these deaths. Actual history supports this interpretation. During the Reformation, when Protestants and Catholics were at odds, they accused each other of unnatural practices that caused miscarriages and stillbirths. During the 1520s and the 1530s Protestant leaders in Bern, Switzerland, sponsored plays that charged Catholic priests with demonic sorcery. Their devilish spells supposedly caused childless women to lose their long-awaited pregnancies.[28] This historical supernatural fear corresponds not only to Daernerys' painful loss but also with Melisandre's witchcraft. Melisandre not only targeted children such as Shireen, but even horrifically mimicked parenthood when she gave birth to the shadow creature that killed Renly Baratheon.

Witch crazes gripped Europe for more than a hundred years, beginning in the late fifteenth century. Much of the fear focused on the harm posed to mothers and young children. Jealous witches were thought to target new mothers and infants with poison or smothering. The midwife or other birth attendants were frequently accused, but fearful communities charged any local woman, even some men, with alleged acts of *maleficium* (harmful magic).[29] Other folklore held that witches nursed demonic helpers in a perverted, horrific contrast to the healthy mothering of human children, then sent these familiars to sour their neighbors' milk or sicken their families. Melisandre's child sacrifices and magical attacks mirror the accusations circulated during the period of European witch hunts.[30] Instead of supporting expectant parents, witches threatened mothers and fathers, endangering families at their most vulnerable.

The parents in Westeros have as many problems as any historical parents in the Middle Ages and Renaissance—maybe even more, because they were raising families in a world where dragons and magic hold sway. Walder Frey might care little for his individual progeny, but few other parents in Martin's world, or in the record of history, are so cavalier. Their children's futures were of the utmost interest to most historical men and women, whether queens or commoners. The same is true in the Seven Kingdoms, where the majority of fathers and mothers care deeply about their families, whether this shows in the iron control of Tywin Lannister or in the coddling of Lysa Arryn. The most successful patriarchs and matriarchs, in history or in Martin's world, both protect their family and prepare their children to become one day strong and successful parents of the next generation.

Notes

1 "The Kingsroad," directed by Tim Van Patten, written by David Benioff and D. B. Weiss, in *Game of Thrones*, season 1, HBO, first aired on April 24, 2011.
2 David Crouch, "Marshal, John (d. 1165)," in *Oxford Dictionary of National Biography*, 2007 [2004] (accessed March 16, 2016 at http://www.oxforddnb.com/view/article/18122).
3 Adam Kosto, *Hostages in the Middle Ages* (Oxford: Oxford University Press, 2012), 40.
4 "No One," directed by Mark Mylod, written by Bryan Cogan, in *Game of Thrones*, season 6, HBO, first aired on June 12, 2016.
5 Wendy Doniger and Gregory Spinner, "Misconceptions: Female Imaginations and Male Fantasies in Parental Imprinting," *Daedalus* 127.1 (1998), 105.
6 W. V. Harris, "Child-Exposure in the Roman Empire," *Journal of Roman Studies* 84 (1994), 6. doi: 10.2307/300867.
7 For more on this topic, see Helle Strandgaard Jensen and Magnus Qvistgaard's chapter in this volume.
8 Philippe Aries, *Centuries of Childhood: A Social History of Family Life*, translated by Robert Baldick (New York: Vintage, 1962), 39–40.
9 Gregory of Tours, *The History of the Franks*, translated with an introduction by Lewis Thorpe (Harmondsworth: Penguin Books, 1974), 521–522.
10 Barbara A. Hanawalt, "Narratives of a Nurturing Culture: Parents and Neighbors in Medieval England," in Barbara A. Hanawalt, *"Of Good and Ill Repute": Gender and Social Control in Medieval England* (Oxford: Oxford University Press, 1998), 162.
11 David Grummitt, "Plantagenet, Arthur, Viscount Lisle (*b.* before 1472, *d.* 1542)," in *Oxford Dictionary of National Biography*, 2008 [2004] (accessed March 16, 2016, http://www.oxforddnb.com/view/article/22355).
12 Kosto, *Hostages in the Middle Ages*, 44–46.
13 Quoted in Steven Ozment, *When Fathers Ruled: Family Life in Reformation Europe* (Cambridge, MA: Harvard University Press, 1983), 133.
14 Bernard Hamilton, *The Leper King and His Heirs: Baldwin IV and the Crusader Kingdom of Jerusalem* (Cambridge: Cambridge University Press, 2005), 43.

15 William E. Welsh, "Death of a Kingmaker," *Military Heritage* 15.3 (2013): 52–69.

16 Jean-Marie Carbasse, "Parricide," in *Encyclopedia of the Middle Ages*, 2016 (accessed November 2, 2016 at http://www.oxfordreference.com/view/10.1093/acref/9780227679319.001.0001/acref-9780227679319-e-2117).

17 Quoted in W. Mark Ormrod, *Edward III* (New Haven, CT: Yale University Press, 2011), 36.

18 Ormrod, *Edward III*, 43–47, 67, 90–91.

19 Björn Weiler, "Kings and Sons: Princely Rebellions and the Structures of Revolt in Western Europe, c. 1170– c. 1280," *Historical Research* 82.215 (2009), 28–30, doi: 10.1111/j.1468–2281.2007.00450.x.

20 N. M. Sutherland, "Catherine de Medici: The Legend of the Wicked Italian Queen," *The Sixteenth Century Journal* 9.2 (1978), 49–52.

21 Frances and Joseph Gies, *A Medieval Family: The Pastons of Fifteenth-Century England* (New York: HarperCollins, 1998), 216–227; Richard Barber, ed., *The Pastons: A Family in the Wars of the Roses* (Harmondsworth: Penguin Books, 1984), 155–158.

22 Jean Flori, *Eleanor of Aquitaine: Queen and Rebel*, translated by Olive Classe (Edinburgh: Edinburgh University Press, 2004), 110–114.

23 Flori, *Eleanor of Aquitaine*, 43–46.

24 Régine Pernoud, *Blanche of Castile*, translated by Henry Noel (London: Collins, 1975), 290.

25 Clarissa W. Atkinson, *The Oldest Vocation: Christian Motherhood in the Middle Ages* (Ithaca, NY: Cornell University Press, 1991), 95.

26 In the novels, Davos has seven sons, four of whom die at the Battle of Blackwater, yet the younger ones are still a live. The television series creates a closer connection between Shireen and Davos.

27 "Queen Elizabeth's First Speech before Parliament, February 10, 1559," in *Elizabeth I: Collected Works*, edited by Leah S. Marcus, Janel M. Mueller, and Mary Beth Rose (Chicago, IL: University of Chicago Press, 2000), 58 n. 9.

28 Glenn Ehrstine, "Motherhood and Protestant Polemics: Stillbirth in Hans von Rüte's *Abgötterei* (1531)," in *Maternal Measures: Figuring Caregiving in the Early Modern Period*, edited by Naomi J. Miller and Naomi Yaveh (Aldershot: Ashgate, 2000), 123–127.

29 Lyndal Roper, *Oedipus and the Devil: Witchcraft, Sexuality and Religion in Early Modern Europe* (London: Routledge, 1994), 209–211.

30 Brian A. Pavlac, *Witch Hunts in the Western World: Persecution and Punishment from the Inquisition through the Salem Witch Trials* (Westport, CT: Greenwood, 2009), 194.

10

"Oh, my sweet summer child"

Children and Childhood in *Game of Thrones*

Helle Strandgaard Jensen and Magnus Qvistgaard

Children are central to a large number of *Game of Thrones'* many narratives, which makes childhood a crucial theme in the series. The realities of a cruel world are often perceived from the point of view of the five Stark children and their half-brother Jon Snow, even if they are only between 3 and 14 years old when the story begins.[1] The emphasis on the children's experience of the fictitious medieval universe only increases after they lose their father and are separated from their mother. Similarly, other children are vital to the *Game of Thrones'* main plot: Joffrey and Tommen Baratheon become kings as young teenagers, and Daenerys Targaryen gives birth to her dragons at the age of 15 in the TV series or 13 in the books. Following the many young characters, the viewer confronts what it meant to be a child in a harsh world where the daily lives of children and adults looked much the same.

In modern society the childhood ideal is that of an innocent, protected age where children's lives consist of school and play, and not much else. Contrary to this, the lives of children and young people in *Game of Thrones* are very similar to those of grownups: they share adult responsibilities; have to fend for themselves from an early age; and sometimes even rule entire kingdoms. Throughout all this, we find out that children can be just as wicked as adults when they fight for power or survival.

Game of Thrones thereby touches on a central question in childhood history posed by the field's founding father, Philippe Ariés: Did childhood exist in the Middle Ages? Was childhood something distinct and different from the adult world? The series also provokes viewers to think about children as independent, historical agents: Are children and young teenagers capable of acting and ruling on their own? What happens when their individual wishes clash with their families' quest for power? These questions about how childhood is narrated and enacted in the *Game of Thrones* universe can be studied by introducing key issues in childhood history related to the later Middle Ages and early Renaissance in Europe.

Game of Thrones versus History: Written in Blood, First Edition. Edited by Brian A. Pavlac.

"Tell Bran he is coming too"

In the series' first episode a deserter from the Night's Watch is captured.[2] According to the law, the punishment for breaking the oath of the Watch is death, and the deserter therefore has to be executed. Ned Stark, Lord of Winterfell and Warden of the North, is to carry out the sentence himself, as is the custom in the northern region—"always the old way," the saying goes. As Ned is preparing to depart, he turns to his ward, Theon Greyjoy, asking him to prepare the horses. He also asks him to "tell Bran he is coming too," thereby indicating that his son Bran, who is ten years old, will join Ned and his older male family members for the execution. "Ten is too young to see such things," Bran's mother, Catelyn, objects. Ned replies: "He won't be a boy forever, and winter is coming." The beheading is then seen from Bran's point of view. The boy stares directly at the kneeling man and does not look away when Ned severs the head in a spray of blood. "You did well," his half-brother Jon Snow comments afterwards. The shock effect of the scene is clear. The modern-day viewer clearly understands that Westeros is harsh, cruel, and unforgiving: very different from our modern, protective societies. By adopting Bran's point of view, *Game of Thrones* efficiently establishes the otherness of Westerosi life and places it in a contrast with what viewers associate with the experience of being a child. This distance between modern childhood and childhood in Westeros is stunning, even more so considering that in the book Bran is seven, not ten. For a modern TV drama aimed at an adult audience, *Game of Thrones* stands out in the extent to which its narrative acknowledges children's point of view. Both the TV series and the books on which it is based emphasize that childhood experiences in medieval and early modern times were very different from what they are today.

Being the son of Ned Stark, Bran is a child of a noble family, as indeed are many of the other key child characters. In the series, most of the major characters come from noble houses. Yet, historically, it is important to remember that noble families were a tiny minority. In medieval Europe, noble families are estimated to have made up between only 0.5 and 10 percent of the total population, depending on country and period.[3] The lives of noble children in the Middle Ages were therefore not typical of most young people, whose lives are unknown and forgotten. This difference is also reflected in *Game of Thrones*. Children with different family backgrounds are introduced in Arya's narrative after her father, Ned Stark, is executed for treason. To save her from being captured by the Lannisters, Yoren, her rescuer, cuts Arya's hair short to make her look like a boy and tells her: "You are Arin, the orphan boy; nobody asks an orphan any questions because nobody gives three shits."[4] Thus, from being the daughter of a major noble, a station in life characterized by strict social control, Arya becomes a nobody, a boy in a million, whom no one sees or cares about.

Arya's change of identity is one of many examples in *Game of Thrones* that demonstrate a point repeated by almost all childhood historians: that "childhood," what we consider to be good, right, and best for children, has changed from time to time and place to place.[5] Even though children do appear to have had some common features that are recognized throughout history (they are less mature, less independent, and less experienced), how childhood is perceived has changed over time.[6] In *Game of Thrones* the changing conditions of childhood are explicitly acknowledged through comparisons of what children born during the "long summer" know of life and what is expected of children who from young age have experienced the rough life during winter. "Old Nan" tells Bran that he, who is a "sweet summer's child," knows nothing of fear, while Ned tells Arya that she has to understand that life, including what is expected of children, is going to be different now that winter is coming.[7]

Childhood History and Parents' Emotional Investment

As an academic field, the history of childhood essentially began with Philippe Ariés' book *Centuries of Childhood* (published in French in 1960 and in English in 1962).[8] In this book Ariés claimed that childhood did not exist in the Middle Ages. From around the age of five, he argued, children were no longer viewed as being different from adults but were counted as part of the general population. Medieval society had no concept of childhood as a special time in life. Not until the fifteenth or sixteenth century, Ariés claimed, did childhood come to be considered as a special stage, different from adulthood. This revolutionary idea provoked many other scholars to investigate children in the past, and thus the history of childhood became a distinct academic discipline. As a result of further research, historians have since rejected Ariés' theory. They have thoroughly demonstrated how medieval laws and religious texts do speak of different stages of childhood as being distinct from adulthood. Today we understand that people in the Middle Ages did in fact have a notion of childhood, that childhood was a special time in the human lifespan, and that children were perceived to be different from adults. Yet historians have also been able to show that this notion was very different from today's concept of childhood. While medieval children were seen as children, not as mini-adults, they still led lives very different from those of moderns.[9]

Ariés' rejection of a medieval concept of childhood, however, was not his most controversial claim. Scholars have criticized him mostly for claiming that medieval parents did not invest emotionally in their children. With very high mortality rates among infants and no conception of childhood as a special time in life, Ariés argued, parents could not afford to care deeply about their offspring. As a result, they treated children with indifference, if not neglect.

In *Game of Thrones* we frequently encounter children as the objects of neglect and cruelty. One of the most extreme examples from the series might be Stannis Baratheon's wife, Selyse, who on the one hand has the bodies of her stillborn sons preserved and kept in her chamber, yet on the other despises her own daughter, Shireen, a lonely and insecure girl. The narrative's point of view makes us strongly sympathize with Shireen. Selyse's moral depravity is further underscored when she sacrifices her own daughter to the Lord of Light, although it is an action that later drives her to suicide. Equally callous is the wildling Craster's treatment of his progeny. Craster not only commits incest with his daughters, but also abandons his own sons to the White Walkers.[10] Further, Old Nan tells Bran about the old days, which were so bad that women smothered their children. Infanticide, we learn, is not accepted in Westeros, yet harsh life during the long winters could drive parents to such extremes.

Contrary to Ariès, sources from all over Europe during the Middle Ages confirm that parents did care about their children. In her book *Childhood in the Middle Ages*, Shulamith Shahar draws on available sources such as coroners' reports, guild and apprenticeship contracts, as well as other legal documents and religious literature to show that parents were affectionate toward their offspring.[11] In *Game of Thrones*, the well-being of children is in fact key to understanding the actions of many adult characters. Parental actions often spring from parents' affection for their children as individuals, not merely as potential heirs. Thus the strictly honorable Ned Stark falsely confesses to having committed treason in order to save his daughters. And, when Tyrion Lannister returns to King's Landing to serve as the Hand of the King, he accuses Cersei Lannister of having mismanaged political affairs but compliments her on her love for her children. In Tyrion's mind this is her "one redeeming quality."[12] After Joffrey kills Ned Stark, the Lannisters' plan to trade the captured Jaime for Sansa and Arya depends on the Stark family's great love of their children.

Childhood in the Middle Ages

Historically, childhood in the Middle Ages was a diverse experience, usually determined by a family's social station, by a child's gender, and by whether the family lived in an urban or a rural area. After infancy, a child's specific age did not overtly determine what activities the child took part in. Children would join in whatever daily tasks their parents or other caregivers would perform.[13] For most children, participating in the family's work replaced any form of formal education, since the household's economy depended on the children's labor. In noble families, children were educated in the home as well, or they were sent to be fostered, or raised, in the household of other ecclesiastical or lay nobles.[14] Although schools did exist in the Middle Ages and became increasingly common throughout the period, they remained the privilege of the elites.

While medieval children most commonly participated in the same activities as adults, humans were nevertheless believed to go through different developmental stages. The boundaries between these stages, however, fluctuated throughout the period. Some scholarly texts divided the human lifespan into three stages: childhood, adulthood, and old age. In other texts there were six or seven stages. One famous example comes from Isidore of Seville (c. 560–636), who lists *infantia, pueritia, adolescentia, iuventus, gravitas,* and *senectus* (roughly the equivalent of infancy, boyhood/girlhood, adolescence, young manhood/womanhood, maturity, and old age).[15]

Infancy was a perilous time for children. Scholars today do not have a great deal of evidence, yet written sources and archaeological findings show that infants and small children were at risk. Infant mortality was high in all strata of society. Leading historians estimate that 20–30 percent of all children died within the first 12 months of life, and 50 percent died before they reached the age of 18.[16] In the colder climates of Scandinavia, to which Winterfell and the Iron Islands in the *Game of Trones* world are similar, it has been estimated that up to 60 percent of all children died before they turned 15.[17] The high mortality rate was not due to parental neglect. Rather children's underdeveloped immune system made them particularly vulnerable to disease. Children living in dense urban settlements were especially exposed to the deadly epidemics that periodically swept through Europe. Similarly, a slum such as Flea Bottom in King's Landing is also probably susceptible to epidemics, because diseases would spread rapidly in its squalid environment.

Once children were out of infancy, the age of seven seems to have been an important turning point in their lives, especially that of boys. Around this age they were better able to participate in the family's work and to act more independently. Reflecting this change, children this old could be punished for some criminal acts, although only at 14 could they be charged as adults.[18] In contrast, inheritance laws show that financial maturity was set at a much later age, 21 being the crucial year for nobles in medieval England. For girls, age was less important than marriage as the decisive point of change in their social status. Marriage also marked an important passage to (real) adulthood for boys, as it meant becoming the head of a household. In general, children's lives, including their significant turning points, were determined more by their gender and family background than by age. For noble children, such as those in *Game of Thrones*, the teenage period was crucial. This was the time when marriages could be consummated, which made girls wives rather than just betrothed. Exactly that sends Sansa Stark into a panic when she has her "flowering," fearful as she is of her marriage to Joffrey ("A Man without Honor," season 2). For noble and aristocratic males, these were the years when they trained to become knights, a rank that they would mostly attain in their early twenties.[19]

Children's Lives: Orphans, Apprentices, and Knights

In *Game of Thrones* we mostly witness the lives of noble children. In the first episode we see how Bran has to practice archery, a skill noble boys were expected to master, as well as how he was taken to the execution to learn justice and bravery. Meanwhile his sisters Arya and Sansa are taught embroidering. These activities reflect the skill sets that noble children in medieval Europe were supposed to learn. Girls would follow the women of their families and boys would follow the men, taking part in the daily tasks of the household.[20] Enculturation was first and foremost a family matter, as the state was too rudimentary to have much power over family life.[21]

Because of the centrality of the family in medieval society, orphans were particularly vulnerable. In *Game of Thrones* the fragility of orphans is reflected in Arya Stark's fall from the comfortable life as an aristocrat's daughter. Gendry, the bastard son of Robert Baratheon, unaware of his lineage, is also disguised as an orphan. In a society with high mortality rates even among adults, a cover story of claiming to be an orphan would have been easily accepted. Furthermore, without an eyewitness or documented proof, it was difficult to establish identity. When Arya claims that the dead Lommy is indeed Gendry because he carries his helmet, there is little way for her captors to know that this is untrue. Medieval laws did exist to protect the rights of orphans, especially if they were to inherit property; but, for orphans at the bottom of society without an extended family to take them in, such as the boys Lommy and Hot Pie, there was no public safety net.[22]

The orphans Lommy and Hot Pie are introduced when Aria, in the disguise of a boy, is drafted for the Night's Watch. They do not belong to noble families but do have some social status as former apprentices. Historically, this would have been all but impossible, since, as orphans, they would not have been able to afford the apprentice fee.[23] In the case of Gendry, it is said that an unnamed lord paid a blacksmith to take him on as an apprentice (but that was probably on behalf of his father, King Robert). In the Middle Ages, however, the vast majority of children—as many as an estimated 90 percent in England—would have been servants in agricultural labor, and it was not unusual for adolescents to stay with other families, as their servants and farm hands.[24] Noble boys could also be fostered with other noble families, as wards learning the skills needed for knighthood. Wardship could serve a dual function. In the case of Theon Greyjoy's stay with House Stark, it provided an education that prepared him for his future rank and ensured the loyalty of his family. Being a servant with another family, whether as an apprentice or a ward, meant freedom from the oversight of the young person's biological family. What has been called "the social childhood" lasted into physical adulthood, because the duties of a parent or guardian were passed on to the master of the household where the service or apprenticeship was carried out.[25]

Since schools were the privilege of the elites in medieval Europe, levels of literacy were very low. Around the year 1500 as many as 90 percent of men and 99 percent of women in England could not read or write.[26] Schools began to appear in England after 1000, most commonly in the rapidly expanding towns. Only boys were allowed to attend school, though noble girls may have learned to read and write in the home. Education was predominantly organized by the church, so children who went to school were primarily expected to learn Latin.

In Westeros it is the Maesters of the Citadel who appear to be responsible for the scholarly education of noble children. As in medieval Europe, formal education and the ability to read seem to be limited to society's higher echelons. In *Game of Thrones* the lack of education proves to be a problem for Ser Davos Seaworth as he climbs the social ladder. Davos, a former smuggler, has never learned to read. But when he is made Hand to Stannis Baratheon, he needs to be able to read documents by which the government is run. His problem is solved by Stannis' daughter, Shireen Baratheon. As a noble girl, Shireen has received a formal education; and, when she learns that her friend Davos cannot read, she sets about to teach him. The two characters' different levels of literacy clearly reflect their differences in social status, and the two form an unusual teacher–pupil relationship. In the case of Arya Stark, her ability to read almost gives away the disguise as a stonemason's daughter that she assumes during her stay at castle Harrenhal.

Children's Lives in Noble Families

In the Middle Ages, noble families not only were more affluent and endowed with military and political power, but also had more children than other families.[27] Children from the higher echelons married at a much younger age; thus advantage was taken of all the woman's fertile years. Although infant mortality was high in all segments of society, once out of infancy noble children had a better chance of survival, since their living conditions were much better than those of poorer people. They had more nutritious food, better housing, and more attention from caregivers. In *Game of Thrones* the importance of the survival of children is constantly evident in the diplomacy between the great noble houses such as Stark, Martell, Frey, and Baratheon. The strength of these dynasties depends on their having children to marry into other noble families, which secures the alliances and wealth they need in order to fortify their positions through generations.

In *Game of Thrones* many girls marry as very young teenagers, a practice that reflects the marriage traditions of medieval noble families, whose children married young as well. Noble girls often wed older men, as is the case in the marriages between Sansa Stark and Tyrion Lannister, and Daenerys Stormborn and Khal Drogo. These marriages also reflect how the betrothal of young children and their later marriage were historically used to secure wealth and political alliances.[28] Parents would therefore carefully arrange their children's marriages in order to ensure that inheritances were kept within the family. So great was the desire to advance the family's fortunes through the marriage of children that the medieval church based marriage vows on the explicit consent of the couple, thereby attempting to avoid forced marriages.

The economic and social interests of noble families made the church's goal of consenting partners impossible to enforce. Children were assets for merging family property and power, which left little room, if any, for marriages based on love. In *Game of Thrones* Robb Stark falls in love with and marries a beautiful foreigner, the field medic Talisa Maegyr. In doing so, Robb breaks his vow of betrothal to one of Lord Walter Frey's daughters, a deal that his mother, Catelyn Stark, had arranged in order to allow Robb's army to cross a strategic river and gain several thousand troops. His love match to Talisa costs him his alliance with the Freys and leads to his violent death.[29]

In the Middle Ages the use of marriage to secure family holdings required legitimate offspring who could legally inherit property. Only children from recognized marriages counted before both secular and canon law. The medieval church forbade polygamy and concubinage, declaring children born out of wedlock to be illegitimate, or literally not lawful.[30] In medieval Europe, several governments helped families to consolidate their holdings by establishing primogeniture. Such a legal policy limited the right of inheritance over an entire estate to the eldest son alone or to the nearest male relative, instead of allowing for the estate to be divided among other siblings or more distant relatives. The drive to have one son inherit an entire kingdom was a strong motive for adopting this policy.

Indeed, the question of legitimate inheritance begins the wars for the Iron Throne of the Seven Kingdoms of Westeros. The discovery of the royal Hand Jon Arryn that Robert Baratheon was not the biological father of Joffrey, Myrcella, and Tommen led to his murder. Then the next Hand, Ned Stark, learned the same and tried to make Robert's brother Stannis the rightful heir. Questioning the legitimacy of the royal succession begins the War of Five Kings.[31]

Ultimately it is children's participation in the struggle for the Iron Throne that makes childhood a central topic in *Game of Thrones*. Just as medieval Europe, Westeros is a harsh and unforgiving place where, as Cersei says, "everywhere in the world they hurt little girls."[32] The point of view of children on violence and injustice effectively highlights the vulnerability of people's lives. The series is truly captivating in how it depicts children not just as victims of a violent political struggle, but as persons with their own agency who consider carefully their own aims. Through the escalating conflict, we follow the Stark children as they fight for survival, vengeance, and justice. Faced with the collapse of the existing political order, they forge a new future for themselves,

Westeros, and their house. Joffrey and Tommen Baratheon also try to shape the kingdom for their house, until they are overcome by murder and despair. The theme of coming of age and the fight for political renewal connect most clearly in Daenerys Targaryan's struggle to rule justly, aided by her dragons. These are windows on childhoods that lie beyond the safe universe of most modern children in the industrialized West and invite reflection on the ever changing conditions for children, their agency, and the very phenomenon of childhood.

Notes

1 On age differences in different versions, see Jessie Heyman, "Game of Thrones Characters Are Much Much Younger Than You Thought," *Vogue*, 2015, April 9 (accessed July 15, 2016 at http://www.vogue.com/13253729/game-of-thrones-season-5-character-ages). For the author's problems with aging, see James Hibberd, "EW Interview: George R. R. Martin talks 'A Dance of Dragons,'" 2011, *Entertainment Weekly*, July 12 (accessed July 15, 2016 at http://www.ew.com/article/2011/07/12/george-martin-talks-a-dance-with-dragons).
2 "Winter Is Coming," directed by Tim van Patten, written by David Benioff and D. B. Weiss, in *Game of Thrones*, season 1, HBO, first aired on April 17, 2011.
3 Jonathan Dewalt, *The European Nobility 1400–1800* (Cambridge: Cambridge University Press, 1996), 23–24.
4 "Fire and Blood," directed by Alan Taylor, written by David Benioff and D. B. Weiss, in *Game of Thrones*, season 1, HBO, first aired on June 19, 2011.
5 Collin Heywood, *A History of Childhood: Children and Childhood in the West from Medieval to Modern Times* (Cambridge: Polity, 2001).
6 Helle Strandgaard Jensen, *From Superman to Social Realism: Children's Media and Scandinavian Childhood* (Amsterdam: John Benjamins, 2017).
7 *Game of Thrones*, "Lord Snow," Season One, directed by Brian Kirk, written by David Benioff and D. B. Weiss, HBO, first aired on May 1, 2011.
8 Philipe Ariés, *Centuries of Childhood*, translated by Robert Baldick (London: Jonathan Cape, 1962).
9 Heywood, *A History of Childhood*; Nicholas Orme, *Medieval Children* (New Haven, CT: Yale University Press, 2001); Shukamith Shahar, *Childhood in the Middle Ages* (London: Routledge, 1990).
10 "The Night Lands," directed by Alan Taylor, written by David Benioff and D. B. Weiss, in *Game of Thrones*, season 2, HBO, first aired on April 8, 2012.
11 Shahar, *Childhood in the Middle Ages*.
12 "The North Remembers," directed by Alan Taylor, written by David Benioff and D. B. Weiss, in *Game of Thrones*, season 2, HBO, first aired on April 8, 2012.
13 Heywood, *A History of Childhood*, 17.

14 Louise J. Wilkinson, "Education," in *A Cultural History of Childhood and Family in the Middle Ages*, edited by Louise J. Winkinson (Oxford: Berg, 2010), 98; Nicholas Orme, *From Childhood to Chivalry: The Education of the English Kings and Aristocracy, 1066–1530* (London: Methuen, 1984), 44–80.

15 J. A. Burrow, *The Ages of Man: A Study in Medieval Writing and Thought* (Oxford: Clarendon, 1986), 82.

16 Deborah Youngs, "Life Cycle," in *A Cultural History of Childhood and Family in the Middle Ages*, edited by Louise J. Winkinson (Oxford: Berg, 2010), 111.

17 Youngs, "Life Cycle," 111–112.

18 Orme, *Medieval Children*.

19 P. J. P. Goldberg, "Family Relationships," in *A Cultural History of Childhood and Family in the Middle Ages*, edited by Louise J. Winkinson (Oxford: Berg, 2010), 21–40.

20 Youngs, "Life Cycle."

21 Richard Huscroft, "The State," in *A Cultural History of Childhood and Family in the Middle Ages*, edited by Louise J. Winkinson (Oxford: Berg, 2010).

22 Goldberg "Family Relationships," 36.

23 Orme, *From Childhood to Chivalry*; Orme, *Medieval Children*.

24 Daniel Pigg, "Children and Childhood in the Middle Ages," in *Handbook of Medieval Culture*, edited by Albrecht Classen (Berlin: De Gruyter, 2015), 170.

25 Barbara A. Hanawalt, *Growing Up in the Middle Ages and the Renaissance: The Experince of Childhood in History* (Oxford: Oxford University Press, 1993), 111; Pigg, "Children and Childhood."

26 Wilkinson, "Education,"108.

27 Young, "Life Cycles."

28 Huscroft, "The State."

29 "Baelor," directed by Alan Taylor, written by David Benioff and D. B. Weiss, in *Game of Thrones*, season 1, HBO, first aired on June 12, 2011. In the novels, Robb's marriage is part of a Lannister plot, which also leads to his death.

30 Huscroft "The State."

31 For more on this topic see the chapter by Pavlac in this volume.

32 "First of His Name," directed by Michelle MacLaren, written by David Benioff and D. B. Weiss, in *Game of Thrones*, season 4, HBO, first aired on May 4, 2014.

11

Writing the Rules of Their Own Game

Medieval Female Agency and *Game of Thrones*

Nicole M. Mares

In the season 6 finale of *Game of Thrones*, Cersei Lannister accomplished what had, just an episode before, seemed impossible: she thwarted the High Sparrow and Margaery Tyrell, her rivals to her son Tommen's attention and affection. As she dresses for her trial by the seven Septons, Cersei is like a knight getting dressed for battle. Moments later, we understand why: she is assassinating her enemies, burning down the institutions that tried to stifle her, and getting ready to battle on virtually alone. While she can't be prepared for the untimely death of her last child, she takes the Iron Throne in his stead, becoming queen and ruler of Westeros, the seeming victor in the game of thrones.[1]

The series *Game of Thrones* depicts a number of powerful women who exercise remarkable agency in determining their own fates. Cersei, in many ways a victim of the circumstances of her birth, still deftly maneuvers the dangerous political landscape of King's Landing. Daenerys Targaryen, used by her family to gain connections to the warlike Dothraki people, leads the Unsullied against rival powers, in a quest to regain the Iron Throne for the Targaryens. Arya Stark, the "tomboy" daughter of the powerful Starks of the North, travels from place to place, implementing her plan of revenge. And Brienne of Tarth moves through the Seven Kingdoms as would a knight, mostly unfettered by the constraints of her sex and gender. But how realistically do these characters represent opportunities for women in the Middle Ages to assert individual identities and agency?

While George R. R. Martin and the producers of the *Game of Thrones* series certainly take liberties in the depiction of female characters in the Seven Kingdoms, the women portrayed in the series do enjoy freedoms that may have been available to certain subsets of medieval women. For instance, both Cersei and Daenerys met social expectations by becoming wives and mothers (though, of course, Daenerys' child did not survive). Their status as widows and mothers gives them an independence that was not available to most women, and their class status empowers them in important ways. Arya, too, comes from the

Game of Thrones versus History: Written in Blood, First Edition. Edited by Brian A. Pavlac.
© 2017 John Wiley & Sons, Inc. Published 2017 by John Wiley & Sons, Inc.

social elite, but, for a period of time, her power emanates from her clothes. That Arya cross-dresses and disguises herself as a boy allows her freedoms in the medieval world. The temporary sacrifice of her identity in Braavos and in the House of Black and White trained her in ways that will only empower her further. Finally, Brienne of Tarth, like Arya, rejects female dress in favor of that of a knight. Her dress, coupled with her stature and demeanor, allows her to navigate the Seven Kingdoms in a "lesbian-like" manner.[2] Thus, while these women seem like extraordinary characters who drive political and social change, their real-life medieval counterparts would have had similar avenues to independence and power available to them. And, like their real-life counterparts, they often see those avenues close in the face of pressures from institutions such as government and religion. But their real-life counterparts would probably have used less poison.

Drama Queens

When viewers watch *Game of Thrones*, they see women playing a number of key roles. Most obviously, women in this series are queens who serve key public and social roles. We see Cersei serving as Queen Regent, a guiding hand in the politics and intrigue at King's Landing. But figures like Margaery Tyrell and Dany link their political roles with that of serving a greater social good. While Margaery might contend that feeding the poor is part of the pantomime of playing the good queen, Dany's efforts at social justice in Mereen are, arguably, much more impactful (and risky). Each of these women has made the most of her position, working behind the scenes and in public to control some aspects of the political sphere in which she is supposed to function.

But the power these women command in the series often comes at a high price: it is a consequence of a certain kind of powerlessness. Cersei, Margaery, and Dany are queens through their bloodlines, their birth, and their families' negotiations for power. In the medieval West, women were key assets in the struggle for power and the creation of political networks. Noblewomen born to the most important families in Europe were used to form alliances through marital networks. Cersei, Margaery, and Dany are all married (at some point) to men they do not love but who will further the political interests of their families. They are essentially bartered by their families for access to the political sphere and a chance at the Iron Throne.

The Queens of the Seven Kingdoms often mask their own ambition with a demure façade. They have to be strong and sweet. Margaery Tyrell does this better than any of the other women in King's Landing, carefully manipulating Tommen while letting him feel like her protector. Cersei, on the other hand, barely masks her ambition, and as time passes her intentions become clearer. This naked ambition pushes her further from the center of power; she is marginalized at court, shamed in public, thrust to the viewing gallery rather than seated at the King's side, and locked away in her chambers protected by her zombie guard.[3]

In the medieval West, women like Cersei who did possess power were often condemned for their ambition and leadership. Take, for instance, Empress Theodora (ca. 497–548), wife to the Roman Emperor Justinian (r. 527–565). She, unlike the main female characters in *Game of Thrones*, came from a poorer background, the daughter of a bear trainer and a dancer. She spent her youth as a performer and courtesan until she met and married the future Roman emperor. But she ascended to the very height of power, practically ruling alongside her husband. Her biographer, Procopius, could not hide his disdain for her in his *Secret History* of Justinian's court.[4] He condemns her, as others do Cersei, for her ambition and her sexuality. Procopius blames Theodora for Justinian's failings and for the political rebellions, plagues, and economic ruin of Byzantium. But Theodora also worked to improve conditions for women, whether by helping ladies at the court or by establishing accommodations for "reformed" prostitutes. She was also an important patron to the Empress Sophia (c. 530–601), her niece. The highly influential Sophia directed many of the economic policies of Byzantium. She also went on to rule the Byzantine Empire as co-regent after her husband, Justin II (r. 565–574), began to suffer bouts of insanity. After her husband's death, she retained the title of "Augusta" and worked to convince Justin's successor, Tiberius, to divorce his wife and marry either her own daughter or herself. After that effort failed, she found herself marginalized, so she plotted to depose him. Her plot failed; Tiberius took away her property and her servants; but she still ended up with her own palace and her own (minor) court to rule.[5]

Like Empress Sophia, the Germanic Queen Amalasuntha (d. 535) was a sixth-century woman who exercised a great deal of authority in her Ostrogothic kingdom on the Italian Peninsula. Amalasuntha served as regent for her son, during which time she declared war, promoted members at court, and served as chief diplomat with other empires. She also advocated moderate views on Christianity and issued laws. Other Germanic queens, like Fredegund of the Franks (d. 597) and Radegund (518–587), demonstrated that women could wield a lot of power in the early Middle Ages, make important alliances, lead troops, and help establish convents.[6] A number of queens in the high and late Middle Ages also serve as examples of warrior queens in the historic past: Matilda of Canossa (1046–1115), a feudal ruler and papal defender; Empress Matilda (1102–1167), who led troops to claim the throne of England; Eleanor of Aquitaine (1122–1204), who went on the Second Crusade with her first husband, Louis VII of France, and joined a rebellion against her second husband, Henry II of England; and, arguably, Isabella of Castile (1451–1504), who worked alongside her husband Ferdinand in reconquering the Iberian Peninsula from the emirate of Granada. Isabella, like Cersei, linked the institution of the church, this time in the form of the Inquisition, with her political power, to vanquish her enemies (although, unlike Cersei, Isabella did not have to destroy the institution with which she partnered).

Each of these women gained access to power by reason of her ancestry, much like Cersei, Margaery, and Dany. And some of these early medieval women, also much like their fictional counterparts, were mothers to heirs to the throne. This was an important factor in allowing them to wield authority over their kingdoms. Amalasuntha and Fredegund had fulfilled their maternal expectations, having given birth to heirs. Their power came as Cersei's had, through their serving as regents for their sons. In their case the burden of reproduction gave them access to power that would normally be beyond their grasps. While Amalasuntha met a grisly end (killed in her bath by her second husband), Fredegund was celebrated at the time of her death with an elaborate funeral.[7] Other queens served as regents for their husbands, as arguably Dany does after Khal Drogo and her son die.[8] Dany's subsequent efforts to get back to Westeros to claim the Iron Throne are reminiscent of Empress Matilda, who fought her cousin Stephen of Blois (1092–1154) for the English throne. Stephen thwarted Matilda's rightful claim to the throne of England as designated heir to Henry I (r. 1100–1135) by claiming it for himself. While her efforts to win back the throne ended in a military stalemate, her son, Henry II (r. 1154–1189), went on to be one of the most important medieval English kings, while she settled in Rouen to administer Normandy.

Ladies under Cover

For women in the lower ranks of the nobility, life could sometimes offer more possibility. They were still often married off to build kinship networks, and younger daughters were sent into a convent. But sometimes these noblewomen exercised a bit more independence. In *Game of Thrones* we see these women represented in the characters of Arya Stark and Brienne of Tarth. These are perhaps the most unrealistic depictions of possibilities available to medieval women.

Unlike her older sister Sansa, Arya Stark was not seen as a valuable link between two powerful families. This gave her more freedoms as a girl, and her father even allowed her to train with a sword. As Arya flees from King's Landing after Ned Stark's execution, she begins her own adventure disguised as a boy.[9] She embarks on a revenge narrative, seeking to destroy those who betrayed her family. Similarly, Brienne of Tarth is on her own journey of revenge, after the Red Woman and Stannis Baratheon murder her patron and king, Renly Baratheon.[10] Brienne, like Arya, never had much of an affinity for dresses and preferred to train as a knight. While both women develop strong affections for men, they are not involved in romantic relationships and instead choose alternative paths for their own lives. Unlike the warrior queens who led armies (or fight atop dragons), they journey, fight, and kill in the battles they have chosen for themselves.

Historian Judith Bennett has argued that a number of medieval western women used gender "disguise," as Arya and Brienne do, as a way to seek expanded opportunities.[11] She writes that any women who did not follow traditional paths were on a gender spectrum that placed them closer to a non-traditional or "lesbian-like" identity.[12] The descriptive term "lesbian-like" women, according to Bennett, does not (necessarily) refer to same-sex desire or sexual contact. Rather they are "women who resisted norms of feminine behavior based on heterosexual marriage."[13] Brienne and Arya embody this non-traditional, "lesbian-like" historical model: they wear men's clothing, they pursue traditionally male paths, and they are uninterested in (traditional) romantic connections.[14] They do not live the lives of "typical" women in the medieval world (or in the Seven Kingdoms, for that matter). In the House of Black and White, Arya escapes traditional gendered expectations and trains with another woman in a commonly male craft (if assassination can be considered a craft). Brienne is a knight who avenges her friend and leader, who swears oaths, and who challenges the fiercest of warriors in battle.

Historically, daughters from the lower gentry or younger daughters in large noble families might not be so rigidly bound by the typical paths of aristocratic women. And, by choosing an alternative path, one that was beyond the bounds of medieval gender conventions, these women fit into Bennett's non-traditional, "lesbian-like" model. Take, for instance, the case of Christine de Pizan (1364–1430), the Renaissance writer and "feminist."[15] Christine was born to an important Venetian family and her father served as physician and astrologer to France's King Charles V (r. 1364–1380). She had the unusual opportunity to be educated in arts and letters, taking advantage of the king's library and archives. While she followed a traditional path to marriage (by the age of 15), Christine eventually accomplished something quite extraordinary: she served as court writer for a number of dukes and, eventually, for the French court of King Charles VI (r. 1380–1422). Widowed at the age of 25, she used her writing to support herself and her children financially. She is most famous for having waded into the humanist *querelle des femmes* ("the woman question"), a Renaissance debate about the nature of women, their sexuality, and their education. The debate, in which she became a leading voice, had been sparked by Jean de Meun's version of *The Romance of the Rose* (c. 1275) and by Giovanni Boccaccio's *On Famous Women* (1374). Christine's seminal text, *Book of the City of Ladies* (1405), defended women against Renaissance humanist claims that they were inferior. For instance, of women's education she wrote (as part of an imagined conversation with Lady Reason):

> I realize that women have accomplished many good things and that even if evil women have done evil, it seems to me, nevertheless, that the

> benefits accrued and still accruing because of good women—particularly
> the wise and literary ones and those educated in the natural sciences [...]
> outweigh the evil. Therefore, I am amazed by the opinion of some men
> who claim that they do not want their daughters, wives, or kinswomen
> to be educated because their mores would be ruined as a result.[16]

Christine celebrated the accomplishments of classical women and made important early contributions to what would become a lengthy feminist debate about social, political, and economic equality for women.

While Christine did what most medieval women were expected to do by getting married and having children, she also accomplished what men were expected to do: she had a career and financially supported her family. As a widow, Christine was more unfettered by gender constraints. According to Judith Bennett, "widows demonstrate clearly how household-status could confound gender-status, since as heads of the households left by their husbands, widows enjoyed certain rights and obligations usually reserved for men."[17] Widows could trade and sell lands, represent households in court, arrange marriages for their children, and stand in court as a guarantor of a debt (a pledge).[18] While it is unclear what advantage Christine took of these other rights and liberties, she debated some of the most prominent male writers of her day. She wrote volumes and volumes of works. Thus, while her life was certainly heteronormative, insofar as it upheld traditional gender roles that were directly derived from biological sex, her life was also non-traditional, "lesbian-like."[19] She fit in both worlds and was allowed to do so mostly because of her social origins.

Brienne's most relevant historical counterpart is, of course, Joan of Arc (Jeanne d'Arc) (1412–1431). Unlike Brienne and Arya, Joan came from the land-owning peasantry of France, but she certainly fits Bennett's model of a non-traditional, "lesbian-like" woman. Joan, who experienced visions of St. Michael, St. Catherine, and St. Margaret at a young age, told the dauphin of France, in the midst of the Hundred Years' War (1337–1453), that a victory in the city of Orléans would lead to his coronation. Dressed in men's armor (though some contend this was a precaution intended to disguise her from the enemy), she helped the dauphin defeat English troops and allies at Orléans. The Dauphin—the heir apparent to the French crown—was to become King Charles VII (r. 1422–1461). She then went on to advise the French army in the defeat of English troops in the Loire Valley, turning the tide of the war. After Charles VII's coronation at Reims on July 17, 1429, Joan continued to aid the French against the English and their allies. Unlike Brienne, who becomes a friend and confidante of Kingslayer Jaime Lannister, Joan met an untimely end, being burned at the stake. Her crimes included one that made her non-traditional, "lesbian-like": wearing male attire instead of dresses. According to historians Katherine L. French and Allyson M. Poska, "biblical law forbade wearing the clothing of the other gender [...] according to the authorities, [Joan] did not dress like a man for religiously acceptable reasons," even though many female saints "wore male clothing to avoid marriage or to enter a monastery against their parents' will."[20] While Brienne's male attire empowers her and allows her to navigate Westeros more freely, it is—in part—what ultimately strips Joan of that ability.

Although Brienne, like Joan, does not appear to be sexually active, Brienne's armor does not erase her sex identity; in many ways it actually emphasizes her female status. And her cross-dressing does not make men forget that she is a woman. In season 3's "Walk of Punishment," Locke, who serves House Bolton, captures Brienne alongside Jaime Lannister. Jaime warns her that she will be raped by Locke's men, and she nearly is, before Jaime negotiates for her to be spared. While the gender roles of Jaime and Brienne, like the relationship between the two, seem to change from minute to minute, at Harrenhal their narrative looks a bit more like that of a traditional heroine in distress and a knight to the rescue than like the story of an equal partnership, reminding viewers of the sex and gender rules that still apply to Brienne, regardless of her outward appearance.[21]

Yara Greyjoy is arguably the most non-traditional, "lesbian-like" character in the Seven Kingdoms. The first woman to stand for the Kingsmoot, Yara is a pirate and a warrior. The first time we meet her, she is dressed as a woman and is the target of the sexual advances of Theon Greyjoy, who does not recognize that she is his sister.[22] But, when we see Yara in subsequent scenes of *Game of Thrones*, she is rather androgynous and dressed in men's attire. It is clear that she is a strong woman, and her strength is magnified as Theon's own strength is diminished at the cruel hands of Ramsay Bolton.[23] We see this when she tries to rescue him from Ramsay in season 4—and much more in season 6, when she is the virile character, while Theon is emasculated (she tells him he might as well kill himself if he doesn't "man up").[24] By the time Theon supports Yara for the Salt Throne at the kingsmoot, it is clear that she is the stronger, more capable sibling from House Greyjoy. And the siblings' subsequent departure from the Iron Islands for Mereen allows Yara to demonstrate her strong leadership and diplomatic abilities. While she is disappointed that she won't be able to rape and plunder once she has allied with Dany, she is committed to leaving a more positive legacy.

There isn't much historical precedent for Yara, but there are a few historical myths that share some features of her story. For instance, in Scandinavia there is a story about Princess Alwilda. She was betrothed to a prince of Denmark, but rather than marry him she disguised herself as a man, commandeered a ship, and took to the seas. After she encountered a ship of pirates without a captain, the men aboard elected her their captain. In the end, Alwilda's ship was confronted by a Danish ship with Prince Alf—her intended—and, impressed by his skills, Alwilda married the prince. While this may be the stuff of legend, the story tells us that women who could transgress boundaries and conquer the seas were held in high regard, much as Yara is clearly a character deserving of respect. But, in the end, those women in the medieval historical past were expected to marry and conform to traditional gender dynamics. While we can't say that the same is true for Yara, the results of the kingsmoot show that the majority of ironmen were not yet ready for a woman's rule.[25]

What women in the non-traditional, "lesbian-like" category show is that, while they may escape traditional gender and sex conventions for a time, their extraordinary accomplishments emphasize their gender and sex even more. Brienne's stature and armor leave everyone she meets struck and intimidated because, under that armor, she remains a woman. Arya's cross-dressing while escaping Westeros emphasizes her vulnerability as a female; for, if she were to be caught, she would surely be victimized by the men around her. And her androgyny in the House of Black and White is undermined by her constant iteration that "a girl has no name."[26] Yara Greyjoy's dalliances in the brothel seem so much more scandalous, her overtures to Dany that much more provocative, as she is a woman.[27] So, while these women may be bucking convention, their rejection of gender convention arguably draws even more attention to their female status.

Women of No Consequence

Joan of Arc was a low-born woman who mingled with kings. While her story is extraordinary in that she was able to influence people at the highest political levels, she is from a population of women who ordinarily exercised their limited authority on a much smaller scale. The overwhelming majority of people in medieval Europe were, like Joan, from the peasantry. We don't see many peasants in *Game of Thrones* (when we do, they often are dead victims) and we hear of them even less. This is fitting in many ways, since they are, essentially, the unseen and unheard in the game for political power. Even though they represented roughly 85 percent of the population, peasants were an unrepresented underclass in medieval society.[28] In *Game of Thrones* the only "peasant" the viewer gets to know is Gilly, the wife and daughter of Craster, who is even more marginalized for having come from north of the Wall.[29] Gilly is a victim until she meets Sam and the other members of the Night's Watch. She is pregnant with her father's child; she is kept in his home, isolated from the rest of the world and routinely raped by him. While most peasants in medieval Europe would not have experienced such a fate, her victimization is symbolic of the kind of powerlessness that peasants, and particularly peasant women, lived with. By the time she is living in Castle Black, Gilly blossoms and exercises more independence and influence over Sam.[30]

Just as it is difficult to learn about the lives of peasants in the world of *Game of Thrones*, so too is it difficult to find out facts about historical peasants in the medieval West. Because of low literacy rates, lack of resources, and the imperative to work to survive, most peasants did not leave written records of their lives. But we are lucky to have a few traces that give us better insight into the lives of peasant women. Judith M. Bennett's *A Medieval Life* studies Cecilia Penifader (1295–1344), a peasant from Brigstock, England.[31] What Bennett emphasizes about Cecilia's gendered experience was that women, from birth, were assigned to "women's tasks."[32] But she uses Cecilia's life to show us what opportunities were available to medieval peasant women. For instance, Cecilia remained unmarried (perhaps fitting the non-traditional, "lesbian-like" paradigm that Bennett embraces), and this meant that she was "an independent tenant and householder." She was able to negotiate "a space for herself between the full dependency of married women and the full autonomy of married men."[33] While Bennett argues that Cecilia's unmarried status could afford her many freedoms, she also notes that "her household was poorer than it would otherwise have been, and she missed the possible pleasures of loving children and a loving husband."[34] Bennett argues that marriage could afford peasant women something that they might otherwise be denied: respect. She claims: "Yes, a wife did not control her own lands or labors, but she could be known as a *goodwife*, respected by her neighbors, appreciated as a wife, and much-loved as a mother."[35] Like aristocratic and noble women, peasant women derived much of their identity from their relationships with men. But what Bennett shows us is that, even though those roles could be confining for many women, there were avenues to power, influence, and pleasure regardless of one's marital and social status. A Gilly could be as powerful and happy as a Cersei or a Margaery—or even more.

Natalie Zemon Davis' *The Return of Martin Guerre* (1983) describes the circumstances of another peasant woman, detailing a compelling court case from 1559 to 1560 in the town of Artigat, France.[36] Bertrande de Rols was a young woman whose husband, Martin Guerre, seemingly frustrated with traditional peasant life, abandoned his wife and child. When he returned several years later, other villagers accused him of being an impostor. Bertrande defended her husband and stood by him, and the court acquitted him of any crime. But, in a retrial, the man who returned to Bertrande proved to be an impostor when the true Martin Guerre appeared in court. Davis argues in her study that Bertrande was able to take control over her own life by accepting the impostor and forging a happy marriage with him. According to Davis, while Bertrande's choices were limited by her sex and social class, by taking in the impostor as her husband she exercised agency and forged her own happiness. Davis aims to make the point that women in the medieval peasant classes, rather than being passive recipients of men's commands, had opportunities to influence their own lives. While historian Robert Finlay dismisses much of Davis' argument as circumstantial and overreaching in that it would assign too much agency to Bertrande, Davis shows that it is certainly possible for peasant women to exercise some choice and to have some authority over their own lives.[37] We can see this in Gilly, who initially has no control over her own life with her father but becomes more assertive, more confident, and happier with Sam.[38]

Limited Success

Women in the Seven Kingdoms, like women in the medieval West, had avenues to power if they took advantage of the limited, but important, opportunities available to them. Through marriage and motherhood, queens could become powerful regents. By not marrying, or through widowhood, women could control more of their own fates and become independent householders, or even soldiers in battle. But, regardless of their class status, opportunities, or advantages, women functioned in relationships with men. Their identities were derived from how they related to their fathers, husbands, sons, and male friends. While history indicates that women successfully maneuvered in this world and could establish some independence, *Game of Thrones* suggests that, regardless of the play for power they can make, women continue to be thwarted by men who are less talented but, by default, more powerful. Sansa, betrayed by all the men she has encountered since her departure from Winterfell, now leans on a few of them to meet her aims. Betrayed by Littlefinger, battered and raped by Ramsay Bolton, Sansa can meet her aims only by leaning on Jon Snow, Ser Davos, and Littlefinger himself.[39] Margaery, who was walking a dangerous line trying to turn the tables on the High Sparrow while manipulating her husband, all in order to save her brother and protect the family name, is swallowed by wildfire.[40] Daenerys arguably relies on the Dothraki and the Unsullied to further her aims and, as she tells her lover Daario, she plans to use marriage as a way to further her political aims.[41] While Dany is arguably flipping sexual and social convention by taking control of her own marital future, she is still recognizing that her path to power entails associating herself to a man. Gilly, rejected by Sam's father but embraced by the Tarly women, chooses to follow Sam to the Citadel, making her home with him and deriving her identity from him.[42] Brienne is almost literally adrift, unable to fulfill her mission to help Sansa, a knight returning from a failed quest.[43] Only two women seem to be winning their own games as they want: Arya and Cersei. Arya, having left Braavos, returns to Westeros, claims her identity, and continues exacting revenge and checking more names off her list.[44] Cersei looked increasingly hemmed in by the High Sparrow and by her son Tommen, who represent the church and the state—that is, the two institutions, both in the fantasy world and in historical reality, that confined women to the roles of wife (or widow) and mother; yet she breaks the confines of gender. Her reputation shattered, her advice no longer sought, Cersei resents her marginalization and blows up the very institutions that had tried to silence her. Our last view of Westeros at the end of season 6 is of a triumphant, though arguably broken, Cersei, dangerous because she has nothing left to lose.[45] While it is unclear where each of these women will end up in the game for the Iron Throne, they are linked to their historical counterparts through the social and gender structures that guide and shape their lives.

Notes

1 "The Winds of Winter," directed by Miguel Sapochnik, written by David Benioff and D. B. Weiss, in *Game of Thrones*, Season 6, HBO, first aired on June 26, 2016.
2 Judith M. Bennett, "'Lesbian-Like' and the Social History of Lesbianisms," *Journal of the History of Sexuality* 9.1/2 (2000), 1–24.
3 "No One," directed by Mark Mylod, written by David Benioff and D. B. Weiss, in *Game of Thrones*, Season 6, HBO, first aired on June 12, 2016.
4 Procopius, *The Secret History*, translated by Peter Sarris (New York: Penguin, 2007).
5 Katherine L. French and Allyson M. Poska, *Women and Gender in the Western Past*, vol. 1: *To 1815* (Boston: Houghton Mifflin, 2007), 134.
6 These early medieval queens could also be quite murderous. Fredegund assassinated her rivals for King Chilperic's affection and attention and likely killed Chilperic himself. She probably assassinated a number of other rivals, including bishops (French and Poska, *Women and Gender*, 147).
7 French and Poska, *Women and Gender*, 146–147.
8 "Fire and Blood," directed by Alan Taylor, written by David Benioff and D. B. Weiss, in *Game of Thrones*, season 1, HBO, first aired on June 19, 2011.
9 "Fire and Blood," HBO.
10 "Garden of Bones," directed by David Petarca, written by Vanessa Taylor, in *Game of Thrones*, season 2, HBO, first aired on June 19, 2011; "Mother's Mercy," directed by David Nutter, written by David Benioff and D. B. Weiss, in *Game of Thrones*, season 5, HBO, first aired on June 14, 2015.
11 Bennett, "'Lesbian-Like.'"
12 Because historians cannot verify a person's sexuality and because medieval women would not have used the term "lesbian" to describe themselves, Bennett categorizes them as "lesbian-like." And in fact many historical women would not have identified as lesbian, had they possessed the terminology. Most likely they would have rejected this term because pre-modern concepts of sexuality were different from our own. But these women did not necessarily buck sexual identities; their different gender-based expectations offered them other kinds of educational, social, and—sometimes—sexual experiences from those today.
13 Bennett, "Lesbian-Like," 9–10.

14 One could argue that the relationship between Brienne and Jaime is a loving relationship. They clearly have mutual affection and a deep, abiding loyalty to each other. Jaime's gift of a Valyrian steel sword and a new suit of armor to Brienne demonstrated a depth of feeling ("Oathkeeper," directed by Michelle MacLaren, written by Brian Cogman, in *Game of Thrones*, season 4, HBO, first aired on April 27, 2014), as did his willingness to let her negotiate with the Blackfish at Riverrun, even though he was there to seize control of the castle ("No One," HBO).

15 The Oxford English Dictionary (OED) defines feminism as "[advocacy] of equality of the sexes and the establishment of the political, social, and economic rights of the female sex" (*Oxford English Dictionary*, s.v. "feminism," 2016, accessed November 2, 2016 at http://www.oed.com/view/Entry/69192?redirectedFrom= feminism, available on subscription). Because feminism did not technically exist in the Renaissance, because Christine did not advocate for broad, sweeping social change, and because she would not have self-identified as a feminist, I use quotation marks here to acknowledge the anachronistic nature of the term.

16 Christine de Pizan, *Book of the City of Ladies*, translated by Rosalind Brown-Grant (London: Penguin Classics, 1999).

17 Judith M. Bennett, *A Medieval Life: Cecilia Penifader of Brigstock, c. 1295–1344* (Boston, MA: McGraw-Hill College, 1999), 124.

18 Bennett, *A Medieval Life*, 125.

19 The OED defines heteronormative as "Of, designating, or based on a world view which regards gender roles as fixed to biological sex and heterosexuality as the normal and preferred sexual orientation" (*Oxford English Dictionary*, s.v. "heteronormative, adj.," 2016, (accessed November 2, 2016, http://www.oed.com/view/Entry/275594?redirectedFrom=heteronormative, available on subscription).

20 French and Poska, *Women and Gender*, 200.

21 "Walk of Punishment," directed by David Benioff, written by David Benioff and D. B. Weiss, in *Game of Thrones*, season 3, HBO, first aired on April 14, 2013. At the beginning, Brienne and Jaime's relationship is one of guardian and prisoner ("Valar Morghulis," directed by Alan Taylor, written by David Benioff and D. B. Weiss, in *Game of Thrones*, season 3, HBO, first aired on June 3, 2012). Later on Brienne encourages a maimed Jaime to stop feeling sorry for himself, so that he may have his revenge on Locke ("And Now His Watch Has Ended," directed by Alex Graves, written by David Benioff and D. B. Weiss, in *Game of Thrones*, season 3, HBO, April 21, 2013) and in another episode Jaime confides in—and seeks comfort from—Brienne, revealing his real motivation for killing "the Mad King," Aerys Targaryen ("Kissed by Fire," directed by Alex Graves, written by Bryan Cogman, in *Game of Thrones*, season 3, HBO, first aired on April 28, 2013).

22 "The Night Lands," directed by Alan Taylor, written by David Benioff and D. B. Weiss, in *Game of Thrones*, season 3, HBO, first aired on April 2, 2012.

23 "The Bear and the Maiden Fair," directed by Michelle MacLaren, written by George R. R. Martin, in *Game of Thrones*, season 3, HBO, first aired on May 12, 2013.

24 "The Laws of God and Men," directed by Alik Sakharov, written by Bryan Cogman, in *Game of Thrones*, season 4, HBO, first aired on May 11, 2014; "The Broken Man," directed by Mark Mylod, written by Bryan Cogman, in *Game of Thrones*, season 6, HBO, first aired on June 5, 2016.

25 While Theon does seem to convince the men of the Iron Islands of Yara's worthiness for the Salt Throne, Euron's appearance allows the men to step back from that approval rather quickly and place a more traditional ruler on the throne ("The Door," directed by Jack Bender, written by David Benioff and D. B. Weiss, in *Game of Thrones*, season 6, HBO, first aired on May 22, 2016).

26 "Home," directed by Jeremy Podeswa, written by Dave Hill, in *Game of Thrones*, season 6, HBO, first aired on May 1, 2016.

27 "The Broken Man," HBO; "Battle of the Bastards," directed by Miguel Sapochnik, written by David Benioff and D. B. Weiss, in *Game of Thrones*, season 6, HBO, first aired on June 19, 2016.

28 Alixe Bovey, "Peasants and Their Role in Rural Life," British Library, n.d. (accessed April 24, 2016, http://www.bl.uk/the-middle-ages/articles/peasants-and-their-role-in-rural-life).

29 "The North Remembers," directed by Alan Taylor, written by David Benioff and D. B. Weiss, in *Game of Thrones*, season 2, HBO, first aired on April 1, 2012.

30 "House of Black and White," directed by Michael Slovis, written by David Benioff and D. B. Weiss, in *Game of Thrones*, season 5, HBO, first aired on April 19, 2015.

31 Bennett, *A Medieval Life*, 114–127.

32 Bennett, *A Medieval Life*, 115.

33 Bennett, *A Medieval Life*, 123–25.

34 Bennett, *A Medieval Life*, 126.

35 Bennett, *A Medieval Life*, 126.

36 Natalie Zemon Davis, *The Return of Martin Guerre* (Cambridge, MA: Harvard University Press, 1983).

37 Robert Finlay, "The Refashioning of Martin Guerre," *American Historical Review* 93.3 (1988), 553–571. Finlay argues in his essay that Natalie Zemon Davis gives Bertrande too much agency. One key component of his argument hinges on Davis' claim that Bertrande surely recognized, sexually, a difference between her husband and the impostor. But Finlay contends that medieval sex was not like modern sex: it happened in the cold and in the dark, with lots of clothes and lots of livestock around (559). He also contends that, because Martin was gone for so many years and the evidence suggests that Martin and Bertrande didn't have a passionate marriage before he left, Bertrande might not have recognized a difference (558). Ultimately Finlay argues that Davis' case is far too circumstantial, based as it is on contextual evidence and on an overinterpretation of the actual evidence—the court records. Finlay suggests that, when looked at more literally, Davis' suppositions have nothing to support them.

38 "The Gift," directed by Miguel Sapochnik, written by David Benioff and D. B. Weiss, in *Game of Thrones*, season 5, HBO, first aired on May 24, 2015.

39 "Battle of the Bastards," HBO.
40 "Blood of My Blood," directed by Jack Bender, written by Brian Cogman, in *Game of Thrones*, season 6, HBO, first aired on May 29, 2016.
41 "Battle of the Bastards," HBO.
42 "Blood of My Blood," HBO.
43 "No One," HBO.
44 "No One," HBO; "The Winds of Winter," HBO.
45 "The Winds of Winter," HBO.

12

The Power of Sansa Stark

A Representation of Female Agency in Late Medieval England

Danielle Alesi

"Like a lady in a song"

Sansa Stark is often considered one of the least popular characters in the *Game of Thrones* series. Many find her boring, submissive, vapid, or weak. Certainly she appears to lack the qualities of other female characters that have captured the audience's attention: Arya's ferocity, Daenerys' realization of her own power, and even Cersei's strength of will and political machinations. It is Sansa's story, however, that most closely mirrors the reality of life for medieval women.

Sansa's life is remarkably similar to that of Elizabeth of York (1466–1503), daughter of King Edward IV (r. 1461–1470, 1471–1483) and Elizabeth Woodville (c.1437–1492). Elizabeth was the first queen to reign after the Wars of the Roses (1455–1485), the dynastic struggle for the English throne that inspired *A Game of Thrones*. Like Sansa, Elizabeth underwent a series of betrothals, suffered the loss of her family together with that of her good name and the death of her brothers, spent time as a political hostage, and was married to the enemy—all while being a potential heir to the throne that stood at the very heart of civil war.

Throughout the series we see Sansa evolve from a sheltered high-born girl into a young woman learning to harness her own agency within the limitations imposed on a lady of her time and class and from the precarious and dangerous political position she finds herself in. Sansa's story is noteworthy because it bears a remarkable resemblance to that of the majority of women in the late medieval period. The typical high-born girl, princess, or queen did not don armor, lead armies, or otherwise subvert the traditional female roles ascribed to her. They were treated as pawns in diplomatic negotiations, traded for property or claims, and given in marriage or held captive on opposite sides of conflicts. They could be hostages in their own homes. They could be victims of marital rape. Sometimes they could have a great deal of power and agency through their children or through the death of their male family members. This was a traditional female power that derived not from swords or from warrior-women who led armies into battle, but was power nonetheless. In studies of female agency, traditional and feminine modes of power should be considered just as legitimate as the power derived from subverting femininity. Thus the power of Sansa Stark and the way her story echoes that of so many women throughout history who have typically gone unnoticed help us understand female agency within the whole of women's history.

A Good Queen

In the study of late medieval and early modern queenship, much attention is given to "bad queens." These are women who subverted the traditional roles ascribed to them and either caused trouble or garnered bad reputations as a result. It is equally important, however, to give credit to women who, in their own time, were considered "good queens." To understand historical reality, norms are as necessary as exceptions. The late medieval and early modern period overflowed with literature, advice books, and chronicles that illustrated what made a good queen "good." Perhaps the emergence of so many "bad queens" caused men to feel as though they needed to write down specifically how a woman in power should behave and what her role should be.

One such instruction manual was *The Game and Playe of Chesse*, published by William Caxton in 1474.[1] It certainly circulated at court and was known by Elizabeth of York and her sisters. The text describes the qualities expected of a queen at that time:

> A queen ought to be chaste, wise of honest people, well mannered, and not curious[;] in nourishing of her children her wisdom ought not only to appear in feat and works, but also in speaking: that is, to wit, that she be secret and tell not such things as ought to be holden secret. Amongst all, she ought to be timorous and shamefast.[2]

Here the traditional role of queens (and aristocratic ladies in general) is clearly prescribed. They were to be, above all, pious and charitable, for their good works and saintly reputations reflected favorably on their male counterparts. In late medieval society, women were considered to be an extension of their male kinsmen, a living representation of their honor, so that the good behavior and charitable actions of noble women were attributed to the moral strength and goodness of the men who ruled them.

As illustrated in *The Game and Playe of Chesse*, queens were expected to play an active role in the education of their children. Through children a medieval queen could access the greatest amount of legitimate power. The similarity between the handwriting and signature of Elizabeth of York and that of her mother, Elizabeth Woodville, suggests that, as queen, the mother played such an active role in her daughter's education that she herself taught her even to write. Close involvement in the rearing of royal children gave queen consorts the ability to establish close relationships with their children and potentially influence them. This could be crucial to the future position of a queen. Kings died. But a queen who was valued by her son, the heir, could retain a position of authority. She could also have far-reaching influence through her daughters and younger sons, who were typically married into foreign kingdoms or given vast lands to rule.

Foreign Queens

After the Norman conquest of 1066, English kings began to acquire brides from other kingdoms, thus securing new lands and alliances. With the arrival of foreign-born queens, the role of a queen consort expanded. A foreign queen was expected to conform to the needs and cultural expectations of her new country, yet remain a representative of her homeland. This new type of queen embodied the peace and prosperity brought about by her marriage; but she was also, in her new country, an exemplar of the culture and an advocate for the land of her birth. Queens could, however, also become scapegoats, blamed both for their homeland's actions and for the actions of their new country, especially if people believed the king to be negatively influenced by his "foreign" wife.[3] In *Game of Thrones*, this is true for Sansa, a foreign princess from the north. In an effort to stem the war, Sansa is used to intercede with her family. She is forced to write a letter dictated by her captors in her new kingdom. Sansa is later beaten and humiliated in front of the court, a scapegoat for her brother's victories against the Lannister army.

During Sansa's time as a political captive in King's Landing, she adopts the tactic of an almost deadpan recitation of necessary lies: "'My father was a traitor,' Sansa said at once. 'And my brother and lady mother are traitors as well.' That reflex she had learned quickly. 'I am loyal to my beloved Joffrey.'" To which Tyrion replies: "'No doubt. As loyal as a deer surrounded by wolves.' 'Lions,' she whispered."[4] This exchange summarizes the situation of any foreign queen: to represent her homeland, while being expected to adopt the values and priorities of her new country.

The Mediator

A queen consort was also expected to play the role of mediator. This highly ritualized and symbolic role was steeped in religious traditions. The queen adopted the role of the Virgin Mary, intercessor to her son, Jesus Christ. Just as kings were God's divine representatives on earth, queens assumed the role of Mary, mediating and intervening on behalf of those who sought the king's mercy. In *A Game of Thrones* Sansa publicly pleads for her father to be allowed to go to the Wall instead of being executed. She tells herself: "Once she was queen, she could persuade Joff to bring Father back and grant him pardon."[5] Sansa is aware that, as queen and not merely a betrothed, she would have more power as an intercessor, despite Joffrey's animosity toward her.

The role of mediator not only provided an avenue for sanctioned female power, it also benefited kings. Intercession was an established method that provided a legitimate excuse for a king to retain his honor and the appearance of strength while granting mercy for political or personal reasons. The credit—or blame—for the decision could be assigned to his wife.

Wedded and Bedded

The issue of Sansa's marriage is introduced from the first episode in *Game of Thrones.* Robert tells Eddard that they shall forge their houses together through a marriage between Joffrey and Sansa. Princesses were typically used as pawns to secure political alliances. Edward IV used Elizabeth of York as a crucial bargaining chip in his domestic and foreign affairs, promising her hand in marriage to various suitors as his political needs shifted.

In 1475 King Edward IV met King Louis XI of France on a bridge near Amiens, to sign the Treaty of Picquigny, which sealed a peace between England and France. This treaty included the betrothal of "the most serene Lady Elizabeth" to King Louis' son, the Dauphin Charles, at a time "when they shall reach marriageable years."[6] Elizabeth was nine and Charles was five when the treaty was signed.

Although Elizabeth was expected to go to France at the age of 12 and to be raised as the future queen of the land, this part of the agreement did not come to pass, just like many other arrangements her father entered into on her behalf.[7] Conflict between Burgundy and France was coming to a head, making the future of the alliance uncertain. King Edward agreed to marry one of his daughters, Anne, to the Burgundian heir, Philip, should Burgundy win in the conflict. In the end, it was England that lost. On December 23, 1482 the Treaty of Arras brought peace between France and Burgundy. It included a betrothal between Dauphin Charles and the three-year-old Margaret of Burgundy. Elizabeth was publicly jilted. Even worse, the blame was laid at Elizabeth's feet, although others had made the decision, as a matter of policy—as was customary for all arrangements of marriages between princes and princesses. A contemporary commentator of these events, Philip de Commines, wrote about the princess: "It was very well known that the girl was a great deal too old for monseigneur the Dauphin," attributing the reason for the snub to Elizabeth's age and unsuitability. Similarly, Sansa was publicly rejected in favor of Margaery Tyrell, in front of the court. In Martin's novel a great show is staged for Joffrey's repudiation of Sansa in favor of the new, politically advantageous match with Margaery.

Both historically and in *Game of Thrones*, young and wealthy heiresses were often betrothed at an early age. In *A Clash of Kings*, Sansa references arrangements for Lady Ermesande—still "a babe seated on her wet nurse's lap"—to be married into the Lannister family.[8] The financial assets and political advantages that such young girls could bring to their husbands made them highly sought-after commodities. Margaret Beaufort, for example, was a close cousin of King Henry VI (r. 1422–1471) and became an extremely wealthy heiress upon her father's death. She was married at the age of 12 to Edmund Tudor, half-brother to Henry VI, who was then 24 years old. But even when a wedding took place with a bride that young, it was the custom to wait for a few more years before consummating the marriage, in order to allow the bride to be old enough to bear a child safely. Unfortunately Edmund refused to wait. He was aware that, if Margaret produced an heir for him, he would own a life interest in her estates. Consequently Margaret became pregnant by the age of 13. The labor was particularly brutal and dangerous, and both Margaret and her newborn son, Henry Tudor, were lucky to survive the ordeal. Ironically, Edmund died before the birth of the son he could not wait to conceive. Margaret never gave birth again, despite several subsequent marriages; she was apparently too damaged and scarred, both physically and psychologically.[9] In *Game of Thrones* Sansa, too, fears the consequences of an early marriage. She is distraught when her first menstrual period arrives. In a desperate attempt to hide the evidence, she tries to cut out the stains. When Shae, her handmaiden, comes in, Sansa cries that she is afraid that the Queen will discover that she can now bear children.[10]

The outcome of Sansa's marriage to Ramsay Bolton can also be compared to Margaret Beaufort's story. In "Unbowed, Unbent, Unbroken" (season 5), Sansa suffers a terrible act of rape from her new husband.[11] Though Ramsay is an extreme caricature of a sadist, rape has been, unfortunately, an ordeal that many women have suffered throughout history. Indeed, rape within a marriage was not even a recognized concept until relatively recent times.[12] Marriage was a transfer of property—a woman—from the father to the husband, and consummation was deemed a legal right of the husband; it was often referred to as "the marriage debt." The law did not consider forced or coerced sex within the institution of marriage to be rape, and a woman could seek no official justice. Henry Tudor, with substantial help from Margaret, eventually became King Henry VII (r. 1485–1509), and Margaret Beaufort became the most important and influential woman in the realm. Upon his ascension, he granted his mother the exceptionally rare status of *femme sole*: a citizen in her own right, with the ability to own property and control her wealth without male interference.[13]

Medieval women were certainly victims of marital rape; hence it is essential to include this tragic subject in discussions of female agency. As Margaret Beaufort and Sansa Stark demonstrate, however, the tragedy of that moment could be effectively surpassed by the actions they took to reassert themselves as women of agency.

"Back to your cage, little bird"

Sansa spends most of the early seasons of the series as the Lannisters' political captive. After her betrothal to Joffrey is dissolved, she is simply called "their ward," although really she was their hostage. In *A Storm of Swords* Sansa is forcibly married to Tyrion Lannister; this was designed to co-opt her claims on the North and to neutralize her ability to make allies with another family, the Tyrells:

> SANSA: You can't make me.
> CERSEI: Of course we can. You may come along quietly and say your vows as befits a lady, or you may struggle and scream and make a spectacle for the stable boys to titter over, but you will end up wedded and bedded all the same.[14]

Sansa never expected to have a claim on the North. Nevertheless, after her older brother Robb dies and her two younger brothers, Bran and Rickon, are presumed dead, she has a viable claim to her ancestral home. Thus these deaths made her a pawn of much higher value.

Similarly, Elizabeth of York was made into a political captive. After the death of her father, King Edward IV, in 1483, she, her mother, and her younger sisters entered the safety of sanctuary. There they spent months hiding from Elizabeth's uncle, Richard III, who had "usurped" the throne. The crown was supposed to go to Elizabeth's brother, the 13-year-old Edward V, who reigned for little over two months and was never crowned. Instead Richard took Edward and his younger brother into his custody in the Tower of London, where they disappeared and were never seen again.

The presumed death of the "princes in the Tower," much like the unknown fate of Bran and Rickon, made Elizabeth of York a claimant to the throne of England and a beacon of hope for her family. But Elizabeth was only a woman, and reports were also being spread that her mother's marriage to Edward IV was not legitimate. Many looked to Henry Tudor as the next heir. It may have been Margaret Beaufort who suggested that the two claimants marry.[15] Such a union would streamline the claims of the Yorkist heir and the Lancastrian heir, uniting the two factions that had been warring for decades. Henry Tudor, publicly "upon his oath, promised that, as soon as he should be king, he would marry Elizabeth, King Edward's daughter."[16] This acknowledgment that Elizabeth's position had changed from marginal to possible heir offered Henry Tudor a method to obtain sovereignty and legitimacy in England.

Learning of the proposed alliance between Elizabeth and Henry Tudor, Richard III reacted much as the Lannisters did at the possibility of a marriage between Sansa and Willas Tyrell. Richard forcibly removed Elizabeth and her sisters from sanctuary and brought them to live at his court, prisoners in their own home. King Richard also began to make marriage plans for Elizabeth. It was widely believed that he was seriously considering marrying his niece himself, both to thwart Henry Tudor and to bolster his own insecure hold on the throne.[17] Before any wedding could occur, however, Henry Tudor invaded England and defeated Richard III in one decisive, history-altering battle at Bosworth Field in 1485. Henry Tudor became King Henry VII, claiming the throne by the medieval right of conquest and by right of his own Lancaster bloodline. Nevertheless, it was not until he married Elizabeth, uniting York and Lancaster, that the throne was secure and the Wars of the Roses were truly over.

Birthright

In *Game of Thrones*, Sansa chooses to marry Ramsay, knowing that the Boltons were responsible for the murder of her mother and brother, the sack and capture of her home, and the loss of her birthright. Her primary motive is, of course, to avenge her family, but it cannot be overlooked that she also has a burning desire to take back Winterfell. Her situation can be compared with that of Elizabeth of York, who, in the interest of her own inheritance and perhaps also to avenge the tragedies that had befallen her own family, married the heir to a dynasty that had been her family's bitter enemy for decades.

One of the most iconic moments for Sansa in the books occurs when she is outside in the Eyrie, building a snow castle in the shape of Winterfell: "She could feel the snow on her lashes, taste it on her lips. It was the taste of Winterfell. The taste of innocence. The taste of dreams."[18] In this moment of self-actualization, Sansa breaks her "King's Landing is my home now" façade. She acknowledges her longing for Winterfell, her desire to return to it. When little Robert Arryn destroys the snow castle with a doll, her rage and vengefulness against anyone who might try to take it away from her lashes out:

> A mad rage seized hold of her. She picked up a broken branch and smashed the torn doll's head down on top of it, then pushed it down atop the shattered gatehouse of her snow castle.[19]

In season 6 Sansa is reunited with Jon Snow at Castle Black. Although it initially appears that she was seeking nothing but refuge and reunion with family, it becomes immediately clear that she is determined to take Winterfell back from the Boltons.

When discussing where they will go next, Sansa begins to try to persuade Jon to raise an army and take back their home: "Winterfell is our home. It's ours. And Arya's. And Bran's. And Rickon's. Wherever they are it belongs to our family. We have to fight for it." Though Jon is reluctant, "I'm tired of fighting," Sansa persists: "If we don't take back the North we'll never be safe. I want you to help me. But I'll do it myself if I have to."[20]

There is little doubt that Sansa's journey from the pawn whimpering "King's Landing is my home" to the player who says "I am Sansa Stark of Winterfell. This is my home. And you can't frighten me" shows one of the most impressive arcs of female empowerment depicted in the series.[21]

"A woman's kind of courage"

Elizabeth of York has often been overlooked by historians, mostly because she is what is considered a "good queen." Her family lineage brought peace and prestige to her husband's reign. She bore children regularly, out of whom two sons (one being the infamous Henry VIII) and two daughters survived, and she was widely considered to be beautiful, kind, religious, and charitable. It has even been said of Elizabeth that she was beloved because she was powerless. Elizabeth of York certainly did not involve herself in politics to the same extent as Elizabeth Woodville (her mother), but that did not mean that she exhibited no power whatsoever. Evidence from letters and inventories of gifts indicates that Elizabeth was a great distributor of patronage during her reign as queen.[22] She often interceded on behalf of others and even admonished powerful lords and courtiers without reference to Henry. She controlled her court and household and the education and upbringing of her royal children. When Yorkist rebellions continued to plague the early years of Henry VII's reign and pretenders claiming to be one of her lost brothers emerged, Elizabeth stood at her husband's side throughout.

Perhaps most significantly, she had a personal and private influence over her husband, the king. This was the method by which it was most likely for a medieval woman to exercise political power: not by exercising her own right, but through intercession, mediation, patronage, and personal influence over powerful men. What makes the study of women like Elizabeth of York so important is that, unlike the women who fully defied gender norms to obtain agency and inspired fascinating and riveting tales, "good" women who operated within the boundaries set by their sex could be just as defiant while still maintaining positive reputations and their personal safety and security.

Sansa survives, then plays "the game of thrones" by using traditional feminine qualities. She uses her "courtesy," her courtly manners and carefully chosen words—polite lies—in order to survive. She is not born with, but later acquires, a political intelligence that grows with her character. Sansa experiences the trials and tribulations that were often thrust upon high-born and royal women in the late medieval period. She is forced into marriages for political purposes. She is a victim of marital rape and abuse. She is held as a political prisoner and treated as a pawn by the great players in the realm. Nevertheless, she survives these trials by using her intelligence and a feminine subtlety that gradually turns her into a strong character, possessed of a fierce determination to avenge her family and to win back the home that has been taken from her. By the time Sansa walks down the steps of the Eyrie in season 4, dressed in a gown she herself has made as a symbolic representation of the identity she has chosen to take control of, she has evolved from pawn to player. This change is fully actualized by season 6, where Sansa not only persuades Jon to raise an army against Ramsay to take back Winterfell, but confronts her abuser, orchestrates his brutal execution, and takes her place at the high table next to her brother, as the Lady of Winterfell.

It surely takes a certain amount of courage to survive as a woman in a man's world. Brienne once said to Sansa's mother, Catelyn: "'You have courage. Not battle courage perhaps, but, I don't know, a woman's kind of courage.'"[23] Surely "a woman's kind of courage" should be considered as valuable as masculine courage, so that women may not feel the need to shed their femininity in order to be perceived as strong. While we applaud women who defy gender norms to achieve their ends, we must also recognize that women throughout history have been powerful and influential, often by operating within the constructs society has set for them. We learn from Sansa Stark, as we learn from Elizabeth of York, that all demonstrations of courage, strength, and agency are legitimate and worthy of study and appreciation.

Notes

1 Alison Weir, *Elizabeth of York: A Tudor Queen and Her World* (New York: Ballantine Books, 2013), 50.
2 Weir, *Elizabeth of York*, 51.
3 Elizabeth Norton, *She Wolves: The Notorious Queens of England* (London: History Press, 2010), 1–12.
4 George R. R. Martin, *A Song of Ice and Fire, Book Two: A Clash of Kings* (New York: Bantam, 2012 [1999]), 51.
5 George R. R. Martin, *A Song of Ice and Fire, Book One: A Game of Thrones* (New York: Bantam, 2013 [1996]), 551.
6 Weir, *Elizabeth of York*, 49.
7 Weir, *Elizabeth of York*, 50.
8 Martin, *A Clash of Kings*, 41.

9 Michael K. Jones, "Margaret Beaufort," in *The Women of the Cousins' War: The Duchess, the Queen, and the King's Mother*, edited by Philippa Gregory (New York: Simon & Schuster, 2011), 241.

10 "A Man Without Honor," directed by David Nutter, written by David Benioff and D. B. Weiss, in *Game of Thrones*, season 2, HBO, first aired on May 13, 2012.

11 "Unbowed, Unbent, Unbroken," directed by Jeremy Podeswa, written by David Benioff and D. B. Weiss, in *Game of Thrones*, season 5, HBO, first aired on May 17, 2015.

12 Jennifer A. Bennice and Patricia A. Resick, "Marital Rape: History, Research and Practice," *Trauma, Violence, & Abuse* 4 (2003), 228–246.

13 Jones, "Margaret Beaufort," 241.

14 George R. R. Martin, *A Song of Ice and Fire, Book Three: A Storm of Swords* (New York: Bantam, 2011 [2000]), 384. Ironically, Tywin Lannister later threatens his daughter Cersei with a forced political marriage, noting that she wouldn't be the first woman dragged into a sept against her will; "The Children," directed by Alex Graves, written by David Benioff and D. B. Weiss, in *Game of Thrones*, season 4, HBO, first aired on June 15, 2014.

15 Weir, *Elizabeth of York*, 99–104.

16 Weir, *Elizabeth of York*, 107.

17 Weir, *Elizabeth of York*, 119.

18 Martin, *A Storm of Swords*, 1101.

19 Martin, *A Storm of Swords*, 1106.

20 "Book of the Stranger," directed by Daniel Sackheim, written by David Benioff and D. B. Weiss, in *Game of Thrones*, season 6, HBO, first aired on May 15, 2016.

21 "Unbowed, Unbent, Unbroken," HBO.

22 Weir, *Elizabeth of York*, 287–293.

23 "The Ghost of Harrenhal," directed by David Petrarca, written by David Benioff and D. B. Weiss, in *Game of Thrones*, season 2, HBO, first aired on April 29, 2012.

Part IV

Religion

13

Continuity and Transformation in the Religions of Westeros and Western Europe

Don Riggs

George R. R. Martin's novel series *A Song of Ice and Fire* and the HBO series *Game of Thrones* based on it depict a complex set of religious institutions and practices that are in many ways parallel to historical reality. Many see medieval Europe as dominated by the Roman Catholic Church, covered by church buildings that ranged from massive cathedrals to small chapels, and filled with clergy, whether popes in their palaces or humble monks eking out a bare existence in far-flung monasteries. This sense of a religious European unity is, however, tempered by constant change within the church, conversion, internal dissension, heresy, and encounters with other, "pagan" religions. Enriched by this historical record, the *Game of Thrones'* religious world creates an alternative reality of its own.

Spirited Away

As the Christian church expanded across Europe during late antiquity, it encountered earlier religions, among the most ancient of which was shamanism.[1] Going back at least 30,000 years, shamanism—which can be described as a kind of animism- was one of the first faiths of our human ancestors, during the Stone Age, when they were hunters and gatherers. The shaman was a person capable of out-of-body experiences or ecstatic trances during which, in the form of an animal, he would visit the spirit world and negotiate a good supply of game. At other times, the shaman would effect a healing through this kind of trance journey. Peoples with shamanic traditions lead a marginalized existence today, being increasingly pushed into inaccessible and inhospitable landscapes, such as the frozen lands north of the Arctic Circle or the impenetrable rainforests. During the Middle Ages there certainly existed shamanic practices on the edges of known civilizations, for instance in the Celtic areas of Spain, France, and England.[2]

Game of Thrones versus History: Written in Blood, First Edition. Edited by Brian A. Pavlac.
© 2017 John Wiley & Sons, Inc. Published 2017 by John Wiley & Sons, Inc.

In *Game of Thrones* the Starks of Winterfell have lost most of the Old Religion of the First Men, but some animistic ideas survive in godswoods (groves) outside the castle. In the grove sits the heart tree—a fictional species called *weirwood*, which has contrasting white bark, red leaves, and sap the color of blood and is marked by a human face carved into the trunk. People believe that the weirwood connects them to the gods, and weirwoods are supposed to be conduits to the nature spirits called Children of the Forest.

A good example of a shamanistic belief is the belief in "warging"—the possession of animals by humans. When Jon Snow discovers a dead direwolf and her newborn pups, each of the Stark legitimate children and Ned's bastard son Jon receives one to raise. Bran, and to a lesser extent Jon and Arya, learn to project their minds into their direwolves, as if they themselves were spirit animals. This is especially significant for Bran. At the beginning of the story Bran suffered a near-fatal fall that cost him the use of his legs, so he can no longer climb the walls of Winterfell, as he used to. In this respect he resembles his namesake in the tales of the *Mabinogion*, who is wounded in the foot by a poisoned spear. His name means "raven," and Alby Stone argues that his character is influenced by the Fisher King of the Holy Grail stories—also a man who cannot move, as his thigh has been wounded.[3] The Celtic name's meaning also links it with the three-eyed raven who teaches Bran Stark, first in his dreams, then in person.[4]

At first Bran has no ancestor or shaman to teach him the art of shamanic binding. Fortunately a Crannogman, Jojen Reed, has "green dreams" (as his ancestors did) and can intuitively direct Bran's development as a "warg"—that is, a person capable of inhabiting an animal's body. Bran sometimes does hate Jojen the taskmaster, as for instance when he has "become" Jojen's direwolf and Jojen calls him out of the trance. "Jojen was always telling him to do things when he opened his third eye and put on Summer's skin."[5]

Jojen insists that Bran should remain a separate entity from the direwolf: "'Bran the boy and Summer the wolf. You are two, then?'... 'Remember that, Bran. Remember *yourself*, or the wolf will consume you.'"[6] Bran's mystical encounters offer two connections with shamanism. First, the "third eye," which features in Bran's dreams in *Game of Thrones*, also appears in shamanic traditions.[7] Second, the literature on shamanism mentions the possibility that a shaman inhabiting the body of an animal might forget his or her human identity and become the animal itself. Anthropologist Rane Willerslev, recounting his experiences among the Siberian Yukaghir, writes that

> taking on the body of another species can [...] only be done for short periods of time and is risky. It is possible that temporarily belonging to an alien species' body can result in the loss of one's own original species identity. [...] A trans-formed individual thus becomes an "Other" and his memories of past experiences are lost.[8]

Bran may well want to become Jojen's direwolf permanently, but Bran's "riding" in Summer's body turns out to be a stage that leads to his narrow escape from the king of winter, and possibly to his ultimately replacing the Three-Eyed Raven, or Last Greenseer.[9]

Lifts Her Leafy Arms to Pray

When nomadic peoples discovered agriculture about 12,000 years ago, they became "sedentary" societies. They abandoned their hunter-gatherer ancestors' wandering in order to settle down in a fixed location and to cultivate crops. These societies developed priesthoods that studied the night sky to keep track of seasonal changes and determine when farmers should irrigate, plant, and harvest. New religions developed a host of gods and goddesses, usually led by a sky-god; we classify them today *polytheistic* ("devoted to many [vs. one] god") precisely on that account. These polytheisms rejected and attacked the earlier shamanistic religions. The Roman historian Tacitus (AD 56–c. 118) records that in AD 60 a Roman army eliminated a large community of Druids, a shamanic priesthood of Celts in what is today Anglesey (in Wales). Tacitus tells us that the new governor of Britain, Paulus Suetonius, led an assault on the Isle of Mons, where his legions were confronted by a Druidic defense:[10]

> Facing them on the shore was the enemy line, a dense array of arms and men, and amongst them rushed women who, like furies, wore funereal clothing, had disheveled hair and brandished torches. Around stood Druids, their hands raised to heaven pouring out terrible curses [...] [the Roman commander snapped the men out of their shock and after defeating the natives] the groves sacred to their barbarous worship were cut down.

Game of Thrones, too, has an instance of a sacred grove's destruction. As Arya Stark is traveling with some of the men of Beric Dondarrion, they visit a place that "had been sacred to the children of the forest."[11] The local people avoid the site, since it is said to be "haunted by the ghosts of the children of the forest who had died here when the Andal king named Erreg the Kinslayer had cut down their grove," leaving a circle of 31 stumps, each so wide that Arya could sleep on one. The Andals had invaded and conquered Westeros centuries before, bringing with them the worship of the Seven to replace the First Men's Old Religion. That there is still strife between the followers of the Old Religion and those who worship the Seven is evident when the company finds shelter beneath the "scorched shell" of a sept, a place of worship for the Seven. Looters had wrecked and robbed it, despoiling images of the Seven. When asked who has committed this desecration, the old septon says: "'Northmen, they were. Savages who worship trees.'"[12]

A New World Order

The rise of Christianity in the Roman Empire of the fourth century AD ended the worship of the Greco-Roman pantheon. Soon after, large groups of barbarians, many of them early Germans or Goths, migrated from Asia into Europe and drove westward in order to invade the Roman provinces of Gaul, the Iberian Peninsula, and ultimately Italy. Many of these tribes had been converted to Christianity, although they often followed a version of it called Arianism. That unorthodox doctrine was named after Bishop Arius (256–336) and held that Jesus was not equal to the Father, since God created the Christ, while the orthodox version of Christianity held that Christ the Son and God the Father were of the same substance. An outsider might not see one jot of difference between the two doctrines. Still, theological disagreements among orthodox Christians and heretical Arians provoked extensive and savage violence for much of the fourth century.[13]

Christianity itself had spread through the Roman Empire as an "illegal," underground religion, surrounded and at times engulfed by Greco-Roman polytheism. In the early fourth century, the Emperor Constantine (r. 306–337) legalized and favored Christianity. As the number of Christians multiplied, Constantine's nephew, Julian "the Apostate" (r. 361–363), attempted to revive the worship of the Greco-Roman gods. Had he succeeded, perhaps the Middle Ages would have included multiple deities, as does the dominant religious system in Westeros. Julian's early death in battle, however, mostly ended any chance of slowing down Christianity's growth.

As Christianity spread throughout the Roman Empire, it reached people called *pagani*—literally "country dwellers" (people who inhabited the *pagi*, rural districts) or "hicks." Since these "pagans" lived far from the urban and commercial centers, Christian missionaries had greater difficulty converting them. In some cases the "pagans" held on to their pre-Christian worship—which contained an element of tree worship.[14] Places holy to an earlier religion, often fountains and pools, were adapted and turned into Christian churches. In northern Spain, for example, a third- or fourth-century temple of the Mother Goddess Cybele became, by the thirteenth century, the church of Santa Eulalia de Bóveda. This chapel, re-dedicated to a Catholic saint, still retained its old wall paintings of plants and birds rather than replacing them with martyrs, apostles, or other Christian figures.[15]

Christians also adopted and transformed elements of Greco-Roman polytheism. Medieval psychology and medicine were based on the theory of the humors, which, roughly speaking, went back to a Hippocratic–Galenic model. In the medieval version each humor was associated with one or more planets: melancholy with Saturn; the jovial red bile with Jupiter; phlegm with the Moon; and yellow bile with Mars, the planet of the god of war.[16] Proper health was believed to come from a proper balance of these humors. More enduring was the survival of the gods of classical antiquity into the Middle Ages (and even into modern times) in the form of astrology and, symbolically, in the planets' names.[17] The names of the days of the week in various modern languages derive from the classical pantheon too, either etymologically or through translation—for example, in English, "Sunday," "Monday," and "Saturday," come from Old English forms that translated the Latin *Solis dies* (day of the Sun), *Lunae dies* (day of the Moon), and *Saturni dies* (day of Saturn); or, in French, *lundi, mardi, mercredi, jeudi, vendredi,* are inherited from the Latin *Lunae dies* (day of the Moon), *Martis dies* (day of Mars), *Mercurii dies* (day of Mercury), *Iovis dies* (day of Jupiter), *Veneris dies* (day of Venus).

Anthropologist Felicitas Goodman argues that, while those who move into cities bring with them their old faith from the forest and from farms, they inevitably become secularized, "sometimes easily, sometimes over several generations." But this loss of religion, this "trance deprivation" is not bearable for people, so in urban environments there appear "cults or movements answering to this need."[18] Medieval Irish literature suggests that celestial signs and portents met this need. Mark Williams points out that "unique celestial phenomena" such as comets and blazing fires in the sky are different from regularly recurring patterns of planetary movement.[19] Planetary movements were already a normal part of rural society's priestly divination of the timing for planting, harvesting, and so on, whereas the unique "fire in the sky" that appears without precedent or warning was interpreted as a sign of major and sudden shift in life on earth.

The Magnificent Seven

At the beginning of the second season of *Game of Thrones*, a portent of red fire in the sky burns so brightly that it can be seen even during the day. Different characters interpret this omen according to their own belief systems. Melisandre, the Red Priestess, seizes the moment for religious warfare. She sees the Red Comet as a sign that Stannis Baratheon, claimant of the Iron Throne, has been recognized as the incarnation of Azor Ahai, a savior foretold of old. She says that her god R'hllor opposes the Seven worshiped by most people in Westeros: "Lord of Light, we offer you these false gods, these seven who are one, and him the enemy."

Of course, those who believe in the Seven consider them to be the true gods. The faithful worship the Seven in temples called *septs* (from the Latin *septem*, "seven"). As in many Roman Catholic churches today, different altars circle the interior of a sept, each with an image and votive candles. The seven Westerosi gods may be derived from our astrology. When Jon Snow is with the wildling woman Ygritte, he finds that those north of the Wall observe the same planets but call them by different names. Jon has "learned the names of the twelve houses of heaven and the rulers of each; he could find the seven wanderers sacred to the Faith."[20] In Western European astrology, the "twelve houses of heaven" are referred to as the signs of the zodiac or the "celestial houses." The "seven wanderers" are the sun, the moon, and the visible planets—a concept reminiscent of that of the "wandering stars" (*stellae errantes* in Latin) as opposed to the "fixed stars" that did not seem to move in relation to each other.[21]

Although St. Augustine (354–430) denounced astrology in late antiquity, in the thirteenth century St. Thomas Aquinas granted it a qualified acceptance.[22] Four fixed signs of the zodiac, Aquarius, Leo, Taurus, and Scorpio, associated respectively with air, fire, earth, and water, may have influenced the representation of the four Christian Evangelists: Matthew, Mark, Luke, and John—an angel, a lion, and bull, and an eagle. These four symbols are frequently found on the title pages of medieval illuminated Bibles and on the tympana of such great medieval cathedrals as the one in Chartres. Astrological symbolism is also built into the thirteenth-century Cathedral of San Miniato del Monte in Tuscany, tying in the church's Christian mysteries with their expression in the signs of the zodiac.[23] Nevertheless, many connections between the pagan gods and Christianity via the astrological planets are indirect, subject to debate, or heretical. In contrast, Martin's Faith of the Seven in *Game of Thrones* puts the seven gods associated with the seven planets directly in the foreground of the religion.

Magic, Miracles, and Sorcery

Records of early Christianity contain many stories of miracles, including dead people resurrected to life. The Acts of the Apostles in the New Testament, for instance, recounts that the apostles Peter and Philip had the power to exorcise evil spirits by the laying on of hands. Philip's miracles even converted one Simon, who practiced magic. In apocryphal texts rejected by Christians, Simon Magus ("the Magician") offers the apostles money in exchange for the secret of their wonders, but Peter rebukes him. The difference between the miracles worked by Christians through their faith and those wonders worked by Simon Magus through his magic may not have seemed significant to people at the time. As the scholar Robert Conner states, "unlike people of today, people of antiquity made no clear distinction between religion and magic, or between medicine and magic."[24] Healing became a common attribute of Christian saints. The Venerable Bede (672/3–735), the medieval English historian, records a miraculous healing performed by Germanus, bishop of Auxerre (378–448):

> In the meantime [...] evil spirits, speeding through the whole island, were constrained against their will to foretell that Germanus was coming, [so that there came] [...] a chief of that region, carrying with him his son,

who in the very flower of his youth laboured under a grievous infirmity; for the sinews of the knee were wasted and shrunk, so that the withered limb was denied the power to walk. [...] [The chief lay his son before the saint] and straightway the blessed Germanus [...] touched the bent and feeble knee and passed his healing hand over all the diseased part. At once health was restored by the power of his touch. [...] The multitude was amazed at the miracle, and the Catholic faith was firmly established in the hearts of all.[25]

Thus even evil spirits can be "compelled," through the power of faith, to foretell the coming of a saint. In Westeros, however, many doubt the power of miracles and magic. Indeed, Tywin Lannister snorts, "sorcery is the sauce fools spoon over failure to hide the flavor of their own incompetence."[26]

Seeing the Light

In *Game of Thrones* there is one faith that disproves Tywin's skepticism. The Red Woman, Melisandre, and the Red Priest, Thoros of Myr, worship the same god, R'hllor, the Lord of Light. Both exercise magical and miraculous powers. Thoros at first seems a buffoon whose "flaming sword" is a stage prop good only to impress the gullible at tournaments. Yet he revives Beric Dondarrion from death repeatedly. Likewise, Melisandre clearly has some power. Davos sees her "give birth" to a maleficent shadow that kills Renly Baratheon. She also fills leeches with royal blood that, when thrown into a fire, seem to engineer the deaths of three of Stannis' enemies. Melisandre's power can even revive the murdered Jon Snow.[27] Her own beauty is a "glamour," masking her withered true self.[28]

The fight between light and darkness or good and evil is integral to Melisandre's religion. The Red Woman is priestess of a dualistic cult in which two gods, one of light and the other of darkness, are pitted against each other up until the final encounter, an apocalyptic fight to the death. Historically, several religions have adopted this kind of dualism. Zoroastrianism is probably the oldest dualistic religion, rising in southwest Asia in the fifth century BC.[29] Christianity also gave birth to a dualistic heresy, gnosticism, in the second century AD. Gnostics claimed that reality was split between God and Satan, Heaven and Earth, Spirit and Matter, and everyone must choose the divine side. Gnosticism influenced Manichaeism, another dualistic religion that arose in Persia in the third century AD. Dualistic beliefs reappeared in the Middle Ages, first as Bogomilism, in the Balkans in the tenth century, then as the Catharism or Albigensianism in southern France, in the twelfth century. In the early thirteenth century Catholic Christians forcibly converted, slaughtered, and exterminated the heretical Cathars, using the inquisition and the Albigensian Crusade.[30]

Melisandre stages her own religious war against other faiths, as mentioned above. She has the sept on Dragonstone destroyed and presides over the burning of the wooden figures of the Seven.[31] Despite the Faith's venerable history in the past of Westeros, its followers "overturned the altars, pulled down the statues, and smashed the stained glass with warhammers." A longsword is thrust into the heart of the image of the Mother.[32] This scene is in many ways similar to one recorded by the Venerable Bede concerning the conversion of King Edwin in AD 627. Edwin's chief priest, Coifi, says:

> "Who more suitably than I can set a public example and destroy the idols that I worshipped in ignorance?" So he formally renounced his empty superstitions and [...] set out to destroy the idols [...] When the crowd saw him, they thought he had gone mad; but without hesitation, as soon as he reached the shrine, he cast into it the spear he carried and thus profaned it. Then, full of joy at his knowledge of the worship of the true God, he told his companions to set fire to the shrine and its enclosures and destroy them. [33]

Revivalism and Popular Uprisings

In the Middle Ages, when the poor became hungry, disgruntled, or critical of the wealth and excesses of the clergy, popular uprisings sometimes arose against the church and the rulers who supported it. The Shepherds' Crusade of 1251, for instance, originally started as a crusade intended to free the Holy Land from Muslim domination, but devolved into attacks on the French church and nobility. The movement, however, "disappeared like smoke."[34] In England, the Peasants' Revolt of 1381 was initiated by impoverished members of the lower clergy, who attacked wealthy members of the church. Soon armed rebels led by the peasant Wat Tyler descended on London, demanding economic and social reforms from the 14-year-old King Richard II. Richard's men killed Wat Tyler and dispersed his followers, after which the king revoked all the concessions he had been forced to sign.[35] A similar Peasants' Rebellion in Germany in 1524–1525 was brutally suppressed by the nobles. Even Martin Luther supported the aristocracy, arguing that it was the duty of peasants to work the land and the duty of the upper classes to keep the peace.[36] Historically, common people did not have the power to enforce fundamental economic and social change.

In *Game of Thrones*, a popular religious movement knows as "the Sparrows" suggests a different outcome. At first, Cersei thinks to use its leader for her own purposes. She makes the "High Sparrow" the new High Septon and allows him to revive the Faith Militant, a popular religious army that had been suppressed centuries before by a previous monarch. Her pride, coupled with the disdain she has for this barefoot rebellion of the poor and uneducated, blinds her to the very real power that the believers have begun to wield. Ironically, the zealots punish Cersei for her sins, shaving her, stripping her, and forcing her to walk barefoot through the streets of King's Landing, while the long-suffering crowds jeer and throw garbage at her.[37] The High Sparrow suggests to her brother, Jaime Lannister, that poor, nameless, and powerless people could unite to overthrow an empire.[38] Given the explosive end to the High Septon at the end of season 6, a popular religious revolt is unlikely to overthrow the monarchy.

Leaving and Returning

For Davos the smuggler, the desecration of the sept on Dragonstone goes too far. To Davos, "the gods had never meant much, though like most men he had been known to make offerings to the Warrior before battle, to the Smith when he launched a ship, and to the Mother whenever his wife grew great with child"; but even he "felt ill as he watched them burn, and not only from the smoke."[39] His faith, in fact, sustained him in a near-death experience. After the Battle of the Blackwater, Davos barely survived drowning by finding a deserted island. When a ship offers rescue from his rock, he says: "The Mother sent her here, the Mother in her mercy."[40] Davos may not be very observant in his worship of the Seven, but its customs and traditions provide comfort and order.

In the Middle Ages, people in need, sorrow, sickness, or trouble also prayed to the Mother, in this case the Blessed Virgin Mary. Our Lady was believed to intercede with her son Jesus on behalf of sinners at the time of their death, to save them from damnation. The *Cantigas de Santa Maria*, for example, is a collection of miracles attributed to Mary and written down in the thirteenth-century scriptorium of the Spanish King Alfonso the Wise (r. 1252–1284). They demonstrate Mary's great mercy and compassion toward those who sought her aid.[41] Even today, Roman Catholics recite the "Hail, Mary," and "Ave Maria" is sung all over the world, both in religious and in secular settings.

A very different kind of deity is the Drowned God of the Iron Islands. The ironmen's Drowned God requires his priests to undergo initiation through the ritual of an actual, not symbolic, drowning. Devotees are held under water until they go limp, then celebrants pull the drowned man onto land, pump his arms and chest, and the High Priest Aeron Damphair gives him the "kiss of life" to resuscitate him.[42] An exception to this pattern is the drowning of Euron Greyjoy, as he becomes King of the Iron Islands; he is drowned and deposited on the beach, then just barely recuperates, all by himself, without any help from the priest.[43] In fact not all those who die are revived; some even die and remain dead. A milder, more modern ritual has newborn children dipped in salt water "that scarce wet the infant's head." The zealot Aeron Damphair, however, scoffs at such watered-down versions of the Old Rite.[44]

Given the similarities between the ironmen and the Vikings, the drowning ritual is possibly analogous to the use of pain in the worship of Odin. He was hanged from the tree Yggdrasill for nine days and nights and gave up one of his eyes in exchange for knowledge. Galina Krasskova asserts that "the only way to gain and master the wisdom of the dead was to die."[45] Seen in this light, the ritual of forcing a man to drown and then be resuscitated is an example of the practice of trial by ordeal.

Reflective of the water dunking of the ironmen, Christianity's main initiation ritual of baptism involves water and submersion. The sacrament of baptism makes the recipient die from the life of sin and be reborn into the life of the church. Almost since the beginning of Christianity, there have been disputes over adult baptism versus infant baptism—as exemplified by John Calvin's support for infant baptism, which has been likened to the Jewish practice of circumcision,[46] and implicit in a recently discovered twelfth-century Spanish image of the infant Jesus being baptized in a font, as opposed to his adult baptism in a river.[47] Whether performed with a few drops on the forehead or with a full-under dunking, baptism remains an essential part of the theology of life and death.

While Westeros is not Western Europe, in certain respects the religious struggles of its inhabitants offer parallels to our history. In some cases, however, Martin's version of shamanism, Druidism, polytheism, and various dualistic and magical manipulations seems larger than what we find in antiquity and the Middle Ages. Both history and *Game of Thrones* question the limits of the human experience: Is there a heaven and a hell? Can we leave the body and return to it? Can we return from death, and remain whole? Aspects of the various religions—from the out-of-the-body experiences of the Starks and their suggestions of a shamanic revival to the hieratic Church of the Seven, which makes no pronouncements on such matters, to the literal death-and-resuscitation rites of the Drowned God among the Iron Men and to the more apocalyptic and sorcery-tinged worship of the Lord of Light—present us with a smorgasbord of suggestions about how to think of life, death, and bodily existence.

Notes

1 Michael James Winkelman, "Shamans and Other 'Magico-Religious' Healers: A Cross-Cultural Study of Their Origins, Nature, and Social Transformation," *Ethos* 18.3 (1990), 320.
2 Kathleen Herbert, *Looking for the Lost Gods of England* (Ely: Anglo-Saxon Books, 1994), 9, 35, 36–38.
3 Alby Stone, "Bran, Odin, and the Fisher King: Norse Tradition and the Grail Legends," *Folklore* 100.1 (1989), 28.

4 George R. R. Martin, *A Song of Ice and Fire, Book Two: A Clash of Kings* (New York: Bantam, 2011 [1999]), 436–437.

5 Martin, *A Song of Ice and Fire, Book Three: A Storm of Swords* (New York: Bantam, 2011 [2000]), 126.

6 Martin, *A Storm of Swords*, 127.

7 Michael Harner, *Cave and Cosmos: Shamanic Encounters with Another Reality* (Berkeley, CA: North Atlantic Books, 2013), 50.

8 Rane Willerslev, "Not Animal, Not Not-Animal: Hunting, Imitation and Empathetic Knowledge among the Siberian Yukaghirs," *Journal of the Royal Anthropological Institute* 10.3 (2004), 634.

9 "The Door," directed by Jack Bender, written by David Benioff and D. B. Weiss, in *Game of Thrones*, season 6, HBO, first aired on May 22, 2016.

10 Cornelius Tacitus, *The Annals*, translated by J. C. Yardley (Oxford: Oxford University Press, 2008), 319–320.

11 Martin, *A Storm of Swords*, 301.

12 Martin, *A Storm of Swords*, 300.

13 Carlos R. Galvao-Sobrinho, "Embodied Theologies: Christian Identity and Violence in Alexandria in the Early Arian Controversy," in *Violence in Late Antiquity: Perceptions and Practices*, edited by H. A. Drake (Hampshire: Ashgate, 2006), 322.

14 Michael Bintley, "The Byzantine Silver Bowls in the Sutton Hoo Ship Burial and Tree-Worship in Anglo-Saxon England," *Papers from the Institute of Archaeology* 21 (2011), 7–8.

15 Church of Santa Eulalia de Bóveda (photo), 2016, Turespaña Website (accessed July 27, 2016 at http://www.spain.info/en/que-quieres/arte/monumentos/lugo/iglesia_de_santa_eulalia_de_boveda.html).

16 Jean Seznec, *The Survival of the Pagan Gods: The Mythological Tradition and Its Place in Renaissance Humanism and Art*, translated by Barbara F. Sessions (Princeton, NJ: Princeton University Press, 1953), 47.

17 Seznec, *Survival of the Pagan Gods*, 42.

18 Felicitas Goodman, *Ecstasy, Ritual, and Alternate Reality: Religion in a Pluralistic World* (Bloomington: Indiana University Press, 1988), 161.

19 Mark Williams, *Fiery Shapes: Celestial Portents and Astrology in Ireland and Wales, 700–1700* (New York: Oxford University Press, 2010), 132.

20 Martin, *A Storm of Swords*, 355.

21 On the notion of *stellae errantes* in antiquity, see Nigel Holmes, "Lucan 7, 425: Planets or Stars?" *Mnemosyne* 51.4 (1998), 447.

22 Benson Bobrick, *The Fated Sky: Astrology in History* (New York: Simon & Schuster, 2005), 82.

23 Fred Gettings, *The Secret Zodiac: The Hidden Art in Medieval Astrology* (London: Routledge & Kegan Paul, 1987), 23–25.

24 Robert Conner, *Jesus the Sorcerer: Exorcist and Prophet of the Apocalypse* (Oxford: Mandrake of Oxford, 2006), 97.

25 Bede, *Ecclesiastical History of the English People*, translated by Leo Sherley-Price (London: Penguin, 1990), 70–71.

26 Martin, *A Clash of Kings*, 492.

27 "Home," directed by Jeremy Podeswa, written by David Benioff and D. B. Weiss, in *Game of Thrones*, season 6, HBO, first aired on May 1, 2016.

28 "The Red Woman," directed by Jeremy Podeswa, written by David Benioff and D. B. Weiss, in *Game of Thrones*, season 6, HBO, first aired on April 24, 2016.

29 See S. A. Nigosian, *The Zoroastrian Faith: Tradition and Modern Research* (Montreal: McGill-Queen's University Press, 1993).

30 Jaye Puckett, "'Reconmenciez novele estoire': The Troubadours and the Rhetoric of the Later Crusades," *Modern Language Notes* 116.4 (2001), 846; Malcolm Lambert, *Medieval Heresy: Popular Movements from the Gregorian Reform to the Reformation* (New York: Barnes & Noble, 1992 [1977]), 105–146.

31 Martin, *A Clash of Kings*, 146–147.

32 Martin, *A Clash of Kings*, 147.

33 Bede, *Ecclesiastical History*, 130.

34 Gary Dickson, "Encounters in Medieval Revivalism: Monks, Friars, and Popular Enthusiasts," *Church History* 68.2 (1999), 273.

35 Elizabeth Hallam, ed., *The Chronicles of the Wars of the Roses* (Wayne, NJ: CLB, 1997), 35.

36 J. M. Porter, "Luther and Millenarianism: The Particular Case of the Peasants' War," *Journal of the History of Ideas* 42.3 (1981), 396–397.

37 George R. R. Martin, *A Song of Ice and Fire, Book Five: A Dance with Dragons* (New York: Bantam, 2011), 854–859.

38 "Home," HBO.

39 Martin, *A Clash of Kings*, 146.

40 Martin, *A Storm of Swords,* 74.

41 Petra Sofie Wirth, "A Study of the Castilian Summaries of Twenty-Five Alfonsine *Cantigas de Santa Maria*, with Special Reference to the Galician Text, Origins, and Illuminations" (MA diss., University of North Carolina at Chapel Hill, 1997), 134.

42 George R. R. Martin, *A Song of Ice and Fire, Book Four: A Feast for Crows* (New York: Bantam, 2006 [2005]), 25.

43 "The Door," directed by Jack Bender, written by David Benioff and D. B. Weiss, in *Game of Thrones*, season 6, HBO, first aired on May 22, 2016.

44 Martin, *A Feast for Crows*, 26.

45 Galina Krasskova, *Runes: Theory and Practice* (Pompton Plain, NJ: New Page Books, 2009), 15.

46 Jill Raitt, "Three Inter-Related Principles in Calvin's Unique Doctrine of Infant Baptism," *Sixteenth-Century Journal* 11.1 (1980), 54.

47 Pamela A. Patton, "*Et partu fontis exceptum*: The Typology of Birth and Baptism in an Unusual Spanish Image of Jesus Baptized in a Font," *Gesta* 33.2 (1994), 79.

14

Religious Violence in *Game of Thrones*

An Historical Background from Antiquity to the European
Wars of Religion

Maureen Attali

In recent seasons, *Game of Thrones* has come under heavy criticism for show-casing detailed acts of violence.[1] These scenes can be disturbing, incomprehensible, or even unbelievable according to current moral standards, but they are nevertheless well documented throughout history. In many of these instances, the scriptwriters and the author of the original novels, George R. R. Martin, have some claim to realistic renderings of actual historical beliefs and events.[2] Elaborate enactments of violence are rarely gratuitous within a culture. They often have a deeper meaning for the people who engage in them, indicating some of the social patterns that organize a community. Several examples of religious violence in *Game of Thrones* demonstrate how such acts deal with specific crises.

In the *Game of Thrones*' world, several religions have coexisted in the Seven Kingdoms for thousands of years.[3] The majority of the Westerosi people belong to the Faith of the Seven. The Andals, an invading people who conquered the land thousands of years before the beginning of the story, first introduced this religion into Westeros.[4] The indigenous religion of the Old Gods of the Forest prevails mostly in the north of the realm, while the inhabitants of the Iron Islands revere the Drowned God. The balance between these religions is upset when a war of succession erupts after King Robert Baratheon's death. One of the contenders for the throne, Stannis Baratheon, is a follower of R'hllor, the god from the eastern continent of Essos. Stannis forces his belief first upon his followers, then proposes to bring it to the lands he conquers.[5] The political conflict of succession progressively turns into a religious one, thus giving birth to specific forms of violence.[6] Three categories will illustrate acts of religious-based cruelty: first, perpetrators who belong to religious orders; second, people whose aim is to gain favor from a divinity; and third, transformative acts that reveal a religious content.

Game of Thrones versus History: Written in Blood, First Edition. Edited by Brian A. Pavlac.
© 2017 John Wiley & Sons, Inc. Published 2017 by John Wiley & Sons, Inc.

The Faith Militant versus Knights Templar

An obvious example of religious violence in *Game of Thrones* is the brutality of certain members of the Faith Militant. The Faith of the Seven used to include two military orders that "dispensed the justice of the Seven."[7] These orders, the Warrior's Sons and the Poor Fellows, were disarmed 300 years before the beginning of the main narrative.[8] In the wake of the War of the Five Kings, there emerged a religious movement known as "Sparrows," which, besides providing food and comfort to the poor, also sought "to defend the bodies and the souls of the common people" by physically assaulting sinners who break the Faith's rules. In a strategic move to undermine the Tyrells' influence at court, Cersei Lannister asks their leader, the High Sparrow, to "restore the religious order" by reviving military groups as the Faith Militant and by becoming the new High Septon.[9]

This kind of military order arising out of religious warfare is reminiscent of the first Christian military orders, which were established as the crusades were getting under way in the eleventh century. Soon after the First Crusade to the Holy Land (1096–1099), a *militia Christi* was approved by the pope after a group of Frankish knights decided to dedicate themselves to the defence of the Holy Sepulchre in Jerusalem, the place where Jesus Christ had allegedly been entombed.[10] This military order, in turn, spurred the creation of the Poor Fellow-Soldiers of Christ and of the Temple of Solomon, commonly known as Knights Templar.[11] In Westeros, too, the rise of the Faith Militant grew out of a spontaneous movement that was legalized afterwards. Both Knights Templar and members of the Faith Militant aimed to protect defenseless and pious people. Both orders required asceticism from their members, demanding vows of obedience, chastity, and poverty. Both included common people as well as noblemen, although within the Templars commoners served as sergeants and took orders from the knights.[12]

In *Game of Thrones*, Lancel Lannister's story hints at repentance and guilt as incentives for people to join such orders and, for some of them, to progress to acts of religious force. Lancel is compromised by two moral failures. First he becomes the adulterous lover of his cousin, Queen Cersei. Second, on Cersei's orders, he treasonously contributes to the death of King Robert Baratheon by pouring him fortified wine during a boar hunt.[13] After getting seriously wounded in battle, Lancel disappears from court and has a religious conversion. Haunted by guilt, he confesses his sins to the High Sparrow and finds "peace in the light of the Seven."[14] As a devout member of the Faith Militant and leader of punitive expeditions, Lancel forces the naked High Septon through the streets to make him atone for breaking the vow of celibacy.[15]

Lancel's path follows a theology of resurrection and redemption. Believers in the Faith of the Seven hold that, when they die, they will be judged according to their deeds in life. In the Faith of the Seven, the Father is the judge and dispatches souls to one of the seven heavens or seven hells.[16] Fearing for their souls, some believers hope to atone for their sins by serving the religious institutions and by upholding the religious requirements of their faith. In medieval Europe the Christian church held similar beliefs. Yet, while church's teachings originally condemned killing as sinful, the crusading movement redefined slaughtering the enemies of God as an act of grace. When Pope Urban II preached the First Crusade in 1095, he declared that the crusaders who had confessed their sins and fought in the crusade would receive plenary indulgence: all their sins would be forgiven.[17] In both cases, we see how religious zeal can result from existential anxiety.

Do ut des: The Gift of Human Sacrifice

One of the most talked-about displays of religious violence in *Game of Thrones* is Stannis Baratheon's sacrifice of his daughter, Princess Shireen. Stannis had Shireen burned at the stake to appease his god R'hllor and thus save his army from starving.[18] Although this episode has not yet taken place in the books, George R. R. Martin has confirmed that he intends for it to happen.[19] The scene is difficult to watch, by the characters and by the audience alike, even though the actual death is not explicitly shown. Shireen's shrill cries for help from the flames mark her suffering, while the camera focuses on the nearly impassive faces of her father and the Red Priestess Melisandre. This horrifying portrayal caused a heated debate in the media, where even reviewers who noted how it fits the show's world also described it as "disturbing," "traumatic," and "upsetting."[20] Nevertheless, this narrative development was not unforeseen: Melisandre had previously sought to sacrifice Gendry, an illegitimate son of King Robert Baratheon, in order to kill royal rivals. As she put it, "a great gift requires a great sacrifice."[21] Also, Melisandre has already sacrificed several "infidels," including Lord Florent, Queen Selyse's brother.

Many reviewers have pointed to the obvious analogy with a famous story in Greek mythology, epic, and tragedy, comparing Shireen's fate with that of Iphigenia, the Mycenaean princess burnt alive by King Agamemnon, her father, in exchange for his appeasing the wrath of goddess Artemis and gaining favorable winds to sail for Troy.[22] In fact human sacrifice in the Graeco-Latin world was not just a narrative device. Such sacrifices were a well-known feature of religions—a feature also related to the institution of gift exchange in antiquity—and the principle behind it, which is summed up in the Latin formula *do ut des* ("I give you so that you will give me"), defines the very concept of *religio* ("religion") as a contractual bond between humans and gods.[23] While human sacrifice was a rare occurrence in the Graeco-Roman world according to surviving sources, it was not unheard of, especially in times of dire need. Twice during the third century BC, the Romans buried alive two pairs of Greek and

Gallic slaves in the Forum Boarium in Rome: first in 228 BC, during the war with the Cisalpine Gauls, and then in 216 BC, after the Punic general Hannibal Barca (247–183 BC) defeated the Roman legions at Cannae.[24] The ancient historians who recorded these events insisted that they were exceptional by Roman religious standards: Livy (59 BC–AD 17) named them *sacrificia extraordinaria* and Plutarch (AD 46–125) considered them to be "innovations." Nevertheless, according to Pliny the Elder (AD 23–79), such sacrifices were still being offered during his lifetime, just as they had since the foundation of Rome.[25]

Shireen's case differs from the ones we encounter in Roman history in two aspects: the status of the sacrificial victim; and the method used to slaughter this victim. Shireen is a princess and the only child of a would-be king, Stannis. He gives her up willingly, and she is burnt alive during a public ceremony. These features are reminiscent of two biblical accounts where first-born children were sacrificed as burnt offerings by their own parents. In one of these accounts, Judge Jephthah offered his daughter as sacrifice, even though he did not intend to; a poorly worded vow made to Yahweh produced this result.[26] In the other account, when the Israelites besieged the city of King Mesha of Moab, Mesha offered his first-born son and heir to be "burnt whole" (this is what *holokaustos* means in Greek).[27]

Another type of offering mentioned in the Bible is the "Moloch sacrifice," in which first-born children were cast through the fire. Originally a Canaanite cult practice, this kind of offering spread through the kingdom of Judah (roughly from the ninth century to 586 BC). Some Judahites performed the sacrifice on a site called Tophet, located in the Ben Hinnom Valley in Jerusalem.[28] The biblical vocabulary used in the narrative, especially in the condemnations voiced by the prophet Ezekiel, makes it clear that the sacrificial victim was killed in this ritual.

Scholars have long considered these biblical accounts historical, not mythological. They describe the systematic sacrifice of first-born children by the adepts of a Canaanite and Phoenician god named "Moloch" in the Bible, but most probably identified with Baal.[29] To support their position, historians draw on Roman literary descriptions of child sacrifices offered by the Carthaginians during the Punic Wars.[30] Several archaeological finds in the Carthaginian Empire seem to support the Roman literary sources: hundreds of infant urn burials with charred bones were discovered in Punic cemeteries, as well as dedicatory inscriptions describing children thrown in the fire in honor of Baal-Hammon and his cult partner, the goddess Tanit.[31] Since the Carthaginians were of the Phoenician descent, scholars have regarded the Roman sources as confirmation of the biblical description of a Canaanite cult.

Nevertheless, recent reassessment of archaeological findings has led scholars to dispute the historical accuracy of the Punic "Moloch sacrifice." The phrasing of the dedicatory inscriptions seems to indicate that the intended human victim was actually replaced by an animal. In addition, anthropologists who comprehensively analyzed a sample of the charred bones found in Carthage concluded that the children had died of natural causes and that their corpses were cremated *post mortem*, as a part of an initiation ritual.[32] The parents who had lost a newborn child thus hoped to offer the infant a chance at the afterlife by turning him or her into an adept of the god.[33] This initiation aspect of the practice also appears in *Game of Thrones'* ritual burnings. According to those who believe in the Lord of Light, fire cleanses people from their sins, so that they join their Lord in "a better place."[34] In supporting Danaerys' rule, Kinvara, the high priestess of the Red Temple of R'hllor in Volantis, hopes that "the dragons will purify non-believers by the thousands, burning their sins and flesh away."[35] A similar belief is found in the Iron Islands. Enemies are drowned as an offering to the Drowned God, but believers who drown by accident or in battle are said to join their god in his underwater palace.[36] Furthermore, to become a priest of the Drowned God, an initiate must survive a sometimes lethal ritual submersion in seawater.[37]

In any case, the ritual death of Shireen in *Game of Thrones* can be seen as a fictionalized version of the "Moloch sacrifice." In fact the theme has often been featured in literature, following the tradition initiated by Gustave Flaubert's historical novel *Salammbô* (1862).[38] *Game of Thrones* emphasizes that religious fanatics were responsible for Shireen's murder.[39] Tragically, the burnt offering accomplished little: Stannis gained the requested good weather, but half his army deserted, leaving him to be defeated and slain.[40]

Desecration and Animalization

A different kind of religious violence is committed during the infamous "Red Wedding." Having struck a bargain with Lord Frey, the Starks attend a wedding devised to create an alliance between the two families. The wedding is a trap: Catelyn, Robb, and his wife are murdered during the wedding feast, while their army is slaughtered outside. Particularly striking is the circumstance that this massive display of violence does not end with the death of the protagonists. The Frey men-at-arms desecrate the corpses. Robb's body is submitted to a particularly elaborate and gruesome *mise en scène*. His body is tied to a horse, with his head cut off and the head of an animal, his direwolf Grey Wind, sewn in its place. He is paraded through the camp by an honor guard of Frey soldiers chanting "Here comes the King in the North!," a title given to Robb by his supporters.[41] The narrative importance of this performance is emphasized by the fact that the scene is afterwards recounted twice. First, in the same episode, a group of four soldiers boast how they managed to prop up Robb's body and sew the direwolf's head onto it. Then, in the opening episode of the following season, Sansa, one of Robb's sisters, voices her shock: "I lay awake all night, staring at the canopy, thinking of *how* they died [...]. Do you know what they did to my brother? How they sewed his direwolf's head on his body?"[42]

The symbolic significance of this desecration is also underscored by the enormous effort expended on it in the midst of the fighting, while the encampment is on fire. Thus manpower is wasted while several men devote themselves to the task. Mutilating corpses of man and wolf does not even give the Frey soldiers a strategic edge in the battle. The violent desecration just deliberately mocks the defeated in the moment, although it might offer a warning to future potential enemies.

In European history, the desecration of human corpses with animal parts was not a widely spread phenomenon. But such acts did happen during the wars of religion from the mid-sixteenth to the mid-seventeenth centuries. Historians and anthropologists who have studied accounts of them, including the propaganda literature of both Catholics and Protestants, have shown how these acts were intended to equate the enemy with an animal, thus denying them their humanity. Mixing human and animal bodily parts to create a hybrid beast demonstrates a dead enemy's monstrosity. The dehumanized enemy becomes a perversion of the normal order, something that legitimizes any amount of violence. Anthropologists call such acts "unveiling violence": they make visible the enemy's innate bestiality and the potential threat he posed before he was killed.[43]

Because of his identification with his direwolf, Robb Stark is the perfect candidate for this treatment. That fictional animal is on the Stark family sigil. From the beginning of the story, Robb and all his brothers and sisters have a pet direwolf each. These animals were regarded not only as wild and dangerous, but also as a nearly mythological, for they had disappeared from the Seven Kingdoms for more than a century.[44] To some, the ability to domesticate a direwolf is a wonder, possibly proof of a great destiny; to others it seems monstrous and evil.[45] The close affinity between the Stark House sigil, Robb, and his animal led supporters to call him the "Young Wolf." Grey Wind's fighting in battles prompted rumors that Robb and the direwolf were one being and that Robb's soldiers ate the flesh of their fallen enemies.[46] In this context, the desecration of his body through the addition of wolf's parts is clearly an unveiling process.

Similarly, in propaganda written by Reformation-era Catholics, Protestants were often labeled "wolves" or "werewolves."[47] This kind of insult often occurs during religious controversy. Robb's religious beliefs in fact contribute to the violence he receives. While most of his enemies, including the Freys, belong to the Faith of the Seven, Robb reveres the Old Gods. This northern religion was little known and consequently prone to nasty rumors and misunderstandings. For perpetrators, fear of their seemingly superhuman foes justified their crimes and absolved them from blame.

The "historical realism" of *A Song of Ice and Fire* and *Game of Thrones* is not limited to similarities between specific scenes of religious violence and their historical precedents. Also shown are the motives and theological beliefs behind the acts of violence. The punishment of sinners by a military order, the sacrifice of a child by her own father, and the desecration of an enemy's corpse are all consequences of specific mindsets, and in *Game of Thrones* they are all portrayed with impressive accuracy.

Notes

1 See Amanda Marcotte, "Cersei's Walk of Shame and *Game of Thrones*' Evolution on Sexual Violence," XX Factor, 2015, June 15 (accessed April 26, 2016 at http://www.slate.com/blogs/xx_factor/2015/06/15/game_of_thrones_has_been_criticized_for_its_portrayal_of_sexual_violence.html), although this article notes some positive aspects.

2 Shiloh Carroll, "Rewriting the Fantasy Archetype: George R. R. Martin, Neomedievalist Fantasy, and the Quest for Realism," in *Fantasy and Science Fiction Medievalisms: From Isaac Asimov to* A Game of Thrones, edited by Helen Young (Amherst, NY: Cambia Press, 2015), 59–76.

3 HBO's promotional featurette "Game of Thrones Season 2: Religions of Westeros," YouTube, 2012, April 16 (accessed April 26, 2016 at https://www.youtube.com/watch?v=DIe0Q3PgcOw).

4 George R. R. Martin, *A Song of Ice and Fire, Book Five: A Dance with Dragons* (New York: Bantam, 2011), 643.

5 "The Night Lands," directed by Alan Taylor, written by David Benioff and D. B. Weiss, in *Game of Thrones*, season 2, HBO, first aired on April 8, 2012.

6 On the notion of religious violence and its definition, see Maurice Bloch, *Prey into Hunter: The Politics of Religious Experience* (Cambridge: Cambridge University Press, 1992).

7 "Sons of the Harpy," directed by Mark Mylod, written by Dave Hill, in *Game of Thrones*, season 5, HBO, first aired on May 3, 2015.

8 George R. R. Martin, *A Song of Ice and Fire, Book Four: A Feast for Crows* (New York: Bantam, 2006 [2005]), 653.

9 "Sons of the Harpy," HBO.

10 Militarized brotherhoods were previously created in the Spanish Peninsula to lead the Reconquista, but they do not belong in this category of military orders, since they included both clerics and lay people and permitted their members to take temporary vows. See Damien Carraz, "Precursors and Imitators of the Military Orders: Religious Societies for Defending the Faith in the Medieval West (11th–13th c.)," *Viator* 41.2 (2010), 91–111, doi: 10.1484/J.VIATOR.1.100793.

11 Anthony Luttrell, "The Earliest Templars," in *Autour de la Première Croisade*, edited by Michel Balard (Paris: Sorbonne, 1957), 195–197.

12 See Christopher Marshall, *Warfare in the Latin East, 1192–1291* (Cambridge: Cambridge University Press, 1996 [1992]), 48–49.

13 "A Golden Crown," directed by Daniel Minahan, story by David Benioff and D. B. Weiss, teleplay by Jane Espenson, David Benioff, and D. B. Weiss, in *Game of*

Thrones, season 1, HBO, first aired on May 22, 2011; "Fire and Blood," directed by Alan Taylor, written by David Benioff and D. B. Weiss, in *Game of Thrones*, season 1, HBO, first aired on June 19, 2011.

14 "The Wars to Come," directed by Michael Slovis, written by David Benioff and D. B. Weiss, in *Game of Thrones*, season 5, HBO, first aired on April 12, 2015.

15 "High Sparrow," directed by Mark Mylod, written by David Benioff and D. B. Weiss, in *Game of Thrones*, season 5, HBO, first aired on April 26, 2015.

16 "The Lion and the Rose," directed by Alex Graves, written by George R. R. Martin, in *Game of Thrones*, season 4, HBO, first aired on April 13, 2014.

17 See Edward Peters, *The First Crusade: The Chronicle of Fulcher of Chartres and Other Source Materials* (Philadelphia: University of Pennsylvania Press, 1998 [1971]), 37.

18 "The Dance of Dragons," directed by David Nutter, written by David Benioff and D. B. Weiss, in *Game of Thrones*, season 5, HBO, first aired on June 7, 2015.

19 Alice Vincent, "*Game of Thrones*: George R. R. Martin always Intended for Shireen to Meet Her Controversial End," *Telegraph*, 2016, 14 March (accessed April 28, 2016 at http://www.telegraph.co.uk/tv/2016/03/14/game-of-thrones-george-rr-martin-always-intended-for-shireen-to0).

20 See, for instance, James Hibberd, "Game of Thrones Showrunner Analyzes That Very Disturbing Death Scene," *Entertainment Weekly*, 2015, 7 June (accessed April 28, 2016 at http://www.ew.com/article/2015/06/07/game-thrones-Shireen).

21 "Second Sons," directed by Michelle MacLaren, written by David Benioff and D. B. Weiss, in *Game of Thrones*, season 3, HBO, first aired on May 19, 2013, Melisandre used leeches to obtain the blood of Robert Baratheon's bastard son Gendry. Only Davos Seaworth's meddling prevented her from killing the royal bastard. See "Mhysa," directed by David Nutter, written by David Benioff and D. B. Weiss, in *Game of Thrones*, season 3, HBO, first aired on June 9, 2013. In George R. R. Martin, *A Song of Ice and Fire, Book Three: A Storm of Swords*, New York: Bantam, 2000, 724–728, she tried to sacrifice Edric Storm, the book's version of Robert's bastard.

22 Several other Greek myths have kings—such as Erechtheus, Hyacinthus, and Leos—who sacrifice their daughters to win a war; see Dennis D. Hughes, *Human Sacrifice in Ancient Greece* (London: Routledge, 1991), 73. On Iphigenia, see Albert Henrichs, "Human Sacrifice in Greek Religion: Three Case Studies," in *Le sacrifice dans l'antiquité*, edited by Jean Rudhart and Olivier Reverdin (Geneva: Vandœuvres, 1980), 198–208. See also Dave Gonzales, "Game of Thrones Goes All Greek Mythology on Shireen," Geek, 2015 (accessed April 28, 2016 at http://www.geek.com/news/game-of-thrones-goes-all-greek-mythology-on-shireen-1624615).

23 *Religio* derives in Latin from *religare* ("to bind fast"). On the subject of gift giving and the meaning of reciprocity, see Walter Burkert, "Offerings in Perspective: Surrender, Distribution, Exchange," in *Gifts to the Gods: Proceedings of the Uppsala Symposium 1985*, edited by Tullia Linder and Gullög Nordquist (Uppsala: Uppsala University Press, 1987), 45.

24 *Plutarch, Lives*, vol. 5: *Agesilaus and Pompey; Pelopidas and Marcellus*, translated by Bernadotte Perrin (Cambridge, MA: Harvard University Press, 1917), 442–443; Livy, *History of Rome: Books 22–23*, translated by Benjamin Foster (Cambridge, MA: Harvard University Press, 1929), 384–387. (Both the Plutarch and the Livy are Loeb texts.)

25 Pliny, *Natural History: Books 28–32*, translated by William Jones (Cambridge, MA: Harvard University Press, 1963), 10–11 (Loeb volume).

26 Judges 11: 29–40. See David Marcus, *Jephthah and His Vow* (Lubbock: Texas Tech University Press, 1986).

27 2 Kings 3: 27. He may have offered the son of a neighboring king; the text is unclear. See Philip Stern, "Of Kings and Moabites: History and Theology in 2 Kings 3 and the Mesha Inscription," *Hebrew Union College Annual* 64 (1993), 1–14.

28 2 Kings 23: 10; 2 Chronicles 28: 3; Jeremiah 7: 31f; 19: 5f; 32: 35. The same practice is mentioned or alluded to at Leviticus 18: 21; Deuteronomy 18: 10; 2 Kings 16: 3; 21: 6; 2 Chronicles 33: 6; Ezekiel 16: 19–21; 20: 31; 23: 37.

29 See e.g. John Day, *Moloch: A God of Human Sacrifice in the Old Testament* (Cambridge: Cambridge University Press, 1989).

30 The most detailed description of such a sacrifice is given by Diodorus of Sicily (first century BC); see Diodorus Siculus, *The Library of History: Volume X, Books XIX.66–XX*, translated by Russel Geer (Cambridge, MA: Harvard University Press, 1954), 178–181 (Loeb volume). For Phoenician and Carthaginian human sacrifice, see Day, *Moloch*, 86–91.

31 See Susanna Brown, *Late Carthaginian Child Sacrifice and Sacrificial Monuments in Their Mediterranean Context* (Sheffield: Sheffield Academic Press, 1991).

32 On the dedicatory inscriptions, see James G. Février, "Essai de reconstitution du sacrifice molek," *Journal Asiatique* 248 (1960), 167–187.

33 Jeffrey H. Schwartz, Frank D. Houghton, Luca Bondioli, and Roberto Macchiarelli, "Bones, Teeth, and Estimating Age of Perinates: Carthaginian Infant Sacrifice Revisited," *Antiquity* 86.333 (2013), 738–745.

34 "The Lion and the Rose," HBO.

35 "The Door," directed by Jack Bender, written by David Benioff and D. B. Weiss, in *Game of Thrones*, season 6, HBO, first aired on May 22, 2016.

36 In Martin, *A Feast for Crows*, 612; Victarion Greyjoy hopes that Talbert Serry, who fought well, will feast "in the Drowned God's watery hall."

37 Martin, *A Feast for Crows*, 23–25. For more on this ritual see the chapter by Riggs.

38 Gustave Flaubert, *Salammbô* (London: Saxon and Co., 1885 [1862]).

39 Christopher Hooton, "Game of Thrones Shireen Death: Showrunners Explain Why Stannis Baratheon Had to Sacrifice His Daughter in Season 5 Episode 9," *Independent*, 2015, June 8 (accessed April 30, 2016 at http://www.independent.co.uk/arts-entertainment/tv/news/game-of-thrones-shireen-death-showrunner-explain-why-stannis-baratheon-had-to-sacrifice-his-daughter-10304780.html).

40 "Mother's Mercy," directed by David Nutter, written by David Benioff and D. B. Weiss, in *Game of Thrones*, season 5, HBO, first aired on June 14, 2015. Ironically,

his death at the hands of Brienne of Tarth also follows from his use of a religious spell to kill his brother Renly and from her sacred vow to avenge Renly with violence.

41 "Mhysa," HBO.

42 "Two Swords," directed by D. B. Weiss, written by David Benioff and D. B. Weiss, in *Game of Thrones*, season 4, HBO, first aired on April 6, 2014.

43 Denis Crouzet, *Les Guerriers de Dieu: La violence aux temps des troubles de religion, vers 1525–vers 1610* (Paris: Champ Vallon, 1990).

44 "Winter Is Coming," directed by Tim van Patten, written by David Benioff and D. B. Weiss, in *Game of Thrones*, season 1, HBO, first aired on April 17, 2011.

45 In "Mhysa," HBO, Lord Bolton and Lord Frey state that what befell Robb was a punishment for assuming this title.

46 "Garden of Bones," directed by David Petrarca, written by Vanessa Taylor, in *Game of Thrones*, season 2, HBO, April 22, 2012. On cannibalism and the process of animalization, see Cătălin Avramescu, *An Intellectual History of Cannibalism* (Princeton, NJ: Princeton University Press, 2009), 93.

47 See for instance Artus Désiré, *Les combats du fidèle papiste, pèlerin romain, contre l'apostat priapiste, tirant à la synagogue de Genève, maison babilonicque des Luthériens: Ensemble la description de la Cité de Dieu assiégée des hérétiques* (Rouen: Robert et Jean du Gort Frères, 1550).

15

Coexistence and Conflict in the Religions of *Game of Thrones*

Daniel J. Clasby

Author George R. R. Martin has said that the religions in *Game of Thrones* are "tweaked or extended" versions of real-world Western religious traditions.[1] In Westeros there are many religious faiths that seem inspired by historical traditions. The Old Gods of the Forest are roughly based on Greek and Roman polytheistic traditions. The followers of R'hllor, the Lord of Light, are similar to the adherents of Manichaeism. They believe that a spiritual world of light exists in constant competition with the material world of darkness, just as the Iranian Mani's (AD 216–274) gnostic prophecies describe. Augustine of Hippo (AD 354–430) also portrayed the world in binary terms, instructing Christians to aspire toward a spiritual "City of God" and to turn away from the earthly city of human sin.[2] Other religious beliefs in Westeros have more tenuous ties to real-life historical counterparts. The Dothraki faith in the Great Stallion, for example, has no obvious link to a specific historical tradition, but the Dothraki themselves might remind viewers of how early Ottoman Muslim clans used cavalry to capture Byzantine Christian lands.

The complexity of religious faiths and traditions in this world suggests a society in very real conflict. Martin and the scriptwriters of *Game of Thrones* have chosen to realize on screen the complexity of religious traditions and faiths that the Western tradition displays. Martin uses religion—much of it inspired by the real-life history of medieval European creeds—as a way to more strongly illustrate the conflict in the Seven Kingdoms. Tensions similar to those between paganism and Christianity, between Islam and Christianity, and within Christianity, including the rise of Protestantism, all serve to lift the drama of the show. Although our historical approaches often reduce the past to binary conflict (Christians versus Jews, Muslims versus Christians, etc.), in the fictional landscape of *Game of Thrones* viewers see a religious cosmos that is both diverse and changing.

Historians understand the Middle Ages as an ever-changing landscape of creativity, technological innovation, political and economic sophistication, and

Game of Thrones versus History: Written in Blood, First Edition. Edited by Brian A. Pavlac.
© 2017 John Wiley & Sons, Inc. Published 2017 by John Wiley & Sons, Inc.

cultural achievement. Popular conception, however, considers the medieval period as the "dark ages," a time when civilization declined after the collapse of the western half of the Roman Empire.[3] The world of *Game of Thrones* plays up the dark ages trope through brutal violence and the collapse of political order into chaos as result of invasions and economic crises that eroded the settled consensus of the Seven Kingdoms under Baratheon rule. *Game of Thrones* resembles the historical Middle Ages of the fifth and sixth centuries, when Western Europe in particular withdrew into local relationships as Rome split and then disintegrated as a center of power and civilization. Invasions, economic crises, and the new political and social order of the late Roman period pitted the relatively young Christianity—as of AD 380 the official religion in empire—against the traditional gods and deities of the popular masses. For a time, Roman modes of life coexisted alongside barbarian society, as Roman legal traditions buttressed the fragmented kingdoms that replaced the centralized Roman political structures. The fusion of the Christian church with the Roman state in the fourth and fifth centuries, and its embracing of imperial trappings, led to veneration for the traditional polytheisitc gods, giving way to a religious climate that appealed to the individual.

Magical Mystical Tour

Similarly, at the peripheries of Westeros, mystical religions took hold of those living in the vacuum of the old political and social order. *Game of Thrones* is filled with interesting and curious religious traditions, most of which seem to suggest that the world of Westeros is a backward, dangerous, and declining place. The variety of these traditions is akin to that of European indigenous religions, which range from the pagan Roman gods to the mystery cults of the Near East and to the tribal beliefs of Celtic groups in northern Europe, which included devotion to war, to motherhood, and to local spirits attached to the natural landscape of northern Europe.[4]

The ancient Romans believed that their official gods and goddesses protected the social and political order; hence they appeased them through codified rituals of prayer and sacrificial offerings. By the beginning of the Christian era, however, the mystical cults of the Near East held greater appeal to those who wanted to put more passion in faith. Historian C. Warren Hollister observed: "As these subterranean ideas floated up to the surface, the elegant, worldly culture of the 'golden age' became more mystical and impressionistic."[5] These "mystery cults" offered passion, drama, emotional ecstasy, and the tight bonds of secret rites (like modern-day campus fraternities and sororities). When the Roman Empire's stability declined, the poor, especially in urban centers, looked increasingly to personalized religions that demanded devotion to specific divinities—such as the cult of the Egyptian Isis, a mother-earth goddess who brought together the forces of nature and magic; Mithraism, a Roman mystery cult of Persian origin with several steps of initiation for its members; and even Christianity, with its promises of salvation in the afterlife.

In *Game of Thrones*, popular superstitious belief systems exist alongside the established and official religions of Westeros. These belief systems are compelling to the people of Westeros. They reveal alternative meanings and interpretations for events that cannot be explained by appeal to natural phenomena or to the traditional religion. Historian Euan Cameron argues that in medieval Europe Christian clergy and theologians also struggled to understand the unexplained facts of daily life—illness, destructive weather patterns—against the backdrop of Christian teaching and in the absence of scientific notions not imaginable before the Enlightenment.[6]

Early Christians used the word "pagan" to designate people with non-Jewish religious traditions. As Prudence Jones and Nigel Pennick tell us, "the early Christians, thinking of themselves as 'soldiers of Christ,' looked down on those who did not follow their religion as mere stay-at-homes, *pagani*."[7] Medieval European Christians thought that they belonged to a culturally unified community called Christendom. The ideology of that conceptual realm rejected pagan traditions and demanded that believers in polytheistic gods convert to Christianity. As a result, pagan traditions fell into relative obscurity until Renaissance humanists brought a quasi-resurgence of the Greek and Roman pantheon through symbolism and art.[8]

In northern Westeros, the Old Gods of the Forest mirror the pagan gods of Europe, who inhabited the natural world in spirit form. This religious belief of the North is a kind of animism that sees spirit gods in lakes, rivers, trees, stones, and the like. A dominant feature of this religious outlook is the need to appease gods who are fickle and mysterious. In a scene during the series' first episode, "Winter Is Coming," Ned Stark, a believer in the Old Gods of the Forest, chides his wife, a practitioner of the Faith of the Seven and an outsider to the North explaining that his homeland and its traditions should not seem so difficult for her, because it is her gods who have all the rules.[9] Here Ned suggests that the dogma of the more modern Faith of the Seven distances believers from the divine.

In contrast, the Children of the Forest and, later, the First Men possess knowledge and the power to communicate directly with the gods and to impart their will, like pagan priests and priestesses. This religious tradition has been relegated to the periphery in *Game of Thrones*, mostly to the north and beyond the Wall, just as in medieval Europe pagan beliefs survived after being suppressed by Christianity.[10] Starting in 340, Constantine's successors began persecuting non-Christians, especially those who practiced pagan sacrifices. By the end of the fourth century the Romans had outlawed paganism. Around 800, in the Frankish kingdom in what is today France and Germany, Charlemagne fought crusading wars against the pagan Saxons, forcing them to convert or die.

And, under various church councils of the eighth and ninth centuries, clerical authorities continued to demand an end to "heathen practices."[11]

Buried, but not Dead

Historians of the Middle Ages have long accepted medieval Europe as a Christian space. Recent research, however, has suggested that magic, folkloric traditions, and the continuance of pre-Christian religion coexisted alongside the powerful medieval church in Western Europe. Among the masses, in fact, pagan traditions likely dominated everyday beliefs about the world around.[12] In her masterful study of French peasant life, *The Return of Martin Guerre*, the historian Natalie Zemon Davis offers a wonderful example of how pagan traditions coexisted alongside Church rites.[13] When young Martin fails to consummate his marriage with his young bride Bertrande, the couple resorts to both folk remedy and clerical intervention to repair Martin's impotence, a condition described in the archival documents as the result of a "spell."[14] Only after a "sorceress" appeared with knowledge on how to lift the spell and the local priest said several masses did Martin father children.[15] As historian Keith Thomas has noted, even the church's doctrine, dogma, and ceremonies could be viewed as a "vast reservoir of magical power" by the large populations of Europe.[16] Martin's priest himself provided special cakes for Martin in order to improve his virility.[17] The power of traditional pagan beliefs and their connection to magic was so powerful that in 1484 Pope Innocent VIII issued the bull *Summis desiderantes affectibus* (*Desiring with Supreme Ardor*), which gave inquisitorial authority to the Dominican friar Heinrich Krämer to root out witchcraft as heresy. It helped to provide a theological foundation for the early modern witchcraft trials, which combined a fear of the devil with magical spells rooted in pagan folklore.[18]

John Van Engen explains how the coexistence of pagan and Christian worked itself out. In an essay in *Religion in the History of the Medieval West* he writes about "Christianizing" or converting old polytheists to a new Christian way of life. The populations of Europe in the early fourth and fifth centuries, many of which had been worshipping Roman gods and goddesses for centuries, needed more than policy and dogma imposed from above. The church was also tasked with reshaping social and moral practices.[19] Christianizing was the beginning of a process of "new associations, expectations, and practices," all the while working to keep that newly baptized Christian brother or sister tied to the social bodies that he or she formerly inhabited.[20] The Roman celebration of Saturnalia, for example, a festival designed to commemorate the god Saturn during which gift giving coincided with hard partying and gambling, turned into Christmas. Another example was the cult of Mithras, popular in among Roman soldiers, who believed that a savior born on December 25 would sacrifice his life for humanity. It likely inspired some liturgical aspects of early Christianity, like the communal meal and the sign of the cross made over the forehead. In sum, Christianizing Europe took time and often resulted in hybrid cultural expressions that blended the familiar and the orthodox into something new. In Western Europe, the whole of medieval society became identified as Christendom by the seventh century. The historian R. W. Southern put it simply: "the Church was a compulsory society."[21] Outsiders like pagans and Jews faced prejudice and violence.

Such ever-present minorities in medieval Europe show, as Van Engen has noted, that the idea of Christendom, a universal Christian Europe, lies on shaky scholarly ground.[22] While Christianity certainly dominated among elites and clerical circles, some in European society embraced folklore traditions that were decidedly non-Christian, as was the case with Renaissance artists who portrayed Greek and Roman gods and goddesses in their art, or as can be seen in the aesthetics of medieval folk dances, which often had participants don animal costumes in commemoration of ancient pagan sacred rites.[23] In Westeros, too, the elites who follow the Faith of the Seven, as they once did the faith of the Old Gods, must concede that the society they preside over often encounters—and sometimes embraces or even worships—foreign religious traditions. Whether it be the religion of the Many-Faced God or of R'hllor, the God of Light, both religions, although originating in Essos, have adherents on the ground in Westeros.

Throne and Altar

In Westeros the Old Gods of the Forest were also replaced by a single-deity religion, called the Faith of the Seven. This religion worships one god with seven faces, or facets of personality: Mother, Father, Warrior, Maiden, Smith, Crone, and Stranger. These seven faces form something like the three-in-one Holy Trinity of Christianity: Father, Son, and Holy Spirit. Like medieval Christianity, the Faith of the Seven developed an orthodoxy that demanded compliance from all social classes and forged an alliance with monarchy. As Cersei says: "Faith and Crown are the two pillars that hold up the world."[24] Atonement for sins and daily practiced rituals are promoted by the High Septon, who is portrayed as a pope-like figure. Under his authority are the Septons and Septas (male and female clergy), who provide liturgical roles, care for the sick and elderly, education, and, in the case of Unella in seasons 5 and 6, take confessions from those they torture. Priests preach from a sacred text: *The Seven-Pointed Star*.

Most people in Westeros, and especially in King's Landing, at least paid lip service to the religion. The Faith becomes a major plot point, however, when, as part of Cersei's plan to disrupt politics in King's Landing, she makes the

High Sparrow the High Septon. She anticipates that his authenticity of faith and action in addressing poverty and criticizing corruption will remove those who stand in the way of her hold on power. His message, one of both repentance and rebellion, aims squarely at the poor and disenfranchised, who will help him realize the dogma of previous church fathers. He seeks a renewal of the religion by returning to repentance and to the roots of the text.

The unification of crown and church in King's Landing in season 6 echoes the interconnection of church and state in medieval Europe. In AD 800, the Frankish King Charlemagne was crowned emperor of the Romans by the pope in Rome. Christianity thus provided continuity with ancient Rome and the legitimation of imperial authority begun by Constantine. This coronation also signifies the delicate balance of power that developed between kings and popes.[25] By joining their interests with the "state" of Christendom, monarchs helped to complete the evangelization of the masses and consolidate their own rule. While Charlemagne forcibly converted outsiders like the Saxons under threat of death, his Christianization program also broadened the power of the ecclesiastical court elite, whose members were charged with helping build schools where children would learn the Christian way of life by assimilating Scripture and civilized behavior. Since post-Roman northern Europe was a world of warring kingdoms, the church needed military power to further its dogma and doctrine. In turn, this "Frankish–Papal alliance" helped stabilize the European frontiers of violence and consolidate rule over large groups of people and swaths of territory.

In *Game of Thrones* Westeros originally had only one head of state: the king. The head of the church, the High Septon, was merely a royal pawn. With the swift rise of the High Sparrow, however, two powers appeared in the realm: one royal, the other clerical. In the season 5 finale of the HBO series *Game of Thrones*, clerical authority won the young king to their side at the cost of the influence of either his mother or his wife. The queen mother, Cersei Lannister, stripped of her clothing and her hair brutally shorn, is shamefully marched through the streets of King's Landing for the crime of incest and adultery, by order of the High Sparrow.[26]

This moment in the episode "Shame" seems likely based on the real-life case of Elisabeth (Jane) Shore, mistress of Edward IV of England, who was forced to make a "walk of shame" after Edward's death. That walk of atonement was really a walk of penance, ordered by Richard III after the death of his brother and sanctioned by the church on account of Elisabeth's conspiracy (political angling against Richard) and promiscuity (she was a mistress to other nobility). In medieval Europe the church often supported this common punishment as a prelude to torture. Public shaming of the accused destroyed their reputation and thus weakened their social status, allowing authorities to exact confessions by torture from those whose past sins had forever shaped their moral character.

It is clear that Martin meant the High Sparrow to resemble the popes of medieval Christianity. Martin commented on the office's revival in King's Landing under the authority of King Tommen I:

> The Sparrows are my version of the medieval Catholic Church, with its own fantasy twist [...] If you look at the history of the church in the Middle Ages, you had periods where you had very worldly and corrupt popes and bishops. People who were not spiritual, but were politicians. They were playing their own version of the game of thrones, and they were in bed with the kings and the lords. But you also had periods of religious revival or reform—the greatest of them being the Protestant Reformation, which led to the splitting of the church—where there were two or three rival popes each denouncing the other as legitimate. That's what you're seeing here in Westeros.[27]

Martin's assessment of medieval church history is broadly drawn and rather cynical in its interpretation of the motivations of church elites. Yet his note about political intrigue shaping historical conflict within the dual spheres of power in Europe—monarchy and aristocracy—strikes a powerful chord. In part, we see the conflict between religious and political authority in the High Sparrow's efforts to reform the Faith of the Seven and ferret out heresy. Unlike the medieval Catholic Church, which maintained a strict doctrinal unity through commitment to orthodoxy, the reformed Faith of the Seven does not seem to have enforced a strict dogma. Only with the High Sparrow's insistence on atonement for sin, especially for lustful behavior and deceitful conduct, does the Faith of the Seven begin to enforce its reformed message. Its power to suppress dissent, however, is limited, since the Faith of the Seven seems to have little resonance outside King's Landing. Still, it is the formal religious belief of Westeros, and so other religious traditions there— such as the Old Gods of the Forest, or the mystical God of Light of Melisandre, the Drowned God of the ironmen, or the Many-Faced God of the Faceless Men—are technically heretical. Its ability to impose orthodoxy seems weak compared to the widespread dominance of the medieval church in Europe.

Is It Heresy If It Succeeds?

Heresy comes in two forms, according to Malcolm Lambert. He calls "real" heresies "a major distortion of orthodox belief or practice," while "artificial" heresies are mostly mystical beliefs championed by groups or individuals who earned attention because they disrupted the popular order, while not necessarily truly challenging orthodoxy.[28] Thus heresy was a relative concept, defined by enemies.

In dealing with its views of heresies, medieval Christianity allowed some acceptance for Greco-Roman polytheism. Although in general the ancients were associated with paganism and idolatry, some could be rescued from suppression (*damnatio memoriae*, literally "condemnation of memory"). Vergil is a good example of this phenomenon. One of Vergil's *Eclogues* (or *Bucolics*)— namely the fourth, which was composed around 42 BC—is a poem about the birth of a boy destined to be savior to the world, and was interpreted by the medieval church as about the birth of Jesus Christ.[29] And since Cicero, Aristotle, Ptolemy, and a handful of other well-known ancient philosophers personified the seven liberal arts, which Charlemagne had revived as the basic curriculum in schools, Christians adapted a few parts of classical scholarship into church teaching.

Other ancient ideas did seriously threaten church dogma and feudal order. One such, Catharism, revived in the twelfth century the ancient heresy of gnosticism. Admittedly the exact ideas of heretics, gnostic or Cathar, are sometimes difficult to pinpoint, since Christians destroyed most of the texts written by heretics themselves. Historians only have polemical attacks by the victors for their research. The belief systems seem based on a Christianized dualism: in a nutshell, that the evil God of the Old Testament was replaced by the good God of the New Testament. Another group of alleged heretics, the Waldensians, founded their creed upon the virtues of apostolic poverty. They demanded that the church and its priests be poor, a practice much resisted by the wealthy and established bishops and popes.

Whether these heresies were "real" in that they actually challenged church orthodoxy or simply represented a threat to the political and social order, the western church committed its considerable power to exterminating them. One method was through the new mendicant (or begging) orders of Franciscans and Dominicans, whose first purpose was to reach the urban poor through preaching, pastoral work, and conversion. The papacy chose to officially recognize these religious orders, despite some of their dangerous leanings toward apostolic poverty.

Another means to root out heresy was through a formal ecclesiastical court system, popularly called the Inquisition.[30] First assembled in 1231, inquisitors travelled across Europe to expose, to arrest, to put on trial, to torture if necessary to get confessions, and then to burn at the stake unrepentant heretics. A variant institution, the Spanish Inquisition, went after Jews and Muslims who remained in Spain after 1492. They had allegedly been baptized Christian, but the Spanish government feared that they secretly continued to practice elements of Judaism or Islam. A Roman Inquisition began in the mid-1500s to prosecute Protestant reformers.

The church in Western Europe did succeed in eliminating some major heresies, such as Catharism. The Waldensians survived, however, and in 2015 Pope Francis I even asked forgiveness for the church's persecution of the group, he himself agreeing with them about eschewing worldly material culture.[31] The Protestant branch of Christianity became so successful through the Reformation that it is no longer considered by the Roman Catholic Church to be a heresy, if it is not deemed quite a legitimate institution to grant salvation either.

In confronting challenges to its orthodoxy in Westeros, the Faith of the Seven uses some methods inspired by the medieval church. Inquisition trials, recantations, confessions, and public shaming, often followed by prison sentences and occasionally execution, are methods by which heresies are rooted out. In Westeros, real heresy consists of public disregard for the priestly class and its doctrinal order on the part of royal and aristocratic authorities, as both Cersei Lannister and Margaery and Lancel Tyrell discover through imprisonment and penance. Yet not all challenges to the faith are defeated; heresies that succeed become relabeled reforms. The believers in the Seven-Pointed Star texts re-created the Faith of the Seven, absorbing their own heretical challenge into the mainstream of the religious tradition.[32] The reformed Faith of the Seven is itself a successful heresy, having defeated and largely replaced the Old Gods of the Forest.

But even the struggles between heresy and reform in the dominant faith of Christendom could not obliterate the superstitious beliefs of the simple people. Historian Euan Cameron reminds us that, even after the Reformation, Protestants and Roman Catholics alike continued to believe in spirits and other-worldly phenomena alongside their church doctrines and dogma: "The Reformation did not abolish the world of fallen angels nor remove the threat of witchcraft and hostile sorcery."[33] While the newness of Protestant Reformation might account for the persistence of superstitious beliefs, part of that persistence should be reconsidered as a rediscovery of those beliefs by elites who had adopted the new faith.

Burning Curiosity

The crises of the Reformation period and new scientific ideas about the social and cultural value of religious traditions in Western history led many to reinvestigate spiritual beliefs outside mainstream Christianity. In response, the mainstream churches fought against these new challenges to their religious order, and this culminated in widespread witchcraft trials during the early modern period.

For example, historian Carlo Ginzburg found how witchcraft could become a common catch-all term in prosecuting heresies that were both remnants and revivals of pre-Christian folklore traditions.[34] Ginzburg studied the *benandanti* ("Good Walkers"), an agrarian cult in the Friuli region of northeastern Italy during the sixteenth and seventeenth centuries, who believed that they did battle at night with witches. He explains how inquisitors at first took the *benandanti*'s belief in visions, night-time meetings and rituals, and general communing with spirits as proof that they were witches themselves.

One can find this curiosity about the dark arts in the world of Westeros, too. Stannis Baratheon, for example, kept the Faith of the Seven as a knight and prince, but he also exploited the magic of the God of Light. Arya Stark joined the House of Black and White to discover the magic inside, finding new purpose—and a new identity—in her training as an assassin. In Braavos, people believe in the Many-Faced God, the god of death. Their belief system holds that all other religions are simply incarnations of their god, death. Additionally, Melisandre reveals herself to be a centuries-old witch through the use of magic of the God of Light. The "Red Woman" evokes the oracles that performed trance ceremonies in the Norse mythological religions of Scandinavia and Iceland. Women who held the position of prophetess sat on raised platforms and went into trances, communing with the natural world spirits or, in some cases, raising corpses from the dead, as Melisandre does with Jon Snow in season 6.[35]

In the world of *Game of Thrones*, the religions of Essos also remind us of the historical framework for the show's drama. The emergence of Daenerys Targaryen and her dragons is a very real threat to the very existence of the Seven Kingdoms that fight for control over Westeros. Targaryen, along with her Dothraki armies, are stand-ins for Islam and its zones of expansion in the Middle East and North Africa in the medieval period. Historically, early medieval Christianity also faced threats from abroad. Conflict over the power of the Islamic caliphate among Muhammad's successors led Tariq ibn Ziyad, under the authority of the Umayyad Empire, to conquer much of the Iberian Peninsula in 711—the first encounter between Islam and European Christianity on European soil. The former Christian Visigoth kingdom there fell to the Muslim invaders from North Africa. Before that, Islam threatened Europe's southern border—along North Africa, the Near East and the Balkans; but now it occupied the western anchor of Christendom. The fear that Islam would spread further into western Europe was not unfounded. Islam had seized territories in the Near East and North Africa that had once been Christian and then converted many of those who lived there to the teachings of Muhammad.

The turning point was the Battle of Tours (or Poitiers), fought in October 732 between the Frankish King Charles Martel and the Iberian Umayyad Emir Abdul Rahman Al Ghafiqi Abd al Rahman. The Christian forces won, ensuring that Islam would not progress farther into Western Europe than the Iberian Peninsula, although Muslim troops temporarily occupied the southern European islands of Malta and Sicily, from the mid-ninth century through the early tenth. But face-to-face encounters were rare before the crusades, leaving Western Europeans with vague rumors and impressions that Christendom might face future attacks from Muslims abroad. In this context, the Christian crusades to the Holy Land and Levant between the eleventh and the fifteenth centuries look like both a defensive measure to protect Christendom's borders and an opportunity to expand Christian presence and influence into Muslim territories.

In contrast, in *Game of Thrones* the Dothraki dream of crossing the sea to conquer Westeros, but the Seven Kingdoms seem blissfully unaware of the gathering storm in Essos. In Essos the numerous religions are localized in towns and villages, except in the so-called Free Cities and in Slaver's Bay—port-cities, urban enclaves where diverse traditions mix. There are, however, religious traditions that define the whole culture. The Dothraki worship the Great Stallion horse god. The choice of the horse as a symbol suggests a connection with the Turks, who had been converted to Islam by the tenth century and whose cavalry forces threatened Christendom's Byzantine border, which finally fell in the fifteenth century. This threat to the boundaries of western Christianity was especially persistent in the Balkans and continued throughout the medieval and early modern periods, until the Ottoman Empire retreated after its failed siege of Vienna in 1683. The menace of Islam was not just military. Conversion to Islam, whether by force or free will, threatened the entire Western way of life.

As *Game of Thrones* progresses, the people conquered by Daenerys Targaryen may undergo a similar conversion, which will affect the political and social lives of the people of Westeros. While Daenerys herself follows no traditional Westeros religions, she has clearly flipped the power structure in Essos. She has elevated a dwarf and a slave girl to high positions of authority and counsel. Most importantly, she has abolished slavery in the territories she conquers and created a formidable citizen army. She is trying to change the Dothraki habits of wanton slaughter and rape. She also destroyed the harpy god symbol over the city of Meereen, sending a signal that the old order of the Ghiscari Empire, especially in Slaver's Bay, had come to an end. Should she conquer mainland Westeros, she will demand that the Seven Kingdoms embrace the new egalitarian principles that seem to drive her actions.

Multifaceted Unity

Clearly the religions featured in *Game of Thrones* have many similarities to history. Yet the series is not just a simple allegorical retelling of the medieval Christian world. In an interview with the comedian John Hodgman, Martin reflected on his real-world inspirations for the religions of *Game of Thrones*:

> The religions are made-up religions, in that sense, imaginative religions. I based them on real world religions, just tweaking it or expanding it a little. The faith of the Seven is of course based on medieval Catholic church and their central doctrine that there is one god. [...] That's the

general process for doing fantasy, is you have to root it in reality. Then you play with it a little; then you add the imaginative element, then you make it largely bigger.[36]

Just as Cersei's penance opens a window into the competing faiths of Westeros, so too the *Game of Thrones* universe ties us to numerous interconnectivities of religious beliefs in the historical West.

Grand narratives about history often reduce the complexities of the past to something easily digestible. Worse, they can ingrain broad social and cultural interpretations about the past that are either completely oversimplified or even untrue. The grand narrative of medieval Christianity once emphasized continuity and unity, especially in Western Europe. The real story, however, is much more complex. Christianity, whether in Western Europe or in the Eastern Roman Empire, Byzantium, was never static. In both settings it arose out of political and social crises and theological disputes that gave rise to institutional and spiritual schisms. Alongside this fluid Christian world, Islam developed in the Mediterranean and Southern Europe, where both religions vied for territorial and political authority. The idea of universal Christendom helped to unify Europe through the wars and political disorder that followed the decline of the Roman Empire. Unity was a way for Christianity to bookend the collapse of Rome with a new order, a process of spiritual renewal.[37] To paraphrase the historian Peter Brown, *diversity*—of political authority, theological doctrine, ethnic and national affiliations—coexisted with a Christianity that ultimately *triumphed* as the cultural unifier on the European continent.[38] Whether the diversity of religious and spiritual beliefs in *Game of Thrones* can be unified by faith remains to be seen, but the vulnerability of the Faith of the Seven at the hands of Cersei Lannister at the end of season 6 would suggest that unity, if it is ever achieved, will come through some other force.

Notes

1 Mirium Krule, "What You Need to Know about the Religions on *Game of Thrones*," *Slate*, 2013, June 14 (accessed June 13, 2016 at http://www.slate.com/blogs/browbeat/2014/06/13/game_of_thrones_religions_old_gods_new_gods_and_more_explained_video.html).
2 See Saint Augustine (Augustine of Hippo), *The City of God*, with introduction by Thomas Merton (New York: Modern Library Classics, 2000).
3 C. Warren Hollister, *Medieval Europe: A Short History* (8th edn., New York: McGraw Hill, 1998), 1–30.
4 Prudence Jones and Nigel Pennick, *A History of Pagan Europe* (London: Routledge, 1997), 86–87.
5 Hollister, *Medieval Europe*, 15.

6 Euan Cameron, *Enchanted Europe: Superstition, Reason, and Religion, 1250–1750* (Oxford: Oxford University Press, 2010), 2–3.

7 Jones and Pennick, *History of Pagan Europe*, 1.

8 Jones and Pennick, *History of Pagan Europe*, 200–212.

9 "Winter Is Coming," directed by Tim van Patten, written by David Benioff and D. B. Weiss, in *Game of Thrones*, season 1, HBO, first aired on April 17, 2011.

10 Jones and Pennick, *History of Pagan Europe*, 161. See the conversation between Osha and Robb in "The Pointy End," directed by Daniel Minahan, written by George R. R. Martin, in *Game of Thrones*, season 1, HBO, first aired on June 5, 2011.

11 Jones and Pennick, *History of Pagan Europe*, 131.

12 See Jacques Le Goff, *Medieval Civilization, 400–1500* (Malden, MA: Blackwell, 1999), 315–324 and John Van Engen, "Christening the Romans," in *Religion in the History of the Medieval West*, edited by John van Engen (Aldershot: Ashgate Variorum, 2004), 20–23 (= chapter 5).

13 Natalie Zemon Davis, *The Return of Martin Guerre* (Cambridge, MA: Harvard University Press, 1983).

14 Zemon Davis, *The Return of Martin Guerre*, 19–20.

15 Zemon Davis, *The Return of Martin Guerre*, 20.

16 Keith Thomas, *Religion and the Decline of Magic: Studies in Popular Beliefs in Sixteenth and Seventeenth-Century England* (London: Penguin, 2003), 45.

17 Zemon Davis, *The Return of Martin Guerre*, 20.

18 Brian A. Pavlac, *Witch Hunts in the Western World: Persecution and Punishment from the Inquisition through the Salem Trials* (Westport, CT: Greenwood Press, 2009), 56.

19 Van Engen, "Christening the Romans," 23–24.

20 Van Engen, "Christening the Romans," 24.

21 R. W. Southern, *Western Society and the Church in the Middle Ages* (London: Penguin, 1990), 17.

22 John van Engen, "The Christian Middle Ages," in *Religion in the History of the Medieval West*, edited by John Van Engen (Aldershot: Ashgate Variorum, 2004), 522 (= chapter 1).

23 Jones and Pennick, *History of Pagan Europe*, 196–197.

24 "High Sparrow," directed by Mark Mylod, written by David Benioff and D. B. Weiss, in *Game of Thrones*, season 5, HBO, first aired on April 26, 2015.

25 "Blood of My Blood," directed by Jack Bender, written by Bryan Cogman, in *Game of Thrones*, season 6, HBO, first aired on May 29, 2016.

26 "Mother's Mercy," directed by David Nutter, written by David Benioff and D. B. Weiss, in *Game of Thrones*, season 5, HBO, first aired on June 14, 2015.

27 James Hibberd, "*Game of Thrones*: George R. R. Martin Reveals Which Religion Inspired the Faith Militant," *Entertainment Weekly*, 2015, May 24 (accessed May 2, 2016 at http://www.ew.com/article/2015/05/24/game-thrones-george-rr-martin-religion).

28 Malcolm Lambert, *Medieval Heresy: Popular Movements from the Gregorian Reform to the Reformation* (Oxford: Blackwell, 1992), xii.

29 Le Goff, *Medieval Civilization*, 170. A translation of Vergil's fourth eclogue can be read online at http://classics.mit.edu/Virgil/eclogue.4.iv.html (accessed October 24, 2016). See also the Loeb volume of Vergil's *Eclogues* in Fairclough's translation (Cambridge, MA: Harvard University Press, 1916).

30 Pavlac, *Witch Hunts in the Western World*, 36–43, 150–153, 166–168.

31 "Pope Francis Asks Forgiveness of Christian Group over Historical Persecution," CNA/EWTN, 2015, July 22 (accessed August 7, 2016 at http://www.catholicnews agency.com/news/pope-francis-asks-forgiveness-of-christian-group-over-historical-persecution-43232). The Waldensians weren't in such a forgiving mood: see Guiseppe Nardi, "Waldensians Reject the Pope's Apology: We Could Not Forgive," Eponymous Flower, 2015, August 25 (accessed August 7, 2016 at http://eponymous flower.blogspot.com/2015/08/waldensians-reject-popes-apology-we.html).

32 Lambert, *Medieval Heresy*, 361.

33 Cameron, *Enchanted Europe*, 12.

34 Carlo Ginzburg, *The Night Battles: Witchcraft and Agrarian Cults in the Sixteenth and Seventeenth Centuries*, translated by John and Anne Tedeschi (Baltimore, MD: Johns Hopkins University Press, 1983 [1966]; the Italian title is *I Benandanti: Stregoneria e culti agrari tra Cinquecento e Seicento*).

35 Jones and Pennick, *History of Pagan Europe*, 150–151.

36 John Hodgman, "John Hodgman interviews George R. R. Martin," *Public Radio International*, 2011, September 21 (accessed October 22, 2016 at http://www.pri. org/stories/2011-09-21/john-hodgman-interviews-george-rr-martin).

37 See Peter Brown, *The Rise of Western Christendom: Triumph and Diversity, AD 200–1000* (rev. edn., Oxford: Wiley Blackwell, 2013), 2–5.

38 Brown, *Rise of Western Christendom*, 2–5.

16

"I shall take no wife"

Celibate Societies in Westeros and in Western Civilization

Kris Swank

To say there's a lot of sex in George R. R. Martin's *Game of Thrones* series is a serious understatement. But often overlooked is the surprising abundance of abstinence. The various groups whose members vow to abstain from marriage or any sexual practice include "the maesters of the Citadel, the septons and septas who serve the Seven, the silent sisters of the dead, the Kingsguard and the Night's Watch."[1] Nevertheless, Martin does not strain believability by creating an unrealistic number of such groups. Each of Martin's celibate orders has a real-world counterpart in western history. From the ancient world to the European Middle Ages (the fifth to the fifteenth centuries) and to the Renaissance (the fourteenth to the seventeenth centuries), some military and religious orders practiced *celibacy* (abstention from marriage). This practice helped guarantee undivided loyalty and obedience to their leaders, since they had no spouses to protect and no legitimate children who should inherit their wealth or status. Other groups practiced *continence* (abstention from all sexual relations) in the belief that suppression of physical desire led to *chastity* (spiritual purity). But, whether the impetus is temporal or spiritual, abstinence is difficult to enforce, in Martin's world and in our own. And when it fails, both history and fiction record scandals.

The Night's Watch and the Roman Legions

The quintessential image of celibacy in Martin's series is Jon Snow atop the frozen Wall. As a brother of the Night's Watch, he is sworn to defend the Seven Kingdoms from the wildlings who inhabit the untamed lands to the north. His oath includes these words: "I shall take no wife, hold no lands, father no

Game of Thrones versus History: Written in Blood, First Edition. Edited by Brian A. Pavlac.
© 2017 John Wiley & Sons, Inc. Published 2017 by John Wiley & Sons, Inc.

children."[2] Maester Aemon explains that the oath is meant to safeguard the brothers of the Night's Watch from falling in love,

> for love is the bane of honor, the death of duty. [...] The men who formed the Night's Watch knew [...] they must have no divided loyalties to weaken their resolve. So they vowed they would have no wives nor children.[3]

The Night's Watch founders had good reason to fear divided loyalties, as examples from throughout the history of the Roman Empire (27 BC–AD 476) prove. Historian Cassius Dio (AD 155–235) recounted how three Roman legions were annihilated by hostile Germanic tribes in Teutoburg Forest (AD 9). The legions were travelling with their wives, girlfriends, children, and servants and had become scattered along the forest track. The presence of families disrupted their discipline, especially their marching formation.[4] The soldiers were massacred as they tried to help their families. Afterwards Roman leaders concluded that the presence of women and children hindered the efficient deployment of the troops. Dio wrote, "men serving in the army [...] could not legally have wives."[5] Men who were already married when they enlisted were obliged to leave their wives behind. This official policy remained in effect for nearly two hundred years, until the reign of Emperor Septimius Severus (r. 193–211).[6]

Nevertheless, official policy is not the same as daily practice. Legionaries often served for extended periods at remote frontier posts, and it proved impossible to prevent them from forming liaisons with local women. Along Hadrian's Wall and in the ruins of other second-century Roman forts, archaeologists have found weaving combs, female ornaments, and shoes indicating that women and children lived alongside the soldiers stationed there.[7] In Westeros, when Samwell Tarly brings Gilly to Castle Black, she performs the same tasks as the women living in the Roman forts: cooking, cleaning, and nursing the babies of high-ranking women. Prostitutes would also have been widely available near Roman forts, just as the men of the Night's Watch seek comfort for hire in nearby Mole's Town. Jon Snow thinks: "That was oath-breaking too, yet no one seemed to care."[8]

Roman leaders didn't seem to care much either. "The ban on marriage did not succeed in imposing a celibate life on Roman soldiers. The emperors and their officers lacked the will, if not the power, to enforce this policy on a frontier army."[9] The Roman legionary was only allowed to marry legally after his 25-year period of military service concluded. Upon discharge, many simply continued to reside where they had served, sometimes marrying their common law wives and legitimizing their children. But, for Martin's Night's

Watch, service is lifelong and the vows of celibacy must last "for this night and all the nights to come."[10]

Kingsguard and the Papal Guard

The Kingsguard of Westeros, the elite royal bodyguard traditionally composed of the seven best knights in the realm, also "had no wives or children, but only lived to serve the king."[11] Yet, as Ser Arys notes, "there have always been men who found it easier to speak vows than to keep them."[12] Several members of the Kingsguard are known to have broken their vows. Jaime Lannister commits incest with his sister Cersei. Ser Arys Oakheart falls in love with the Dornish Princess Arianne, while Ser Terrance Toyne's love affair with a king's mistress costs both their lives.[13] Ser Lucamore Strong has three wives and sixteen children before his own Sworn Brothers castrate him, and the king banishes him to the Wall.[14] Writing to a fan, Martin observed: "Sometimes the best knights are not eager to take such stringent vows, and you have to settle for who you can get."[15]

In contrast, there is at least one elite historical bodyguard that has always been able to attract high-quality recruits. The Swiss Guard at the Vatican was founded in 1506, when 150 soldiers were invited to Rome as the security force for Pope Julius II (r. 1503–1513). A tradition was established, and in 2006 the Guard celebrated its 500th anniversary. The force currently consists of 110 men, all Swiss nationals and all practicing Roman Catholics. Like Martin's Kingsguard, the unmarried Swiss guardsmen are sworn to celibacy and continence. Unlike the Kingsguard, a Vatican guardsman who is at least 25 years old and holds the rank of corporal (or a higher one) may be allowed to marry after three years of service.

The Swiss Guard is exclusively male. In Westeros, however, Renly Baratheon broke an ancient tradition when he appointed a woman, Brienne of Tarth, to his Kingsguard. Women warriors also played a role in western history. Homer's *Iliad*, for instance, the famous epic about the Trojan War composed in another "dark ages"—probably in eighth century BC—describes the all-female Amazon warriors as the "peers of men."[16] The Roman historian Cornelius Tacitus (c. AD 56–c. 118) wrote that Boudicca, queen of the Iceni tribe in Britain, led a revolt against Roman forces in AD 60 with "more women than warriors" in her army, "women, in black attire like the Furies, with hair dishevelled, waving brands."[17] In the present day, over a dozen industrialized nations—including, as of December 2015, the United States[18]—allow women to serve in military combat roles. The Pontifical Swiss Guard, however, is not likely to admit women anytime soon. As Commander Elmar Theodor Maeder stated: "The Swiss Guard has stood the test of time for 500 years, so why should we change anything?"[19]

The Religious Orders of Westeros and Medieval Europe

The most obvious parallels between the celibate orders of Westeros and the West are displayed by the "Godsworn" (septons and septas) of the Faith of the Seven on the one side and Roman Catholic priests, monks, and nuns on the other. Septons who preside in septs (the Faith's houses of worship) are analogous to Roman Catholic priests in their parish churches, while some orders of the Godsworn roughly correspond to Christian monastic orders. The "Begging Brothers" of Westeros are similar to the mendicant friars of medieval Europe, while the contemplative "Brown Brothers" are comparable to cloistered monks. The female septas, like medieval nuns, can either join contemplative houses or be sent as governesses to noble families, like Septa Mordane, who instructs Sansa and Arya Stark. Those who join the Godsworn take lifelong vows of poverty, chastity, and obedience, as Loras Tyrell does in the Great Sept of Baelor. He declares,

> My only remaining wish is to devote myself to the Seven. [...] I will abandon the Tyrell name and all that goes with it. I will renounce my lordship and my claims on Highgarden. I will never marry and I will never father children.[20]

Since the first century of Christianity, many men and women have devoted their lives to Christ, renouncing wealth and worldly trappings in favor of simple living and prayer. *The Rule of Saint Benedict*, a book of monastic regulations developed by the founder of western monasticism, Benedict of Nursia (c. 480–550), instructs adherents, among other things, to "*renounce yourself in order to follow Christ* [...] *clothe the naked, visit the sick* [...] devote yourself often to prayer.*"[21] It also commands followers to "*discipline your body*" and warns: "*Do not gratify the promptings of the flesh.*"[22]

But not all religious houses enforced such strict behavior:

> At one time the monks of Italy's Farfa abbey openly recognized their concubines. In France, the monks of Trosly were nearly all married, and each monk of St. Gildas at Ruits abbey "supported himself and his concubines, as well as his sons and daughters."[23]

It may surprise modern readers that clerical celibacy was not universally practiced during Christianity's early history. In the Celtic church, which flourished in the British Isles in the first half of the first millennium, "both sexes inhabited abbeys and monastic foundations, which were known as *conhospitae*, or double houses, where men and women lived raising their children in Christ's service."[24] The community of St. Brigid of Kildare in Ireland was founded as one such mixed community in the late fifth century.[25] And, although celibacy was expected of high church officials, marriage among parish priests was tolerated in the early church. In parts of Spain, for instance, "it was commonplace for priests to have wives."[26] Likewise, in "early medieval Scandinavia, married priests were common, and several Icelandic bishops were married, the last being Magnus of Skálholt, who died in 1237."[27]

Periodic church reforms included the gradual expansion of the rules that enforced religious celibacy. Double monasteries were forbidden at the Second Council of Nicaea (AD 787).[28] The papal reforms of the eleventh century penalized both married priests and the children of those priests.[29] "The Lateran decrees of 1123 and 1139 thus transformed clerical marriage from a legally tolerated institution into a canonical crime."[30] Not all married priests accepted these reforms unquestioningly. Bishops who announced the reforms were driven out "with jeers and blows." One archbishop "was stoned by his indignant clergy," while others "simply did not dare to publish the celibacy decrees for fear of their lives."[31]

Sodomy was another form of sexuality that concerned the church in the Middle Ages. The term "sodomy" derives from the biblical story of the godless town of Sodom, which God destroyed for its sins, along with the nearby town of Gomorrah. Under that term the medieval church included various sexual practices deemed irregular and unnatural, including masturbation, same-sex relations, and bestiality.[32] Legal consequences varied by time and place, but sodomy could carry the death penalty in some parts of medieval Europe.[33] Once clerical marriage was banned, "there were anxieties that if clerics were celibate they would all become sodomites."[34] *The Rule of Saint Benedict* suggests that sodomy was a concern in the monasteries as well, for it mandated:

> The monks are to sleep in separate beds. [...] If possible, all are to sleep in one place [...] in groups of ten or twenty under the watchful care of seniors. A lamp must be kept burning in the room until morning. They sleep clothed, and girded with belts of cords.[35]

In *The Book of Gomorrah* (c. 1049), the Italian monk Peter Damian warned: "Vice against nature creeps in like a cancer and even touches the order of consecrated men."[36] When Henry VIII of England (r. 1509–1547) broke away from the Roman Catholic Church, allegations of sodomy in monasteries were among the pretexts that were used to justify his closure of over 600 religious communities—a process known as "the Dissolution of the Monasteries" (1536–1541).[37] Although these allegations, being politically motivated, may have been embellished or even falsified, they do indicate that some people at the time held the view that sex was prevalent in monasteries and convents. By contrast, even though readers of *Games of Thrones* learn that "Septon Utt likes little boys," there are few allegations of sexual misconduct leveled against the septons and septas of Westeros.[38]

The High Septon and the Pope

Just as septons and septas are analogous to the monks and nuns of the Roman Catholic Church, the High Septon of the Faith of the Seven is comparable to the pope. The Roman Catholic faithful call the pope the "Vicar of Christ upon earth," while the faithful in Westeros call the High Septon the "Voice of the Seven on Earth." The pope sets forth the creed of his church, directs its manner of worship, and, as chief judge and pastor, interprets canon law regarding religious, social, and family life.[39]

The personal character of popes varied widely: some were saints, others were sinners. John XII (r. 955–964), "who was elected pope at the age of eighteen, led such a debauched life that he was a scandal even in the debauched Roman society of the tenth century."[40] John reportedly "turned the Lateran [Palace] into a brothel [...] no respectable woman dared any longer make a pilgrimage to Rome, for fear of falling into the power of the Pope."[41] John died at the age of 27 and in the company of a married woman, being killed by either a stroke or blows to his head from an outraged husband.[42] Benedict IX (r. 1032–1048) was accused of multiple adulteries, rape, sodomy, bestiality, and of sponsoring orgies. Popes Paul II (r. 1464–1471), Sixtus IV (r. 1471–1484), Leo X (r. 1513–1521), and Julius III (r. 1550–1555) all allegedly had homosexual lovers. While these accusations may have been propaganda invented by rival political factions, they cannot be simply dismissed.

Perhaps history's most notorious pope is Alexander VI (r. 1492–1503). Born Rodrigo Borgia, he allegedly fathered at least seven illegitimate children while a cardinal. He used these young Borgias as political pieces in his own "game of thrones," to increase papal political power in the Italian Peninsula during the Renaissance.[43] The two most famous offspring are Lucrezia (1480–1519), whom Alexander married off advantageously three times, and Cesare (1498–1507), whom Alexander appointed cardinal at the age of 18 and then unleashed to control the Papal States. Niccolò Machiavelli (1469–1527) admired Cesare, using him as the model of the modern ruler in his treatise on politics and power, *The Prince*.[44] The Borgias' political enemies circulated scandalous (though unverified) gossip: incest between Pope Alexander and Lucrezia, entertainments featuring animals breeding, and the infamous Banquet (or Ballet) of Chestnuts in the Vatican where 50 prostitutes "stripped naked and entertained their hosts with lewd gymnastics involving chestnuts, all of this followed by a rollicking orgy."[45]

Certainly nothing in *Game of Thrones* approaches this level of sexual deviancy and corruption. In the television series, one High Septon is a frequent customer at Littlefinger's brothel, where he likes to role-play "worshipping" prostitutes costumed as the Seven gods. Zealous brethren known as "Sparrows" burst into the brothel and drive the High Septon naked through the streets, hissing "sinner, sinner."[46] Cersei replaces him with a new High Septon, the so-called "High Sparrow," who encourages reforming zeal. The High Sparrow resembles a similar figure from Renaissance Florence: Girolamo Savonarola, the celibate Dominican friar (1452–1498). Savonarola preached against the hedonism and materialism of his day. His calls to oust Alexander Borgia prompted the pope to declare Savonarola a heretic, and soon enough the Florentines had the friar burned at the stake.[47] The High Sparrow's accusations against Cersei Lannister likewise lead to his own fiery demise.

The Faith Militant and the Knights Templar

In *A Feast for Crows*, readers meet two additional religious orders that have direct counterparts in historical Europe. The Warrior's Sons and the Poor Fellows— collectively known as "the Faith Militant"—flourished in Westeros hundreds of years prior to the events of Martin's series. As Cersei Lannister explains:[48]

> The Warrior's Sons were an order of knights who gave up their lands and gold and swore their swords to His High Holiness [the High Septon]. The Poor Fellows [...] they were humbler, though far more numerous. Begging brothers of a sort, though they carried axes instead of bowls. They wandered the roads, escorting travelers from sept to sept and town to town.

These religious soldiers are clearly patterned after the religious military orders of monk-knights that emerged during the medieval crusades in the Holy Land (1096–1291); in Spain, as part of the Reconquista of the Iberian Peninsula (c. 1094–1309); and in the Baltic (c. 1147–1290). Like monastic monks, monk-knights took religious vows to live under special rules of poverty, chastity, and obedience. But, like secular knights, they also took up swords to fight. Orders such as the Hospitallers originally protected Christian pilgrims in their journey to the Holy Land, just as the Poor Fellows of Westeros escort travelers to the sept and into town. Eventually religious military orders carved out their own territories to rule.

The most famous and influential of these orders was the Poor Fellow-Soldiers of Christ and of the Temple of Solomon, commonly called the Knights Templar. The original or "primitive" Rule of the Templars, issued by the Council of Troyes in 1129 (and supposed to incorporate the Latin Rule of 1128 attributed to Bernard de Clairvaux), forbade Templars from becoming fathers, or even godfathers. Any emotional attachment outside the order could lead to conflicting loyalties. The Rule also prohibited sexual contact of any kind, "that the flower of chastity is always maintained among you."[49] Templars were cautioned to "avoid at all costs the embraces of women, by which men have perished many times" and were forbidden even to kiss their own mothers, sisters, or aunts.[50] By 1187 the Rule referred to sodomy as one of nine offences for which a brother could be expelled from the order. Brothers were instructed to always journey in pairs, but when they stayed at an inn they were not to go into each other's rooms.[51] Married men were allowed to join the Templars, but only as associate members (*confrères*).

While the Templars were an exclusively male organization, other Christian military orders admitted women, for example the Teutonic Knights, the Santiago Knights, and the Knights Hospitaller, whose nuns or "nursing sisters" ministered to the sick and the injured.[52] Nursing sisters became so entrenched in European society that in Catholic nations such as France nuns provided the bulk of nursing care until the early twentieth century. Although convents were disbanded in England during the Dissolution of the Monasteries, female charge nurses in British hospitals are still addressed as "Sister" today. Until the late 1960s, British nurses were, like nuns, required to remain unmarried. Christine Hancock, who qualified as a nurse in 1966, recalled: "one of my friends was not only married but pregnant and hadn't told anybody apart from us because she would have had to leave."[53] But some of the old taboos were lifted throughout the 1960s and married sisters gradually became tolerated.[54]

Despite their stringent rules against sexual relations, the Templars were plagued by allegations of heretical and homosexual practices. The French King Philip IV (r. 1285–1314) trumped up such allegations in order to destroy the Templar order and seize their wealth for himself. Relying on the testimony of an expelled Templar knight and twelve spies planted inside the order, Philip's troops surprised and arrested the Templar Master, Jacques de Molay, along with 15,000 others, on the night of October 12, 1307.[55] As many as 138 men were interrogated or tortured and 36 of them died, while only three confessed to the charges of homosexual practices.[56] In *Game of Thrones*, the earlier incarnation of the Faith Militant was also crushed by an envious king. When the organization chose the wrong side in a rebellion, Maegor the Cruel offered bounties for the scalps of Warrior's Sons and Poor Fellows. Both groups were banned in Westeros for 300 years until the "High Sparrow" revived them during the reign of King Tommen.[57] Cersei Lannister's destruction of their temple, however, signals a bleak future for the Faith Militant.

The Silent Sisters and the Caretakers of the Dead

Martin's novels also feature the order of "silent sisters," who are sworn to the service of the Stranger, the divine aspect of Death in the Faith of the Seven. Called "Death's handmaidens," the sisters take vows of silence and abstain from sexual relations. As one knight says:

> A man would need to be a fool to rape a silent sister. [...] Even to lay hands upon one [...] it's said they are the Stranger's wives, and their female parts are cold and wet as ice.[58]

The silent sisters' primary function is the cleansing of corpses. Cersei explains: "Theirs is a serene life, a life of prayer and contemplation and good works. They bring solace to the living and peace to the dead."[59] In medieval Europe, too, monks and nuns washed the dead and clothed them in clean garb for burial. *The Rule of Saint Benedict* instructs monks to "bury the dead. Go to help the troubled and console the sorrowing."[60]

The silent sisters also practice mummification. Upon Tywin Lannister's death, they "removed Lord Tywin's bowels and organs, drained his blood [...] every care was taken [...] his body was stuffed with salts and fragrant herbs."[61] Mummification is typically associated with the funeral rites of the ancient Egyptians, performed by the priests of the god of embalming, Anubis.[62] However, mummification was not completely forgotten in medieval and Renaissance Europe. The *Collectanea historica* (1585), a history of Basel Cathedral in Switzerland, describes the mummification of Queen Anna of Habsburg, who died in 1281. The procedure was similar to that used by the silent sisters.[63] Other mummies known to have been buried in Basel include a woman who died of syphilis, five children, a participant in the Council of Basel (1431–1449), and David Joris, a wealthy Dutch immigrant who died in 1556. Joris' mummified body was later disinterred, drawn, quartered, and publicly burned when it was discovered that he had belonged to a heretical sect.[64]

The Maesters and the Dons

Our last group of celibates, the maesters, are sometimes called "the knights of the mind."[65] Maester Luwin, for example, is tutor to the Stark boys, caretaker of Winterfell's ravens, resident healer, and Ned Stark's most trusted retainer. He offers to teach Brandon Stark "history, healing, herblore [...] the speech of ravens, and how to build a castle, and the way a sailor steers his ship by the stars."[66] As Lady Dustin says, "every great lord has his maester, every lesser lord aspires to one. If you do not have a maester, it is taken to mean that you are of little consequence."[67]

In *Game of Thrones* maesters are an all-male order of learned counselors who study at the university-like Citadel in Old Town. When Gilly and Little Sam try to follow Sam inside the Citadel's library, a scribe exclaims: "No women or children!"[68] The maesters are actually an amalgamation of several retainers common in the noble houses of medieval Europe: tutor, political advisor, scribe, lawyer, astrologer, and physician. Every lord who could afford it would have employed not one, but an entire retinue. A maester puts aside his family name and "the hope of children."[69] Instead, he must be single-mindedly loyal to the particular castle where he's been appointed. Although Maester Luwin has served the Starks of Winterfell for many years, when Theon Greyjoy seizes the castle, Luwin assures him: "so long as you hold Winterfell I am bound by oath to give you counsel."[70]

In the early Middle Ages, education was centered in monasteries and cathedral schools, since the clergy had preserved education and literacy after the fall of Rome. By the High Middle Ages education began to resemble the guild system, with masters and apprentices. In the twelfth century some masters chartered universities as self-governing entities, perhaps desiring independence from the cathedrals (and from the bishops who ran them). Among the earliest were the University of Bologna (1088), the University of Paris (c. 1200), Balliol College (1263) and Merton College (c. 1265) at Oxford, and St. Peter's College ("Peterhouse") in Cambridge (1284). Despite their nominal independence, the European universities technically remained part of the church.

The discipline of medieval colleges was also modeled after the monasteries. The statutes at Peterhouse, for example, required dons (or learned masters) to be "honourable, chaste, peaceable, humble and modest."[71] They were also required to be celibate. When a Parisian scholar named "John" divorced his wife in 1290, officials warned that revoking the divorce would result in his being "deprived of the function of teaching at Paris in the faculty of arts."[72] Perhaps the most famous case of a medieval scholar breaking his vow of celibacy involves Abélard and Héloïse. When Canon Fulbert of Notre Dame hired the renowned cathedral school master Peter Abélard (1079–1142) to tutor his niece Héloïse d'Argenteuil (c.1090–1164), the two soon fell in love. Abélard wrote:[73]

> Under the pretext of study we spent our hours in the happiness of love, and learning held out to us the secret opportunities that our passion craved. Our speech was more of love than of the books which lay open before us; our kisses far outnumbered our reasoned words.

Héloïse fell pregnant and the lovers were secretly married. The outraged Fulbert hired men to assault and castrate Abélard. In shame and despair, Abélard retired to a monastery and Héloïse to a convent. Although they exchanged letters over the next 20 years, they only saw each other one more time.[74]

Other university students and masters were accused of rape or sodomy. In 1269 a Paris court denounced scholars and clerics who "atrociously wound or kill many persons, rape women, oppress virgins, break into inns."[75] When Italian scholar Benvenuto da Imola (c. 1320–1388) visited Bologna in 1375, he reported: "I found vermin born from the ashes of sodomites, who contaminated the entire University."[76] At Oxford, in 1737, the Reverends John Swinton and Robert Thistlethwayte were accused of perpetrating or attempting "sodomitical practices" on undergraduates.[77] In Westeros, too, it's whispered that maesters are sexually permissive. Lady Dustin gossips: "Walys Flowers had [...] an archmaester of the Citadel for a father, it was rumoured. The grey rats are not as chaste as they would have us believe."[78] When Tyrion Lannister finds a naked girl in Grand Maester Pycelle's bed, he asks, "does the Citadel approve of you bedding the serving wenches?"[79]

After the English Reformation (c. 1525–1549), fellows at both Oxford and Cambridge continued to be members of the church. Although King Edward VI (1537–1553) did allow Anglican priests to marry, Queen Elizabeth I (1533–1603) reestablished celibacy for university dons, "commanding that no women be allowed into the universities on any pretext."[80] The prohibition against marriage for university fellows remained in force until the Universities of Oxford and Cambridge Act of 1877 gave each college the discretion to establish its own rules regarding matrimony. In *Game of Thrones*, Sam Tarly, a brother of Night's Watch, will be doubly bound to celibacy if he ever attains the rank of maester. Yet, even the dutiful Sam breaks his vows with Gilly.

There are other celibate groups in *Game of Thrones*: priests of the Blind God, court eunuchs like Varys, as well as Grey Worms and the Unsullied. They, too, have real-world models in the priests of the Phrygian goddess Cybele and in the imperial and military eunuchs of Byzantium.[81] But these are more prevalent in the cultures of Essos than of Westeros. As for the celibate societies of Westeros—the Night's Watch, the Kingsguard, the Godsworn, the Faith Militant, the silent sisters, and the Maesters of the Citadel—they clearly have models in the ancient and medieval worlds, particularly in the medieval Catholic Church. Not surprisingly, Martin drew extensively on Roman Catholic institutions. He was born and raised a Roman Catholic himself and attended Marist High, a Roman Catholic school in Bayonne, New Jersey. Although he calls those years "not the happiest of my life," they provided him with a firm grounding in Roman Catholic history.[82] Along with his knowledge of the history of ancient Rome, the Middle Ages, and the Renaissance, Martin's Roman Catholic background gives *Game of Thrones* textural depth and realistic characters. The celibate societies of Westeros are entirely believable on account of the dramatic narrative, but also thanks to their historical parallels. If anything, Martin hasn't yet fully plumbed the depths of clerical misconduct and scholarly sodomy or all the high church orgies that can be found in the pages of western history.

Notes

1 George R. R. Martin, *A Song of Ice and Fire, Book Three: A Storm of Swords* (New York: Bantam, 2000), 261–262.
2 George R. R. Martin, *A Song of Ice and Fire, Book One: A Game of Thrones* (New York: Bantam, 1996), 435–436.
3 Martin, *A Game of Thrones*, 552–553.
4 Cassius Dio, *Roman History*, vol. 7: *Books 56–60*, translated by Earnest Cary (Cambridge, MA: Harvard University Press, 1924), 45 (Loeb text).
5 Cassius Dio, *Roman History*, 429.

6   Peter Garnsey, "Septimius Severus and the Marriage of Soldiers," *California Studies in Classical Antiquity* 3 (1970), 46, doi: 10.2307/25010598.

7   Garnsey, "Septimius Severus and the Marriage of Soldiers," 46; for more on Hadrian's Wall and the wall it inspired in Westeros, see the chapter by de Ruiter in this volume.

8   Martin, *A Game of Thrones*, 648.

9   Garnsey, "Septimius Severus and the Marriage of Soldiers," 47.

10 Martin, *A Game of Thrones*, 436.

11 Martin, *A Game of Thrones*, 64.

12 George R. R. Martin, *A Song of Ice and Fire, Book Four: A Feast for Crows* (New York: Bantam, 2005), 192.

13 Martin, *A Feast for Crows*, 192.

14 Martin, *A Feast for Crows*, 193.

15 George R. R. Martin, "The Kingsguard," *The Citadel: So Spake Martin*, 1999, May 22 (accessed June 25, 2016 at http://www.westeros.org/citadel/ssm).

16 Homer, *The Iliad*, edited by Louise R. Loomis, translated by Samuel Butler (New York: Walter J. Black, 1942), 47.

17 Publius Cornelius Tacitus, *The Annals*, translated by A. J. Church and W. J. Brodribb (London: Macmillan, 1876), 272 and 269.

18 Ashley Fantz, "Women in Combat: More Than a Dozen Nations Already Doing It," CNN.com, 2015, August 20 (accessed June 25, 2016 at http://www.cnn.com/2015/08/20/us/women-in-combat-globally); Eric Bradner, "US Military Opens Combat Positions to Women," CNN.com, 2015, December 3 (accessed June 25, 2016 at http://www.cnn.com/2015/12/03/politics/u-s-military-women-combat-positions).

19 Andreas Keiser, "Faithful Swiss Guard Stands the Test of Time," SWI, 2006, May 7 (accessed July 8, 2016 at http://www.swissinfo.ch/directdemocracy/faithful-swiss-guard-stands-the-test-of-time/5168642).

20 "The Winds of Winter," directed by Miguel Sapochnik, written by David Benioff and D. B. Weiss, in *Game of Thrones*, season 6, HBO, first aired on June 25, 2016.

21 St. Benedict, *The Rule of Saint Benedict*, edited by Timothy Fry with a preface by Thomas Moore (New York: Vintage, 1998), 12–13.

22 St. Benedict, *The Rule of Saint Benedict*, 12–13.

23 Elizabeth Abbott, *A History of Celibacy* (New York: Scribner, 2000), 103.

24 Peter Tremayne, "Fidelma's World," International Sister Fidelma Society, n.d. (accessed June 29, 2016 at http://www.sisterfidelma.com/fidelma.html).

25 Tremayne, "Fidelma's World."

26 Emma Mason, "Celibacy Bitterly Contested in 11th Century," *BBC History Magazine*, 2013, August 14, HistoryExtra.com (accessed June 27, 2016, http://www.historyextra.com/news/sex-and-love/celibacy-%E2%80%98bitterly-contested-11th-century%E2%80%99).

27 Birgit Sawyer and Peter Sawyer, *Medieval Scandinavia: From Conversion to Reformation, circa 800–1500* (Minneapolis: University of Minnesota Press, 1993), 172.

28 Charles Joseph Hefele, *A History of the Councils of the Church*, vol. 5 (London: T. & T. Clark, 1896), 385.

29 David Noble, *A World without Women: The Christian Clerical Culture of Western Science* (New York: Knopf, 1992), 124.

30 James A. Brundage, *Law, Sex, and Christian Society in Medieval Europe* (Chicago, IL: University of Chicago Press, 2009), 220.

31 Brundage, *Law, Sex, and Christian Society in Medieval Europe*, 221.

32 R. B. Parkinson, *A Little Gay History: Desire and Diversity across the World* (New York: Columbia University Press, 2013), 60. Modern scholars and theologians assert that the real crime of Sodom was not related to deviant sexuality but rather to inhospitality; see Mark D. Jordan, *The Invention of Sodomy in Christian Theology* (Chicago, IL: University of Chicago Press, 1997).

33 Parkinson, *A Little Gay History*, 60.

34 Mason, "Celibacy Bitterly Contested in 11th Century."

35 Benedict, *The Rule of Saint Benedict*, 30.

36 Peter Damian, *Book of Gomorrah: An Eleventh-Century Treatise against Clerical Homosexual Practices*, translated by Pierre J. Payer (Waterloo, Ontario: Wilfred Laurier Press, 1982), 27.

37 "Henry VIII: February 1536, 26–29," in *Letters and Papers, Foreign and Domestic, Henry VIII*, vol. 10: *January–June 1536*, edited by James Gairdner (London: Her Majesty's Stationery Office, 1887), 135–160, in *British History Online* (accessed June 21, 2016 at http://www.british-history.ac.uk/letters-papers-hen8/vol10/pp135–160).

38 George R. R. Martin, *A Song of Ice and Fire, Book Two: A Clash of Kings* (New York: Bantam, 1999), 669. On how the rise of the High Sparrow in season 5 increases those allegations, however, see the chapter by Attali in this volume.

39 George Joyce, "The Pope," in *The Catholic Encyclopedia*, vol. 12 (New York: Robert Appleton Company, 1911), 260 (available at http://www.newadvent.org/cathen/12260a.htm). Christopher M. Bellitto, *101 Questions and Answers on Popes and the Papacy* (New York: Paulist Press, 2008) offers a more balanced modern overview of papal history.

40 John O'Malley, *A History of the Popes: From Peter to the Present* (Lanham, MD: Rowman & Littlefield, 2010), xi.

41 Ferdinand Gregorovius, *History of the City of Rome in the Middle Ages*, vol. 3, translated by Annie Hamilton (4th edn., London: George Bell & Sons, 1895), 340.

42 Gregorovius, *History of the City of Rome in the Middle Ages*, 351.

43 G. J. Meyer, *The Borgias: The Hidden History* (New York: Bantam Books, 2013), 239.

44 Niccolò Machiavelli, *The Prince*, translated by W. K. Marriott (London: J. M. Dent, 1908): chapter vii. For more on Cesare, see the chapter by della Quercia in this volume.

45 Meyer, *The Borgias*, 324.

46 "High Sparrow," directed by Mark Mylod, written by David Benioff and D. B. Weiss, in *Game of Thrones*, season 5, HBO, first aired on April 26, 2015.

47 Meyer, *The Borgias*, 222.

48 Martin, *A Feast for Crows*, 423.

49 Judith Mary Upton-Ward, *The Rule of the Templars: The French Text of the Rule of the Order of the Knights Templar* (Woodbridge, Suffolk: Boydell Press, 1992), 36.

50 Upton-Ward, *The Rule of the Templars*, 36.

51 Upton-Ward, *The Rule of the Templars*, 29.

52 Desmond Seward, *The Monks of War: The Military Religious Orders* (rev. edn., London: Penguin, 1995), 95, 152, 165, and 67.

53 Adrian O'Dowd, "Nursing in the 1960s: 'The Ward Sisters Were Pretty Fierce,'" *Nursing Times*, 2008, February 4 (accessed June 26, 2016 at http://www.nursing times.net/nursing-in-the-1960s-the-ward-sisters-were-pretty-fierce/577485.article).

54 O'Dowd, "Nursing in the 1960s," 2008.

55 Seward, *Monks of War*, 211.

56 Seward, *Monks of War*, 213.

57 Martin, *A Feast for Crows*, 458.

58 Martin, *A Feast for Crows*, 64.

59 Martin, *A Feast for Crows*, 483–484.

60 St. Benedict, *The Rule of Saint Benedict*, 12.

61 Martin, *A Feast for Crows*, 241.

62 For more on Egyptian mummification, see Robert M. Brier and Hoyt Hobbs, *Daily Life of the Ancient Egyptians* (2nd edn., Santa Barbara, CA: Greenwood, 2008), 51–58.

63 Bruno Kaufmann, "Mummification in the Middle Ages," in *Human Mummies: A Global Survey of Their Status and the Techniques of Conservation*, edited by Konrad Spindler, Harald Wilfing, Elisabeth Rastbichler-Zissernig, Dieter ZurNedden, and Hans Nothdurfter (Vienna: Springer-Verlag, 1996), 231.

64 Kaufmann, "Mummification in the Middle Ages," 233.

65 Martin, *A Game of Thrones*, 484.

66 Martin, *A Game of Thrones*, 485.

67 George R. R. Martin, *A Song of Ice and Fire, Book Five: A Dance with Dragons* (New York: Bantam, 2011), 495.

68 "The Winds of Winter," HBO.

69 Martin, *A Clash of Kings*, 15.

70 Martin, *A Clash of Kings*, 690.

71 Oswald Hunter-Blair, "University of Cambridge," in *Catholic Encyclopedia*, vol. 3 (New York: Robert Appleton Company, 1908), 211.

72 Noble, *A World without Women*, 153.

73 Peter Abélard, *Historia calamitatum: The Story of My Misfortunes, an Autobiography*, translated by Henry Adams Bellows with an introduction by Ralph Adams Cram (Saint Paul, MN: Thomas A. Boyd, 1922), 18.

74 Noble, *A World without Women*, 143–146.

75 Noble, *A World without Women*, 156.

76 Original quotation translated into English by the author: "*Perocchè nel 1375 essendo io a Bologna nello Studio* […] *trovai de' vermi nati dalle ceneri de' sodomiti, che contaminavano tutto quello Studio*": Luigi Rossi Casè, *Di Maestro Benvenuto da Imola, commentatore dantesco* (Pergola: Gasperini Editori, 1889), 81.

77 *A Faithful Narrative of the Proceedings in a Late Affair between the Rev. Mr. John Swinton, and Mr. George Baker…* (London: Britannia in the Old Baily, 1739), i.

78 Martin, *A Dance with Dragons*, 496.

79 Martin, *A Clash of Kings*, 308.

80 Hastings Rashdall, *The Universities of Europe in the Middle Ages*, vol. 2, part 2 (Oxford: Clarendon, 1895), 647. Noble, *A World without Women*, 154.

81 Abbot, *A History of Celibacy*, 319–320 and 324–326.

82 George R. R. Martin, "Student Journalist," Bayonne, Life & Times: George R. R. Martin's Official Website, n.d. (accessed October 22, 2016 at http://georgerrmartin.com/life/bayonne.html).

Part V

The Background

17

By Whisper and Raven

Information and Communication in *Game of Thrones*
Giacomo Giudici

When we speak about the power of information and communication, we immediately think of the modern world: newspapers, intelligence agencies, television, the internet. Although medieval in setting, *Game of Thrones* is certainly aligned with this contemporary thirst for the latest news. The show's world is bursting with dense webs of short- and long-distance communication. Considering the convoluted events that determine who lives and who dies, "knowing things" is crucial. This chapter compares the use of information and communication management in the exercise of power in *Game of Thrones* with that of our historical past.

The tension between knowledge and power is clear very early in the series. A dramatic stand-off takes place at the very beginning of the second season. Petyr Baelish (aka Littlefinger) confronts Cersei Lannister. He implies that he knows about Cersei's carnal relationship with her brother Jaime and taunts that "prominent families often forget a simple truth [...] knowledge is power." In response, Cersei orders the guards that are escorting her to seize Littlefinger and cut his throat. Just before the order is executed, she replies: "Power is power."[1] Two seasons later, Tyrion Lannister asks Varys (aka the Spider) to lie when Cersei and Tywin Lannister inquire about Tyrion's affair with Shae, a prostitute. Varys refuses: "How long do you imagine your father and sister would let me live if they suspected me of lying? I have no pet sellsword to protect me, no legendary brother to avenge me: only little birds who whisper in my ear."[2]

Littlefinger and Varys have something in common. They both manage to acquire immense influence in King's Landing even though they have humble origins (they are the lord of a minor holding and a former slave, respectively). This is unusual, because normally only those who belong to important houses are able to succeed in a world where blood (both in the sense of lineage and in the sense of violence) is king. Instead, Littlefinger and Varys succeed because they assemble a vast network of spies, thus mastering two tremendously

Game of Thrones versus History: Written in Blood, First Edition. Edited by Brian A. Pavlac.
© 2017 John Wiley & Sons, Inc. Published 2017 by John Wiley & Sons, Inc.

important assets: information and communication. Indeed, their belief that knowledge is power and that "whispering birds" can be more effective than either a powerful army or the right lineage is well placed.

Historically, spy networks evoke the Cold War confrontations between Russia and the West, fictionalized in James Bond movies. But classified information is not the only kind of information valued in the contemporary world. People want as much information as possible, obtained as fast as possible. This trend picked up speed with 24-hour news networks (CNN in 1980) and has continued thanks to the internet and smartphones. But, over the past 20 years, historians have realized that the frenzy for information and communication goes back much further than London's or Paris' vibrant eighteenth-century cafés—the point in history at which, according to older schoolbooks, people would have become eager to keep up with the news. The ability to collect and disseminate the latest news actually dates back to the Later Middle Ages.[3] Scholarly interest in these developments has flourished. Recently a Dutch scholar sought to list all the articles and books dealing with medieval communication that had been published just since the 1960s: the result was a 658-page volume.[4]

The Spoken Word

How much of an interest in information do the medieval-like characters in *Game of Thrones* show? How do they inform themselves? How vast is the arsenal of communication methods at their disposal? To start, let us note that one of the top officials in the government of the Seven Kingdoms bears the title of Master of Whisperers. He serves as a chief adviser to the ruler (or to his/her advisers) in matters of intelligence and espionage. This position, which has no medieval analog, indicates two things. First, information trafficking is essential for moving the story along. Second, the word "whisperer" unequivocally defines an oral mode of communication.

In the sixth season it is finally revealed that the "whispers" the Master collects are nothing but poor children (what Varys calls "little birds"), the illiterate par excellence.[5] Nowadays we typically associate the concepts of "intelligence" and "espionage" with a recorded document, either in writing or in an audio format. In our contemporary mindset, information is trustworthy and long-lasting evidence only if it is recorded. In contrast, the politics of *Game of Thrones* is consistently deployed in an oral universe. Even though the written word does have its place in the story (as we shall see), the characters' first choice of a means of communication is word of mouth.

Why prefer the spoken word? It is certainly better for keeping secrets. Words written on paper or parchment can easily fall into the hands of enemies. Oral communication does not leave evidence. Catelyn Stark wants to send a written message about her suspicions that the Lannisters have tried to kill Bran Stark. Instead of doing that, she personally rides all the way from Winterfell to King's Landing, because she fears interception.[6] Later on Littlefinger tells Cersei that he has "so urgent" a message that he "could not trust the words to a raven."[7] Therefore a three-level hierarchy of urgency emerges for communication. First, the spoken word is used for the most burning matters. Second, ravens carrying tiny scrolls (which will be discussed below) convey pressing messages. (Ravens give rise to the saying "dark wings, dark words," since urgency often accompanies bad news.) Third, bearers carrying letters by horse or by foot suffice for messages that do not demand extreme secrecy or quick delivery.

The recurrent use of oral methods makes communication less traceable and more secure, but it both causes an explosion of voices, rumors, and gossip and produces a multitude of listeners. As a consequence, no character really feels alone, especially in the chaotic King's Landing. Ears are everywhere. This sensation can be very annoying, as it is for Sansa Stark, who shelters in the capital's godswood (a place of worship dedicated to the Old Gods of the Forest), complaining that it is "the only place where people do not talk" to her.[8] Even worse, "everyone knows everything about everyone," as Loras Tyrell effectively puts it.[9] Networks of intelligence, however, are much more Machiavellian than Loras' simple claim might suggest. When Tyrion is in the royal dungeon, he tells his servant Podrick that "they" will start to follow him after his visit. "Who will?" Podrick asks, and Tyrion agitatedly replies: "They, they, the ominous they. The man pulling the strings. Or woman. My father."[10]

The importance of the spoken word in an atmosphere of volatile information and communication is not unique to the tumultuous medieval world of *Game of Thrones*. Historians, who once assumed the clear primacy of writing over orality in medieval politics, have learned to treat ephemeral forms of communication much more seriously. In recent years, several publications dedicated to "gossip and rumor" and "interactions between orality and writing" have appeared.[11] This last theme is crucial: scholars now agree that medieval men and women, living in a face-to-face society, considered writing to be largely unreliable unless it was based on a trusted, or convincing, or authoritative voice. Such skepticism was certainly well placed. In England, the period from the Norman conquest (1066) to the reign of Henry II (1154–1189) has been defined "the golden age of forgery"; but in the following centuries, too, the practice of counterfeiting writings remained so common as to become a Renaissance "quasi-profession," exercised by people called *jarkmen* (also known as *bianti* or *pitocchi* in Italy).[12]

The same skepticism about the written word is definitely justified in the Seven Kingdoms as well. If someone sends multiple ravens to spread news as propaganda, the news is received in one of two ways. It is either controversial (Stannis disclosing the incestuous relationship between Cersei and Jaime Lannister) or false (Ramsay Bolton declaring that Roose Bolton has been poisoned by unidentified "enemies").[13] In contrast, delivery of a letter by hand is supported by the words of its bearer, and this feature enhances the message's credibility. The importance of this difference is demonstrated when Davos Seaworth resists Stannis Baratheon's order to go to Winterfell. He complains that "a boy with a scroll" could easily deliver the message that Stannis wants him to bring to Jon Snow. Stannis, however, pointedly replies: "And if Jon Snow refuses the boy with a scroll, what does the boy say?"[14]

In general, viewers get the feeling that politics and society in *Game of Thrones* are often too cruel and violent to bother with sophisticated writings. Cersei, for example, bluntly reminds Tyrion that the "piece of paper" Tywin has given him—that is, the decree of appointment as Hand of the King—won't keep him safe if he tries to overpower her, just as (she adds) a similar piece of paper did not save Eddard Stark.[15] And Doran Martell, prince of Dorne, is stabbed to death just after he is given to read the account of Myrcella's murder—a startling juxtaposition between thought and action.[16]

The Written Word

Written documents are far from useless, however. They may be less secure or dynamic than the spoken word, but they are nonetheless necessary for administration and long-distance communication. In Westeros, the idea of writing is strictly connected to that of authority. Writing presents, first and foremost, a visual hallmark: the show is called *Game of Thrones*, but it could well be renamed *Game of Desks*. Almost all characters with distinctively political roles share a symbol of power: a desk with quill, an inkpot, papers, and registers. When Cersei wants to bolster her role as Queen Regent in front of Olenna Tyrell, she sits at her desk holding a quill and writing. (Olenna is not impressed, though: "Put your pen down, my dear; we both know you are not writing anything.")[17] If it were a game of desks, first-rate political strategist Tywin Lannister would certainly be the winner, although Jon Snow quickly gets his office and desk after he is elected Lord Commander of the Night's Watch. In contrast, the former Lord Commander, Alliser Thorne, is seldom (if ever) shown writing or reading, a sign of his ignorant and harsh way of running Castle Black.

These desk riders are often reading dispatches brought by ravens as couriers. Using ravens to carry messages is one of the signature features of *Game of Thrones*. As noted above, they deliver urgent written messages. The ubiquity of ravens demonstrates the need for a plausible way to bridge the immense distances of the world depicted in the show. It also suggests an awareness of the importance of a reliable communication infrastructure. Historically, even though they never constituted the backbone of any long-distance communication system (as they do in the show), messenger birds, especially pigeons, have nonetheless been used in every period of history, from the crusades down to World War I.[18] Wikipedia even has pages dedicated to the most heroic pigeons![19]

But all those messages cannot clutter the desks forever. Storing them some-where can promote a tool of government called "bureaucracy," namely rule or power (ancient Greek *kratos*) through records kept in cupboards (French *bureaux*). Throughout history, the use of writing has varied in frequency and not all polities resorted to writing with the same intensity. In medieval Europe, for example, the bureaucracy of many Italian communes was already in full swing by the beginning of the 1200s, following a process that scholars describe as a "documentary revolution." Yet it took much longer, around three centuries after the Norman conquest of 1066, for the writing technology to take full root in England.[20] In *Game of Thrones*, the corridors of power in King's Landing resemble the offices of Italian communes, filled as they were with letters, char-ters, and administrative registers; and in Braavos (a flourishing financial center, seat of the powerful Iron Bank) officials are proud of their "books filled with numbers." By contrast, in the more isolated castles of Westeros or in the hinter-lands of Essos, hardly any writing is shown at all. The case of Meereen is par-ticularly striking: Daenerys Targaryen and her aides try to establish their authority in the city through a vast array of communication tactics, but none of them uses ink and paper.

Stages, Scrawls, Seals, and Songs

Meereen offers a place to analyze other kinds of communication used in *Game of Thrones*. The events in Meereen show how communication, instead of being words spoken or written in private, is inherently *public*. Scholars are currently investigating the use of public spectacle as communication in the medieval and early modern world. Shared sociopolitical spaces offer insight into the interac-tion between the authorities and their subjects (the elite and the common people). Such spaces "physically" show that all strata of society played an active (although unequal) role in the political debate.[21]

One example of public communication occurs when the champion chosen by the Meereenese Masters fights Daario Naharis (Daenerys' champion) over control of the city.[22] Just before the duel starts, the Meereenese champion shouts insults: the Unsullied are "an army of men without men parts" and Daenerys herself is "no woman at all, but a man who hides his cock in his own asshole." These slanders remind us of the Trojan hero Aeneas challenging the Greek hero Achilles before battle in the Trojan War (*Iliad*, Book 20). Ser Barristan Selmy urges Daenerys to ignore the champion's "meaningless words," but Ser Jorah Mormont points out to Barristan that words "are not meaning-less if half the city you intend to take is listening to them." According to Jorah, therefore, the truthfulness of words matters less than their public perception.

Daenerys immediately learns the lesson. After Daario has killed his opponent, she makes a passionate speech, calling for a rebellion of the Meereenese slaves against the Great Masters. In a carefully studied move, she orders the hundreds of broken collars that slaves wore on their necks to be catapulted into the city.

Daenerys' conquest of Meereen triggers an upheaval of the existing social order and an intense propaganda war. On the one hand, the Masters form an insurgency group called Sons of the Harpy and designed to reestablish their supremacy. They claim responsibility for their actions by leaving harpy-shaped golden masks at the scenes of their murders. On the other hand, a number of former slaves want to eliminate the Masters, and their intimidating graffiti ("Kill the Masters") become iconic. Think graffiti are a twentieth-century phenomenon? Think again. The ruins of ancient Pompeii still display political graffiti, and the public in cities like medieval and early modern Rome and Venice chose specific statues (*Il Pasquino* and *Il Gobbo* respectively) to inscribe or attach polemic and irreverent messages.[23]

Daenerys stands between these factions and tries to keep order through public and theatrical shows of authority rather than through administrative or bureaucratic actions. First she has more than 150 Masters crucified. Public executions, sadly, have always been an effective form of communication. Then she wants to stage a public burial for an Unsullied who was murdered by the Sons of the Harpy. Funerals, too—from funeral pyres in *Beowulf* (written between 700 and the early 1000s), where burning symbolized the disruption of social order, to IRA funerals in Northern Ireland, which catalyzed political demands, protests, and violence—are a very important ceremony, full of sociopolitical meanings. Later on Daenerys chooses to marry Hizdahr do Loraq, the scion of an ancient family of Masters, taking advantage of his relationship with Meereen's still thriving elite. Meanwhile she holds public audiences during which she hears her subjects' grievances. Audiences are held in King's Landing, too, but there an official takes notes, whereas in Meereen no one compiles a record of any kind.[24]

Historically, the role of kings and queens as providers of justice was an important pillar of medieval king- and queenship.[25] They often fulfilled this role by holding public audiences. For instance, King Louis IX (commonly known as "Saint" Louis) of France (r. 1226–1270) was famous for holding an informal court of justice under an oak tree in the Vincennes forest. There he would listen to the grievances of his subjects and try to right their wrongs.[26] In similar fashion, the chief secretary of the Sforza dukes of Milan between 1450 and 1480, Cicco Simonetta, reminded duchess Bianca Maria Sforza née Visconti (1425–1468) that holding audiences was most important for maintaining widespread political consensus.[27]

Game of Thrones also uses another non-verbal form of communication, namely sigils. While the term "sigil" comes from the late Latin for "seal" (*sigillum*), which secures a closed document, Martin uses it to designate the Westerosi version of heraldic badges or coats of arms. Every house of Westeros has a distinct visual symbol, and these are important. Knowledge of sigils helps characters orient themselves within their world. Bran Stark, for example, is trained to recognize sigils (and the mottos connected to them).[28] The sight of a sigil immediately provokes pride, relief, hatred, or terror, depending on the sigil and who sees it.

Heraldry had the same function for medieval knights. For instance, heraldic banners rallied troops, while coats of arms also helped combatants enclosed in helmets distinguish between allies and enemies, whether in a tournament or on the battlefield. During the Italian Wars (1494–1559) the invading French kings of the House of Valois battled not only with swords, but also with brushes, as they painted their coats of arms on the walls of the cities they conquered. During the same period, the intellectuals surrounding Emperor Charles V (r. 1519–1556) actively worked to turn the imperial symbol of the eagle into a sort of "global brand." In the early sixteenth century, print made it much easier to reproduce and spread such iconic emblems.[29]

Songs are still another important medium of communication. In *Game of Thrones* they are not just sung for musical enjoyment; they also express political feelings. "The Rains of Castamere" is perhaps the most powerful song in the show. As a sort of Lannister anthem, it tells of that family's extermination of an opposing family. As soon as the song starts being played at the infamous Red Wedding, the Starks realize that they have been betrayed by their hosts. Similarly, overhearing one verse of the same song is enough to irritate Oberyn Martell beyond reason.[30] Historically, these situations are well documented. We have texts of songs that celebrate victorious sieges, libel popes and bishops, satirize the behavior of kings, criticize the mores of the time, and so forth. It is easy to imagine performing this song as a means to antagonize opponents and enemies.[31] Historians use the tag "song culture" to indicate that singing in premodern times was much more than a form of entertainment.[32]

The Materiality of Writing and Writings

A recent field of study, the "materiality of writing and writings," examines the physical features of documents themselves and how people handle written documents. Generally speaking, scholars describe how all sorts of texts provide insights not just through their content, but also through their form. Over recent decades, the encounter between material culture studies (which focus on the meaningfulness of physical "things") and textual objects (books, but also letters and charters) has revealed more cultural, social, and political history.[33]

In this context, characters in the *Game of Thrones* act against historical practice when they regularly refuse to close documents, especially after season 1. Rolled writings were the norm in antiquity, when texts were written predominantly on papyrus scrolls. And they were also common in the Middle Ages, especially for legal documents. The Anglo-American Legal Tradition (AALT) has an internet site with over 6 million digitized "rolls" and other English documents between 1217 and 1800 that are held in the National Archives in London.[34] Anyone can now easily look at plea rolls, memoranda rolls, pipe rolls, liberate rolls, feet of fines, early chancery proceedings, exchequer accounts, patent rolls, close rolls, fine rolls and state papers, to name just some of the records. But folded documents also made up a significant amount of these bureaucratic records.

Experts specialize in the study of the technology of folding and securing paper or parchment to function as its own closure—now referred to as "letterlocking."[35] It is odd that something as simple as a folded piece of paper is so hard to spot throughout the series of *Game of Thrones*. The choice of rolling rather than folding could not have been accidental; it must be a deliberate practice that contributes to shaping meanings.

Considering the complexity and dangerousness of the *Game of Thrones'* world, rolls offer very insecure letterlocking techniques. Scrolls are excellent for presentation. They give a beautiful representation of intimacy and privacy. In other words, scrolls are appropriate if, like Oberyn Martell, one uses them to enclose fancy poems and to show off to impress Cersei.[36] They are a horrible choice, however, for sending sensitive information on a long, difficult journey. Scrolls are frailer than codices and other folded formats; they are easily crushed, and it is quite easy to see into the scrolls' ends.

Even more, consider the way documents are typically sealed on *Game of Thrones.* There are several close-up shots of sealed documents, usually focusing on the wax sigils (the show's version of wax seals of coats of arms) that identify a document's sender. Unfortunately, everyone who seals a document in *Game of Thrones* seems to be an utter amateur. Characters are content merely to pour some wax on top of the paper and then press a stamp down on it, without allowing the seal to go *underneath* the document's overlap and stick it down. If one uses this latter method, which is historically more accurate, the seal must be *broken* in order to open a document. The paper is securely fastened, and the intended recipient can see immediately whether someone else has already read it. For example, in "High Sparrow," Littlefinger notices that a raven message from Cersei has been already read by Roose Bolton.[37] Clearly, anyone can peel off a seal that is placed just on top of a document. The seals can even pop open all of a sudden, on their own. In many cases viewers see opened documents with intact seals still attached to them, something that any medieval person with a minimum expertise in document and letter writing would no doubt have considered astonishing.

Speaking more generally, the paper used for documents in *Game of Thrones* contrasts with the more common material used in the Middle Ages: parchment. Made of prepared animal skin (usually sheep), parchment is water-resistant and durable. Until at least the mid-fifteenth century, parchment was, without doubt, the only writing material that guaranteed medium- and long-term preservation of writings. Only during the Renaissance did paper improve in quality and became more reliable.[38]

Another surprising (and illogical) feature of written documents in *Game of Thrones* is that they are sometimes written on see-through paper. It does not take Varys' fine intellect to realize that dispatching a document that can be partially read even without opening it is a bad idea. In contrast, late medieval diplomats made sure that no writing could be seen from the outside. They used bifolia (big sheets of paper, folded to create four writable leaves) even if they were going to write on only one leaf. Once folded, the blank leaves helped conceal the letters' contents. Since, historically, paper—and especially parchment—were rather expensive commodities, the willingness of diplomats to "waste" it with blank pages proves that they were really concerned for the security of their communication exchanges.

Of course, characters in *Game of Thrones* do show some concern for the security of the written word. As mentioned above, Catelyn Stark and Littlefinger avoid committing anything to writing, for fear of interception. When characters do write, they have three choices to circumvent the potential dangers caused by the nature of the material (see-through paper or parchment) and the choice of format (rolling rather than folding). First, they can pick an exceptionally trustworthy bearer. Second, they can opt for opaque containers in which to enclose their letters (although this is never shown). Third, they can use coded messages. In season 1, Theon Greyjoy suggests that an innocent-seeming birthday message intercepted by the Starks (by shooting down the raven that was carrying it) may actually conceal some hidden meaning.[39] Coded messages played a huge role in late medieval and early modern diplomacy and espionage, so much so that desperate ambassadors sometimes begged their masters *not* to change the cipher too often. The task of ciphering and deciphering was extremely time-consuming, and learning a new code too frequently just made it even more extenuating.[40]

Despite their misuse of paper and seals, many characters in *Game of Thrones* are highly skilled document handlers, as a few scenes demonstrate. Tyrion, for example, is once seen shutting some documents into a beautiful secrétaire, a piece of furniture that was commonly found in the rooms of wealthy people who dealt with writings on a daily basis.[41] In another episode, Littlefinger is shown hiding a message in his sleeve, a move meant to highlight his astuteness: this was certainly part of the repertoire of medieval diplomats and spies.[42] In general, the format of raven messages (small, horizontal, easy to hide) fits the politics of the show.

Overall, information- and communication-related themes feature prominently in *Game of Thrones*. This in itself is a cutting-edge characteristic of the show. In addition, the management of information and communication has a strong internal logic and a number of highlights demonstrate that the creators did their history homework. The balance between the spoken word, the written word, and other forms of communication is more than historically "plausible": it is both clever and sophisticated. First, the spoken word is the fundamental form of communication for conducting political affairs. Second, the written word is not used uniformly but varies depending on the level of development of each place in Westeros and Essos. Finally, other forms of communication, public and symbolic, have a prominent role in the socio-political arena. These elements reflect the results of recent scholarly research. Only the representation of the materiality of writing and writings seems implausible (especially considering the lack of security measures). Nevertheless, the series creates alternative strategies (trusted bearers, letter containers, coded messages) that compensate.

Notes

1 "The North Remembers," directed by Alan Taylor, written by David Benioff and D. B. Weiss, in *Game of Thrones*, season 2, HBO, first aired on April 1, 2012.
2 "The Lion and the Rose," directed by Alex Graves, written by George R. R. Martin, in *Game of Thrones*, season 4, HBO, first aired on April 13, 2014.
3 See Joah Raymond and Noah Moxham, eds., *News Networks in Early Modern Europe* (Leiden: Brill, 2016). Their work shows that a proper European-wide news network emerged beginning from the 1450s (p. 7), but the postal networks that made its development possible appeared earlier, between the late fourteenth and the early fifteenth century (see pp. 26–27 and 32 for Italy and France).
4 Marco Mostert, *A Bibliography of Works on Medieval Communication* (Turnhout: Brepols, 2012).
5 "Oathbreaker," directed by Daniel Sackheim, written by David Benioff and D. B. Weiss, in *Game of Thrones*, season 6, HBO, first aired on April 6, 2014.
6 "The Kingsroad," directed by Tim Van Patten, written by David Benioff and D. B. Weiss, in *Game of Thrones*, season 1, HBO, first aired on April 24, 2011.
7 "Unbowed, Unbent, Unbroken," directed by Jeremy Podeswa, written by Bryan Cogman, in *Game of Thrones*, season 5, HBO, first aired on May 17, 2015.
8 "Two Swords," directed by D. B. Weiss, written by David Benioff and D. B. Weiss, in *Game of Thrones*, season 4, HBO, first aired on April 6, 2014.
9 "The Wars to Come," directed by Michael Slovis, written by David Benioff and D. B. Weiss, in *Game of Thrones*, season 5, HBO, first aired on May 8, 2016.
10 "Breaker of Chains," directed by Alex Graves, written by David Benioff and D. B. Weiss, in *Game of Thrones*, season 4, HBO, first aired on April 20, 2014.
11 Claire Walker and Heather Kerr, eds., *Fama and Her Sisters: Gossip and Rumour in the Early Modern World* (Turnhout: Brepols, 2015); Luca Degl'Innocenti, Brian Richardson, and Chiara Sbordoni, eds., *Interactions between Orality and Writing in Early Modern Italian Culture* (London: Routledge, 2016).

12 See Alfred Hiatt, *The Making of Medieval Forgeries: False Documents in Fifteenth-Century England* (London/Toronto: British Library/University of Toronto Press, 2004), 22 and Miriam Eliav-Feldon, *Renaissance Impostors and Proofs of Identity* (Basingstoke: Palgrave Macmillan, 2012), 215–217.

13 Stannis' scene is in "The North Remembers," HBO. Ramsay's scene is in "Home," directed by Jeremy Podeswa, written by Dave Hill, in *Game of Thrones*, season 6, HBO, first aired on May 1, 2016.

14 "The Dance of Dragons," directed by David Nutter, written by David Benioff and D. B. Weiss, in *Game of Thrones*, season 5, HBO, first aired on June 7, 2015.

15 "What Is Dead May Never Die," directed by Alik Sakharov, written by Bryan Cogman, in *Game of Thrones*, season 2, HBO, first aired on April 15, 2012.

16 "The Red Woman," directed by Jeremy Podeswa, written by David Benioff and D. B. Weiss, in *Game of Thrones*, season 6, HBO, first aired on April 24, 2016.

17 "Unbowed, Unbent, Unbroken," HBO.

18 Susan B. Edgington, "The Doves of War: The Part Played by Carrier Pigeons in the Crusades," in *Autour de la Première Croisade: Actes du Colloque de la Society for the Study of the Crusades and the Latin East (Clermont-Ferrand, 22–25 juin 1995)*, edited by Michel Balard (Paris: Sorbonne, 1996), 167–175. For the use of pigeons during the World War I and II, see Royal Pigeon Racing Association, "Pigeons in War," 2016 (accessed May 12, 2016 at http://www.rpra.org/pigeon-history/pigeons-in-war).

19 E.g. Cher Ami, awarded the French Croix de Guerre (visit https://en.wikipedia.org/wiki/Cher_Ami); G. I. Joe (visit https://en.wikipedia.org/wiki/G.I._Joe_(pigeon)); and Mary of Exeter (visit https://en.wikipedia.org/wiki/Mary_of_Exeter; all pages accessed July 8, 2016). The last were both awarded the Dickin Medal.

20 Michael Clanchy, *From Memory to Written Record: England 1066–1307* (Oxford: Wiley Blackwell, 2012 [1979]).

21 See e.g. John A. Agnew and James S. Duncan, eds., *The Power of Place: Bringing Together Geographical and Sociological Imaginations* (Boston: Unwin Hyman, 1989). A classic case study is Richard Trexler, *Public Life in Renaissance Florence* (New York: Academic Press, 1980).

22 "Breaker of Chinas," directed by Alex Graves, written by David Benioff and D. B. Weiss, in *Game of Thrones*, season 4, HBO, first aired on May 17, 2015.

23 See Filippo De Vivo, *Information and Communication in Venice: Rethinking Early Modern Politics* (Oxford: Oxford University Press, 2007), 136–142.

24 "A Golden Crown," directed by Daniel Minahan, written by David Benioff and D. B. Weiss, in *Game of Thrones*, season 1, HBO, first aired on May 22, 2011.

25 On justice as a pillar of medieval kingship, see e.g. Maria Cecilia Gasposchkin, "Boniface VIII, Philip the Fair, and the Sanctity of Louis IX," *Journal of Medieval History*, 29 (2002), 1–26, doi: 10.1016/S0304–4181(02)00054–4.

26 Jean sire de Joinville, *The Memoirs of the Lord of Joinville: A New English Version by Ethel Wedgwood* (London: John Murray, 1906), 21 (accessed July 27, 2016 at https://archive.org/details/memoirsoflordofj00joinuoft).

27 Jane Black, *Absolutism in Renaissance Milan: Plenitude of Power under the Visconti and the Sforza, 1329–1535* (Oxford: Oxford University Press, 2009), 53.

28 "The Wolf and the Lion," directed by Brian Kirk, written by David Benioff and D. B. Weiss, in *Game of Thrones*, season 1, HBO, first aired on May 15, 2011.

29 See Silvio Leydi, *Sub umbra imperialis aquilae: Immagini del potere e consenso politico nella Milano di Carlo V* (Florence: Olschki, 1999), especially 26–28.

30 "Two Swords," HBO.

31 See Thomas Wright, ed., *The Political Songs of England from the Reign of John to that of Edward II* (London: Printed for the Camden Society by J. B. Nichols and Son, 1839).

32 See e.g. Rosa Salzberg and Masimo Rospocher, "Street Singers in Italian Renaissance Urban Culture and Communication," *Cultural and Social History* 9 (2012), 9–26, doi: 10.2752/147800412X13191165982872.

33 On the materiality of books, see David Pearson, *Book as History: The Importance of Books beyond Their Texts* (London/Newcastle, DE: British Library/Oak Knoll Press, 2011). On letters, see James Daybell, *The Material Letter in Early Modern England: Manuscript Letters and the Culture and Practices of Letter-Writing, 1512–1635* (Basingstoke: Palgrave Macmillan, 2012). On charters, see Jessica Berenbeim, *Art and Documentation: Documents and Visual Culture in Medieval England* (Toronto: PIMS, 2015).

34 Anglo-American Legal Tradition: Documents from Medieval and Early Modern England from the National Archives in London, 2015 (accessed July 10, 2016 at http://aalt.law.uh.edu).

35 The term "letterlocking" was coined in 2009 by Jana Dambrogio (MIT Libraries), who, together with Daniel Starza Smith (Lincoln College, Oxford), has kindly helped with the last section of this chapter. See the site http://www.janadambrogio.com/letterlock, as well as the Twitter profile @letterlocking, Twitter hashtag #PreserveTheFolds and the Youtube channel Letter Locking offer more information on these often overlooked material features of letters.

36 "Oathkeeper," directed by Michelle MacLaren, written by Bryan Cogman, in *Game of Thrones*, season 4, HBO, first aired on April 27, 2014.

37 "High Sparrow," directed by Mark Mylod, written by David Benioff and D. B. Weiss, in *Game of Thrones*, season 5, HBO, first aired on April 26, 2015.

38 An exciting research project at the University of Groningen, titled Paper Princes, studies the late medieval transition from a parchment to a paper "media environment"; see "Exploring the role of paper in early modern diplomacy and statecraft, ca. 1460–1560" on the project's website (accessed October 25, 2016 at http://www.paperprinces.org/about.html).

39 "Baelor," directed by Alan Taylor, written by David Benioff and D. B. Weiss, in *Game of Thrones*, season 1, HBO, first aired on June 12, 2011.

40 See Paul Dover, "Deciphering the Diplomatic Archives of Fifteenth-Century Italy," *Archival Science* 7 (2007), 310, doi: 10.1007/s10502–008–9065-y. On coded messages and ciphers, see Alan Stewart, "Francis Bacon's Bi-Lateral Cipher and the

Materiality of Early Modern Diplomatic Writing," in *Diplomacy and Early Modern Culture*, edited by Robyn Adams and Rosanna Cox (Basingstoke: Palgrave Macmillan, 2011), 120–137.

41 "The Children," directed by Alex Graves, written by David Benioff and D. B. Weiss, in *Game of Thrones*, season 4, HBO, first aired on June 15, 2014.

42 "The Wars to Come," directed by Brian Kirk, written by David Benioff and D. B. Weiss, in *Game of Thrones*, season 5, HBO, first aired on May 15, 2011.

18

What's in a Name?

History and Fantasy in *Game of Thrones*

Sara L. Uckelman, Sonia Murphy, and Joseph Percer

Names: On the Border between History and Fantasy

What's in a name? More specifically, what's in a medieval name, a modern name, or a fantasy name? On the one hand, it might seem strange to ask how historical the names in *Game of Thrones* are, given that both the books and the television series are fiction, stories of imagination. On the other hand, nowhere is the border between history and fantasy more blurred than in our perceptions of personal names. Because of the strong influence of the Middle Ages on authors of contemporary fantasy, readers often believe that names in modern fantasy stories are medieval in origin or reflect medieval sensibilities. This belief is not entirely misguided, as we can see by looking to the history of the genre of fantasy, but it is not entirely justified either.

Modern fantasy was significantly influenced and its course directed by two figures: William Morris (1834–1896) and J. R. R. Tolkien (1892–1973), themselves significantly steeped in medieval European culture and literature.[1] Morris' books *The Wood Beyond the World* (1894) and *The Well at the World's End* (1896) are widely regarded as the first fantasy novels, set in an entirely invented fantasy world.[2] Morris' books were explicitly written in the style of medieval romances and many of their characters have ordinary medieval names, such as *Ralph, Ursula, Blaise,* and *Richard.* Other characters have distinctly Scandinavian names, such as *Morfinn* and *Gandolf,* and were likely influenced by the translations of Icelandic sagas that Morris completed in the 1860s and 1870s.[3] Morris greatly influenced Tolkien, not only in literary genre and style, but also in names. It is no coincidence that the similar names *Gandolf/Gandalf* appear in works by both authors.[4] Tolkien's academic work in historical linguistics is well known, and many of the names of his characters—such as *Gandalf, Thorin, Frodo, Theodred,* and *Peregrine*—are in fact genuine medieval names, and many more—such as *Eowyn, Eomer, Samwise, Hamfast*—are constructed along the lines of extant medieval names, most of

Game of Thrones versus History: Written in Blood, First Edition. Edited by Brian A. Pavlac.
© 2017 John Wiley & Sons, Inc. Published 2017 by John Wiley & Sons, Inc.

them Old English in origin. Further, many of Tolkien's names that are not medieval are explicitly distinguished from the medieval ones by being drawn from one of his constructed, non-human languages such as Quenya, Sindarin, or Khuzdul. Given the works of these two influential figures, readers could easily assume that names in fantasy fiction that are not clearly marked out are medieval or plausibly medieval.

The strong influence of the Middle Ages on early fantasy fiction has had repercussions, particularly on authors such as George R. R. Martin who are interested in building a large fantasy world, as Tolkien did. So how historical are the names of people in *A Song of Ice and Fire* (the books) and in *Game of Thrones* (the television show)?[5] One might think that mere participation in the fantasy genre gives insufficient reason to even ask this question, given that fantasy implies the imaginary. Certainly one would not expect the names of the Dothraki people, or names of Old Valyrian origin to be medieval, given that the languages from which they are drawn are recently constructed languages, not historical.[6] Almost by definition, then, Dothraki and Valyrian names will not be medieval names any more than Quenya or Sindarin names are, and for the same reasons. But the vast majority of the names in the books and television episodes are Westerosi, an unspecified vernacular that draws on elements of contemporary English. With these names, then, we can consider the extent of the influence of names and naming practices from the European Middle Ages. This will be more than a mere catalogue of elements that are medieval and elements that are not. While such a catalogue is interesting—and indeed this chapter discusses the historicity of individual name elements—the question "Are the individual name elements medieval?" takes too narrow a view of what counts as "historical." We must also compare the way names are constructed and used with historical practices, considering broader questions such as "Are the patterns and types of names used medieval?" and "Are the ways the names are used medieval?" This will better reveal the extent to which names in *Game of Thrones* and in *A Song of Ice and Fire* are based on history.[7]

What's in a Medieval Name?

We begin by introducing the basics of medieval naming practices and some terminology used in onomastics (the study of names), just to set up a benchmark against which we can discuss Martin's names. By "the Middle Ages" or "medieval" we understand, roughly, the period from 500 to 1500. Our geographic frame of reference is all of Europe, though most examples are taken from the British Isles, because they will be the most familiar. Despite this breadth of time and space, naming patterns were surprisingly homogeneous. The same types of constructions and the same types of usage can be found across different languages and at different times. This uniformity gives us reason to look at broad practices and patterns of naming—and not just at individual elements.

In the Middle Ages people generally had a single given name, perhaps with an additional byname or bynames. These bynames originated as literal descriptions of a person—"bishop of Urgell," "son of John," "clerk," "red," "from London"—unlike names today, where one doesn't expect *John Smith* to be a smith or *Jane Moore* to live on a moor. Literal bynames can be classified into four main types:

1) Relational bynames indicate the bearer's relationship to someone else, for example "son of," "wife of," "nephew of," "sister of." Of these, the most common type was the patronymic byname, which indicated the bearer's father's given name ("Richardson").
2) Occupational bynames indicate the bearer's job, for example "goldsmith," "weaver," "thatcher," "butcher."
3) Locative bynames indicate the bearer's place of origin, for example "of London," "from the hill," "the Scotsman."
4) Other bynames include a wide variety of descriptions, from English *Small* to German *Spring in Czeug* ("jumps in stuff") to Old Norse *meinfretr* ("stinkfart").

A consequence of the literal nature of bynames is that one person could have different bynames in different contexts. *Ralph* might be *fitzStephen* "son of Stephen" in the context of his father's will, but *le Bordwreghte* "the table maker" when signing an apprentice contract, or *Beribroun* "brown as a berry" among his friends. A second consequence of this literalness is the fact that names were not fixed in a single language. *Henry of London* may have been known by that name among his English-speaking friends, but when writing in Latin he would have signed his name *Henricus de Londonia* and when traveling in France he would have answered to *Henri de Londres*, or even *Henri l'Anglois* (the Englishman).

Over time, these literally descriptive nicknames transmuted into the fixed, inherited surnames we are familiar with nowadays. How this happened varied depending on time and place, but often the mechanism was simple: If *Simon the Smith* had a son, he would likely follow in his father's footsteps, and thus he, too, would be *the Smith*. In other contexts, inheritance of surname was closely linked to ownership of land, and hence to social class. As land was handed down from father to son, so was the byname that referred to the land. There is a clear correlation between inherited surnames and social class: those from the upper classes were more likely to develop "dynastic" names such as the Lancasters, the Tudors, the Guelphs, the Visconti, the de' Medici, and so on.

This transition from literal bynames to fixed, inherited surnames impacted women's names upon marriage. When bynames were literal descriptives, women did not generally change their name upon marriage: *Joan la Baxtere* "the female baker" wouldn't change her occupation simply by marrying *William le Weber* "the male weaver." Similarly, *Alice* the daughter of *Henry* would still be the daughter of *Henry* even after marrying *Adam Thompson* "son of Thomas." But when surnames were used primarily to indicate membership in a particular family, or lines of inheritance, then women started taking their husband's surnames.[8]

This background material provides a number of dimensions along which we may assess the historicity of the names in *Game of Thrones*. Are bynames literal descriptives or fixed family surnames? Can examples of all four types of bynames be found? Do people's names vary depending on the context of use? Does a person's class affect the types of names used? The extent to which these and other questions can be answered "yes" determines the extent to which we can say that the names in *Game of Thrones* represent fantasy or history.

Medieval Elements in the Names of *Game of Thrones*

Slightly over 2,000 people are named in the books of *A Song of Ice and Fire*, many of them minor characters that are mentioned only once or appear only in appendices. The vast majority of these characters have a single given name and a single, fixed, inherited surname, perhaps along with a descriptive nickname. Some are referred to just by a given name, their byname or surname (if they had any) not being known to the reader or viewer. Similarly, a few are referred to simply by title and surname, such as *Lord Ashford*, *Lord Cafferen*, *Lord Caswell*, and *Lord Staunton*, while a handful are known only by descriptions, such as the *Lady of the Leaves*, the *Daughter of the Dusk*, the *ghost of High Heart*, and the *Veiled Lady*.

Slightly more than half of the given names bear no resemblance to actual medieval names and are clearly invented. These include the names of non-Westerosi peoples, for example the Dothraki and people from the Summer Isles and the Slaver's Bay city-states of Astapor, Yunkai, and Meereen. Such names, and the cultures they come from, occupy much the same role in the *Game of Thrones* universe as Quenya and Sindarin names do in Tolkien; as the Dothraki speak an explicitly constructed language, it is unsurprising that names in this population group are almost all invented. Even when names from invented languages are identical with historical European names—such as *Drogo*, the name of both a son of Charlemagne and a twelfth-century French saint[9]—they bear this resemblance accidentally, because of the narrow pattern along which the Dothraki masculine given names are constructed (generally two syllables ending -*o*).

Surprisingly, the next largest group of constructed or invented names comes from a Westerosi family, the Targaryens, the former ruling family of the Seven Kingdoms, and their cadet branch, the Blackfyres. Almost all Targaryen given names—many of which can be identified by the characteristic *ae* vowel combination (*Aemon/Aemond, Daeron, Jaehaerys*, etc.)—are invented. They bear little resemblance to medieval European names, beyond the *ae* vowel combination found in medieval Welsh dialects. This anomaly can be explained by looking at the historical roots of the family. Although Targaryens ruled the Seven Kingdoms, they originally came from Essos, where the historical language is Valyrian, which, like Dothraki, is an explicitly fictional, constructed language.

Setting aside the Targaryens, about one third (more than 600) of the given names of people from Westeros are either actual or plausible medieval names. Many are identifiable with modern English names such as *Alan, Catelyn, Jon* and its variants, *Jeyne* and its variants *Richard/Rickard*, or *Robert*. Similarly, nicknames like *Beth, Cat, Jack, Meg, Nan, Ned*, and *Robin* are identifiably English.[10] Other less obvious names, like *Drogo*, also have medieval origins: *Axell, Ellery, Hobb, Jarman* (or *Jarmen*), *Melicent*, and the various forms of *Quenten/Quentin/Quenton/Quentyn*.[11]

The next largest class contains names constructed by taking a real historical name and changing a letter or two, usually a vowel, in such a way that the result is not consistent with medieval spellings. The most common change is the switch of *y* for *i*. This switch is found in medieval English names, where *Martyn* is a plausible variant of *Martin, Alyce* of *Alice, Denyse* of *Denise, Myles* of *Miles*, and so forth.[12] This substitution is not, however, found in German, where *-fryd* is not a plausible variant of *-fred* or *-frid*. As a result, names such as *Manfryd, Osfryd*, and *Sigfryd* fall on the unhistorical side of the fence. Another common respelling pattern is the substitution of *-ae-* for another vowel, for example, *Maerie, Margaery, Aemma, Aelinor*, and *Aemon*. These spellings are not medieval but they all derive from medieval names (*Mary, Margery, Emma, Elinor*, and *Éamonn*).[13] Sometimes a consonant is swapped; Perhaps the best-known bearer of such an altered name is *Eddard Stark. Eddard* is neither a medieval name nor a plausible variation, but it clearly derives from the medieval name *Edward*. The connection is particularly apparent given *Eddard's* nickname *Ned*, the usual medieval English pet form.[14] Other medieval names of Old English origin, *Edmund* and *Edwin*, are reflected in the names *Emmon, Edmyn*, and *Edwyd*.[15]

The final class of names that are not obviously invented contains elements that were used in medieval style as bynames or surnames, and not as given names. One example is the well-known *Game of Thrones* given name, *Brandon*. This name originates from various medieval English places named *Brandon*, a word constructed from Old English *brōm* "broom" and *dūn* "hill."[16] In the Middle Ages, *Brandon* could have been incorporated into a locative byname meaning "from Brandon," but it wasn't used as a given name until modern times. Many people erroneously believe *Brandon* to be related to the given name *Brendan*, the name of a saint ultimately of Old Irish origin, but the two names are completely separate.[17] Interestingly, just as *Eddard* is not medieval but *Ned* is, the diminutive *Bran* is a medieval given name even though *Brandon* is not. The name is identical with *bran*, the word for "raven, crow" in medieval Irish.[18] This connection is fitting, given Bran's identification with the Three-Eyed Raven. Other given names that originally derive from names of cities or places include *Clarence* (from Latin *clarensis* "of/from Clare"), *Co(u)rt(e)nay* (France), *Desmond* (Ireland), *Mortimer* (France), and *Walder* (from Old English *weald* "woods, forest").[19]

Names of Nobles, Names of Peasants: Dynasty and Inheritance

Around three quarters of the characters in *Game of Thrones* have some sort of byname, and most of them have relatively "modern"-style names in that they have one single fixed surname that is generally shared with other members of their family. The surnames of the eight main Westerosi houses—*Arryn, Baratheon, Greyjoy, Lannister, Martell, Stark, Tully, Tyrell*—which, along with the Targaryens of Essos, make up around one tenth of the characters, are medieval, pseudo-medieval, and invented in roughly the same distribution as the given names; *Baratheon, Lannister*, and *Targaryen* fall on the far-right, invented side of the spectrum. On the historical far left, *Stark* is a medieval nickname deriving from Old English *stearc* or Old High German *stark* "firm, unyielding," *Martell* can either be a nickname of *Martin* or a name derived from Old French *martel* ("hammer, war mace"), and *Tyrell* is a derivative of Old French *tirer* ("to pull, draw").[20] As we noted earlier, the use of inherited "dynastic" names is closely linked to the upper classes, which had wealth, land, and status worth keeping in the family. It is thus not surprising to see that the main characters, who come from these noble houses, have inherited surnames.

Perhaps the least historical of all the names and naming patterns found in *Game of Thrones* are the surnames of bastards born to parents of high birth. These names are given according to a rigid and fixed pattern. All such bastards born in a particular area of the Seven Kingdoms have the same surname: *Flowers* (the Reach), *Hill* (the Westerlands), *Pyke* (Iron Islands), *Rivers* (the Riverlands), *Sand* (Dorne), *Snow* (the North), *Stone* (the Vale of Arryn), *Storm* (the Stormlands), and *Waters* (the Crownlands), though some bastards were recognized and then took their father's surnames (e.g., *Ramsay Snow*, recognized as *Ramsay Bolton*). The only remotely similar medieval practice was the occasional use of the byname *FitzRoy* ("son of the king") by recognized illegitimate children of English kings. Apart from this, no consistent or specific type of naming pattern was used for bastards. In medieval Europe, particularly among noble families, bastardry was not considered the moral slight that it is considered nowadays. Bastards were often recognized by their fathers or adopted by uncles. For example, Lorenzo de' Medici adopted his brother's illegitimate son, Giulio de' Medici (later Pope Clement VII). Other illegitimate de' Medici include Ippolito de' Medici, a grandson of Lorenzo, who was Lord of Florence between 1523 and 1527. Pope Clement replaced Ippolito with another illegitimate de' Medici, Alessandro, who was recognized as the son of Lorenzo II, grandson of Lorenzo, but may have been the son of Clement himself.[21]

Outside of the noble houses, it is sometimes difficult to tell whether a byname is being used literally or whether it is inherited. This is the case when only one character bears the name, or when no information about the character's parents or descendants is provided. In this group we can include bynames such as *Browntooth, Blackthumb, Stackspear,* and *Tangletongue,* each of which could be interpreted as a straightforward descriptive or as an inherited surname. There are also bynames of locative origin, such as *of Duskendale, of Myr, of the Hill,* and *of the Vale.* In other cases bynames have a specific connection to the person beyond simple family membership, and the use of such bynames shows a clear difference between the dynastic names used by nobles and the types of names used by the lower classes. For example, consider the names of singers, a specific lower-class group that illustrates three of the four types of medieval bynames as well as fixed, inherited surnames: *the Blue Bard* and *the Rhymer* (occupational); *of Braavos, of Cuy, of Eysen, of Oldtown,* and *of Sevenstreams* (locative); *Silvertongue* and *Whitesmile* (descriptive); *Costayne* and *Frey* (inherited). Only patronymic bynames are omitted (indeed, they are conspicuously rare across all contexts in *Game of Thrones*).

A Rose by Any Other Name: The Role of Nicknames

Across all social classes, however, there is ample evidence of the medieval practice of literal bynames borne on the basis of some significant characteristic or event. Examples include *the Kingslayer* (Ser Jaime Lannister), *the Imp* (Tyrion Lannister), *Stormborn* (Daenarys Targaryen), and *of the Blackwater* (Ser Bronn). Some of the literal nicknames are historical medieval bynames; some are consistent with medieval practices without being themselves explicitly found; and some follow invented, ahistorical patterns. For example, *Imp* itself is a medieval word, but in Middle English it had a very different connotation from the one it has today. While the modern word connotes mischief and trick-siness, this connotation is lacking in the Middle English usage.[22] Originally the word literally meant "a shoot, sprig" of a plant or a tree. It was used metaphori-cally to indicate the scion of a family (usually noble), or more generally some-one representative of some class.[23] The metaphorical use of the term then shifted to mean "child," and then further to designate someone "short" or "small." Tyrion, the dwarf, is known as *the imp* due to his short stature.

Examples of names that are constructed in an ahistorical fashion include *Shieldbreaker, Ironmaker,* and *Bonebreaker*: these do not follow the standard pattern of constructing action-based bynames in English, where the verb is put before the noun, as occurs in *Stackspear* (noted above), as well as in the familiar historical name *Shakespeare*. To be constructed in a medieval fashion, these three names would have to be *Breakshield*, *Makeiron*, and *Breakbone*. Then they would be in keeping with the actual medieval nicknames *Brekelaunce* "break lance," *Brekeleg* "break leg," *Brekespere* "break spear," *Makedance* "make dance," and *Makejoye* "make joy."[24]

For the most part, the *Game of Thrones* narrative does not say explicitly how individuals received their nicknames, whether they were chosen by the bearers themselves or cast upon them by others—though presumably people would only adopt pejorative nicknames themselves in special circumstances. The principal use of such bynames was to remove ambiguity, particularly when multiple people in a narrow context shared a given name. This is the case with the *Frey* family, many of whose members are named *Walda* or *Walder*. To gain clarity, they attached distinguishing nicknames, such as *Fair Walda, Fat Walda, White Walda, Big Walder, Black Walder, Little Walder,* and *Red Walder*. A different reason for using a nickname rather than a dynastic name is the intention to disguise oneself. One noteworthy example is *Arya Stark*, known variously as *Arry, Weasel, Salty,* and *Cat of the Canals*. Arya rejects not only her family name but also her whole persona, in order to become an assassin working for the Faceless Men. They repeatedly want her to recognize that "a girl has no name." Rather than become "No One," however, Arya Stark of Winterfell reclaims her name and title when she leaves the temple and strikes out on her own.[25]

Fantastical History or Historical Fantasy?

This chapter has only touched on a few aspects of the names and naming patterns in *Game of Thrones*. It completely ignores the names of places, objects, animals, and more. The evidence of personal names, though, clearly demonstrates that there are many historical echoes both in the individual name elements and in the ways names are constructed and used. Nevertheless, only a small percentage of the personal names echo history: more than half bear little resemblance to medieval European naming patterns. Martin's character names, in contrast with those of some of his predecessors, are overall more fantastical than historical and, where there are historical influences, they often are no more than happenstance.

Notes

1 L. Sprague de Camp, *Literary Swordsmen and Sorcerers: The Makers of Heroic Fantasy* (Sauk City, WI: Arkham House, 1976).

2 Lynn Carter, ed., *Kingdoms of Sorcery* (Garden City, NY: Doubleday, 1976), 39.

3 Michael W. Perry, ed., *On the Lines of Morris' Romances: Two Books that Inspired J. R. R. Tolkien:* The Wood beyond the World *and* The Well at the World's End (Seattle: Inkling Books, 2003), 9.

4 Perry, *On the Lines of Morris' Romances*, 63.

5 In this chapter, '*Game of Thrones*' is used to refer to the books and the television show collectively.

6 For more on creating the languages, see the DVDs "Creating the Dothraki Language," in *Game of Thrones: The Complete First Season* (Home Box Office, Inc., 2014) and "Creating the Valyrian Language," in *Game of Thrones: The Complete Third Season* (Home Box Office, Inc., 2014). See also David J. Peterson, *Art of Language Invention: From Horse-Lords to Dark Elves, the Words Behind World-Building* (New York: Penguin Books, 2015).

7 For a brief discussion of his naming practices, see "Game of Thrones: A Dance of Dragons and the Winds of Winter Original Trilogy, George R. R. Martin and Robin Hobb—Exclusive Event!" 2014, August 26 (accessed October 25, 2016 at https://www.youtube.com/watch?v=tXLYSnMIrXM&feature=youtu.be), beginning with his declaration: "Names are hard." Also listen to his discussion in "The Bear Swarm! Podcast, "Episode 136—George R. R. Martin and a Song of Ice and Fire," 2010, November 22 (accessed August 7, 2016 at http://www.bearswarm.com/episode-136-george-r-r-martin-and-a-song-of-ice-and-fire).

8 In England, the practice of women taking their husbands' surnames was established in urban centers by the fifteenth century; see Richard McKinley, *The Surnames of Oxfordshire* (London: Leopard's Head Press, 1977), 191.

9 See "Drew," in *Dictionary of Medieval Names from European Sources* (hereafter *DMNES*), edited by Sara L. Uckelman (edn. 2016, no. 4, at http://dmnes.org, accessed October 27, 2016). Names can be found by their initial, under "Browse" (thus "Drew" will be found at http://dmnes.org/2016/4/name/Drew).

10 See "Alan," "Elizabeth," "Joan," "John," "Katherine," "Margaret," and "Robert," in *DMNES*; "Catin" and "Nanson," in P. H. Reaney and R. M. Wilson, *A Dictionary of English Surnames* (Oxford: Oxford University Press, 1995); and "Margaret" in E. G. Withycombe, *Oxford Dictionary of English Christian Names* (3rd edn., Oxford: Oxford University Press, 1977).

11 See "Absalon," in Gunnar Knudsen, Marius Kristiansen, and Rikard Hornby, *Danmarks Gamle Personnavne*, vol. 1: *Fornavne* (Copenhagen: G. E. C. Gads Forlag, 1936); "Germain," "Milicent," and "Quentin," in *DMNES*; "Hillary" and "Hob," in Reaney and Wilson, *A Dictionary of English Surnames*; "Quentin," in Withycombe, *Oxford Dictionary of English Christian Names*.

12 See "Alice," "Denise," "Martin," and "Miles," in *DMNES*.

13 See "Eleanor," "Emma," "Margaret," and "Mary," in *DMNES*; "Émann," in Donnchadh Ó Corráin and Fidelma Maguire, *Irish Names* (Dublin: Lilliput Press, 1990).

14 See "Edward," in Withycombe, *Oxford Dictionary of English Christian Names*.

15 See "Edmond" and "Edwin," in Withycombe, *Oxford Dictionary of English Christian Names*.

16 See "Brandon," in *Cambridge Dictionary of English Place-Names*, edited by Victor Watts (Cambridge: Cambridge University Press, 2004).

17 See "Brénainn," in Ó Corráin and Maguire, *Irish Names*.

18 See "Bran," in Ó Corráin and Maguire, *Irish Names*.

19 See "Clarence," "Courtenay," "Mortimer," and "Walder," in Reaney and Wilson, *Dictionary of English Surnames*; "Desmond," in Withycombe, *Oxford Dictionary of English Christian Names*.

20 See "Martel," "Stark," and "Tirrell," in Reaney and Wilson, *A Dictionary of English Surnames*.

21 Ferdinand Schevill, *History of Florence: From the Founding of the City through the Renaissance* (New York: Frederick Ungar, 1936).

22 *Oxford English Dictionary*, 2016 [1899] (at http://www.oed.com), *s.v.* "imp, n.," especially senses (4) and (5).

23 *Middle English Dictionary*, 2001–2014 (at http://quod.lib.umich.edu/cgi/m/mec/med-idx?type=id&id=MED22157), *s.v.* "impe, n."

24 See "Breaklance," "Breakleg," "Breakspear," and "Makejoy," in Reaney and Wilson, *A Dictionary of English Surnames*.

25 "No One," directed by Mark Mylod, written by David Benioff and D. B. Weiss, in *Game of Thrones*, season 6, HBO, first aired on June 12, 2016.

19

Setting up Westeros

The Medievalesque World of *Game of Thrones*

Gillian Polack

The medieval setting that George R. R. Martin has created is an important feature of his successful series *A Song of Ice and Fire* and of *Game of Thrones*, the television series based on it. Martin taps into the popularity of fantasy novels that use aspects of the Western European Middle Ages. He has built a world that links together pageantry, war, and glamor. Westeros and Essos may come across to viewers as authentically medieval. Fictional medievalism, however, is seldom an accurate depiction of the Middle Ages. Martin creates a vibrant fictional world with a medievalism that is inspired by history but enhanced by fantasy.

Martin introduces his world in great detail from the outset of the first book in the series. The audience must be persuaded as soon as possible that the fictional universe is plausible and interesting. This chapter concentrates on the very first book in the series, since it is there that Martin sets up his universe. Fans can accept *A Song of Ice and Fire* sometimes differs from the TV series. The process of world building in a book is quite different from its development in a TV series. The costumes Martin describes in the book, for instance, are interpreted by specialist costume designers and do not always reflect what Martin intended. Given the many differences between the books and the televised presentation, this chapter explores the medievalist world of A Game of Thrones as imagined only in the Martin's first book in the series.

Since Martin gives more detail about the northern part of Westeros and this place will be prominent in the discussion. And, although much of the interest in fan circles has centered on Martin's use of medieval chronicles and his adaptation of historical events, this chapter looks at the everyday aspects of characters' lives. It focuses on clothing, on courtliness, and on the courtesies of everyday life, paying some attention to social structures, cosmology, religion, and the military.[1]

Looking at *Game of Thrones* with a historian's gaze is quite different from seeing it through a fan's eyes. To a historian, Martin's world is not believable.

Game of Thrones versus History: Written in Blood, First Edition. Edited by Brian A. Pavlac.
© 2017 John Wiley & Sons, Inc. Published 2017 by John Wiley & Sons, Inc.

It is in fact preposterous in places. Why does the Great Hall in a castle that is heated by natural hot springs need a fire so big and bellowing that one cannot breathe? How can an economy operate on gold and iron coinage? The standard in the Middle Ages was in fact silver. Where does the knowledge of platinum come from, when its existence and use were not common in Europe until well after the Middle Ages? How does Cersei's double-decker wheelhouse, too big to get through castle gates, move over narrow and badly kept roads? Why are artistic representations of human faces dependent on non-medieval conventions of realism?[2]

All of these items have artistic reasons (for instance, the wheelhouse is an early demonstration of how far Cersei's demands will affect the lives of others), although none has clear historical evidence or justification. The difference between what makes credible medieval-based fantasy and what we know from the historical Middle Ages helps us understand how Martin works and why his world seems functional even when it isn't quite authentically medieval.

In a realistic medieval universe, Martin's explanatory detail would be verifiable with our current knowledge of the Middle Ages. In other words, historians could find sources to prove it as potentially accurate. Martin, however, leans very heavily on heroic fantasy mechanisms to make his universe credible to readers. In fact his level of detail is very uneven and is used more to reinforce plot or character and to bring action sequences to life than to re-create a functional medieval society. When he does give detail, it is most commonly about weapons. There are also significant descriptions of meals, unusual objects, and strange places.

Martin uses visual pageantry in his choice of what should be described. This matches the visceral pageantry he uses in his treatment of violence. The greatest amount of detail about Martin's world is given in the opening chapters of the first book. Introducing and building up the setting this way gives the impression of a very thick, densely observed world, which Martin can add to but does not need to repeat later.

Titles, Blazonry, and Armor

Let us look first at social structure and status. "Ser" is used to indicate knighthood, a form close to the historical use of "sir" or "sire," which was standard from about the fourteenth century on. This is a small thing, but critical. It's something that most readers associate with the Middle Ages, even when they know little else. Martin uses "Lady" in a similar way: he is clever about using the "known" Middle Ages.

To reinforce social structures, Martin does not use only titles but also blazonry. Blazonry is the formal use of colors and figures in heraldry as visual symbols designed to identify noble families, both in medieval Europe and

Westeros. European heraldry began just before the twelfth century and was firmly established by the thirteenth. It arose out of the need to identify armored soldiers on the battlefield but also defined the lineages, or ancestry, of noble families.[3] In *Game of Thrones* Martin carefully distinguishes each family through distinctive insignia. Each dynasty has its own form of medieval heraldry, which includes a kind of coat of arms called a "sigil." The sigils give Martin's world an immediate visual structure. Colors that dominate a sigil, such as the red and gold of the Lannisters, are often repeated in livery—the clothing worn by members and retainers of the corresponding House. The livery gives pageantry, while the blazonry gives distinctiveness: readers are easily able to determine the loyalties of the rather large cast when they have colors and devices to assist them. In much the same way, sports teams use uniforms and mascots to helps viewers distinguish them. Given that family and political loyalties are the basis of the plot in *Game of Thrones*, heraldry makes the story easier to follow, while reinforcing its medievalism. The importance of these symbols is emphasized by the opening credits of the TV series, which show the major families' sigils on cities and castles and next to the actors' names.[4]

If Martin's heraldry roughly reflects the Middle Ages, are the arms and weapons in *Game of Thrones* also authentically medieval? Martin is very specific about some kinds of arms and surprisingly vague about other crucial elements. The first shield mentioned in the novels is "a great wood-and-leather shield blazoned with the same striding huntsman he wore on his surcoat."[5] This description sounds quite precise, but does "great" refer to height or is it relative to much smaller (and unmentioned) shields? Round shields made of wood and leather were common throughout the Middle Ages, but one cannot assume that the "great shield" was round. The actual appearance of the shield may not, however, be crucial. Just by including one genuine facet of a medieval shield (its fabrication), Martin gives a sense of the Middle Ages. This isn't the same as being able to pin down a specific place or a date. It's not the Middle Ages, but it is definitely characteristically medieval.

Other details about arms and armor also evoke rather than replicate the Middle Ages. In one instance, Martin describes a spectacular "steel helm, shaped like a bull's head, with two great curving horns."[6] It's not a standard military helmet: not the stark Norman helm with its clean lines and simple nosepiece, nor the great helm of the fourteenth century, which covered the whole head in claustrophobic fashion. It mostly resembles, in fact, a specific helmet owned by King Henry VIII of England (r. 1509–1547): steel, with vast curving horns. Henry's helmet, fashioned by one of the leading armorers of his century, was meant for display, perhaps at parades before tournaments.[7] Martin's, crafted by the apprentice smith Gendry, is meant for combat. Perhaps Martin is not interested in distinguishing between show armor and practical fighting gear. Or perhaps differentiation between the ornamental and the practical is not important; the helmet gives the feeling of a medieval world.

In the novels, Martin deals in a similar way with plate armor. He talks about "plate" in a general way. He does not mention specific pieces of plate (such as greaves, cuisses, gauntlets, or gorgets) or the body parts they protected (calves, thighs, hands, necks). Without specific details, it is impossible to pinpoint a specific historical period. But this tells us something about Martin's world: it exists outside our time. Martin's world does not, however, exist outside our cultural space. People think of plate armor as "medieval" (even if it actually developed only in the very late Middle Ages and Renaissance). So, each time armor is mentioned, the reader's sense of being in the real Middle Ages is reinforced.

Martin's plate armor is thus not the reality of history as we know it; it is tempered by pop culture. Its reality is that of an heroic fantasy novel. The historical evolution of armor is significant in military history, reflecting new tactics and weapons. The actual use of plate is not relevant, however, to Martin's narrative: what *is* relevant is the sense of dressing like a medieval knight. Plate armor is only used as a prop, to show the seriousness of the fighting and the wealth and social position of the knight.

Clothes Make the Man

Likewise, armor and clothes help define characters and their role in the plot. They are shortcuts to understanding and save long descriptions. For instance, Ser Waymar Royce appears only briefly, in the prologue of the first novel.[8] In addition to his chain mail, his clothing is described in much detail. It's luxurious. One particular garment indicates both his personality and the symbolic importance of his fate to the future of Westeros. His cloak is "sable, thick and black and soft as sin." This suggests that the fur is not simply a lining or a trimming, but is the whole cloak. In contrast, when a renegade is executed, his furs are described as "ragged and greasy."[9] The telling detail is not about showing an accurate medieval cloak; it is about the difference between extreme wealth and extreme poverty, ostentation and bare necessity, vanity and desperation.

Clothing helps indicate Martin's choice to create atmosphere rather than accuracy. He tends to overlook the issue of practicality. He has men wearing tall boots indoors rather than historically realistic house shoes.[10] When surcoats are introduced, Joffrey wears one that has both padding and embroidery, but no surcoat is described in the historical fashion of being worn over armor.[11] Martin gives Ned a doublet laced at the back, then has him commit a Renaissance faux pas: he buckles on a longsword without putting any mail over the doublet, or a surcoat over the mail.[12] Few readers are likely to object. The clothing is more than sufficiently Hollywood-style medieval.

Moreover, Martin is not afraid to use medieval and Renaissance interchangeably. He has Catelyn disguise herself by lacing a bodice.[13] This is more indicative of the sixteenth century than of the late medieval period (1300–1500). Some might not think that the difference of a hundred years is significant. Consider, however, the difference between the leg-of-mutton sleeves of the 1890s and the blue jeans of the 1990s. But, again, accuracy is not the point. Catelyn is not in fact a medieval or a Renaissance figure; she is someone from a mythical Middle Ages that draws on popular images—a "Renaissance Faire" woman. In the *Game of Thrones* world, the use of color is at its height during moments of ostentatious display, such as the tournament where Sansa's eyes greedily alight on sight after sight.[14] Martin describes color and pageantry.

Color Him Heroic

With his flair for atmospheric color, Martin gives some attention to making his society real. He draws an item with lightning strokes, to give it a moment of focus: a dirk, for instance, that "tastes of cold iron";[15] Jon Snow mucking out the stables in lieu of showing the amount of horse training that the fighters needed; the "soft metallic slither of the lordling's ringmail" to demonstrate how tight it was and illustrate how mail works.[16] Not detail, exactly, or accuracy, but color that gives a sense of reality.[17] We're not fixed in time and place the way an historian would anchor us; the small and telling details provide instead a sea anchor. As all sea anchors, it moves with the sea.

Martin's understanding of the European past (not always the medieval past) shapes the sense of the real. He creates Valyrian steel and describes it so clearly that it resembles Damascene steel. Damascene steel is the name that medieval crusaders gave the swords of their Arab enemies, which sliced through their own, lower-quality swords. The epithet derived from the name of Damascus, the capital city of Syria, and this kind of steel was used to manufacture swords in the Near East from antiquity through the early modern era. The swords had distinctive patterns of mottling reminiscent of flowing water. Their blades were legendary: tough, resistant to shattering, and capable of being honed to a razor-sharp edge.[18]

In the case of Eddard Stark's sword Ice, however, Martin ensures that we know it was created using magic along with smithwork. Ice is clearly a sword of power, wielded by heroes. It fits a mythical concept of a sword for heroes. Heroes have special abilities; no ordinary warrior is capable of fighting with such a sword. The medieval equivalent would be a sword like Roland's Durendal in the French epic *La Chanson de Roland*. Durendal is imbued with a very medieval power: it contains a holy relic.[19] Thus *Game of Thrones* relates more strongly than usual to a past recognizable by historians, alluding both to the swords of crusaders and to those of medieval legendary figures. Martin is not in fact giving us either history or a reinvented Middle Ages; he is using aspects of medieval legend to create pageantry and drama. Ice is magical, like King Arthur's Excalibur.[20]

Pageant and epic drama are more important to Martin than the petty details of keeping a weapon sharp, armor unrusted, and clothing practical. When Martin creates a scene, it must be a moment with color and atmosphere. For instance, he describes how the Kingslayer slew Aerys Targaryen, the king:

> "*Kingslayer*," he pronounced carefully. "And such a king he was!" He lifted his cup. [...] "And to the sword that opened his throat. A *golden* sword, don't you know. Until his blood ran red down the blade. Those are the Lannister colors, red and gold."[21]

The color is important, for it gives the style of the man who wields the sword. The technical means of maintaining a gold sword are simply not relevant. Nor are technical descriptions, which is why so much detail that would establish a precise period and place is simply not given. The mention of red blood also conjures a vivid image, immediately juxtaposed with the blazonry of the Lannisters. Color counts. It matters so much that a personality can be determined by the colors the person chooses. For instance, "Lord Renley's new armor, the green plates with the golden antlers" sums up his position—one of not great importance but of much beauty.[22] In Martin's reality, the element of display helps give a large cast defining features.

Green Men, Gods and Wildlings

From the beginning, Martin introduces a sense of religious belief into his world. Within the first few pages, a frightened character whispers a prayer "to the nameless gods of the wood."[23] While the Westeros gods are usually plural and seldom named, Martin's Green Men have a particular link to our Middle Ages. Martin describes the Green Men several times. For example, those on the Isle of Faces are described as keeping silent watch. Their worship has been lost in the south, but the godswoods they inhabit are still numerous.

Martin's is an interesting fantasy interpretation of the medieval Green Men. The Green Man should not be confused with the green lord from the Middle English romance *Sir Gawain and the Green Knight*. Green Men are artistic representations, usually sculptures, that show a face surrounded by, or made from, green leaves. Foliage often sprouts from their nose, mouth, or nostrils, sometimes carrying flowers or fruit. The Green Man appears to be a symbol of spring and rebirth and consequently could seem to be a pagan nature spirit. Yet Green Men decorated Christian churches, small and large, from the fifth century to early modern times. The source of this motif is unknown, and the motif itself may not have served any religious function at all, save to decorate religious buildings. Nevertheless, Green Men are evocative and mysterious and translate well into the setting of the godswood, where they are carved into trees.

In *Game of Thrones* religion is important. Belief shapes the actions of some characters. The different religions also strengthen the reader's understanding of the cultures in Westeros. But the religions in *Game of Thrones* are neither those of medieval Christianity nor the remnants of the ancient paganism and Judaism infused into it. Yes, there are some similarities to Christian practice: there is anointing with oils in a form of baptism, and there is worship with a censer and incense done by a priesthood.[24] Nevertheless, for much of the time, Martin's religion serves quite a different purpose. It reinforces a sort of folkloristic Middle Ages, as described by Brian Stableford.[25] Such aspects give flavor to Martin's world.

Like the Green Men, the wildlings are another example of a folkloric element used in *Game of Thrones*:

> The wildlings were cruel men, she said, slavers and slayers and thieves. They consorted with giants and ghouls, stole girl children in the dead of night, and drank blood from polished horns. And their women lay with Others on the Long Night to sire terrible half-human children.[26]

The mythology behind evil women sleeping with strange beings comes from the medieval legend of Brutus. The initial story of Brutus (without the full development of the evil maidens, which was added slightly later) was recorded by the medieval historian Geoffrey of Monmouth (c. 1100–c. 1155). According to Geoffrey, Brutus was the great-grandson of Aeneas, the legendary Trojan prince who fled after the fall of Troy and, after much wandering, founded the city of Rome. Needless to say, no surviving account from antiquity mentions this Brutus. Nevertheless, according to Geoffrey, Britain was named after this character. Clearly Geoffrey wanted to prove that Britain was directly connected to the Roman Empire, remembered in the Middle Ages as a time of legendary greatness. Perhaps Martin connects Westeros with medieval Europe in a similar way.

Laying Down the Law

One area where the relationship between Martin's world and history is particularly tenuous involves legal systems. In Martin's world, they are more the stuff of Robin Hood ballads than anything authentically medieval. In introducing his world, Martin describes a legal judgment as the very first event in it; and that judgment leads to a beheading for desertion. But the legal system is incomplete. The accused is condemned without as much as a hearing, let alone a trial; he is given only the opportunity to say a few last words, which are ignored, before the blade comes down with finality through his neck. There are hints of a medieval reality (justice is done "in the king's name," the court of final appeal is the king, and trial by combat is possible as a defense when all else fails), but there is no actual system underpinning the references: occasional references act as the whole of the system. The one significant trial in the series, Tyrion's for murdering Joffrey, is a mockery of judicial procedure, entirely rigged to produce a guilty verdict.[27] This lack of jurisprudence further indicates why Martin's society lacks the depth of the known Middle Ages.

In *Game of Thrones*, the idea of the king's justice is a concept of absolute power. There is no other court of appeal to solve complex legal problems. Justice is a personal justice. In medieval England, however, a whole system of courts and assizes developed, especially after the reign of King Henry II (r. 1154–1189). The king's court, which was at the top, gave the king significant power; but it did so within an administrative and legal framework. His judiciary promoted trained lawyers, the circuit court, a grand jury, and trial by a jury of one's peers—innovations then but commonplace now. A working legal system helped keep England stable.

And quite early people questioned royal absolute power, although opposing it led to significant unrest. In 1215 rebellious barons famously forced King John to limit his power by imposing the Magna Carta. The war over this pact only ended because of John's sudden death. A generation later, the "Oxford Parliament" or "Mad Parliament" of 1258 forced John's heir, King Henry III (r. 1216–1272), to agree to provisions that limited his absolute power by a council of barons led by Simon de Montfort, earl of Leicester. When that agreement collapsed, the Second Barons' War (1264–1267) erupted, ending in a bloody victory for the king and the victory of the legal system over taking the law into one's own hands. An even longer disruption of stability occurred during the struggle for the English crown between the House of York and the House of Lancaster—what is known as the Wars of the Roses (1455–1485). The political unrest of this period substantially inspired *A Game of Thrones*. Similarly, in Martin's world the politics at the heart of the story is family politics. *Game of Thrones* has at its core the dysfunctional, violent, sprawling, and complex families that dominate history during a state of unrest or uncontrollable war. Westeros is an anarchic society.

Missing Manners

When we think of the Middle Ages, we often think of courtliness and courtesy. Martin's characters, however, do not always exhibit this kind of good behavior. Although Sansa displays proper upbringing, she seems to be the exception. Joffrey is seldom constrained by manners and social obligations. Eddard Stark is a decent person, but not a polite one: he attends his first meeting as King's Hand with little or no grace. Ironically, the characters who most espouse courtly behavior and courtesies are in fact the spies and traitors in the story.

Littlefinger is an excellent example. This is directly contrary to modes of behavior among the upper classes in the Middle Ages: courtesy was critical. In a society of trained killers, as the knights were, good manners smoothed out social relations, so that everyday encounters would not wind up in bloodshed.

But displays of being raised well are seldom important to Martin. Far more important is narrative tension, which does not arise from polite courtesies and good manners. Drama is achieved when social niceties have broken down, feuds are unleashed, or civil war breaks out. Such collapses happen more easily when interaction leads to violence rather than to polite niceties. Indeed, Martin obtains much of his dramatic tension by making his characters suffer. Obtaining drama from suffering is a common fiction trope, reaching its climax in the tragic death of the hero. Martin pushes his society into heroic fantasy and high drama.

The constraints of historical authenticity would complicate this heightened portrayal. Much of history, like most of our lives, is pedestrian and routine. But we crave to be entertained by extremes. Most people's consumption of history even leans toward the violent, as our culture's penchant for the perennially popular American Civil War or World War II illustrates. Although well informed by history, Martin doesn't try to make his world authentically medieval. That isn't necessary to furthering the drama. Yet he does make it believably medievalesque. Human drama is what makes the series great—not the more or less accurate details of medieval heraldry, weapons, religions, or law courts. Martin's painted backdrop of history, the costumes and props, are secondary to his story, which is about complicated people making hard choices in tough times. Nevertheless, staging this drama in a medievalesque world makes *A Game of Thrones* utterly enthralling.

Notes

1 This essay draws on research for our recent book: Gillian Polack and Katrin Kania, *The Middle Ages Unlocked: A Guide to Life in Medieval England, 1050–1300* (Stroud: Amberley Publishing, 2015).

2 For these examples, see George R. R. Martin, *A Song of Ice and Fire, Book One: A Game of Thrones* (London: HarperVoyager, 1998), 49, 327, 6, 192, 40, 277 (in this order).

3 Polack and Kania, *The Middle Ages Unlocked*, 29–30.

4 The credits also attach made-up sigils to the names of the production staff, most amusingly for Executive Producer Carolyn Strauss, whose last name means "ostrich" in German; see "The Wars to Come," directed by Michael Slovis, written by David Benioff and D. B. Weiss, in *Game of Thrones*, season 5, HBO, first aired on April 12, 2015.

5 Martin, *A Game of Thrones*, 260.

6 Martin, *A Game of Thrones*, 280.

7 The Royal Armouries Collection, "The Horned Helmet," 2016 (accessed November 5, 2016 at https://collections.royalarmouries.org/object/rac-object-2623.html).

8 Martin, *A Game of Thrones*, 3; he also features in the cold open of the series; see "Winter is Coming," directed by Tim Van Patten, written by David Benioff and D. B. Weiss, in *Game of Thrones*, season 1, HBO, first aired on April 17, 2011.

9 Martin, *A Game of Thrones*, 14.

10 Martin, *A Game of Thrones*, 51–53.

11 Martin, *A Game of Thrones*, 73.

12 Martin, *A Game of Thrones*, 277.

13 Martin, *A Game of Thrones*, 171.

14 Martin, *A Game of Thrones*, 295 ff.

15 Martin, *A Game of Thrones*, 8.

16 Martin, *A Game of Thrones*, 264.

17 Or perhaps a sense of fantasy, since Martin suggests that "we read fantasy to find the colors again": George R. R. Martin, "On Fantasy," in On George (on his website), 2016 (accessed October 28, 2016 at http://www.georgerrmartin.com/about-george/on-writing-essays/on-fantasy-by-george-r-r-martin, accessed August 3, 2016).

18 Polack and Kania, *The Middle Ages Unlocked*, 165.

19 *The Song of Roland*, translated by Glynn Burgess (New York: Penguin, 1990).

20 For more on Arthur, see *Medieval Folklore: An Encyclopedia of Myths, Legends, Tales, Beliefs, and Customs*, edited by Carl Lindahl, John McNamara, and John Lindow (Santa Barbara, CA: ABC-Clio, 2000) and N. J. Lacy, *The New Arthurian Encyclopedia* (New York: Garland Publishing, 1996).

21 George R. R. Martin, *A Song of Ice and Fire, Book Two: A Clash of Kings* (London: HarperVoyager, 1999), 581–582.

22 Martin, *A Game of Thrones*, 279.

23 Martin, *A Game of Thrones*, 8.

24 Martin, *A Game of Thrones*, 23.

25 Brian Stableford, "Narrative Structures in Science Fiction," in *Reading Science Fiction*, edited by James Gunn, Matthew Candelaria, and Marleen S Barr (Basingstoke: Palgrave Macmillan, 2009), 33–34.

26 Martin, *A Game of Thrones*, 13.

27 "The Laws of Gods and Men," directed by Alik Sakharov, written by Bryan Cogman, in *Game of Thrones*, season 4, HBO, first aired on May 11, 2014.

Appendix

List of Books and Episodes

A Song of Ice and Fire, by George R. R. Martin, book series from Bantam Books	
A Game of Thrones	1996
A Clash of Kings	1999
A Storm of Swords	2000
A Feast for Crows	2005
A Dance with Dragons	2011
The Winds of Winter	to be announced

Game of Thrones television series on HBO

Season One	Episode			
Episode Title		**directed by**	**written by**	**airdate**
Winter Is Coming	1	Tim Van Patten	David Benioff and D. B. Weiss	April 17, 2011
The Kingsroad	2	Tim Van Patten	David Benioff and D. B. Weiss	April 24, 2011
Lord Snow	3	Brian Kirk	David Benioff and D. B. Weis	May 1, 2011
Cripples, Bastards, and Broken Things	4	Brian Kirk	Bryan Cogman	May 8, 2011
The Wolf and the Lion	5	Brian Kirk	David Benioff and D. B. Weis	May 15, 2011

(Continued)

Game of Thrones versus History: Written in Blood, First Edition. Edited by Brian A. Pavlac.
© 2017 John Wiley & Sons, Inc. Published 2017 by John Wiley & Sons, Inc.

(Continued)

Episode Title	Episode	directed by	written by	airdate
A Golden Crown	6	Daniel Minahan	Story by: David Benioff and D. B. Weiss; Teleplay by: Jane Espenson and David Benioff and D. B. Weiss	May 22, 2011
You Win or You Die	7	Daniel Minahan	David Benioff and D. B. Weis	May 29, 2011
The Pointy End	8	Daniel Minahan	George R. R. Martin	June 5, 2011
Baelor	9	Alan Taylor	David Benioff and D. B. Weis	June 12, 2011
Fire and Blood	10	Alan Taylor	David Benioff and D. B. Weis	June 19, 2011

Season Two	Episode			
Episode Title		**directed by**	**written by**	**airdate**
The North Remembers	1	Alan Taylor	David Benioff and D. B. Weiss	April 1, 2012
The Night Lands	2	Alan Taylor	David Benioff and D. B. Weiss	April 8, 2012
What Is Dead May Never Die	3	Alik Sakharov	Bryan Cogman	April 15, 2012
Garden of Bones	4	David Petrarca	Vanessa Taylor	April 22, 2012
The Ghost of Harrenhal	5	David Petrarca	David Benioff and D. B. Weiss	April 29, 2012
The Old Gods and the New	6	David Nutter	Vanessa Taylor	May 6, 2012
A Man Without Honor	7	David Nutter	David Benioff and D. B. Weiss	May 13, 2012
The Prince of Winterfell	8	Alan Taylor	David Benioff and D. B. Weiss	May 20, 2012
Blackwater	9	Neil Marshall	George R. R. Martin	May 27, 2012
Valar Morghulis	10	Alan Taylor	David Benioff and D. B. Weiss	June 3, 2012

Season Three	Episode			
Episode Title		**directed by**	**written by**	**airdate**
Valar Dohaeris	1	Daniel Minahan	David Benioff and D. B. Weiss	March 31, 2013

Dark Wings, Dark Words	2	Daniel Minahan	Vanessa Taylor	April 7, 2013
Walk of Punishment	3	David Benioff	David Benioff and D. B. Weiss	April 14, 2013
And Now His Watch Is Ended	4	Alex Graves	David Benioffand D. B. Weiss	April 21, 2013
Kissed by Fire	5	Alex Graves	Bryan Cogman	April 28, 2013
The Climb	6	Alik Sakharov	David Benioff and D. B. Weiss	May 5, 2013
The Bear and the Maiden Fair	7	Michelle MacLaren	George R. R. Martin	May 12, 2013
Second Sons	8	Michelle MacLaren	David Benioff and D. B. Weiss	May 19, 2013
The Rains of Castamere	9	David Nutter	David Benioff and D. B. Weiss	June 2, 2013
Mhysa	10	David Nutter	David Benioff and D. B. Weiss	June 9, 2013

Season Four	Episode			
Episode Title		**directed by**	**written by**	**airdate**
Two Swords	1	D. B. Weiss	David Benioff and D. B. Weiss	April 6, 2014
The Lion and the Rose	2	Alex Graves	George R. R. Martin	April 13, 2014
Breaker of Chains	3	Alex Graves	David Benioff and D. B. Weiss	April 20, 2014
Oathkeeper	4	Michelle MacLaren	Bryan Cogman	April 27, 2014
First of His Name	5	Michelle MacLaren	David Benioff and D. B. Weiss	May 4, 2014
The Laws of Gods and Men	6	Alik Sakharov	Bryan Cogman	May 11, 2014
Mockingbird	7	Neil Marshall	David Benioff and D. B. Weiss	May 18, 2014
The Mountain and the Viper	8	Alex Graves	David Benioff and D. B. Weiss	June 1, 2014
The Watchers on the Wall	9	Neil Marshall	David Benioff and D. B. Weiss	June 8, 2014
The Children	10	Alex Graves	David Benioff and D. B. Weiss	June 15, 2014

(Continued)

(Continued)

Season Five	Episode			
Episode Title		**directed by**	**written by**	**airdate**
The Wars to Come	1	Michael Slovis	David Benioff and D. B. Weiss	April 12, 2015
The House of Black and White	2	Michael Slovis	David Benioff and D. B. Weiss	April 19, 2015
High Sparrow	3	Mark Mylod	David Benioff and D. B. Weiss	April 26, 2015
Sons of the Harpy	4	Mark Mylod	Dave Hill	May 3, 2015
Kill the Boy	5	Jeremy Podeswa	Bryan Cogman	May 10, 2015
Unbowed, Unbent, Unbroken	6	Jeremy Podeswa	Bryan Cogman	May 17, 2015
The Gift	7	Miguel Sapochnik	David Benioff and D. B. Weiss	May 24, 2015
Hardhome	8	Miguel Sapochnik	David Benioff and D. B. Weiss	May 31, 2015
The Dance of Dragons	9	David Nutter	David Benioff and D. B. Weiss	June 7, 2015
Mother's Mercy	10	David Nutter	David Benioff and D. B. Weiss	June 14, 2015

Season Six	Episode			
Episode Title		**directed by**	**written by**	**airdate**
The Red Woman	1	Jeremy Podeswa	David Benioff and D. B. Weiss	April 24, 2016
Home	2	Jeremy Podeswa	Dave Hill	May 1, 2016
Oathbreaker	3	Daniel Sackheim	David Benioff and D. B. Weiss	May 8, 2016
Book of the Stranger	4	Daniel Sackheim	David Benioff and D. B. Weiss	May 15, 2016
The Door	5	Jack Bender	David Benioff and D. B. Weiss	May 22, 2016
Blood of My Blood	6	Jack Bender	Bryan Cogman	May 29, 2016
The Broken Man	7	Mark Mylod	Bryan Cogman	June 5, 2016
No One	8	Mark Mylod	David Benioff and D. B. Weiss	June 12, 2016
Battle of the Bastards	9	Miguel Sapochnik	David Benioff and D. B. Weiss	June 19, 2016
The Winds of Winter	10	Miguel Sapochnik	David Benioff and D. B. Weiss	June 26, 2016

Index

Game of Thrones versus History: Written in Blood, First Edition. Edited by Brian A. Pavlac.
© 2017 John Wiley & Sons, Inc. Published 2017 by John Wiley & Sons, Inc.

Moloch sacrifice, 188–9
  see also human sacrifice; sacrifice
monarchy *see also* kingship; queenship
  absolute, 258
  and religion, 58, 59, 61, 78, 150,
    199–201
monasteries, 213, 218
Monasteries, Dissolution of the,
    213, 216
Mongols 98
monks, 212–14, 217
Mooton, Lord, 80
moots, 58
moral principles, 76–7
Mordane, Septa, 19, 29, 212
Mormont, Lyanna, 59
Mormont, Jorah, 42, 113, 231
Morocco, 118
Morris, William, 241
Moses, 33, 35
motherhood, 125–32, 134–5, 137–8,
    147, 150, 156
Muhammad, 204
Mulay Isma'il, 118
mummification, 217
Muslims, 24, 53, 97, 99, 101, 180,
    195, 202
Myr, 98
mystery cults, 196–7
mythologizing, 74
"myths," 1–2

n

Naharis, Daario, 42, 156, 231–2
names, 12, 241–50
  dynastic, 244, 246–7
  given, 243–5
  nicknames, 243–8
  and occupation, 243–4
  women's, upon marriage, 243–4
Naples, 33
narratives
  grand, 206

revenge, 150, 156
"story so far," 9–11
narrators, 3
Narrow Sea, 10, 41
National Archives, London, 234
nature, 74
nature spirits, 174 *see also* Children of
    the Forest
near-death experiences, 181
Near East, 196, 204, 255
necromancy, 106
Nennius, 74
Netherlands, 26
Neville, Anne, 21
Neville, Richard, "the Kingmaker", earl
    of Warwick, 8, 130–1
New Testament, 78, 178, 202
Nicaea, Second Council, 213
nicknames, 243–8
Night King, 9
Night's Watch, 10, 23, 76, 77, 88,
    90, 154
  Arya's draft into the, 142
  and the assassination of Jon Snow, 92
  and celibacy, 209–11, 219
  and chivalry, 52–4
  deserters, 39, 77, 138
  erosion of the values of, 53
  oath, 209–10
  protective function, 92
  and the White Walkers, 9
  and the wildlings, 85, 92, 209
Nizaris, 101–2
nobility, 7 *see also* aristocracy; elites
  and blazonry, 252–3
  children of the, 138, 141–5
  and chivalry, 51–2
  and knighthood, 48–9
  names, 246–7
  women, 150–1
nomadic peoples, 175
"non-fiction," 2
Norfolk, duke of, 132